Family Law
Problems and Documents

Editorial Advisory Board
Aspen Law & Business
A Division of Aspen Publishers, Inc.

Richard A. Epstein
James Parker Hall Distinguished Service Professor of Law
University of Chicago

E. Allan Farnsworth
Alfred McCormack Professor of Law
Columbia University

Ronald J. Gilson
Charles J. Meyers Professor of Law and Business
Stanford University
Marc and Eva Stern Professor of Law and Business
Columbia University

Geoffrey C. Hazard, Jr.
Trustee Professor of Law
University of Pennsylvania

James E. Krier
Earl Warren DeLano Professor of Law
University of Michigan

Elizabeth Warren
Leo Gottlieb Professor of Law
Harvard University

Bernard Wolfman
Fessenden Professor of Law
Harvard University

Family Law
Problems and Documents

J. Eric Smithburn
Professor of Law
Notre Dame Law School

Aspen Law & Business
A Division of Aspen Publishers, Inc.

Copyright © 1997 by J. Eric Smithburn

All rights reserved
Printed in the United States of America

ISBN 1-56706-500-7

This publication is designed to provide accurate and authoritative information in regard to the subject matter covered. It is sold with the understanding that the publisher is not engaged in rendering legal, accounting, or other professional services. If legal advice or other professional assistance is required, the services of a competent professional person should be sought.

> —From a *Declaration of Principles* jointly adopted by a Committee of the American Bar Association and Committee of Publishers and Associations.

No part of this publication may be reproduced or transmitted in any form or by any means, electronic or mechanical, including photocopy, recording, or any information storage and retrieval system, without permission in writing from the publisher. Requests for permission to make copies of any part of this publication should be mailed to:

Permissions
Aspen Law & Business
A Division of Aspen Publishers, Inc.,
1185 Avenue of the Americas
New York, NY 10036

1 2 3 4 5

To Aladean

Summary of Contents

Contents . . . . *ix*
Foreword . . . . *xvii*
Preface . . . . *xix*
Introduction . . . . *xxi*

Chapter One.	Marriage and Family 1	
Chapter Two.	Antenuptial Agreements 17	
Chapter Three.	Procreation Decisions 23	
Chapter Four.	Parent-Child Relationship 35	
Chapter Five.	Children Born Out of Wedlock 49	
Chapter Six.	Adoption 51	
Chapter Seven.	Family Torts 65	
Chapter Eight.	Decisions About Children and Families—The State's Role 75	
Chapter Nine.	Dissolution of Marriage 141	
Chapter Ten.	Mediation in Dissolution Cases 275	
Chapter Eleven.	Family Law Practice and Professional Responsibility . . . 277	
Appendix.	Statutes and Uniform Acts 287	

Contents

Foreword . . . . *xvii*
Preface . . . . *xix*
Introduction . . . . *xxi*

Chapter One

Marriage And Family 1

- A. The Nature of Marriage and Family 1
  - 1. Definition of Marriage 1
    - **PROBLEM 1**: *Johnson and Johanson v. Eldridge*. 1
  - 2. Definition of Family 3
    - **PROBLEM 2**: *Peacock Realty Inc. v. Lyndon Hayes*. 3
- B. State Regulation of Marriage 4
  - 1. Right to Marry 4
    - **PROBLEM 3**: *In re John Wilson and Jasmine Rafhiq*. 4
  - 2. Intimate Association 4
    - **PROBLEM 4**: *Hidalgo v. Michiana State Attorney General*. 4
- C. Marriage Formalities And Legal Qualifications 6
  - 1. Bigamy: Legal Versus Deemed Widow 6
    - **PROBLEM 5**: *In re Estate of Doolittle Walter Ditty*. 6
- D. Enforcing Promises to Marry 7
    - **PROBLEM 6**: *Emily v. James* 7
- E. Common Law Marriage 8
    - **PROBLEM 7**: *In re Estate of Harley Thomas*. 8
- F. Annulment 10
  - 1. Fraud as to Qualifications 10
    - **PROBLEM 8**: *In re Marriage of Conway* 10
  - 2. Fraud in Inducement 13
    - **PROBLEM 9**: *Barryless v. Barryless* 13

G. Extending Marital Rights to Unmarried Cohabitants 13
   1. Loss of Consortium. 13
      PROBLEM 10: *Shuler v. Morrison* 13
   2. Child's Action for Loss of Parental Consortium 14
      PROBLEM 11: *Templin v. Sparticus Airlines*. 14
   3. Palimony. 15
      PROBLEM 12: *Muriel v. Arthur*. 15

Chapter Two

Antenuptial Agreements 17

PROBLEM 13: Antenputial Agreement—Preparation. 17
PROBLEM 14: Antenuptial Agreement—Enforcement 19

Chapter Three

Procreation Decisions 23

A. Contraception and Sterilization 23
   1. Wrongful Pregnancy 23
      PROBLEM 15: *O'Hara v. Holder*. 23
B. Abortion 24
   1. Contractual Rights 24
      PROBLEM 16: *In re Marriage of Robertson* 24
   2. State Regulation 25
      PROBLEM 17: *Gomez v. State of Michiana and Women's Clinic*. 25
C. Assisted Conception 26
   1. Gestational Surrogacy. 26
      PROBLEM 18: *In re Baby Bo* 26
   2. Surrogate Birth. 27
      PROBLEM 19: *Consultation with Jane Ray*. 27
   3. Artificial Insemination. 31
      PROBLEM 20: *In re Benjamin* 31
   4. Rights of Artificial Insemination Donor (AID) 32
      PROBLEM 21: *Terry v. Ainsworth*. 32
   5. Artificial Insemination by Husband (AIH) 33
      PROBLEM 22: *Cadewell v. Michiana State Department of Correction*. 34

Chapter Four

Parent-Child Relationship 35

- A. Action to Establish Paternity 35
  - **PROBLEM 23**: *In re Paternity of Heather Hodson* 35
- B. Rebutting the Presumption of Paternity 36
  - 1. Reverse Paternity—Action by Wife 36
    - **PROBLEM 24**: *In re Marriage of Sherry (T.) B. and Gary T./ Lucy T. v. Gary T.* 36
  - 2. Reverse Paternity—Action by Husband 45
    - **PROBLEM 25**: *Little v. Little* 45
- C. Equitable Parent Doctrine 46
  - **PROBLEM 26**: *In re Marriage of Janet M. and Zachary D.* 46

Chapter Five

Children Born Out Of Wedlock 49

- **PROBLEM 27**: *In re Paternity of Albert Sparks* 49
- **PROBLEM 28**: *In re Paternity of Darrell Dutile* 50

Chapter Six

Adoption 51

- A. Same-Race Placement 51
  - **PROBLEM 29**: *In re Adoption of R.K.O.* 51
- B. The Interstate Dimension 52
  - **PROBLEM 30**: *In re Adoption of Baby Gail* 52
  - **PROBLEM 31**: *Bur v. Crack* 54
- C. Psychological Parents 55
  - **PROBLEM 32**: *In re Adoption of T.L.C.* 55
- D. Lesbian Adoption 59
  - **PROBLEM 33**: *In re Adoption of S.S. and W.S.* 59
- E. Indian Child Welfare Act 61
  - **PROBLEM 34**: *In re Blackfoot* 61
- F. Adoption of Adults 62
  - **PROBLEM 35**: *In re Adoption of Mollie Sue Sage* 62

Chapter Seven

Family Torts 65

- A. Parental Immunity 65
  - **PROBLEM 36**: *Freeman v. Jones* 65
- B. Domestic Violence 66
  - **PROBLEM 37**: *State v. Heldarco* 66
- C. Violence Against Women Act 72
  - **PROBLEM 38**: *Murphy v. Murphy* 72
- D. Wiretapping 72
  - **PROBLEM 39**: *In re Marriage of Rodriguez* 72
- E. Passive Parent Action 73
  - **PROBLEM 40**: *Jackson v. Jackson* 73

Chapter Eight

Decisions About Children — The State's Role 75

- A. Claims Against the State — 42 U.S.C. Section 1983 75
  - **PROBLEM 41**: *Lightfinger v. Michiana DROP* 75
- B. Physical Abuse 77
  - **PROBLEM 42**: *In re Ruth Ann Collins, a Child Alleged to Be a Child in Need of Services* 77
- C. Fetal Abuse 95
  - **PROBLEM 43**: *State v. Fitzgerald* and *In re Baby John, a Child Alleged to Be a Child in Need Of Services* 95
  - **PROBLEM 44**: *In re Mary Jones* 96
- D. Child Neglect 97
  - **PROBLEM 45**: *In re Leonard R. Bowman, a Child Alleged to Be a Child in Need of Services* 97
- E. Indian Child Welfare Act 135
  - **PROBLEM 46**: *In re Blackstone* 135
- F. Medical Treatment of Children 135
  - **PROBLEM 47**: *State v. Anderson* 135
- G. Termination Of Parental Rights 137
  - **PROBLEM 48**: *In re Termination of Parent-Child Relationship Between Leonard R. Bowman, Child, and Bonnie and Clyde Bowman, Parents* 137

Contents

Chapter Nine

Dissolution Of Marriage 141

- A. Subject Matter Jurisdiction 141
  - **PROBLEM 49**: *Fisher v. Fisher* 141
- B. Personal Jurisdiction 154
  - **PROBLEM 50**: *Fisher v. Fisher* 154
- C. Death and Loss of Jurisdiction 154
  - **PROBLEM 51**: *In re Marriage of Crosby* 154
- D. Grounds and Defenses: The Fading of Fault 155
  1. Fault Divorce 155
     - **PROBLEM 52**: *Kilmer v. Kilmer* 155
  2. No-Fault Divorce 157
     - **PROBLEM 53**: *In re Marriage of Barton* 157
  3. Jewish Divorce 158
     - **PROBLEM 54**: *Rubin v. Rubin* 158
- E. Attorney-Client Relations in Divorce Cases 158
- F. Right to Divorce 159
  - **PROBLEM 55**: *Manilow v. Pension Board* 159
- G. Spousal Support: Alimony or Maintenance 161
  1. At Dissolution 161
     - **PROBLEM 56**: *In re Marriage of Farrell* 161
  2. Modification of Alimony Order 163
     - **PROBLEM 57**: *In re Marriage of Perry* 163
  3. Necessaries Rule 178
     - **PROBLEM 58**: *Southby Community Hospital v. Sherer* 178
- H. Bankruptcy: Discharge of Marital Obligations 178
  1. Property Division or Support of Spouse or Child? 178
     - **PROBLEM 59**: *In re Marriage of Perry* 178
  2. Dischargeability of Attorney Fees 185
     - **PROBLEM 60**: *In re Howard W. Ganglinger, Debtor* 185
- I. Custody of Minor Children 187
  1. At Dissolution 187
     - **PROBLEM 61**: *In re Marriage of Gardner* 187
  2. Homosexual Parent 195
     - **PROBLEM 62**: *Ginger v. Ginger* 195
  3. Joint Custody 196
     - **PROBLEM 63**: *In re Marriage of Morgan* 196
  4. Non-Marital Relationships 205
     - **PROBLEM 64**: *Fontes v. MacNamara* 205

	5.	Parental Alienation Syndrome	206
		PROBLEM 65: *In re Marriage of Wallace*	206
	6.	Modification of Custody Order	207
		PROBLEM 66: *In re Marriage of Goddard*	207
		PROBLEM 67: *In re Marriage of Porter*	208
	7.	Petition by the Child	210
		PROBLEM 68: *In re Sammy H.*	210
J.	Visitation		211
	1.	Rights of Custodial and Non-Custodial Parents	211
		PROBLEM 69: *In re Marriage of Rockaway*	211
	2.	The AIDS Issue	213
		PROBLEM 70: *Carson v. Carson*	213
	3.	Grandparent Visitation	214
		PROBLEM 71: *In re Marriage of Daley*	214
	4.	Visitation by Third Parties	215
		PROBLEM 72: *In re Marriage of Sherry (T.) B. and Gary T.*	215
	5.	Termination of Visitation	216
		PROBLEM 73: *In re Marriage of Houser*	216
K.	Domestic Violence		225
		PROBLEM 74: *In re Marriage of Custer*	225
L.	Battered Women's Syndrome		227
		PROBLEM 75: *Dobbs v. Dobbs*	227
M.	Removal of Child from Jurisdiction		227
		PROBLEM 76: *In re Marriage of O'Neil*	227
N.	Interstate Custody Disputes		229
	1.	Uniform Child Custody Jurisdiction Act and Parental Kidnapping Prevention Act	229
		PROBLEM 77: *In re Marriage of Tried*	229
O.	International Custody Disputes		230
	1.	Hague Convention and International Child Abduction Remedies Act	230
		PROBLEM 78: *In re Application of Fiona Bindra*	230
		PROBLEM 79: *In re Marriage of Singh*	236
P.	Child Support		236
	1.	Federal Intervention	236
		PROBLEM 80: *In re Marriage of Morgan*	236
	2.	Enforcement and Modification of Child Support Order	251
		PROBLEM 81: *In re Marriage of Rose*	251
	3.	Emancipation	255
		PROBLEM 82: *In re Marriage of Rose*	255
	4.	Education Expenses—Private School	255
		PROBLEM 83: *In re Marriage of Tidmarsh*	255

5.	College Expenses	256
	PROBLEM 84: *Meyer v. Meyer*	256
6.	Child Support Recovery Act	257
	PROBLEM 85: *United States v. Balboa*	257

Q. Division of Property 257
  1. Defining Equitable Distribution 257
     PROBLEM 86: *Gibbons v. Gibbons* 257
  2. What Constitutes Marital Property? 258
     PROBLEM 87: *In re Marriage of Mumfort* 258
  3. Person or Property? 260
     PROBLEM 88: *Scribner v. Scribner* 260
  4. Lien Avoidance 260
     PROBLEM 89: *In re Hanes* 260
  5. Valuation of Assets 261
     PROBLEM 90: *Fester v. Fester* 261
  6. Qualified Domestic Relations Orders 262
     PROBLEM 91: *Harris v. Harris* 262
  7. Future Interests—Pensions 267
     PROBLEM 92: *In re Marriage of McDougal* 267
  8. Community Property 268
     PROBLEM 93: *Rollins v. Rollins* 268
  9. Social Security Income 269
     PROBLEM 94: *In re Marriage of Robinson* 269
  10. Worker's Compensation 269
      PROBLEM 95: *In re Marriage of Branch* 269
  11. Application of RICO 270
      PROBLEM 96: *In re Marriage of Sarducci* 270
  12. Negotiation of Settlement Agreement 271
      PROBLEM 97. *In re Marriage of Miller* 271

Chapter Ten

Mediation In Dissolution Cases 275

PROBLEM 98: *In re Marriage of Gardner* 275

Chapter Eleven

Family Law Practice And Professional Responsibility 277

A. Family Law Practice 277
  1. Role of Guardian ad Litem 277

		PROBLEM 99: *In re Woods*........................277
	2.	Attorney-Client Relations....................278
		PROBLEM 100: *In re Marriage of Constant*............278
B.	Professional Responsibility......................282
	1.	Attorney-Client Relationship..................282
		PROBLEM 101: *In re Bellows*....................282
	2.	Conflicts of Interest.......................283
		PROBLEM 102: *In re Matthews*..................283
	3.	Ethical Dilemmas........................284
		PROBLEM 103: *In re Marriage of Hosinski*...........284
	4.	Contingent Fee..........................285
		PROBLEM 104: *Ketch v. Alstott*..................285

Appendix

Statutes And Uniform Acts....................287

Defense of Marriage Act..........................287
Uniform Premarital Agreement Act....................287
Uniform Parentage Act............................288
Uniform Putative and Unknown Fathers Act..............290
Uniform Status of Children of Assisted Conception Act.......292
Uniform Adoption Act............................294
Interstate Compact on the Placement of Children..........303
The Indian Child Welfare Act.......................305
Uniform Marriage and Divorce Act....................307
Uniform Child Custody Jurisdiction Act................314
Parental Kidnapping Prevention Act...................321
Hague Convention on Civil Aspects of International Child Abduction...323
International Child Abduction Remedies Act.............327
International Parental Kidnapping Act..................328
Uniform Interstate Family Support Act.................328
Child Support Recovery Act........................338
Full Faith and Credit for Child Support Orders Act.........338

Foreword

Fifty years ago, family law was a narrow field. The legal principles involved, although vitally important for affected individuals, were relatively few and, for the most part, quite straightforward. How things change! Today, at the threshold of the twenty-first century, family law has been transformed from a legal backwater into an enormously complex, expanding, and important specialty. The family law attorney for the next millennium must know much more than the law of marriage and divorce. The modern practitioner grapples with fundamental principles of constitutional law, the increasing impact of federal law on the family, the intricacies of conflicts of law and interstate agreements affecting children, and, as the world continues to shrink, with international law.

Professor Smithburn's *Family Law: Problems and Documents* provides students with an excellent introduction to the complex theoretical, practical, and ethical issues that await them in practice. The Problems in this book address the full range of issues in contemporary family law, from child custody and property division to such cutting-edge issues as assisted conception and domestic violence.

Law students benefit from the mind-stretching experience of theoretical analysis. Yet students crave instruction in the practical reality of lawyering: "Tell me the nuts and bolts of family law." This book achieves a wonderful blend of theory and practice. Many of the problems are accompanied by the everyday documents, reports, letters, and pleadings used in the real world of family law. With this challenging book, students can get their feet wet in the modern practice of family law.

John E.B. Myers
Professor of Law
University of the Pacific
McGeorge School of Law

Preface

It occurred to me several years ago that in addition to reading appellate opinions, the family law student should also work with practice materials and discuss problems. This book provides the student with an opportunity to expand case and policy analysis to include problem-solving and advocacy on behalf of a client in a family law case. Family law continues to be an area where the trial court often has broad discretion and the judge's rulings are reviewed by the abuse-of-discretion standard. There is, of course, substantial coverage in the book of Problems where the federal or state constitution or statutory law limit the trial judge's freedom to decide. This book requires the student to review most of the Problems in the trial setting and to develop an understanding of the nature of judicial decision-making in the family law context.

The book begins with Problems in traditional and non-traditional marriage, which provide the student with an opportunity to explore the ecclesiastical underpinnings and other definitional sources of the law of marriage and family as a basis for state marriage regulation, and to review the Supreme Court's constitutionalization of marriage and family law. Once grounded in the concepts of state support for traditional marriage, disfavor of divorce, family privacy, and individual privacy within the family unit, the student may segue into the issues of private ordering by parties versus state regulation, presented by the Problems on antenuptial agreements, alternative forms of marriage, cohabitation and surrogacy agreements, and decisions on procreation. The Problems on establishing the parent-child relationship, the rights of children born out of wedlock, adoption, family torts, and the state's role in protection of at-risk children expose the student to the interface between issues of family privacy and the system of public law (often the juvenile court). There is extensive coverage of dissolution of marriage and its incidents—spousal and child support, child custody and visitation, and division of property and mediation. The final chapter contains several Problems on family law practice and professional responsibility. These Problems permit students to reflect on the subjects studied in the course in the sometimes difficult context of reconciling the client's expectations of role behavior (of counsel) with the lawyer's personal beliefs about ethical and moral questions. Finally, there is an appendix of statutes and uniform acts for student use.

I'm most grateful to my Notre Dame Law School students, whose thirst for practical insight into family law issues broadened my perspective and got me started on this project. I further wish to thank Dean David T. Link of Notre Dame Law School for his support and Rosemary Burke, J.D. 1992, Notre Dame Law School, for her research assistance.

Special words of thanks go to the following persons: James DeMarco, J.D. 1994, Notre Dame Law School, and Meighan A. Templin, J.D. 1996, Notre Dame Law School, whose assistance with research, drafting and organization of the text was invaluable; my secretary, Marlou Hall, for her patience and diligence in typing the manuscript; and to my wife, Aladean DeRose-Smithburn, for her support in many ways throughout the project.

J. Eric Smithburn
February 1997

Introduction

The Problems in these materials place the student in the role of counsel representing a client involved in a family law dispute. Each of the Problems is followed by several questions. The primary use of the Problems and questions will be to stimulate class discussion. This may be done on an informal basis by the student being asked to state an argument for a party, analyze a point of law or policy, or answer one of the listed questions. It is expected that the Problems will be used in connection with assigned reading in a casebook or handout material. There is an appendix of statutes and uniform acts for student use.

In some of the Problems, the professor may also assign roles to be played by students in a class simulation. The formality of a simulated hearing may vary from assigning students to present arguments while remaining in their seats to having the students sit at counsel table and advocate to the court (with the professor serving as judge). The Problems that contain pleadings, reports of experts, and other exhibits are well suited for simulated hearings. The professor may also assign written motions, memoranda of law, and certificates of service to be filed with the court (the professor's secretary serves as clerk) and arguments to be presented in a classroom simulation. If a simulated hearing is assigned, the hearings are conducted in the courts of Hoynes County, Michiana (unless otherwise stated in the Problem). It is assumed that, unlike other jurisdictions, Michiana has no family law statutes or case law (unless otherwise provided in the Problem). Instead, the courts of Michiana have discretion to choose the applicable substantive law on a case-by-case basis. Student counsel may be required to submit to the trial court written memoranda, that summarize applicable federal law, pertinent standards and uniform acts, rules of professional responsibility, and the law of the other fifty state jurisdictions on the issues presented. Each Problem is considered a case of first impression in Michiana, therefore a memorandum should include a synopsis of the prevailing view on the issues and other minority positions and trends in the law. Michiana rules of practice and pleading, which are identical to the Federal Rules of Civil Procedure, state that written memoranda are to be not less than eight nor more than twelve properly numbered typed pages (excluding title pages, appendices, and certificate of service) and include the following sections:

1. facts
2. questions presented
3. summary of law (an objective statement of "what the law is")
   a. majority view

    b. minority view(s)
    c. trend(s) in the law
 4. choice of law (the advocacy part—"what the law should be")
    a. reasons—law and policy
 5. answers to questions

The Michiana rules of evidence and advocacy are identical to the Federal Rules of Evidence. The student should provide signatures for all documents and writings in the Problems and assume that they are authentic. Each set of documents filed for an assigned Problem must include a properly executed certificate of service on opposing counsel. In some Problems, where a hearing is scheduled, certain preliminary questions may arise which require a separate hearing on the matter.

The preliminary question(s) may be raised by counsel filing a written motion and serving opposing counsel with a copy of the motion, notice of hearing, and certificate of service. Where a pretrial conference is required, the professor will provide instructions to counsel. To increase student participation in a simulation, the professor may reserve time at the end of class for the other students to question the student counsel about their analysis, arguments, and so forth. Also, the professor may announce before the class that after the hearing three students will be assigned to deliberate and decide the case, as a three-judge panel, and submit a written opinion at the next class.

If a simulated hearing is assigned, the professor may designate alternative rules of practice and procedure and applicable law of a specific state.

In all of the Problems, YR-0 is the year of the hearing, YR-1 the preceding year, etc. YR+1 is next year, YR+2 is two years from now, etc.

J. Eric Smithburn
February 1997

Family Law

Problems and Documents

Chapter One

Marriage and Family

A. THE NATURE OF MARRIAGE AND FAMILY

1. Definition of Marriage

Problem 1

Johnson and Johanson v. Eldridge

Terry Johanson (Terry) and Shawn Johnson (Shawn) are a homosexual couple living in Southby, Hoynes County, Michiana. They have been lovers for four years, since Shawn moved in with Terry after Shawn's divorce. Shawn's daughter, Charlotte, has lived with the couple since her father moved in with Terry. Shawn and Terry are concerned that Charlotte's natural mother, Tracy, who has had visitation rights limited by the court because of her alleged physical and emotional abuse of Charlotte since the divorce, might try to take custody of Charlotte if Shawn dies. Everyone else in Shawn's family loves Terry, and would be supportive of him as Charlotte's surviving parent.

Michiana has never recognized a homosexual marriage. Consequently, Shawn and Terry have not been able to legalize their relationship, particularly with regard to Charlotte. Charlotte is seven years old and, according to a psychologist's assessment, is strongly reliant on both Shawn and Terry for parental support. In nearly all respects, Terry and Shawn live as a married couple, and share parenting duties. Shawn and Terry feel that the best solution, both legally and in terms of family cohesion, is for them to marry.

Terry, a paralegal who works as a law librarian, researched the appropriate Michiana marriage statute. On the theory that the statute permits same-sex marriage because the legislature would have stated a gender bias if it had wanted to prevent homosexual marriage, Shawn and Terry went to the Clerk of Hoynes County to apply for a marriage license. Samuel Eldridge, Clerk of Hoynes County, refused to allow Shawn and Terry to fill out a license application, stating that they were unqualified to marry. When Terry asserted that the laws were gender-neutral and intended no sexual orientation bias, Eldridge threw Terry and Shawn out of his office, stating that "the law doesn't intend for sick people like you to be married."

Shawn and Terry filed a lawsuit in the Hoynes Superior Court, requesting declaratory and injunctive relief against Eldridge in his official capacity. Shawn and Terry seek a declaration by the court that they may be married and a permanent injunction requiring the Clerk of Hoynes County to accept marriage license applications from all homosexual couples who otherwise meet the qualifications for marriage. Shawn and Terry base their claims on Title 10 of the Michiana Domestic Relations statutes and on Title 1 of the Michiana civil rights statute, which was recently amended to make illegal any discrimination against homosexuals. (The relevant portion of the statutes follow this Problem.)

MICHIANA REVISED STATUTES

Title 10. Domestic Relations

Section 1001—**Who May Not Marry.** The following marriages are prohibited in Michiana and shall be void ab initio: marriage between any person with his or her grandparent, grandparent's spouse, spouse's grandparent, child's spouse, son, daughter, aunt, uncle, sibling, cousin within one degree of consanguinity, or any child under the age of sixteen without written consent of both of the child's parents. The marriage of any persons either of whom has been previously married and whose previous marriage has not been terminated by decree of divorce is void ab initio. No person may marry another who is formally decreed an idiot or lunatic. Any marriage procured by force, fear, or fraud shall be void ab initio. Any marriage into which either of the parties to which shall be incapable, from physical causes, of entering into the married state, shall be void.

Section 1002—**Who May Marry.** Any persons not excluded under section 1001 of this Code may apply to the clerk of the county in which they reside for a marriage license. Having fulfilled such regulatory requirements as shall be enacted under this title, the couple may use said license to marry before an authorized minister, judge, justice of the peace, or other authorized official for the county in which one of them resides.

Title 1. Civil Rights

Section 112—**Discrimination** (amended, June 1, YR-2). No officer of the state in his official capacity may discriminate against any person on the basis of race, color, religion, national origin, gender, sexual orientation, age, marital status, personal appearance, political affiliation, physical or mental handicap, or source of income.

Questions

1. What is the definition of "marriage"? What are the definitional sources for marriage?
2. What is the relationship between marriage and family?
3. How has characterization of marriage as a relationship or higher status, arising out of a contract to marry but not a contract itself, affected the law's response to would-be married couples?
4. What authority does the state have to regulate marriage? Why is the state vested with that authority? What limits, if any, should there be on the state's control over marriage?
5. Under the Michiana marriage statute alone, do Shawn and Terry have a right to marry? What are some pertinent rules of statutory construction that may help answer this question?

6. Are Charlotte's circumstances a proper consideration for the court in this case?

2. *Definition of Family*

Problem 2

Peacock Realty, Inc. v. Lyndon Hayes

Ramon DeRosa, Lyndon Hayes, and Fleur Hayes, Lyndon's minor daughter from a prior marriage, shared an apartment in Southby, Michiana, from YR-8 to March 21, YR-0, when Ramon died as a result of complications for Acquired Immune Deficiency Syndrome (AIDS). In YR-8, at a ceremony attended by a few friends and Fleur, Ramon and Lyndon exchanged rings and expressed their commitment of love and loyalty to each other for life. Ramon and Lyndon, who were considered by their friends to be a happily married couple, had executed wills in which each left his entire estate to the other; and their wills also named Fleur as alternate devisee and legatee if one predeceased the other. Lyndon and Fleur provided care for Ramon, and Lyndon handled Ramon's personal and business affairs during the final months of his life. When Ramon died, his name alone was on the lease to the rent-controlled apartment the two men and Fleur shared since YR-8. Section 101(d) of the Southby rent control law provides noneviction protection to those who are either the

surviving spouse of the deceased tenant, or some other member of the deceased tenant's family who has been living with the tenant [of record].

Pursuant to Section 101(d), the landlord, Peacock Realty, Inc., filed a complaint to evict Lyndon, claiming that Lyndon was not a member of Ramon's family. Lyndon filed a counterclaim against Peacock for injunctive and declaratory relief. Lyndon claims he should have succession rights even though his name wasn't on the lease.

Questions

1. At the time of Ramon's death, were Ramon and Lyndon married? If so, what distinguishes their marriage from other committed cohabitation arrangements? If not, what elements required for marriage did they lack?
2. Assume that Ramon suffered much discomfort during his last three months in the hospital and that Harvey, Ramon's brother, moved in with Lyndon and Fleur. After Ramon's death, a dispute arose between Lyndon and Harvey over the rights to the apartment. Who has the stronger claim?
3. Assume that, prior to his death, Ramon moved to West Dakota to obtain treatment for his illness and that Lyndon quit his job to join Ramon. Would Lyndon's voluntary departure disqualify him from unemployment benefits under a scheme that allows benefits to those workers who quit "with good cause"?

4. Should the definitions of "marriage" and "family" vary depending on the legal context of the problem (e.g., rent control, zoning ordinance, or unemployment compensation)?

B. STATE REGULATION OF MARRIAGE

1. Right to Marry

Problem 3

In Re John Wilson and Jasmine Rafhiq

You are a sole practitioner specializing in criminal and constitutional law. One of your first criminal clients was John Wilson, whom you represented in a rape case. John was convicted of statutory rape and sentenced to six years in prison in YR-3. Because of his involvement in a prison yard fight last summer, John was convicted of battery and assaulting a prison guard. Based on his sentence arising from the prison yard incident, John will not have a parole hearing until March, YR+10, and he is not scheduled for release until July 21, YR+18.

John's rape conviction stems from his relationship with Jasmine Rafhiq, his high school sweetheart. He and Jasmine met in YR-4, when John was a high school senior and Jasmine was a fourteen-year-old sophomore. John and Jasmine quickly became friends, and before long they were romantically involved. Shortly after John graduated from high school, the couple became engaged. Despite vehement opposition from Jasmine's father, the couple planned a wedding for the Saturday following Jasmine's eighteenth birthday.

Jasmine became pregnant during John's fall semester college break. When Jasmine's father found out about the pregnancy, he became outraged. He called the Hoynes County Prosecuting Attorney and demanded that the prosecutor press statutory rape charges against John. Jasmine was fifteen years old at the time she became pregnant. John was convicted and sentenced to six years in prison on the same day his daughter, Amber Rafhiq Wilson, was born.

John contacted you six weeks ago. Since then you have been in contact with Jasmine more than five times. Jasmine turned eighteen last week, and now she and John want to be married. Both have expressed a desire for their daughter, Amber, to have a legal father. John and Jasmine have further confirmed their life-long commitment to each other and their desire to live together as a family as soon as possible.

Billy Mixter, John's prison warden, has expressed to you his disapproval of prison marriages, especially for John. During a recent telephone conversation, Mr. Mixter told you, "John Wilson is a crook. He's dangerous and he's bad. He beat up one of my guards, and he's not remorseful. I don't trust him, and I won't let him get married. Not on my watch, buddy boy!" Mr. Mixter then referred you to the Michiana State Prison Code, which allows for prison marriages "unless the prison warden determines that the marriage poses a threat to legitimate prison interests."

John and Jasmine request you to help arrange for their marriage as soon as possible.

Chapter One. Marriage and Family

Questions

1. Who is your client? Can you represent both Jasmine and John?
2. How fundamental is the right to marry?
3. What right does the state have to deny John and Jasmine's marriage? Can Warden Mixter prevent the marriage solely for prison security reasons? Can he prevent the marriage because he personally doesn't trust John?
4. What legal action might you file on the couple's behalf?
5. What are the benefits (economic and otherwise) of marriage to John, Jasmine and Amber?
6. If the couple is allowed to marry, should they be allowed to consummate the marriage? If so, how can the state reasonably prohibit sexual relations for other inmates?
7. Should the fact that John's imprisonment is based on his rape of Jasmine play any role in the legal determination of whether John and Jasmine may marry?
8. Review Problem 1. Is there a constitutional right for homosexuals to marry? What are the implications of prisoners' rights to marry on gay couples? *See Turner v. Safley,* 482 U.S. 78 (1987).

2. Intimate Association

Problem 4

Hildago v. Michiana State Attorney General

Maria Hildago graduated from Michiana University School of Law in YR-2, and, after a two-year clerkship with the Michiana Supreme Court, Maria was offered a job with the Michiana Attorney General's office. Two weeks later, the attorney general learned that Maria planned to take part in a Jewish "marriage" ceremony with her lesbian partner. The ceremony was to be conducted by a rabbi and is recognized by the branch of Judaism to which Ms. Hildago and her partner belong. The attorney general promptly withdrew the job offer to Maria, claiming that there would be a conflict between Maria's conduct and Michiana marriage laws, which would preclude her ability to represent the State of Michiana. Assume that Michiana has adopted the Uniform Marriage and Divorce Act.

Maria filed suit alleging that the withdrawal of her job offer is a violation of her constitutional right to intimate association under the First Amendment of the U.S. Constitution.

Questions

1. Does Maria have a fundamental right to "marry" her partner?
2. Does the State of Michiana have a legitimate interest in not wanting to employ Maria?
3. When balancing the state's interests against Maria's right to intimate association, should the court apply a rational basis test or the same strict scrutiny standard that applies when a state restricts conventional marriages?

C. MARRIAGE FORMALITIES AND LEGAL QUALIFICATIONS

1. *Bigamy: Legal Versus Deemed Widow*

Problem 5

> ### In Re Estate of Doolittle Walter Ditty

Doolittle Walter Ditty (known to his friends and fans as "Doo Wah"), a rock musician, and Madonna Shutt, a country music singer, were married in Southby, Michiana, on July 19, YR-9. The Dittys, who continued to live in Michiana, had two children, Shamus and Denise. The strains of travel and long working hours took their toll on the marriage, and in YR-3 Doolittle said to Madonna, "So long, Babe, Doo Wah Ditty is headed for New York City." Doolittle and Madonna divided their assets, and Doolittle executed the necessary documents to transfer certain real and personal property to Madonna. Shortly after moving to New York, Doolittle received the following letter from Madonna:

> Dear Doo Wah,
>
> The lawyer says that since we agree on everything, the divorce is automatic. So there's nothing more to do. Thanks for the support money.
>
> Madonna

No formal legal action was taken in Michiana to dissolve Doolittle and Madonna's marriage. In January of YR-1, Doolittle married Petula in New York. Doolittle and two other members of his band were killed in an automobile accident in May of YR-0. Doolittle and Petula had no children. Doolittle's will devised and bequeathed all of his property to Petula and named her as executrix.

Madonna retains counsel to file a claim for spousal benefits under the Social Security Act. Petula also files a Social Security claim. For the purpose of this Problem, assume that Michiana does not recognize common law marriage.

Questions

1. Is Madonna entitle to benefits as the surviving spouse under the Social Security Act? Is Petula? *See* 42 U.S.C. Sections 402, 416.
2. Who is the "deemed widow" in this case? Which woman is the "legal widow"? To whom should the law show a preference when competing claims are brought?
3. What effect would a letter to Doolittle from Madonna, dated June, YR-1, renouncing her Social Security benefits, have on her claim? What about a letter from Petula? Assume that Doolittle doesn't mention Madonna or the children in his will. Does Madonna have a right to a statutory share of Doolittle's estate?
4. What protection does the law provide for second spouses who have no knowledge of a prior marriage or the nonexistence of a prior divorce?

D. ENFORCING PROMISES TO MARRY

Problem 6

Emily v. James

James and Emily were married and lived in Southby, Michiana, for six years before their divorce in October of YR-10. There were two children, Scott and Melissa, born of the marriage. After the divorce, Emily and the two children moved to suburban Chicago, Illinois. Nearly three years later, in May of YR-7, James wrote the following letter to Emily:

Dearest Em,

I still love you, Honey. Please bring Scott and Melissa home where you belong. I was wrong. Let's start over. I love you and miss you, and I promise I'll do my part this time. It'll be forever share and share alike, fifty-fifty, okay? I await your reply.

Devotedly,

Jim

In July of YR-7, Emily quit her job as a tenured secondary public school teacher, and she and the children moved back to Southby to live with James. James, Emily, and the children lived together from July of YR-7 until March of YR-1, when Emily and the children moved out of the "family home," as Emily describes it. James had purchased this spacious house in his own name on August 2, YR-7. On the same day, James placed a 1.5 carat diamond ring on Emily's finger, stating "Here's to us, Honey." From YR-7 to YR-1, Emily was employed thirty hours a week as a dental office assistant and receptionist. She made contributions from her personal savings of approximately $12,500 for improvements on the home, purchased furniture and other household items, and performed the homemaking duties.

Emily maintains that on several occasions during this period she appealed to James without success to "make it legal" and marry her, for her and the children's security. Emily also has the following letter, dated June 2, YR-7, inside an envelope postmarked Chicago, Illinois, June 3, YR-7:

Dear Jim,

I've thought long and hard about your May 7 letter. You know, we had our share of problems, but you were always a man of your word. I've learned how precious honesty is, Jim. You've made me an offer I can't refuse, Love. The kids and I are excited about us being a family again. You'll love the wedding dress I bought. Let's go back to Beck Chapel and get it right this time.

Yours,

Em

In March of YR-1, James admitted to Emily that he was having an intimate affair with Carl, a male friend he had met at the YMCA. The next day, Emily and the children took their clothes and personal effects and moved into an apartment in Southby. Carl moved in with James a few days later and continues to live with James.

James has rejected Emily's requests for a settlement. Emily seeks advice on what cause(s) of action for mending a broken heart and recovery of damages she may have against James.

Questions

1. What possible causes of action does Emily have against James?
2. Should the court regard Emily's lawsuit as an unenforceable claim against an unmarried cohabitant and subject to a motion to dismiss?
3. If Michiana recognizes the action for breach of promise to marry, what damages should be recoverable?
4. Assuming common law marriage is not recognized in Michiana, would recognition of Emily's claim be tantamount to reinstating the cause of action in the jurisdiction?
5. Assume that Emily had been having a secret affair with Len, James's business partner, for three years before James's affair with Carl was discovered. What effect would this have on Emily's breach-of-promise-to-marry action?
6. What if, after a few days with Carl, James asks him to leave and offers to marry Emily. Does Emily still have a claim against James on the original breach of promise to marry?
7. What are some possible defenses in a breach-of-promise-to-marry action?
8. Felix and Jolene become engaged after a two-year courtship. Felix surprises Jolene on her birthday with a dozen roses, a bottle of Dom Pedro champagne, two tickets to the opera, and a two-carat diamond ring. For Christmas that year, Felix buys his fiancée a fur coat and gives her a hefty down payment towards the purchase of a new sports car. Two weeks before the wedding, Jolene tells Felix she wants to call off the wedding. Felix threatens her that if she does, he will sue her for breach of promise to marry and take back all the gifts he has given her. Jolene agrees to go through with the wedding. Three months after the wedding, Felix sues for divorce and adds a claim for anticipatory breach of promise to marry. What result?

E. COMMON LAW MARRIAGE

Problem 7

In Re Estate of Harley Thomas

Harley Thomas, a farmer, and his wife, Dorothy, were divorced in Green Mountain, Iowa, On March 15, YR-6. Two children were born of the marriage, Lester in YR-17 and Bernice in YR-15. During the Summer of YR-7, Harley sold his farm equipment and livestock and moved to Southby, Michiana. In September of YR-7, Harley obtained employment at an ethanol plant

Chapter One. Marriage and Family

in Southby. The following month, Harley met Ellen Love at a Halloween party. In January of YR-6, Ellen, who was living with her mother, moved her furniture to Harley's house and began living with him. On February 14, YR-6, at a surprise party for Ellen attended by family and friends, Ellen read aloud her Valentine from Harley, "Be mine, Ellen, 'til death do us part." Ellen replied, "Oh, Harley, I will! I will!" Harley and Ellen opened a joint checking-savings account at First Source Bank, purchased two certificates of deposit in joint names, and stated on all of their employment and personal records that the other was to be contacted in case of emergency. In YR-5, Harley had surgery to remove a malignant lung tumor. From YR-5 to April of YR-1, Ellen provided constant care for Harley, which during YR-1 included bathing and feeding him. On April 17, YR-1, Harley was hospitalized. He died on April 20. Ellen was named as executrix in Harley's will. Lester and Bernice, who never came to Michiana to see their father during his illness, have filed a petition with the Hoynes Probate Court to disqualify Ellen as Harley's personal representative. The petition alleges that Ellen is not Harley's common law wife and that, under the circumstances, she is unable to perform the duties of executrix without a conflict of interest. Harley's will makes the following specific bequests:

1. To Ellen:
   a. one-half interest, as tenant in common, in Arbor Acres
   b. all of the household furnishings
   c. 1.5k. diamond ring
2. To Lester:
   a. one-half interest, as tenant in common, in Arbor Acres
   b. silver dollar collection in lockbox at First Source Bank
3. To Bernice:
   a. ruby ring
   b. sapphire ring
   c. $2,000

There is also $7500 in a savings account in Harley's name, which Ellen claims goes into the will's residuary clause, to which Ellen claims she is entitled as Harley's common law wife. Lester and Bernice state that, as Harley's children, they are entitled to receive the $7500. The Michiana Department of Revenue informs Ellen's attorney that Ellen, as a non-family member, is required to pay 10 percent inheritance tax on the total value of Harley's bequests to her (as Harley's common law wife, she would pay no tax). In June of YR-2, Harley quitclaimed his land contract interest in a parcel of real estate to Ellen. Harley had made a down payment of $750, and Ellen made ten subsequent monthly payments of $100 each. The Department of Revenue claims that the full market value ($15,000) of this parcel of real estate should be included in Harley's gross estate, as a gift made in contemplation of death, on which Ellen, as a non-family member, should pay inheritance tax.

Questions

1. What is common law marriage? What are the legal requirements for a common law marriage?
2. Should courts recognize common law marriage? What policy reasons favor common law marriage? What policy reasons support requiring formalities for marriage?

3. What is the main legal impediment to Ellen and Harley being married on February 14, YR-6? What is the significance of removal of the impediment?
4. What effect would Ellen's status as Harley's common law wife have on the distribution of the $7500 under the will's residuary clause?
5. Does the policy promoting marriage apply to this case, where Harley is deceased?
6. Assume that Michiana does not recognize common law marriage. Is Ellen still entitled to the specific bequests under the will? Why or why not?
7. What effect does the common law marriage determination have on the federal tax question? Must there be an independent federal determination as to marital status?
8. Suppose Harley and Ellen first lived in Oregonia, which recognizes common law marriage, and they met all of Oregonia's requirements for a common law marriage. Thereafter, Harley and Ellen moved to North Virginia, a state that doesn't recognize common law marriage. Should Ellen still be treated as Harley's common law wife?
9. Assume Michiana recognized common law marriage in YR-6 but does so no longer. What result?
10. How can a rule be consistently applied to distinguish between common law marriages and committed cohabitation arrangements?
11. Does refusal to adopt common law marriage reflect any racial or ethnic prejudice by the judiciary or legislature?
12. What effect does the AIDS epidemic have on common law marriage?

F. ANNULMENT

1. Fraud as to Qualifications

Problem 8

> ## In Re Marriage of Conway

PART A

Karen and Wayne met at a singles bar in Southby, Michiana, in November of YR-1. During their brief courtship, Wayne told Karen that he was recently divorced and employed as a manufacturer's representative for Canco Corporation, located in Mason, Michiana, forty miles west of Southby. Wayne also stated that his mother died following the divorce and, as her sole heir, he would soon inherit approximately $250,000. On December 30, YR-1, Karen sent the following letter to her mother:

Dear Mom,

Sorry I couldn't be home for Christmas. Wayne had a business meeting on the 26th, so we had to stay in Southby. He's a wonderful guy—

successful and confident. He's been married, but has no children and no debts. Wayne promises to be a good provider. Guess I'm lucky to have found him. Love to all,

Devotedly,

Karen

Karen and Wayne were married on January 27, YR-0. To Karen's dismay, Wayne cancelled their honeymoon trip to Atlantic City, New Jersey, because of an important business deal. In early February of YR-0, Karen closed her money market account and purchased two $10,000 one-year certificates of deposit, her entire savings, in joint name—Karen and Wayne—with rights of survivorship. They also opened a joint checking-savings account at National Bank of Southby. Shortly after moving into Southridge Apartments, Karen received several phone calls from Wayne's creditors. Karen complained to Wayne that nearly all of her salary as a registered nurse was being used to support the couple. Wayne stated that he would be in Chicago on business for the next two days and didn't want to discuss personal matters. On February 20, Karen called Canco Corporation to speak with Wayne. She was told that Wayne had been discharged from his position with Canco in August of YR-1. Karen also found a copy of Wayne's divorce decree, dated July 16, YR-1, in which Wayne was ordered to pay $60,000 in debts arising from the marriage. Wayne's creditors have filed lawsuits totaling $100,000 against Wayne. Wayne admits that he lied to Karen about his employment and future inheritance. Karen files a complaint for annulment.

Questions

1. What is annulment? How is annulment different from divorce?
2. What criteria should be considered by a legislature when it distinguishes between annulment and divorce?
3. Is fraudulent misrepresentation as to financial status a sufficient basis for annulment? If so, what must be proven?
4. What effect would the annulment issue have on the status of Karen and Wayne's jointly held funds?
5. If Karen cannot obtain an annulment, which of her assets might be subject to Wayne's creditors?
6. In view of recognition by the courts of private ordering between marriage partners, should fraud as to money or property be included in the "essentials of marriage" test?

PART B

A few weeks after their wedding, Wayne tells Karen that the reason he lost his job at Canco in August of YR-1 was that he refused to submit to a test for AIDS. Wayne admits that he would not take the test because he felt ill in July and August of YR-1 and feared that he might have AIDS. After learning that Wayne had tested positive for the HIV virus, Karen moved into the guestroom of their home and refused to engage in sexual intercourse with him. On June 10, YR-0, Wayne showed Karen a letter from his doctor, dated the same day, stating that he did not have full-blown AIDS and that his disease was in remission. Karen, however, again refused to have sexual contact with Wayne. On October 27, YR-0, Karen gave birth to a baby boy, Alexis. Medical tests show that Alexis and Karen are HIV negative and that Alexis is a healthy baby. Karen files a complaint for annulment.

Questions

1. Is Wayne's failure to disclose his exposure to AIDS a sufficient cause for annulment? What if Wayne had known he was HIV positive when he and Karen were engaged?
2. What if instead of testing positive for the HIV virus, Wayne suspected in August of YR-1 that he had genital herpes, which was confirmed in a letter from Wayne's doctor on June 10, YR-0?
3. If Karen obtains an annulment from Wayne, does Alexis become an illegitimate child?
4. Can someone with a terminal illness have the capacity to marry? Suppose Wayne is a healthy member of the Hemlock Society and he told Karen before the wedding that he planned to kill himself in YR+1. Would Wayne have the capacity to marry? What if he had not told Karen?

PART C

Assume that (rather than the facts in Part B) Wayne tells Karen that the reason he lost his job at Canco Corporation in August of YR-1 was that he was caught smoking marijuana with Julian, another employee at Canco. Wayne states that he became romantically attracted to Julian in July of YR-1 and had sexual relations with Julian once in February of YR-0. After learning of Wayne's relationship with Julian, Karen moved into the guest room and refused to engage in sexual intercourse with Wayne. On June 10, YR-0, Wayne showed Karen a letter of June 10 from his doctor, stating that tests showed Wayne to be HIV negative. Wayne attends weekly therapy sessions with Dr. Anthony DeRosa, a clinical psychologist, who states in his report that Wayne exhibits "bisexual tendencies, which may be altered through a regular regimen of treatment." On October 27, YR-0, Karen gave birth to Alexis, a healthy baby boy. Karen files a complaint for annulment.

Questions

1. Is drug addiction a valid ground for annulment under the Uniform Marriage and Divorce Act (UMDA)? (*See* the UMDA in the Appendix.)
2. Is homosexuality or bisexuality, as described in this Problem, grounds that under the UMDA go to the essentials of the marriage?
3. What if, instead of annulment, Karen divorced Wayne and received an alimony order in the divorce decree. Thereafter, Karen married Roger and obtained an annulment of this voidable marriage to Roger based on fraud. May Karen now reinstate her alimony payments from Wayne pursuant to the divorce decree?

Chapter One.   Marriage and Family

2. Fraud in Inducement

Problem 9

Barryless v. Barryless

On November 24, YR-1, William and Ethel Barryless were married after a four-year courtship. During a Christmas Eve argument, Ethel told William that she didn't love him and in fact had never loved him.

William sues to annul the marriage. William claims that he proposed marriage to Ethel in reliance on her representations that she loved him, and since love is essential to the existence of a marital relationship, Ethel's statements constitute a fraud on the formation of the marriage.

Ethel files a motion for summary judgment on William's suit and also files an independent petition for dissolution of the marriage. Ethel neither admits nor denies the claim that she never loved William, despite her representations to that effect.

Questions

1. Are misrepresentations about love a proper basis for annulment of a marriage?
2. Suppose Ethel is a multimillionaire stock broker and a graduate of the Harvard Business School. William gave up his education to put Ethel through school and he currently works as a manager for Pizza Hovel. If William obtains an annulment, should he be entitled to alimony or spousal support?

G. EXTENDING MARITAL RIGHTS TO UNMARRIED COHABITANTS

1. Loss Of Consortium

Problem 10

Shuler v. Morrison

Howard Whitley and Peggy Shuler lived together at Meadow Park Apartments in Southby, Michiana, since shortly after their graduation from Central High School in June of YR-2. Howard and Peggy had a joint checking account and shared all of their living expenses. On February 14, YR-1, Howard proposed a June 15, YR-1, marriage and gave Peggy an engagement ring. Peggy made arrangements with her pastor to conduct the wedding ceremony, rented a hotel suite for the reception, and ordered the invitations. On March 15, YR-1, Peggy informed Howard that she was pregnant. On November 21, YR-1, Peggy gave birth to a baby son, Howard Whitley, Jr. On May 5, YR-1, Howard and

Peggy were riding Howard's Harley Davidson motorcycle west on Interstate 65 in northern Michiana when the Harley was sideswiped by a YR-1 Oldsmobile Cutlass Sierra driven by Carl Morrison. Peggy claims that she suffered serious emotional trauma when she witnessed Howard being thrown from the Harley and killed. Peggy alleges that Carl Morrison's negligence caused loss of consortium and severe distress.

Questions

1. What legal remedies should Peggy pursue against Carl Morrison?
2. Should Carl's duty of care be different simply because the victim and plaintiff hadn't formalized their relationship with a wedding ceremony?
3. What are the public policy issues that must be balanced in this case?
4. Does Howard Whitley, Jr. have any remedies against Carl?
5. How would Peggy's claims be affected if Michiana recognized common law marriage?
6. Assume that Peggy was not on the motorcycle when Howard was killed, but that she watched in horror from a safe distance as Howard was struck by Carl's car. Would Peggy be entitled to recover damages for emotional distress? *See Dillon v. Legg*, 441 P.2d 912 (Cal. 1968).
7. Is the claim for loss of consortium a proper question for the judiciary, or is it an issue for the legislature?

2. *Child's Action for Loss of Parental Consortium*

Problem 11

Templin v. Sparticus Airlines

In YR-1, Judy Templin was killed in an airplane crash as a result of the negligence of Sparticus Airlines. Judy was survived by her only daughter Meighan, who was ten years old at the time of her mother's death. As provided in the guardianship terms of Judy's will, Judy's brother, Michael Smith, was granted custody of Meighan. While Judy's estate was being probated, Michael approached Judy's attorney, who suggested to Michael that it might be worthwhile for Meighan to file a loss-of-consortium claim against Sparticus Airlines. The attorney told Michael that a few states had recently recognized this relatively new cause of action and that a judgment for Meighan would eliminate any future financial difficulties.

Questions

1. As discussed in Problem 10, courts recognize a cause of action for loss of consortium as between spouses. What are the differences between a husband-wife relationship and a parent-child relationship that would warrant a cause of action for loss of consortium in one case and not the other?

Chapter One. Marriage and Family

2. What arguments should Sparticus Airlines make to oppose the court recognizing a cause of action for Meighan's loss of consortium?
3. How would recognition of this cause of action be beneficial or harmful to society?

3. Palimony

Problem 12

Muriel v. Arthur

In September of YR-4, Arthur, an automobile salesman, who had been separated from his wife, Wendy, for one year, and Muriel, a real estate broker, orally agreed that they would live together in Arthur's home, combine their incomes, and share living expenses. Arthur and Muriel also agreed that any other property accumulated by either or both of them while they lived together would be considered jointly owned property. Muriel openly discussed with friends her relationship with Arthur, whom she described as "ambitious, confident, and a terrific lover." Arthur and Wendy were divorced on March 15, YR-2. Arthur and Muriel kept a joint checking-savings account and executed new wills, each making a specific bequest of $10,000 to the other. The parties also made equal contributions to the down payment on a parcel of real estate with title in the name of Arthur, who made the monthly mortgage payments. Muriel has custody of her five-year-old daughter, Laura, from a previous marriage. Arthur and Laura have an affectionate relationship, and since YR-2 she has referred to Arthur as "Daddy." On several occasions, among friends at the country club, Arthur has said, "I'm stickin' with a good thing. Muriel is better in bed than a good cigar." Muriel left her position with the real estate agency in January of YR-1 in order to spend more time as a homemaker. In July of YR-1, Arthur changed the locks on the house and told Muriel, "I've been taken to the cleaners once, and it won't happen again. Pack up all of your stuff and hit the road." YR-4 to YR-1 were profitable years for the automobile industry; consequently, Arthur acquired substantial income during his cohabitation with Muriel. Muriel admits that she knew Arthur was married when she and Arthur entered into their agreement in YR-4. Assume that Michiana has no fornication statute.

Questions

1. What is a palimony claim? What bearing do these claims have on the state's interest in protecting marriage?
2. What effect, if any, does Arthur's marital status have on Muriel's right to recover in contract?
3. Should the court distinguish between cases involving two unmarried cohabitants and those involving an unmarried person cohabiting with a married person?
4. If Arthur had returned home to Wendy in early March of YR-2, would Muriel be entitled to recover on her palimony claim?
5. What is the "meretriciousness test"? Is it realistic and workable?
6. What legal principles should be applied to the division of property acquired during the cohabitation?

7. If Michiana had a fornication statute, how does it affect division of the parties' property?
8. Would Muriel recover if she sued Arthur for breach of their cohabitation contract?
9. How would the doctrine of common law marriage affect the parties' rights?
10. Without palimony, what rights would Muriel have?
11. What distinguishes palimony from common law marital alimony?
12. Assume that Muriel marries Arthur with the good faith belief that Arthur has never been married. Upon learning of Arthur's marriage to Wendy, does Muriel have any legal recourse? What is the putative spouse doctrine?
13. What practical advice should you give a client who wants to enter into a cohabitation agreement?

Chapter Two

Antenuptial Agreements

Problem 13

Antenuptial Agreement—Preparation

Kenneth (Ken) Olsen, age forty-five, and Stella Kramer, age forty-four, plan to be married on May 22, YR-0. Ken has three daughters, Molly, age seventeen, Mary, age fifteen, and Mandy, age eleven. His wife from a previous marriage, Kate, has custody of the three children. Ken makes monthly child support payments. Stella has two children, a son, Carl, age twenty-four, and a daughter, Candice, age twenty-two, from her previous marriage to Morris. Both children live outside Stella's home. Carl is married to Kim.

Ken is a partner in the Southby office of Winters and Lytle, a large public accounting firm. He has listed the following income and property:

1. Real estate located at 1421 Greenbriar Manor, titled in the name of Kenneth Olsen, appraised in YR-0 at $400,000 (mortgage balance of $125,000), and household furnishings at $85,000 (including antiques from Olsen family)
2. Prudential Securities Moneymart account no. 34112—$190,000
3. United States Savings Bonds—Series EE—100 bonds purchased between September, YR-2, and May, YR-1 (80 bonds at $200 face value, 20 bonds at $100 face value)
4. Winters and Lytle group life insurance policy no. 2151-G, control no. 52636, through James Peacock Mutual Life Insurance Company, valued at $100,000
5. Common stocks—held by A.G. Emerson, Inc.
   a. 1000 shares of Sears Roebuck
   b. 500 shares of Chrysler
   c. 500 shares of Michiana National Bank
   d. 500 shares of Rostel Industries
   e. 250 shares of Procter and Gamble
6. A.G. Emerson, Inc. Moneymarket account no. 15432—$85,000
7. Present salary of $185,000 per year
8. Expected pension of $90,000 a year for life, beginning at age sixty
9. Expected inheritances from Mr. and Mrs. Robert Olsen, Ken's paternal aunt and uncle, and Mrs. Florence Hendley, Ken's maternal aunt.

Ken saves approximately $40,000 per year from his income. He has not taken any of his federal gift tax exemption.

Stella is an elementary school teacher in Morton, Michiana, with annual income of $35,000 and has the following property:

1. Real estate located at 6147 Cherry Tree Lane, Morton, Michiana, titled in the name of Stella Kramer, appraised in YR-0 at $80,000 (no mortgage), and furnishings at $8,000 (including antiques from the Kramer family)
2. Metropolitan Life Insurance variable annuity no. 89-9635415, valued at $10,000
3. Jefferson Life Insurance Company variable annuity no. 0839954160 and policy no. 0086281950, valued at $10,000
4. MacDonald Carey Company account no. 386-10201 in names of Stella Kramer, Carl Kramer and Candice Kramer, valued at $10,000
5. Expected inheritances from Stella's mother, Mrs. Lucille Baxter, and grandmother, Mrs. Maude Knight
6. Teachers Credit Union savings account no. 78-657708—$5,000

Ken wants to enter into an antenuptial agreement with Stella and has made an appointment for both of them to consult with his attorney, J.T. Ryan, on April 22, YR-0. Stella recently agreed with Ken to sign an antenuptial agreement, which would classify the parties' assets as separate property and not subject to equitable distribution in the event of a divorce. (The professor may provide confidential instructions to the students assigned to play the roles of Ken and Stella in a class simulation.) For the simulation, assume that Michiana has adopted the Uniform Premarital Agreement Act (UPAA). (*See* the UPAA in the Appendix.)

Questions

1. Assume that you are Ken's lawyer and Ken makes an appointment for you to meet with him and Stella to advise them and prepare their antenuptial agreement. What will you say to Ken and Stella at this meeting?
2. What is an antenuptial agreement? How does it fit within a public policy environment that is designed to encourage marriage and discourage divorce? Are antenuptial agreements merely preludes to divorce? Should they be void per se?
3. What are the various subjects covered in a typical antenuptial agreement? What law governs the enforcement of antenuptial agreements?
4. What criteria should be used to determine the validity of an antenuptial agreement?
5. Suppose Ken forgets to tell Stella about the savings bonds and the Chrysler stock. What effect will this omission have on the validity of the parties' antenuptial agreement?
6. What options aside from an antenuptial agreement exist for Ken and Stella?
7. Suppose Ken and Stella enter into a valid antenuptual agreement, and three years later they divorce. What effect would the antenuptual agreement have on the division of their marital property?
8. Suppose Ken and Stella execute a valid antenuptial agreement that proposes to give Stella all of Ken's stock on divorce or death. Ken has a prior will bequeathing his stock to his children. Ken dies on the honeymoon. What result?

Problem 14

Antenuptial Agreements—Enforcement

The following is Ken and Stella's Antenuptial Agreement:

ANTENUPTIAL AGREEMENT

THIS AGREEMENT made between Kenneth Olson (hereinafter referred to as Ken) and Stella Kramer (hereinafter referred to as Stella);

Witnesseth:

(a) The parties are contemplating their marriage.

(b) Ken has been previously married and divorced and by his previous marriage he has three children, Molly, Mary, and Mandy. Stella has been previously married and divorced and by her previous marriage has two children, Carl and Candice.

(c) In anticipation of marriage, the parties desire to fix and determine by Agreement the rights and claims which will accrue to each of them in the estate and property of the other by reason of their marriage. Ken and Stella further desire to fix their obligations to each other should there be a separation or divorce between them. They wish to accept the provisions of this Agreement in lieu of and in full discharge of settlement and satisfaction of all such rights and claims. Without the benefit of this Antenuptial Agreement the parties would not marry.

(d) At all times herein, Ken has been represented by his legal counsel, J.T. Ryan. Stella has consulted once with independent counsel, but is not represented by counsel and hereby waives further consultation with counsel. Ken and Stella also acknowledge that he and she are conversant with all of the wealth, property, estate and income of the other, and that each is aware of his or her respective rights in the premises. Ken has listed his current assets in Schedule "A," and Stella has listed her current assets in Schedule "B;" both Schedules attached hereto and made part hereof. (See Problem 13.)

NOW, THEREFORE, in consideration of the premises and of the marriage, and in further consideration of mutual promises and undertakings hereinafter set forth, Ken and Stella agree:

1. **Separate Property.** Each party shall during his or her lifetime keep and retain sole and separate ownership, control, and enjoyment of all property, real or personal, now owned and acquired before the marriage, free and clear of any future claim by the other of any kind or nature, except for any gifts given by one to the other during the marriage. Such property shall be designated by the parties and hereinafter referred to as "separate property":

The following shall be considered Ken's separate property:

   a. Real estate located at 1421 Greenbriar Manor, titled in the name of Kenneth Olsen, appraised in YR-0 at $400,000 (mortgage balance of $125,000), and household furnishings at $85,000 (including antiques from Olsen family)
   b. Prudential Bache Moneymart account no. 34112—$190,000
   c. United States Savings Bonds—Series EE—100 bonds purchased between September, YR-2, and May, YR-1 (80 bonds at $200 face value, 20 bonds at $100 face value)
   d. Winters and Lytle group life insurance policy no. 2151-G, control no. 52636, through James Peacock Mutual Life Insurance Company, valued at $100,000
   e. Common stocks however held

1) 1000 shares of Sears Roebuck
2) 500 shares of Chrysler
3) 500 shares of Michiana National Bank
4) 500 shares of Rostel Industries
5) 250 shares of Procter and Gamble

f. A.G. Emerson, Inc. Moneymart account no. 15432—$85,000
g. Expected pension of $90,000 a year for life, beginning at age 60
h. Expected inheritances from Mr. and Mrs. Robert Olsen, Ken's aunt and uncle on his father's side of the family, and Mrs. Florence Hendley, Ken's aunt on his mother's side of the family.

The following shall be considered Stella's separate property:

a. Real estate located at 6147 Cherry Tree Lane, Morton, Michiana, titled in the name of Stella Kramer, appraised in YR-0 at $80,000 (no mortgage), and furnishings at $8,000 (including antiques from the Kramer family)
b. Metropolitan Life Insurance variable annuity no. 89-9635415, valued at $10,000
c. Jefferson Life Insurance Company variable annuity no. 0839954160 and policy no. 0086281950, valued at $10,000
d. MacDonald Carey Company account no. 386-10201 in names of Stella Kramer, Carl Kramer, and Candice Kramer, valued at $10,000
e. Expected inheritances from Stella's mother, Mrs. Lucille Baxter, and grandmother, Mrs. Maude Knight
f. Teachers Credit Union savings account no. 78-657708—$5,000

2. **Gifts or Transfers of Separate Property.** Ken and Stella shall have the unlimited right to dispose of his or her separate property by gift, transfers to or in trust, or by will during his or her lifetime without interference by the other party.

3. **Earned Income as Separate Property.** The parties hereby further designate as separate property or nonmarital property all income, including salary, bonus, stock rights, deferred compensation, or any other emolument of any nature or description and/or other property which will be received by Ken as a result of performance by Ken of personal services for others and all such property which is received by Stella as a result of performance by her of her personal services for others.

4. **Affirmative Action Required to Create Marital Property.** Further, both Ken and Stella specifically reject the concept of unintentional creation of marital property or unintentional transmutation of nonmarital or separate property into marital property. Accordingly, all property acquired by either spouse subsequent to the marriage shall be separate property to be taken in joint tenancy, tenancy in common, or any other form of co-ownership, as evidenced by a written instrument.

5. **Waiver of Rights of Surviving Spouses.** Each party hereby waives, discharges, and releases any and all claims and rights he or she may acquire as a lawful spouse by reason of the marriage, including without limitation, by recitation, the following rights:

(a) To share in the estate of the other upon the latter's death, whether by way of dower, curtesy, widow's allowance, statutory allowance, or distribution in intestacy; and

(b) To elect to take against any will and testament or codicil of the other party; and

(c) to act as personal representative, executor or administrator of the other party's estate.

6. **Divorce or Legal Separation.** The parties agree that, in the event a Decree of Divorce or Judgment of Dissolution of Marriage or Judgment of Legal Separation shall be entered in a proceeding between them, both parties shall, and do

hereby, waive, release, and relinquish any and all rights to maintenance, alimony, or support for themselves, both temporary and permanent, whether past, present, or future, whether in installments or in gross.

7. **Affirmation of Fairness.** Ken and Stella expressly state that they have freely and voluntarily entered into this Agreement of their own volition, free from any duress or coercion and with the full knowledge of each and every provision contained in this Agreement and the consequences thereof. Each party expressly states that no representation has been made by the other party or by his or her attorney other than that which is contained in this Agreement. The parties, after carefully considering the terms and provision of this Agreement, state that they believe same to be fair, reasonable, and not unconscionable.

8. **General Release.** Except as otherwise provided in this Agreement, each party hereby forever waives, releases, relinquishes, and quitclaims to the other all rights of alimony, maintenance, dower, homestead, marital property, and all other support of property rights that he or she may have otherwise had upon marriage as husband, wife, widower, widow, or otherwise, which would exist under present or future law in this or in any other state or country, to or in, or against the property of the other party or his or her estate, whether now owned, owned at the time of marriage, or acquired at any time after the marriage by such other party.

IN WITNESS WHEREOF, Ken and Stella now sign this Agreement, this _____ day of _____, YR-0.

_____
Kenneth Olson

_____
Stella Kramer

Witness:_____

Witness:_____

This instrument was prepared by J.T. Ryan, Attorney at Law, Suite 511, Clinton Building, Southby, Michiana 146617.

Questions

1. Should the court look to the time the premarital contract was executed or to the time of the divorce or death of a party when determining whether the agreement is enforceable? What factors should the court consider?
2. What if Ken, in listing his assets (see assets listed in Problem 13), leaves out his Barclay's account (balance of £100,000 or $160,000) in London? Would this lack of disclosure render the agreement unenforceable under the Uniform Premarital Agreement Act (UPAA)?
3. Are the accrued interest and dividends for Ken's bonds and stocks separate property? If not, how should this property be characterized?
4. If Ken and Stella both move into Ken's house and Stella makes payments on the house out of her earnings, how should this impact the characterization of the real estate?

5. In order for a premarital agreement to be enforceable, it must be fair. Is this agreement fair? If at Ken's request Stella quits her job in order to be a homemaker, would this agreement still be fair if the parties later divorce?
6. Assume that Stella is diagnosed with osteoporosis, which significantly impedes her daily activities and employment possibilities, and that Ken has filed a petition for dissolution of marriage. Is Stella prevented by the parties' prenuptial agreement from receiving spousal support from Ken at dissolution? How should the court rule under the UPAA? (*See* UPAA in the Appendix.)
7. Is the requirement of independent counsel satisfied?

Chapter Three

Procreation Decisions

A. CONTRACEPTION AND STERILIZATION

1. Wrongful Pregnancy

Problem 15

O'Hara v. Holder

Brian and Anne-Marie O'Hara, residents of Southby, Michiana, are the parents of two children, Liam, age eight, and Willie, age six. Anne-Marie is employed part time at F.S. Absolute Realty and also takes care of the domestic work in the O'Hara home. Brian is employed full-time as a computer salesman with Diskland in Southby. On the advice of their doctor, Brian and Anne-Marie decided to have no more children. The doctor prescribed an oral contraceptive, Alinol. When Anne-Marie delivered the written prescription to the pharmacist, Ivan Holder, in October of YR-1, she was mistakenly given the drug Actinol, a strong antihistamine. Anne-Marie took the Actinol as directed, and two months later the doctor confirmed that she was pregnant. On July 5, YR-0, Anne-Marie gave birth to twin boys, Paddy, a healthy child, and Sean, diagnosed by the family pediatrician as mildly mentally retarded. The births were not without complications, however, and the doctor now recommends that Anne-Marie undergo a hysterectomy.

Questions

1. What are the differences in the following causes of action: wrongful pregnancy, wrongful birth, and wrongful life?
2. What cause(s) of action do the O'Haras have against Holder?
3. If the O'Haras file an action for wrongful pregnancy, should it be allowed?
4. How are damages computed in a wrongful pregnancy action?
5. Assume Anne-Marie and Brian file a wrongful pregnancy action against Holder. Holder moves to dismiss on the grounds that Anne-Marie should have obtained an abortion or pursued an adoption and thereby mitigated damages. The O'Haras are morally opposed to abortion. How should the court rule on Holder's motion?

6. Should the O'Haras be allowed damages for the cost of rearing Paddy? What about Sean?
7. Anne-Marie wishes to bring an action because of Sean's retardation. On whose behalf should the lawsuit be brought? Who are the defendants, and what damages should be alleged in the complaint?

B. ABORTION

1. Contractual Rights

Problem 16

In re Marriage of Robertson

Rita Mayrose and Flynn Robertson met during law school at Michiana University in the Fall of YR-2. Rita was active in law student government and served as president of the university chapter of Women's Pro Choice Coalition. Following their graduation in late May of YR-1, Rita and Flynn were engaged to be married. The following month, Rita and Flynn executed an antenuptial agreement, which contained the following provisions:

> ... That Rita and Flynn are desirous of having natural born children of their marriage;
> The parties agree that no decision to terminate Rita's pregnancy shall be made without written consent of both parties. ...
> WHEREAS the parties desire to fix, limit, and determine their respective rights by this agreement, which each party acknowledges as fair and equitable. ...

Rita and Flynn were married in December of YR-1. On February 4, YR-0, Rita told Flynn that the doctor confirmed that she was approximately two months pregnant. Flynn responded, "A child! Oh, Honey, that's wonderful!" Rita informed Flynn that the time was not right for a child and she intended to have an abortion. Rita and Flynn had several heated arguments in which Flynn stated that Rita could not have an abortion without his written consent, and Rita insisted that, notwithstanding their antenuptial agreement, she had a legal right to an abortion.

On February 11, YR-0, Flynn filed a petition for dissolution of marriage, requesting sole custody of the parties' child, expected to be born during the first week of September, YR-0. Flynn also filed a petition for a restraining order to enjoin Rita from having an abortion.

Questions

1. Can Flynn enforce the antenuptial agreement? (*See* the Uniform Premarital Prenuptial Agreement Act in the Appendix.)
2. Assume Michiana has a statute requiring the father's consent before a woman may obtain an abortion. Regardless of the antenuptial

Chapter Three. Procreation Decisions

agreement, can Flynn use the statute to stop Rita from having an abortion?
3. Assuming that Rita plans to leave town to have an abortion, should habeas corpus relief be available to Flynn? Is there a "person" to be brought before the court for habeas corpus purposes?
4. What legal remedies does Flynn have if Rita obtains an abortion?
5. Should husbands have any legal standing in their wives' reproduction decisions?

2. State Regulation

Problem 17

Gomez v. State of Michiana and Women's Clinic

On December 28, YR-1, Elena Gomez, age nineteen and unmarried, learned from her doctor in Southby, Michiana, that she was four weeks pregnant. Elena requested the doctor's assistance in arranging for an abortion as soon as possible. The doctor informed Elena of the following Michiana statute:

> Section 111. Any woman who seeks a first trimester abortion shall be examined by a licensed physician and complete a clearance questionnaire, which shall be signed by the doctor and filed with the health department in the county where the abortion is performed. The abortion shall not be performed until the county health department has issued a certificate of clearance to a licensed clinic or hospital on or before the end of the first trimester. The department's failure to certify an abortion by the end of the first trimester, after a questionnaire has been filed pursuant to this section, constitutes a waiver to prevent a first trimester abortion.

The doctor completed the required examination and clearance questionnaire and mailed the document to the Hoynes County Health Department on December 29, YR-1.

During the following month, Elena attended counseling sessions for psychological problems related to her pregnancy and experienced physical complications such as headaches, morning vomiting, constipation, and extreme fatigue, which caused her to miss several days at her secretarial job. On January 30, YR-0, Elena called the women's clinic on the telephone and pleaded to have an abortion. She was informed that she had not yet been "cleared" by the health department. Elena retains legal counsel to file a complaint for declaratory judgment that Section 111 is unconstitutional, and a claim against the State of Michiana and women's clinic for damages.

Questions

1. Is the Michiana statute constitutional?
2. Can a state enforce a waiting period for women who desire to obtain an abortion?

C. ASSISTED CONCEPTION

1. Gestational Surrogacy

Problem 18

In re Baby Bo

Rex and Eve were married in June of YR-8. They have tried without success to have a child. Eve has endometriosis, and, following her second surgery in YR-2, the gynecologist and surgeon agreed that life-threatening complications could result if Eve became pregnant. In January of YR-1, Eve told Rex, "I don't want to spend another Christmas without a child." Rex and Eve placed an ad in the Chicago *Tribune* offering $15,000 to a woman who would agree to carry a fetus produced by in vitro fertilization of Eve's egg with Rex's sperm, carry the child to term, surrender the child to Rex and Eve, and renounce all parental rights to the child. Darlene, who is married and has three children, ages four, eight, and ten, responded to the ad with the following letter:

Dear Rex and Eve,

This letter is in response to your recent ad in the Chicago *Tribune*.
Having consulted with my attorney, I hereby agree to carry the fetus and give birth to a child for the $15,000, as advertised, over and above all medical and hospital expenses.
I look forward to receiving written confirmation of our agreement.

Sincerely,

Darlene

pc: Arnold Attorney

Rex and Eve sent a reply letter to Darlene accepting the financial terms in her letter and confirming the parties' agreement that Darlene would act as the surrogate mother. In March of YR-1, Rex and Eve received the following letter from Darlene:

Dear Rex and Eve,

I was delighted to receive your recent confirmation of our agreement.
This will be the second time I've served as a surrogate mother. I delivered a healthy baby girl in YR-3 for a nice young couple. I was artificially inseminated with the sperm of Edward J. Young. The contract was prepared by Surrogate Services, Inc., in Southby, Michiana. I also attended the counseling sessions required by the contract. This letter will serve as my authorization for Surrogate Services to release documents or other information about me.
I look forward to seeing you at the clinic.

Sincerely,

Darlene

pc: Arnold Attorney

Chapter Three. Procreation Decisions

On February 11, YR-0, Darlene delivered a healthy baby boy, identified in hospital records as "Baby Bo," and received a check from Rex and Eve for $15,000. On February 12, Darlene told Rex and Eve that she had had "a change of heart." She returned the check, stating, "As the boy's mother, I have parental rights, and I intend to keep him as my own." Rex and Eve refused the check and threatened immediate legal action.

Questions

1. What legal action should Rex and Eve take? What are the possible theories of relief?
2. What arguments can Darlene make in her defense?
3. Are pregnancy and childbirth proper subjects for contract law? If so, how much of a woman's reproductive and child-rearing rights may she properly contract away? If not, what rights do genetic donors have regarding the child?
4. If Darlene succeeds in keeping Baby Bo, what are Rex and Eve's rights and obligations with respect to the child?
5. Assume Michiana has adopted the Uniform Parentage Act. (*See* Appendix.) Under the Act, who will obtain custody of Baby Bo? What result if Michiana does not recognize the Uniform Parentage Act?
6. Suppose Darlene refused to renounce her parental rights to Baby Bo merely because she wanted $25,000 instead of the $15,000 in the contract. How should Rex and Eve respond? How do Darlene's actions affect her claim to Baby Bo?
7. What difference would it make if Darlene was an unwed mother receiving public assistance payments?
8. Under what circumstances should courts enforce surrogacy contracts?
9. Suppose the court invalidates the surrogacy contract. What other rights do Rex and Eve have regarding Baby Bo? *See In re Baby M.*, 537 A.2d 1227 (N.J. 1988).
10. What effect would the Uniform Status of Children of Assisted Conception Act—Alternative A—have on the outcome of this case? What about Alternative B? (*See* Appendix.)

2. Surrogate Birth

Problem 19

Consultation with Jane Ray

The following is the transcribed recording of an initial client consultation with Ms. Jane Ray. The consultation occurred at 9:30 A.M. last Thursday, March 3, YR-0.

CLIENT CONSULTATION: MITCHELL MCDUDE, SENIOR PARTNER, MCDUDE, STANLEY & MCDUDE, WITH A POTENTIAL CLIENT NAMED JANE RAY

Questions by Mr. McDude:

Q: It is currently Thursday, March 3, YR-0. 9:30 A.M. I am Mitchell McDude of McDude, Stanley & McDude. This is a client consultation with Jane Ray. The purpose of this meeting is to determine whether we may be able to help Ms. Ray with a legal matter. Miss Ray, do you understand that this consultation is being recorded?

A: Yes.

Q: Do you further understand that this consultation is entirely confidential, that we may not ever use it against you in any way, and that its sole purpose is to help us serve you better by sharing this conversation with those lawyers in our firm who will be handling the legal research in this case, and that no one will hear this tape without your permission and that at your request we will destroy this tape?

A: Uh-huh.

Q: Thank you. Now, then, would you please state your name.

A: Jane Ray.

Q: Where do you live, Miss Ray?

A: I live at 1034 South Bland Street in New Carter, Michiana.

Q: How old are you, Miss Ray?

A: Twenty-three.

Q: Are you married?

A: No.

Q: Do you have any children?

A: Three; ages five, six, and eighteen months.

Q: Are you employed?

A: Yes. I work for McDougall's Department Store. I'm a security guard there.

Q: That's fine. What we would like to do is figure out what your legal problem is. Before we started this tape, you told me about a contract you entered into with a Mr. and Mrs. Fowler. Would you please describe how you know them?

A: I work with Stephanie Fowler at McDougall's. She manages the lingerie department. My job is sometimes to chase the teenage boys out of her department.

Q: Okay. Thank you. Now then, when did you enter into the agreement you told me about, and what was the agreement?

A: Well, Stephanie and I got to talking when I worked in her department. I found out she and her husband couldn't have kids, something about her uterus not being able to take the egg. Anyways, she told me that they couldn't have kids, even though they could conceive them.

Q: When was that?

A: About a year ago.

Q: Okay. Go on.

A: Well, they, I mean Stephanie, told me they were looking for someone to be a surrogate parent for them.

Q: When did she say this?

A: About eleven months ago—yeah, eleven months ago. I remember because it was right after the Spring sale, Stephanie told me that she and her husband were looking for somebody to carry their child for them.

Q: Did she ask you to bear their child for them?

A: No. She told me that they would bear the child, but they wanted somebody whose uterus wouldn't reject the fetus.

Chapter Three. Procreation Decisions

Q: Did she ask you to do that?
A: Not at first. She told me they were looking for somebody through their church. Last May she asked me. We'd gotten to be pretty close by then.
Q: Did you agree?
A: She told me that she and her husband had been to see a lawyer. Her husband's a doctor, so he knew how surrogate parenthood works. She said that the lawyer told her that they could enter into a contract with someone to carry their baby to term. She gave me a contract to look over and sign.
Q: When was this?
A: Memorial Day Weekend.
Q: What were the terms of the contract?
A: Here. [Hands McDude contract, which follows this Problem.]
Q: [Reads contract.] I see. What is this handwritten portion [underlined text in language of the contract]?
A: That's where I wrote in that they had to pay my medical expenses for the pregnancy. My last pregnancy was pretty expensive, because I was sick.
Q: Okay. We'll look over the contract later. Am I correct in saying that you wish not to abide by the contract?
A: I want to keep my baby. Stephanie and her husband are getting divorced. They're using the baby as a weapon to fight each other. I love this baby; I'm the one who will give birth to it. I'll care for it just like I have my other three babies. They don't want the baby, they just want to use it to hurt each other. I want it.
Q: Have they lived up to their part of the contract?
A: They've paid me $9,000. They don't have to pay me the last thousand or the fifteen grand for my kids' trust until the baby is born. I'll give them back the nine thousand. I don't need the money that bad. I haven't spent it. I want this baby and they don't.
Q: Have you lived up to the other terms of the contract?
A: Yes. Except I missed the doctor for once while I was at Disney World with my mom and my kids. I saw him right after I got back, and they said it was okay.
Q: Have you asked the Fowlers if they would be willing to cancel the contract?
A: Yeah, but they won't. They said that even if they divorce it's still their baby, so they get to keep it. I told them I'd give the money back, but they said no, it was their baby and that was that. The baby's due in three weeks. It's already dropped. I don't have much time. Can I go to court to have them say the contract is no good?
Q: That we'll have to look into. Miss Ray, you've given us all the information we need now. May I copy your contract?
A: Sure. Are you going to take my case?
Q: We're going to give it a thorough investigation, and then tell you what we can do for you. In the meantime, hold onto that contract. I'm going to turn off the tape now. Okay?
A: Okay.

TAPE ENDED.

Questions

1. Who is the child's natural mother?
2. In what ways does this Problem differ from Problem 18?
3. Assume Michiana has a surrogate parenting act that makes it a misdemeanor for parties to enter into surrogacy contracts. Who may be prosecuted under the act?

4. What result under the Uniform Parentage Act? (*See* the Act in the Appendix.)
5. What result under the Uniform Status of Children of Assisted Conception Act? (*See* the Act in the Appendix.)
6. With technology advancing so rapidly in the surrogacy field, how should the law treat surrogate parent contracts?
7. Should the intent of the parties at the time of the agreement be the deciding factor in these cases?

CONTRACT

On this 31st day of May, YR-1, the parties enter into this contract for services. The parties of the first part, Robert and Stephanie Fowler, agree to pay to the party of the second part, Jane Ray, good consideration to be listed below for her services as surrogate mother to their child.

Said services shall be as follows: At a date to be agreed by the parties, Ms. Ray shall admit herself to Hoynes County Hospital to meet with Dr. Ronald McDonal. Dr. McDonal will give Ms. Ray a thorough medical examination, including a gynecological examination. Upon finding her suitable to maintain a pregnancy, Dr. McDonal will inject into Ms. Ray's uterus a fluid sample containing several zygotes begotten of Mr. and Mrs. Robert Fowler. Such procedure shall be repeated monthly for three months or until Ms. Ray becomes pregnant. If Ms. Ray becomes pregnant, she shall carry the child until term. During her pregnancy, she shall visit Dr. McDonal twice each month for such prenatal care as Ms. Ray, Dr. McDonal, and Mr. and Mrs. Fowler agree is necessary and beneficial. Upon giving birth to the child, Ms. Ray shall have sixty hours within which to sign an affidavit to be given to Ms. Ray by Mr. Fowler, such affidavit relinquishing all of her rights as parent to the child. Within sixty hours of birth, Ms. Ray shall deliver the child to Mr. and Mrs. Fowler's custody. She shall not visit the child thereafter, except with the Fowlers' mutual agreement.

In return for said services, should Ms. Ray submit herself for said treatments but not become pregnant, Mr. and Mrs. Fowler agree to pay her the sum of $1000. If Ms. Ray becomes pregnant and fulfills all the conditions precedent to this contract, Mr. and Mrs. Fowler shall pay Ms. Ray the sum of $10,000, in ten monthly payments of $1000 each, starting the month Ms. Ray becomes pregnant. *Mr. and Mrs. Fowler shall pay all medical expenses for Ms. Ray relating to the pregnancy.* In addition, Mr. and Mrs. Fowler agree to establish a trust fund of $15,000. Such trust fund shall inure to Ms. Ray's children, to be used for their education.

Conditions Precedent to this contract:

1.) That Ms. Ray become pregnant by the zygotes begotten by Mr. and Mrs. Fowler.
2.) That Ms. Ray carry the child to term.
3.) That Ms. Ray not smoke or consume alcohol or illicit drugs during her pregnancy.
4.) That Ms. Ray deliver the child to Mr. and Mrs. Fowler within sixty (60) hours of birth, and within such time sign and notarize an affidavit relinquishing all parental rights to the child.

WHEREFORE, said parties agree to enter into this contract.

          Robert J. Fowler   5/31/YR-1
          Stephanie Fowler   5/31/YR-1
          Jane Doe Ray   5/31/YR-1

3. Artificial Insemination

Problem 20

In re Benjamin

Harry, a lumber dealer, and Emma (Em), a registered oncology nurse, were married in June of YR-5. In YR-2, their physician advised that it was extremely unlikely that Em would become pregnant from Harry's sperm. Em grew depressed about the prospects for a childless marriage. She confided in her friend, Chad, a medical student assigned to the oncology unit at Hoynes General Hospital, that she would like to have Chad's child. Em and Chad agreed that a child with their genetic material would be a worthwhile contribution to civilization. Em stated in a letter to Chad that if the artificial insemination worked, she wanted Chad someday to see the "little miracle they created" and "be a role model for the child." Chad wrote back to Em, stating "I will always be there for you, Em, through thick and thin, and I'll support our child, if necessary." Em and Harry agreed that Em would be inseminated artificially with semen donated by Chad. The written agreement, signed by Em, Harry and Chad, provided in pertinent part as follows:

1. That Em, Harry, and Chad have consulted with legal counsel and willingly sign the agreement with full knowledge and understanding.
2. That Harry consents to Em, with assistance from a licensed physician, being artificially inseminated with semen donated by Chad.
3. That Em and Harry agree to pay Chad $2,000 on the date that a licensed physician confirms that Em is pregnant.
4. That Harry will be recognized and treated in law as the natural father of a child conceived by said artificial insemination.

The applicable Michiana statute provides in part as follows:

1. If, under the supervision of a licensed physician and with the consent of her husband, a wife is inseminated artificially with semen donated by a man not her husband, the husband is treated in law as if he were the natural father of a child thereby conceived. . . .
2. The donor of semen provided to a licensed physician for use in artificial insemination of a woman other than the donor's wife is treated in law as if he were not the natural father of a child thereby conceived.

On January 15, YR-1, Em gave birth to a healthy baby boy, Benjamin. On December 1, YR-1, Harry was killed in an automobile accident. In July of YR-0, Em became engaged to marry Fred, a former business partner of Harry. On August 1, YR-0, Chad came to Em's home to discuss his visitation with Benjamin. Em refused Chad's visitation with Benjamin, denied any prior agreement with Chad, and stated that she planned to marry Fred and that Fred was agreeable to adopting the child.

Chad files a filiation action in the Hoynes County Probate Court, seeking to establish parental rights with respect to Benjamin.

Questions

1. What rights does Chad have with respect to his petition being filed under the following circumstances:
   (a) for visitation prior to Harry's death;
   (b) for visitation after Harry's death and before Em's marriage to Fred;
   (c) for visitation after Em's death, before her marriage to Fred, and a provision in Em's will naming Claire as Benjamin's guardian;
   (d) for visitation after Em's marriage to Fred and before Fred's adoption petition is filed;
   (e) for visitation after the adoption petition is filed;
   (f) for visitation after the adoption order (assuming Chad didn't know about the adoption).
2. What rights does Benjamin have to learn the identity of his biological father and to have visitation with Chad in each of the situations in Question 1?
3. Is Em an appropriate party for the protection of Benjamin's rights, or should the court appoint one or both of the following:
   (a) legal counsel to represent Benjamin;
   (b) a special advocate (CASA) or guardian ad litem (GAL) to represent Benjamin's best interests.
4. What legal responsibilities does Chad have toward Benjamin?
5. If Harry had not died, what would Chad's responsibilities toward Benjamin have been?
6. On what theory might the Michiana artificial insemination statute be unconstitutional?
7. Under the Michiana statute, which sperm donors would be denied their parental rights?
8. Assume Chad had tested positive for the HIV virus at the time he donated his sperm but negligently failed to notify Em of his condition. Do Benjamin or Em have a claim against Chad?

4. *Rights of Artificial Insemination Donor (AID)*

Problem 21

Terry v. Ainsworth

In YR-10, Amelia Ainsworth, a single woman with no imminent prospects for marriage, decided that she wanted to have a child. After considering the use of a licensed sperm bank, she chose instead to enlist a friend to donate some sperm, with which she planned to inseminate herself. Tom Terry was a longtime close friend of Amelia for whom she had a great deal of respect. Amelia explained to Tom that she wanted to a have a child and that she hoped to find a sperm donor whom she already knew, so that she would know as much as possible about the person's background. Amelia and Tom agreed that Tom would provide Amelia with sperm but that Tom would have no contact or involvement with the child. It was also agreed that Amelia would be responsible for all of the expenses relating to the pregnancy and for the care and support of the child.

Chapter Three. Procreation Decisions

In YR-9, Amelia gave birth to Rollie, a healthy baby boy. In YR-5, when Rollie began to ask about his father, Amelia made arrangements for the child to meet Tom. Over the next four years, Tom visited Rollie frequently and developed a relationship with the child. In YR-1, Tom asked for permission to take Rollie to visit Tom's family. Amelia was uncomfortable with Tom's proposal and told Tom that such an arrangement would be a breach of their agreement. She then refused to let Tom see the child at all.

After making several unsuccessful attempts to see Rollie, Tom filed a filiation petition in order to pursue a formal order for visitation with Rollie.

Questions

1. Does Tom, or did he ever, have the right to file a petition as the father of Rollie? Does it matter that no formal written agreement was made in this case?
2. What arguments should Amelia make to oppose Tom's right to establish paternity nine years after Rollie's birth?
3. Does Tom have a constitutional right to establish a parent-child relationship with Rollie?
4. What legal advice should lawyers give to clients who wish to utilize artificial insemination?

5. *Artificial Insemination by Husband (AIH)*

Problem 22

Cadewell v. Michiana State Department of Corrections

Thadius Johnson was imprisoned following a murder conviction in YR-10 and will not be eligible for parole until YR+15. Wilma is his long-time girlfriend and the mother of his son, Odell, who was born in YR-11. In YR-5, Thadius and Wilma were married in a prison wedding service. Wilma now wants to have another child, and, as Thadius is now forty-five years old, he and Wilma are concerned that if they have to wait until Thadius is released from prison, they will be too old to have another child. Therefore, Thadius and Wilma have petitioned the Department of Corrections of the State of Michiana to allow Thadius to artificially inseminate his wife while he is still in prison. The State of Michiana, however, has refused this request. Thadius has decided to bring suit against the State of Michiana, alleging that its refusal to allow him to inseminate his wife is a violation of his constitutional right to procreative freedom.

Questions

1. Does a prison inmate have a constitutional right of procreative freedom?
2. What arguments should the State of Michiana make to justify not allowing Thadius to artificially inseminate his wife?

3. Would the state have a more compelling argument if Thadius were a female inmate requesting to be artificially inseminated? Does this inquiry bring to light any equal protection considerations?

Chapter Four

Parent-Child Relationship

A. ACTION TO ESTABLISH PATERNITY

Problem 23

In re Paternity of Heather Hodson

Arnold Painter, a lawyer, and Sandra Hodson, an elementary school teacher, lived together in a nonmarital relationship from November of YR-2 to May of YR-1, during which time they engaged in sexual intercourse. In September of YR-1, Sandra gave birth to a baby girl, Heather, and recently Sandra filed a paternity action naming Arnold as Heather's father. Sandra states, "When Arnold and I lived together, he would ask me nearly every day if I had taken my pill. He was obsessive about it. I gave him my word that I would take the pill and I did. He never once offered to pay for my prescription. There's no doubt about it, Arnold is Heather's father." Arnold states that by not taking the pill Sandra lied and deceived him and therefore her paternity action should be dismissed. Arnold also states that he recently received the following letter from Tom Osborne, dated November 2, YR-1:

> Dear Arnold,
>
> I heard that Sandra is filing a paternity action against you. I guess you should know that after you left Chuckie's last New Year's Eve, Sandra got pretty drunk. She had sex with me and Drake that night. We were all pretty messed up. I'd hate to see you take the rap if it's not your kid. Let me know if I can help.
>
> Tom

Sandra states that she didn't engage in sexual intercourse with anyone but Arnold during the time they lived together.

Questions

1. Who has standing to file a paternity petition? (*See* the Uniform Parentage Act in the Appendix.)
2. Who is a presumed father? Is there a presumed father in this case?

3. Is Tom's letter admissible to disprove Arnold's paternity? What about testimony by Tom or Drake? Suppose a judge rules testimony of Tom and Drake is inadmissible. Is Sandra's testimony, thus uncontroverted, sufficient to prove Arnold's paternity?
4. What burden of proof exists in paternity cases? Can that burden be shifted?
5. What types of evidence are admissible to prove/disprove paternity?
6. Suppose Sandra had a reputation in the community for promiscuity. Should such character evidence be admissible to disprove paternity?
7. Assume Sandra's paternity petition is granted based solely on her accusations regarding Arnold's paternity. Arnold appeals on due process grounds. What result?
8. What constitutional rights do indigent putative fathers have in paternity proceedings?
9. Is misrepresentation as to birth control a valid defense to paternity?
10. Assume Sandra files a paternity petition naming Arnold as Heather's father, but her petition is denied. May Heather's guardian ad litem later file a paternity petition against Arnold?
11. Assume Sandra had already filed separate unsuccessful paternity petitions against Tom and then Drake. In both those cases, evidence was presented that Sandra had slept with Tom, Drake, Steve, Arnold, and Sven during the relevant period. In what ways could the prior petitions affect a suit against Arnold?

B. REBUTTING THE PRESUMPTION OF PATERNITY

1. Reverse Paternity—Action by Wife

Problem 24

In re Marriage of Sherry (T.) B. and Gary T./Lucy T. v. Gary T.

Sherry (T.) B. and Gary T. were married on February 14, YR-8, in Southby, Michiana. Five months before their marriage, Sherry was pregnant with Lucy, who was born on June 19, YR-8. Sherry told Gary before and after their marriage that he was not Lucy's father. Gary nevertheless established a loving parent-child relationship with Lucy and treated her as his own child. Sherry and Gary were divorced in the Hoynes Superior Court on January 6, YR-6. The decree of dissolution provided, inter alia, that there was one child born of the marriage, Lucy T.; that Sherry T. was granted the permanent care and custody of the minor child; that Gary T.'s support obligation was $95.00 per week; and that Gary T. was entitled to reasonable visitation with Lucy, to be arranged by the parties, including two continuous months during the summer. Gary exercised his visitation rights three times between January 6, YR-6, and May 10, YR-6, the date of Sherry's remarriage to Paul B., her high school boyfriend, who she says is Lucy's "real father." Sherry states that at the final dissolution hearing on January 6, YR-6, she told her lawyer that Gary T. was not Lucy's father, and her lawyer advised her not to say anything about it. In June of YR-6, Sherry filed a petition to remove Lucy from Michiana to Chicago, Illinois,

Chapter Four.   Parent-Child Relationship

where Paul had obtained a job and the couple planned to live. The court granted Sherry's request to remove Lucy from the jurisdiction and continued the visitation order of January 6, YR-6.

From the summer of YR-6 through YR-1, Sherry prevented Gary from visiting Lucy. Sherry refused to answer Gary's letters, and when Gary called her on the telephone to inquire about visiting Lucy, Sherry said to him, "I told you from the beginning, you're not Lucy's father, so leave us alone." Gary responded by filing a verified information for a rule to show cause each spring from YR-5 through YR-0, alleging that Sherry should be found in contempt for violating the court's January 6, YR-6, order on visitation.

The Hoynes Superior Court found Sherry in contempt in June of YR-5, May of YR-3, June of YR-2, May of YR-1, and May 17, YR-0, for willfully and intentionally violating the court's visitation order of January 6, YR-6. In each instance, Sherry failed to appear for hearing, and the court ordered a body attachment. Sherry was never apprehended in Illinois and brought before the Hoynes Superior Court in Michiana (each body attachment was issued for a period of 180 days). Gary paid child support on a regular basis from January 6, YR-6, to May of YR-3. He is currently delinquent in payment of support in the sum of $1,500.00.

In late May of YR-0, during a "secret trip" with Lucy to Southby, Michiana, to visit with relatives, Sherry was picked up on the May 17 body attachment and held in the Hoynes County Jail. You receive a telephone call from Sherry and meet with her at the jail. Sherry tells you that Gary T. is not Lucy's father and asks you to do anything possible to help her. You decide to file in the Hoynes Probate Court, in Lucy's name, by her mother, a complaint for declaratory judgment that Gary T. is not Lucy's biological father; and also a motion for an order of HLA testing of Gary T., Sherry (T.) B., and Lucy T. (The motion and order for HLA testing follow this Problem.) Prior to the hearing in Hoynes Probate Court (June 6), counsel for the parties receive the results of the HLA tests from Dr. Sonia M. Stephens, of Michiana University (Dr. Stephens' letter and affidavit follow this Problem.) Sherry's attorney may call as a witness Dr. Franklin Moses, a sociologist who will testify consistent with his letter, which follows this Problem. The court has appointed an attorney to serve as guardian ad litem (GAL) and legal counsel for Lucy. Paul, who is presently separated from Sherry and unemployed, has been granted leave by the court to intervene.

Questions

1. Why did Gary file the information for a rule to show cause against Sherry?
2. Who is the legal father of Lucy?
3. Who is the biological father of Lucy?
4. What scientific tests are available to prove or disprove paternity? Are the results of such tests determinative?
5. What is "reverse paternity"? Who has standing to file this cause of action?
6. What significance does the testimony of Dr. Moses have in this case?
7. Suppose the Michiana court rules that Gary is not Lucy's father but also rules that Sherry is an unfit parent (based on her prolonged contempt of court). What result for Lucy? How should Gary respond?
8. Should a blood relationship be the conclusive factor concerning parental rights?

9. *See* Section 4 of the Uniform Parentage Act in the Appendix. Should Michiana allow the rebuttal of a presumption of paternity? If so, by what standard? If not, why not? What alternatives exist for natural fathers?
10. What policy reasons support the presumption of paternity? Are those policies viable in an era of advanced technology?
11. Does the court-appointed attorney have a conflict of interest?
12. Assume that, instead of filing an information for a rule to show cause, Gary files in Hoynes Superior Court a complaint for declaratory judgment that he is not Lucy's natural father, based on the following: (a) at the final dissolution hearing on January 6, YR-6, Gary told his attorney that he wasn't sure whether or not he was Lucy's father, and his attorney advised Gary not to "open up a can of worms"; (b) the results of the HLA tests; (c) Gary's testimony regarding Sherry's statements; and (d) Lucy's best interests. What result on this complaint? What role would a GAL play in this kind of case?

STATE OF MICHIANA, COUNTY OF HOYNES
IN THE HOYNES PROBATE COURT

L.T., et al.,   )
)
        Plaintiff,   )
)   Cause No. K-6106
    vs.   )
)
G.T.,   )
        Defendant.   )

MOTION FOR ORDER OF H.L.A. TESTING

Petitioner, L.T., et al., pursuant to MC 31-6-6.1-8, respectfully requests that this court issue an order requiring the parties to this action, L.T., G.T., and S.B., to undergo the Human Leukocyte Antigen (H.L.A.) tissue test.

The moving party, L.T., requests that this particular test be performed because it is recognized as the test having the highest degree to exclusionary accuracy as to paternity. Petitioner further requests that the test be performed by qualified physicians at the Michiana University Medical Center Histocompatibility Laboratory, which is the only medical center in the State of Michiana that is qualified to and regularly engages in this procedure.

WHEREFORE, Petitioner requests that the parties be ordered to undergo a Human Leukocyte Antigen (H.L.A.) tissue test at the Michiana University Medical Center Histocompatibility Laboratory in accordance with the requirements issued by said laboratory.

_____
Attorney for Petitioner

CERTIFICATE OF SERVICE

I hereby certify that I served a true and complete copy of the foregoing Motion for Order of H.L.A. Testing upon _____, by depositing the same in the United States mail, first-class postage prepaid, this _____ day of _____, YR-0.

_____
Attorney for Petitioner

STATE OF MICHIANA, COUNTY OF HOYNES
IN THE HOYNES PROBATE COURT

L.T., et al.,)
       Plaintiffs,)
) Cause No. K-6106
  vs.)
)
G.T.,)
       Defendant.)

ORDER FOR ORDER OF H.L.A. TESTING

    Hearing having been held on Petitioner L.T.'s Motion for Order of H.L.A. Testing, and the Court having heard arguments by counsel and being duly advised in the premises, now finds that said Motion should be granted.
    IT IS THEREFORE ORDERED, ADJUDGED, AND DECREED that the parties, L.T., S.B., and G.T., whose actual names are designated elsewhere in the pleadings of this case, and which parties are the minor child, her natural mother, and her mother's spouse at the time of her birth, respectively, submit themselves to the Human Leukocyte Antigen (H.L.A.) tissue test. It is further ordered that said H.L.A. test be performed upon the parties at the Michiana University Medical Center Histocompatibility Laboratory, Dolton, Michiana, at the soonest time and date that said Laboratory can accommodate this testing. Said test shall be conducted in accordance with the stringent controls required by evidentiary rules as to chain of custody and proper identification.

                                                              _____
                                                               Judge, Hoynes Probate Court

Date: _____

FRANKLIN B. MOSES, PH.D
Sociologist
814 North Main Street
Southby, Michiana 46617

May 28, YR-0

Attorney at Law
1404 National Bank Building
Southby, Michiana 46601

Re: Sherry T. and daughter Lucy T.

Dear Attorney:

I have been asked by your office for my professional opinion as to whether the best interests of the child, Lucy T., daughter of Sherry T., are to be served as she conforms to court orders which will have her commence a two-month visitation with Ms. T's former husband; which visitation will be interrupted by brief weekly visits with her mother; and which visitation will commence on or about July 2, YR-0, after there had been no visitations with subject parent, Gary T., for several years. To accommodate your request, I have conducted two interviews with Sherry T. and one with Lucy.

Lucy appears to be a normal, healthy, intelligent, and sensitive child. She exhibits no remarkable problems of a behavioral nature. Lucy understands the meaning of "divorce," "custody," and "visitation." She has some understanding that the court has ordered the proposed visitation with her mother's ex-husband, but denies that this man is her father. Lucy emphatically stated that she would not go with, or stay with "that man"; that he was "bad" -- by which she meant bad because he would force her to do something against her own desires; and that if she were forced to go with him she "would not go anyway." Efforts to encourage Lucy to compromise her stand on this issue were not productive. Her comments were all made in a calm, firm, unemotional fashion.

Sherry T. made it immediately evident to the counselor that she was unqualifiedly opposed to forcing her daughter to do something which was totally against Lucy's wishes, or, in her opinion, Lucy's interests. She pointed out a history of indifference and under-involvement in the child's life, except at moments when Ms. T. was involved herself in one issue or another with her ex-husband. She further suspects some interest in the child may relate more to the ex-husband's mother than to her ex-husband himself.

On the basis of these interviews, it is clear that a visitation plan, as ordered, would not meet the best interests of this child. The promulgation of visitation is too abrupt; the duration of it is too protracted; and -- most importantly -- there has been no prior effort made to reduce the strain and anxiety which would be generated in this child, if she were forced to participate in an experience about which she is terribly apprehensive. The mere fact that some of her concern about the visitation has been aggravated by her mother's protective stance, does not make the problem faced by the child a less serious one.

It would be my recommendation that the date for the promulgation of visitation be deferred for a period of time, during which period the mother and the ex-husband, in the best interests of the child, attempt to resolve their differences concerning the plan for Lucy's visitation. Furthermore, at some point in the near future, Lucy herself should obtain counseling in order to reduce her fears and anxieties concerning proposed visitations. If I am not mistaken, I believe that such recommendations, should they be understood to be in the best interests of the child, could be court-ordered.

My qualifications in the area of juvenile counseling are as follows: I received my M.A. in YR-31 and Ph.D. in YR-17 in sociology from Michiana University, my area of specialization being family disorganization. The subject of my thesis was parent-linked delinquency. I have been an instructor of sociology on the subject of family relations for many years and am currently teaching at Southby State University.

From YR-26 to YR-20, I was Superintendent of Parkside Detention Home. From YR-20 to YR-17, I was the Chief Probation Officer of Hoynes County. I have maintained a private counseling practice for a period of thirty years and have frequently been requested to report to the courts in northern Michiana concerning the welfare of children in various domestic cases regarding visitation and child custody.

Sincerely,

Franklin B. Moses, Ph.D.
Sociologist

HISTOCOMPATABILITY LABORATORY

Michiana University Medical Center

University Hospital 116/3339 W. North Street, Dolton, Michiana 46224

Director: Sonia M. Stephens, M.D., F.A.C.P.

June 8, YR-0

Dear Attorneys:

Enclosed you will find in affidavit form the results of the HLA test in the paternity case of Lucy T. and Sherry B. vs. Gary T. I hope these results are useful to you in your deliberations in this case.

I'm quoting you below an article in regard to the HLA testing and its interpretation, especially in paternity cases, which you might find of interest.

Sincerely,

Sonia M. Stephens, M.D., F.A.C.P.
Professor of Medicine

SMS/js

Reference: P.I. Terasaki, Journal of Family Law 16:54, 1977-78.
Resolution by HLA Testing of 1,000 Paternity Cases Not Excluded by ABO Testing.

HISTOCOMPATABILITY LABORATORY

Michiana University Medical Center

University Hospital 116/3339 W. North Street, Dolton, Michiana 46224

Director: Sonia M. Stephens, M.D., F.A.C.P.

AFFIDAVIT

Comes now Sonia M. Stephens, and being duly sworn states:

(1) She is a licensed medical doctor in the State of Michiana, and the Director of the Histocompatibility Laboratory at the Michiana University Medical Center at University Hospital, Dolton, Michiana.

(2) She has personal knowledge of all statements contained herein, and all statements concerning medical matters are based upon her knowledge and expertise as a medical doctor.

(3) On 10/16/YR-0, she supervised and conducted an HLA blood test on Gary T., Sherry B. and Lucy T., birthdate 5/19/YR-8, which gave the following results:

	HLA-A	HLA-B	HLA-C
Gary T.	A1,2	B8,18	C-,-
Sherry B.	A28,31	B15,40	Cw3,-
Lucy T.	A28,33	B14,15	Cw3,-

(4) Her interpretation of these findings is that Lucy inherited from her mother the combination (or haplotype) of HLA-A28,B15,Cw3, and therefore the remaining haplotype of GLA-A33,B14,Cw- from her biological father.

(5) Gary T. does not have these antigens and is thereby excluded as being the biological father of this child.

Chapter Four. Parent-Child Relationship

(6) Any child of Gary T. should have one of the following haplotypes: HLA-A1,B8, or HLA-A1,B18, or HLA-A2,B8 or HLA-A2,B18. Lucy T. does not have any of these haplotypes and this only more excludes Gary T. as being the biological father of this child.

Further Affiant Saith Not.

Sonia M. Stephens, M.D., F.A.C.P.

Subscribed and sworn to before me, a Notary Public in and for the County of Warren and State of Michiana, this eighth day of June, YR-0.

_____
Notary Public

My Commission Expires:

_____

2. *Reverse Paternity—Action by Husband*

Problem 25

Little v. Little

In YR-8, Mona and Greg Little were married. A few weeks after the wedding, Mona and Greg decided that they did not want to have children, and Greg had a vasectomy. In YR-3, Mona became pregnant and gave birth to a daughter, named Jenny. Mona admitted to Greg that she had an affair, but claimed that the man was from another state and there was no chance she would ever see him again. Greg decided that he would forgive Mona and try to save the marriage. For the next two years, Greg and Mona seemed to be happily married, and Greg treated Jenny as if she were his own child. In YR-1, Greg learned that Jenny's father was not a man from out of state but Mona's boss, Clayton, with whom she was having a continuing affair. Greg immediately filed for divorce, making no claims to custody or visitation with Jenny. Soon after the divorce was filed, Mona sued Clayton for child support, and Clayton in turn joined Greg in the action, claiming that Greg, having held Jenny out to be his own child since birth, was estopped from denying paternity.

Questions

1. Who generally has standing to dispute the legitimacy of a child?
2. May the presumption that a child born during wedlock is the child of the mother's husband be rebutted? What standard of proof is needed to rebut the presumption? Is there a time limitation on when this rebuttal must be made?
3. May a party be estopped from rebutting the presumption?
4. What is the policy behind estopping a party from disputing the legitimacy of a child?

C. EQUITABLE PARENT DOCTRINE

Problem 26

In re Marriage of Janet M. and Zachary D.

Janet M. and Zachary D. (Zach) met in June, YR-4, when Janet responded to a television ad placed by Zach. At the time they met, Janet, a thirty-eight-year-old graduate student, was approximately three months pregnant as the result of artificial insemination. Janet and Zach were married October 2, YR-4, in Southby, Michiana, when Janet was seven months pregnant. After their marriage, the couple sought legal advice as to whether Zach should adopt the baby. Both their attorney and the Office of the Friend of the Hoynes Circuit Court advised them that adoption was not necessary. A healthy baby boy, Jeremy, was born two months later. Zach participated in the birthing experience, coaching Janet and assisting in Jeremy's delivery. Zach was listed on Jeremy's birth certificate as his father.

For the first six months of their marriage, Janet maintained a residence in Southby while she completed her studies. Jeremy lived with Janet, while Zach commuted from Minden, Michiana, to visit during the week and on weekends. Following graduation, the family was reunited when Janet was employed as an associate professor at Michiana University at Southby. Although he was not Jeremy's biological father, Zach actively assumed the role of fathering, caring for Jeremy while Janet was working, taking Jeremy to the zoo and the park, putting him to bed in the evening, and providing financial support for his care.

By their second anniversary, the marriage was in trouble, and the couple was seeking marital counseling. In April, YR-1, Janet filed a petition for dissolution of the marriage. Janet requests full custody of Jeremy, with denial of rights of parenthood to Zach, including visitation. Janet is willing to assume full financial support of her son.

Questions

1. Who is Jeremy's father?
2. What is the equitable parent doctrine? How should it be applied in this case?
3. Should Zach be granted or denied parental rights regarding Jeremy? Why?
4. Was it malpractice for the parties' attorney to suggest that adoption was unnecessary? Was it ethical? Were the actions of the Office of the Friend of the Court proper?
5. If the court rules that Zach should be treated as Jeremy's father, at what point in Jeremy's life is Zach considered the father? At what point in Jeremy's life would Zach be responsible for child support?
6. What equitable issues could Zach raise against Janet's petition?
7. How does the presumption of paternity in the Uniform Parentage Act operate in this instance?
8. If Janet's motion to deny Zach's parental rights succeeds, can a guardian ad litem file a petition on behalf of Jeremy for support from Zach?

Chapter Five

Children Born Out of Wedlock

Problem 27

In re Paternity of Albert Sparks

Lula Sparks gave birth to Albert ("Bertie") out of wedlock on April 10, YR-5. Cleon Baker is the child's putative father, although paternity has not been legally established. In YR-3, Cleon married Denise, an elementary school teacher, who is unable, for medical reasons, to have children. Cleon is the only child of Kermit Baker, a vice president and trust officer for National Bank of Southby, Michiana, and Dorothy Baker, deceased.

In January of YR-0, Lula was laid off at her assembly line job with AM General in Southby. Lula has recently borrowed money from a few friends to make ends meet. Cleon has made gifts of clothing and toys during his rare visits with Bertie, but otherwise he has not supported the child. In August of YR-1, Cleon came to visit Bertie and found the child alone and crying in his bedroom. Bertie told Cleon that Roxie, the babysitter, left him alone. Cleon stayed with Bertie until Lula returned home four hours later. After a heated argument, Cleon threatened to go through court to get custody of Bertie. During the past six months, Cleon has been highly critical of Lula as a parent. Lula describes herself as an agnostic but permits Bertie to attend Sunday School with the neighbors' children. Cleon is an usher in the Community Baptist Church in Southby.

Lula does not wish to receive public assistance (AFDC, food stamps, etc.) funds because, as she states, "No one in my family has taken a government handout, and I won't be the first."

Assume that in Michiana a paternity action must be brought within six years from the date of the child's birth.

Questions

1. What rights does Cleon have at this time?
2. What should the lawyer tell Cleon during his first interview?
3. Are there any legal obstacles to Cleon filing a filiation action to establish paternity?
4. What effect would a paternity judgment have on the parties' custody rights and child support obligations?

5. What other legal considerations are there for the parties at this time?
6. May Lula sue Cleon for child support? What kind of action could she bring?
7. Would the Michiana statute of limitations be a bar to either Lula's or Cleon's petition for establishing paternity? How would the statute of limitations affect Bertie's rights?
8. Should illegitimate children be given all the same legal rights regarding support and inheritance as children born of marriage? If so, how does such a rule fit within the policy of encouraging marriage?
9. What is the contractual basis for equalization of the rights of non-marital children with marital children?
10. What are Bertie's rights in this case?

Problem 28

In re Paternity of Darrell Dutile

In YR-1, Bridgett O'Malley became pregnant with Frank Dutile's son. Bridgett and Frank were not married at the time, and when Bridgett told Frank she was pregnant, he denied he was the father and told Bridgett she was on her own. Bridgett in turn told Frank, "You just wait until the baby is born. I'll have a paternity test done and prove this child is yours. You'll be paying child support for the rest of your life."

Two months into Bridgett's pregnancy, Frank was killed in an automobile accident. There were few assets in Frank's estate, but he was insured under the Social Security Act, and therefore his child would be entitled to "child's insurance benefits." Bridgett knew that the baby might be entitled to these benefits but thought she had to wait until after the baby was born to file a paternity claim.

After Darrell was born three months ago, human leukocyte antigen (HLA) tests were performed and Frank was determined to be the father. Bridgett came to you for advice about how to file the paternity action. Your research uncovered a Michiana statute of limitations requiring a paternity claim to be filed within six months of the father's death.

Questions

1. What are the prospects of success for Darrell and Bridgett? Could this law be in violation of the Equal Protection Clause? Does it unfairly burden children born out of wedlock? Would it be a different case if the time limit was two months? Eighteen months? Six years?
2. What policy considerations would prompt Michiana to enact such a law? Are there less restrictive means of meeting these policy goals?

FAMILY LAW TRIAL SCHEDULE

All trials will be held in the Buchanan County General District Courtroom
Buchanan County Courthouse
3rd Floor

Wednesday, April 14, 2004, 2:00 – 5:00 **TRIAL A: Slovin v. Slovin**	Plaintiff: Attorneys: Witnesses:	Rita Slovin Kelly Cutler/Amanda Burke Rita Slovin—Mindy Mullins Serena Phillips—Geri Spindel Rowena Marks--_____
	Defendant: Attorneys: Witnesses:	Michael Slovin Kim Miller/Gerald Arrington Michael Slovin—David Bruno Alan Brucker—Lonnie Ayers Thoren Elkind--_____
Wednesday, April 14, 2004, 5:30 – 8:30 **TRIAL B: Slovin v. Slovin**	Plaintiff: Attorneys: Witnesses:	Rita Slovin Chris Bledsoe/Russell Egli Rita Slovin—Amy Voyles Serena Phillips—Jill Overton Rowena Marks--_____
	Defendant: Attorneys: Witnesses:	Michael Slovin Patricia Basham/Nancy Coulling Michael Slovin—Stephen Jones Alan Brucker—David Yeaman Thoren Elkind--_____
Monday, April 19, 2004, 4:30 – 7:30 **TRIAL C: In the Interest of Grace Kyles**	Plaintiff: Attorneys: Witnesses:	State of Nita, County of Darron Stephen Jones/Michael Mounts Rollin Bradley--_____ Dr. Alamar—Amanda Burke Ellen (Allen) Nyman—Stacey Beans
	Defendant: Attorneys: Witnesses:	Cynthia Kyles Mindy Mullins/Beth Bowersock Cynthia Kyles—Kelly Cutler Dr. G. Benton—Gerald Arrington Ramona McKenzie--_____

Wednesday, April 21, 2004, 2:00 – 5:00
TRIAL D: Slovin v. Slovin

Plaintiff: Rita Slovin
Attorneys: David Yeaman/David Bruno
Witnesses: Rita Slovin—Jean Ann Lilly
Serena Phillips--_____
Rowena Marks—Barbara DeFilippis

Defendant: Michael Slovin
Attorneys: Carolyn St. Clair/Lonnie Ayers
Witnesses: Michael Slovin—Russell Egli
Alan Brucker--_____
Thoren Elkind—Nancy Coulling

Wednesday, April 21, 2004, 5:30 – 8:30
TRIAL E: Slovin v. Slovin

Plaintiff: Rita Slovin
Attorneys: Ollieloretta Shepherd/Jeff Kessler
Witnesses: Rita Slovin—Beth Bowersock
Serena Phillips--_____
Rowena Marks—Kim Miller

Defendant: Michael Slovin
Attorneys: Barbara DeFilippis/Stacey Beans
Witnesses: Michael Slovin—Michael Mounts
Alan Brucker—Chris Bledsoe
Thoren Elkind--_____

Thursday, April 22, 2004, 4:30 – 7:30
TRIAL F: In the Interest of Grace Kyles

Plaintiff: State of Nita, County of Darros
Attorneys: Geri Spindel/Amy Voyles
Witnesses: Rollin Bradley--_____
Dr. Alamar—Jeff Kessler
Ellen (Allen) Nyman—Ollieloretta Shepherd

Defendant: Cynthia Kyles
Attorneys: Jill Overton/Jean Ann Lilly
Witnesses: Cynthia Kyles—Pat Basham
Dr. G. Benton--_____
Ramona McKenzie—Carolyn St. Clair

*Each side will be allotted 1 ½ hours to complete the case. Objections will not be included in time limitations.

Feb 5, 2004

Tooker v. Lopez 1969
Center of gravity or grouping of contacts theory under which the courts apply the law of the state which b/c of its relationship or contact or with the occurance or the parties has the greatest concern with specific...

3 step process
1) necessary to isolate the issue
2) identify the policies embraced in the laws in conflict
3) to examine the contacts of the respective jurisdictions to ascertain which has a superior interest in having its policy or law applied.

※ Negligence - place of the wrong, place of the injury.

→ last year's exam question.

Page 185 Notes
"False conflict" one state has a interest in the litigation & the other does not.

Neumeier v. Kuehner 1972
   pg. 188.

Cause of action: torts
Choice of law theory: evolving.
Forum: NY
Plaintiff: ONT
Defendant: NY
Place of Injury: ONT
NY's interest:
ONT's interest

Guest statutes in Conflicts settings

pg. 191   Neumeier Rules.
★   1) when guest/passenger host/driver
very   and care are domiciled in ~~same~~
important   same state the law of such state
            governs.

2's 3   2) when guest/passenger and host/
place of   driver are domiciled in DIFFERENT
injury   states the law of the state
             of injury controls when 1) injury
             in guest's home state and law
             permits recovery and 2) when
             injury is in host's home state
             law does not permit recovery.

3) When guest/passenger and host/driver are domiciled in different states, the law of the state of injury generally controls unless displacing place of injury law would advance the relevant substantive law purposes without impairing the smooth working of the multi-state system or producing great uncertainty for litigants.

Which Neumier Rule did the ct. actually apply?
  P - injured in home state but law did not favor P.
    D = place of injury

#3 rule: so they applied place of injury

What rules in Schultz?
- court makes distinction between
- conduct-regulating rules and
- loss-allocating rules

- with conduct-regulating rules, locus/situs state will usually have "predominant" concern.

Schultz v. Boy Scouts of America, Inc. (p 197.)

loss allocating or conduct regulating before you look @ Neumier rules.

Cooney v. Osgood Machinery, Inc 1993

Pg. 211 the public policy exception should be considered only after the ct. has first determined under choice of law principles, that the applicable substantive law is not the forum's law.

The first Neumier rule applies when the parties share a common domicile, in that situation the law of common domicile.

Bodea v. Trans Nat Express
731 NYS 2d 113

- The 3rd Neumier rule Applies in other situation:

NY's Public Policy Exception
only considered when other state's substantive law applies & Not forums.

Exam question — In Schultz required important contacts b/w the parties

Feb 6, 2004
Second Restatement pgs. 47-48

can use in torts & in contracts → section 6 General Principals
145 General Tort Principals & Contacts
156 Presumption that Place of Injury controls conduct
146 Presumption that Place of Injury controls in Personal Injury cases unless other state has more Significant Relationship under section 6 (pp. 58, 216

Will be tested over this.

Know to discuss this go through contacts talk about these principles, etc.

Most tort sections contain a presumption
Know diff. sections & what they are as in Section 146 that place of injury controls unless other state has more sign. relationship under section 6 to the occurrence
- about & how to apply that

Bad Faith Insurance — some states say it is tort & others say it is a contract. Need to know b/c in torts can get punitive damages & can't in a contract case.

Bates v. Superior Court pg. 214
Cause of action: tort for breach of good faith
Choice of law theory: 2d Restatement
Forum: AZ
Plaintiff: AZ
Defendant: OH
Place of Injury: AZ

Second Restatement sections used in Bates
Section 6 - General Principles

Section 145 pg. 216

1) Place of where injury occurred.
   AZ
2) Place of conduct
   OH
3) Domicile π - AZ Δ = OH
4) Center of Relationship
   OH

pg. 46 & 47 sections laid out.

Chambers v. Dakotah Charter, Inc. (p 220)

cause of action: negligence
choice of law theory
              2nd restatement
Forum: South Dakota.
π = SD
Δ = SD
Place of Injury MO.

π is barred if π's negligence is even slight.
ct. characterized case as dealing with damages not conduct.

Chambers case § section 6
only two relevant factors from section 6
    1) Policies of interested states

    2) Relevant interests of states in determining the issue.

pg. 254

Johnson v. Spider Staging Corp. 1976
cause of action: wrongful death / product liability
choice of law theory: 2d Restatement
Forum: WA
π - KS
Δ - WA
Place of Injury KS

Section 175 Wrongful Death

Note 2 on pg. 228
Notes are subject to the exam questions.

Hataway v. McKinley 1992
cause of action: wrongful death Negligence
choice of law theory: 2nd restatement
Forum TN
π - TN
Δ - TN
Place of injury - ARK

pg. 240

Feb 11, 2004

- Bonnlander v. Leader National Ins. (Handout 1)
Cause of action: contract
Forum: Kentucky
Choice of law theory: restatement 2nd
Place of event: KY
Plaintiff: ID
Defendant: Driver - KY
Issues: Id or Ky
Holding: Restatement 2nd 188, 193.
* Section 193 know for the exam.

Bonnlander on Torts.
- The only contacts w/ Kentucky are that the accident occurred here & tortfeasor resided here.
  Any significant contact was enough to allow Kentucky law to apply.

Arnett v. Thompson
Ohio couple had accident in KY.

Looking for existence of KY contacts. If accident occurs in KY there is enough contact from that fact alone to justify applying KY law.

Also if Ky residents of KY is the only relationship

of the case to another state is that the accident happened there it is enough contact for the case to have KY laws apply.

✱ weighing of gov. interest analysis → wouldn't be answer @ all. it would design. contacts for KY.

Haggarty v. Cadeno
cause of action: tort
Forum: New Jersey
Place of event: New Jersey
Place of garage: New York
Plaintiff: New Jersey
Defendant 1: Driver from FL.
Defendant 2: car rental place: Delaware: NY.
• If you own the key you are responsible therefore you can be sued.
  Determative law is that of the state w/ the greatest interest governing the particular issue.

• If no conflict False conflict.
 1st step in gov. interest analysis
 1) Is there a conflict 2) identify gov. policies

Feb 11, 2004

of each state's how those policies are affected by each state's contacts to the litigation's to the parties.

If A state's contacts are not related the policies underlying law then that state does not possess an interest in having its law apply.

Do Gov's have an interest in this litigation.

Class Actions

Castano v. American Tobacco p. 270

Not very important

 cause of action:
 Forum:
 Choice of law theory:
 Place of event:
 Plaintiff:
 Defendant:
 Issues:

Footnote pg. 271 Footnote 10.
Footnote pg. 273 Footnote 15.

Feb 13, 2004
 Review Notes on TWEN site
Lefler's Better sounder rule of law - ?!
 what sets him apart.

Section 6 General Principals
Very important → important to any of the issues being applied.

- People can only have one domicile

Escape Devices
* Public Policy

* Procedural v. substantive

applying other states law to other states
depacage

characterizing the issue.

Feb 17, 2004

Choice of law theories for Contracts.
1) Vested Rights / traditional / First Restatement
Lex Loci Contractus VA/TN.

2) Currie's Govt. Interest Analysis + 2nd Restatement
NJ

When contract does not have a choice of law provision / use one of these!

3) Grouping of Contacts (Auten) + 2nd restatement NY

4) Leflar's Choice-Influencing Considerations
NW.

5) 2nd restatement / Most significant Relationship

escape devices still available even though we are dealing with contracts. some tort devices apply in contracts.

First Restatement

place of contracting — Place of Making - validity, interpretation, or construction of a contract is governed by substantive law of the lex loci contractus - place of contracting

(place of contracting) place where final act to make contract

✱ on exam — binding occurs.
　　　　offer accepts signature.

<u>Place of Performance</u> — the law of the place of performance determines the questions of the breach.

<u>Exceptions</u>
　　Parties expressly provide otherwise that another states' law will apply.

Chesapeake Supply & Equip. Co. (Handout 2)

Look to the terms of the contract.

All about validity of the contract decided that it WAS in MD.

When looking @ public policy looking @ Forum's public policy.

Mere differences in law are not enough must be repugnate.

Pro Football Inc. v. Paul (Handout 2)
are professional athletics subject to Workman's comp.
Cause of action: Workman's comp.
Choice of law theory: First Restatement
Forum: VA
Plaintiff:
Defendant:
Final Act: reporting for duty, physical exam
final act are not always the signature of a contract.

Tenn.'s twist on Traditional Approach.
law presumes to have intended to contract pursuant to the laws of the state in which the contract was entered into

Exceptions
1) Parties expressly chose another state's law to apply and
2) contract is to be performed in another state & parties envision that state's law will apply.

A.J.J Enterprises v. Weizer
  unpublished case.
cause of action - Contract
Choice of law theory: 1st restatement (TN style)
Forum - TN
Plaintiff - 40 states (did business)
Defendant - NC
Where contract made - Absent provision in contract
TN will apply lex loci
Trial Ct. thought Florida law applied.
employee changed terms in counter offer
counter offer became a contract when it was
signed & accepted in NY.

Not going to be just an offer &
acceptance.

NY's Approach - Background 597 NYS 2d 904.

NY. { lex loci delicti
      place of the tort place of injury
      contract made or performed.

Auten v. Auten pg. 283

cause of action: contract

After several yrs. women sued for support & maintenance under a separation agreement executed in 1933.

Choice of law theory: NY grouping of contracts.
Plaintiff - Eng.
Defendant - Eng (temporary visa).
contracts connections: eng.

NY's Approach to Contracts

"center of gravity" or "grouping of contracts" choice of law theory applied in contract cases.

- Under this approach the spectrum of specific contacts. Section 188 of the 2nd restatement of contracts.

on exam →
1) Place of contracting
2) Place of negotiation
3) Place of performance
4) Location of the subject matter of the contract, and
5) domicile of the contracting parties.

pg. 300.

Chapter Six

Adoption

A. SAME RACE PLACEMENT

Problem 29

In re Adoption of R.K.O.

Robert Kevin Obucho was born on January 23, YR-2. His mother, a single woman and an undocumented alien from Niger, gave birth to Robert in Southby Memorial Hospital's emergency room after twenty hours of labor. Knowing she could not afford to keep the child and that she had to return to Niger, the mother left the baby in his crib in the maternity ward, along with a note giving him his name, Robert Kevin Obucho.

When it was discovered that Robert's mother had disappeared, the hospital staff immediately called the Michiana Department of Public Welfare. After the search for Robert's mother proved futile, the DPW took Robert into its custody and placed him in foster care with Patrick and Clair O'Reilly, a married couple who had recently emigrated to the United States from Dublin, Ireland.

On October 26, YR-1, the O'Reillys, who were unable to have children of their own, filed a petition to adopt Robert. In their adoption papers, the O'Reillys stated that they would keep the child's name, Robert Kevin, according to the wishes of his natural mother.

The O'Reillys had had a falling out with the DPW over foster care compensation during the summer of YR-1. The caseworker in charge of Robert's case decided that the O'Reillys' response to the dispute was so inappropriate that she recommended that DPW oppose the O'Reillys' adoption. Further, she stated in her placement recommendation report that the O'Reillys never acknowledged the racial differences between themselves and Robert, and that Robert would be better placed in an African-American home.

Michiana's adoption statute provides as follows:

> In any adoption proceeding involving a minor, the court must place the child's best interests ahead of all other interests. In analyzing these interests, the court must consider the following factors: (1) the child's age; (2) the stability of the adopting family; (3) economic and other resources available to the adopting family; (4) existence of love and affection among those involved; (5) family relationships between the child and the adopt-

ing family; (6) race of the parties; (7) religion of the parties; and (7) any other factors significant in that proceeding.

Questions

1. Is race a permissible consideration in adoption proceedings? If so, how significant should it be compared to other considerations? If not, why not?
2. May race be the sole factor in adoption proceedings?
3. Assume this case arose under the Indian Child Welfare Act and that Robert's mother is known to be a member of the Comanche Tribe. What result in this case?
4. If the O'Reillys' adoption petition fails, do they have a cause of action against the DPW? If so, on what grounds?

B. THE INTERSTATE DIMENSION

Problem 30

In re Adoption of Baby Gail

In December of YR-1, Suzanne Huff, a resident of Brighton, Ohio, who was unmarried and pregnant at the time, sent a Christmas card to her friends Jerome and Carolyn Burns in Southby, Michiana, in which she wrote, "I'm going to have a baby in a few months and I want to give it up for adoption. Can you tell me what to do or help me?" Suzanne is employed as a bartender at Harvey's, a restaurant-tavern in Brighton. In January of YR-0, Suzanne received a letter from Jane Gamboa, a resident of Southby, stating that she and her husband, Don, were interested in adopting Suzanne's baby and that the Gamboas would be pleased to pay all medical and hospital expenses, attorney fees, and court costs related to the child's birth. Suzanne wrote back to Jane as follows:

Dear Jane,

The baby is due in three weeks. I'm so glad that Jerome and Carolyn found you. It will be necessary for you to come to Brighton, Ohio, to pick up the baby after birth. My home telephone number is 312-289-6664. I will have the baby at Good Samaritan Hospital, 701 E. Drexel in Brighton. The telephone number at the hospital is 312-234-7514. Please bring whatever legal papers are needed. Also, please fax me (317-235-5517) copies of these papers ASAP so I can go over them with my attorney. Thanks and God bless.

Yours truly,

Suzanne Huff

On January 27, YR-0, Suzanne met with her attorney and showed him the form faxed to her by the Gamboas. Suzanne and the attorney discussed

Chapter Six. Adoption

Suzanne's desire to have the Gamboas adopt the baby. Handing Suzanne the consent form, the attorney stated, "This will work fine. Good luck." Suzanne gave birth to a baby girl on January 30, YR-0, and the following day, in the presence of a notary public, signed the consent-to-adoption form provided by the Gamboas. The hospital records show that Suzanne named Ronald T. Lane as the father of Baby Gail. Ronald Lane was doubtful of his paternity of the child, but he nevertheless paid for prenatal care and childbirth expenses. Lane moved from Brighton to Reno, Nevada, in early January, YR-0, is employed as a pit boss at Peppermill Casino in Reno, and has paid no further child support for Baby Gail. Lane made no further attempt to contact Suzanne or Baby Gail following his departure for Nevada. On February 2, YR-0, Don and Jane took the baby (identified in hospital records as "Baby Gail") and returned to Southby. On February 3, YR-0, Jane sent the following note to Good Samaritan Hospital:

To the Doctors and Nursing Staff:

Words can't express our gratitude for the good care you gave our Baby Gail during and after her recent birth at your hospital. This adoption is our dream come true. Thanks for everything.

Don and Jane Gamboa

Don and Jane are both employed full time, Don as an attorney for a title insurance company and Jane as a secretary for a collection agency. In YR-3, Don had been dismissed from his position as deputy city attorney for the City of Southby, Michiana, for charges of sexual harassment involving an eighteen-year-old secretary. On February 5, Don and Jane filed an adoption petition and the signed consent form in Hoynes Probate Court in Southby, Michiana, and set the matter for hearing, with no notice served on any state agency in Ohio or Michiana. Meanwhile, on February 5, YR-0, Suzanne consulted another attorney and stated that she wants to revoke her consent to the adoption and obtain custody of her daughter. On February 6, in Brighton, the new attorney filed a custody petition and revocation of consent to adoption, with no notice to Don and Jane or any state agency, and obtained custody and revocation orders for Suzanne.

Assume that Michiana has adopted the Uniform Adoption Act, and that Ohio and Michiana have adopted the Interstate Compact for the Placement of Children and the Uniform Child Custody Jurisdiction Act.

Questions

1. What is the purpose of the Interstate Compact on the Placement of Children (ICPC)? (*See* the Appendix.)
2. Does the ICPC apply to non-agency adoptions, as in this case?
3. Are the Gamboas a "sending agency" under Article II of the ICPC?
4. Did the Gamboas follow the proper procedure for bringing Baby Gail into Michiana for adoption?
5. What sanctions does the ICPC provide for sending agencies that fail to comply with its procedures?
6. What should Suzanne do in order to enforce the Ohio custody and revocation orders in Michiana?
7. Will Suzanne's revocation of consent invalidate the Gamboa's adoption action? Is lack of notice fatal to her revocation claim? If Suzanne succeeds, what recourse do the Gamboas have?

8. In an adoption proceeding, to whom should notice be given? (*See* the Uniform Adoption Act in the Appendix.)
9. Should violation of a provision of the ICPC result in the denial of an adoption petition? Why or why not?
10. *See* the Uniform Child Custody Jurisdiction Act (UCCJA) in the Appendix. The UCCJA is designed to determine the proper forum and choice of laws for child custody matters. Under the UCCJA, which state is the proper forum for adjudicating Baby Gail's case as of October 3, YR-0? Must the other forum dismiss its proceeding?
11. Does the Parental Kidnapping Prevention Act (PKPA) apply in this case? (*See* the Appendix.)
12. What are Ronald Lane's rights in this proceeding?

Problem 31

Bur v. Crack

On April 1, YR-3, in Jasper County, East Dakota, Connie Frode gave birth to a baby girl, whom she named Chastity. Ms. Frode was unmarried at the time. On April 6, Ms. Frode signed a voluntary relinquishment of parental rights form, giving up her rights to Chastity under East Dakota law. On the form, Ms. Frode named Alex Hamilton, her current boyfriend, as Chastity's father.

On April 10, YR-3, Felix and Sandra Crack, residents of New City, Michiana, petitioned the Jasper Juvenile Court to adopt Chastity. The court granted the Cracks custody and revoked the parental rights of Ms. Frode and Mr. Hamilton. Chastity has lived with the Cracks in Michiana since that time.

On May 19, YR-3, Ms. Frode filed a request in the Jasper Juvenile Court to revoke her relinquishment of parental rights. She claimed she had lied on the release form when she named Alex Hamilton as Chastity's father, and that Chastity's real father was in fact her former boyfriend, Arin Bur. Mr. Bur filed an affidavit of paternity in support of Ms. Frode's request. Ms. Frode and Mr. Bur were married on July 10, YR-3, after learning that she was again pregnant by him.

On June 7, YR-3, Mr. Bur filed a petition to intervene in the Cracks' Jasper County adoption petition. The Cracks moved to revoke Mr. Bur's parental rights on the grounds of falsity or, in the alternative, abandonment. On November 30, YR-3, the Jasper Juvenile Court denied Connie (Frode) Bur's May 19 petition on equity grounds. At the same time, however, the court made a factual determination on the basis of an HLA test that Arin Bur is Chastity's biological father, that because of this fact he is entitled to parental rights unless the Cracks can show abandonment, and that the Cracks have failed to show abandonment. The judge denied the Cracks' motion to revoke Mr. Bur's rights. The court further denied the Cracks' adoption petition because the natural father had not relinquished his rights. The court refused to apply a standard of the child's best interests because of its holding that Mr. Bur had not abandoned Chastity. The court revoked the Cracks' custody and ordered Chastity to be returned to the Burs.

The Cracks appealed from this judgment. They maintained their custody of Chastity during the appeal. On October 10, YR-2, the East Dakota Court of Appeals affirmed the juvenile court's ruling. On March 3, YR-1, the East Dakota Supreme Court denied certiorari.

The Cracks filed the current petition in the Hoynes Superior Court of New City, Michiana, on March 31, YR-1. The petition, filed under the Uniform Child

Custody Jurisdiction Act, requests that the Michiana court assume jurisdiction, based on Chastity's best interests, and modify the East Dakota order. The Cracks base their claim on the fact that Chastity has lived in Michiana virtually nonstop since shortly after her birth, that the Burs are unfit parents, and that Chastity's best interests would be served by Michiana assuming jurisdiction. Mr. Bur filed a motion to quash, based on lack of jurisdiction, stating that the full faith and credit clause of the U.S. Constitution requires the Michiana court to dismiss the Cracks' petition on res judicata and collateral estoppel grounds. Additionally, Mr. Bur claims that the Cracks are in violation of the Parental Kidnapping Prevention Act, 28 U.S.C. Section 1738A. He requests quick determination of these issues so Chastity may be returned to her family.

Questions

1. Can Michiana assume jurisdiction under the Uniform Child Custody Jurisdiction Act?
2. Must the Michiana court quash the proceedings on res judicata grounds under the full faith and credit clause of the U.S. Constitution?
3. Was it proper for the East Dakota court to find for Mr. Bur on the facts shown?
4. May a natural father undo an otherwise valid adoption if the adopting parents inadvertently fail to terminate the natural father's parental rights? Even in situations where the adopting parents have no idea and no way of knowing about his paternity? Should some form of statute of limitations be applied to such situations? If so, how long?
5. *See* the Uniform Adoption Act in the Appendix. What effect would Arin's consent to the adoption, obtained after the adoption proceedings were concluded, have had on the validity of the adoption?
6. Must an adopting couple give notice of adoption proceedings to every man the natural mother slept with nine months before the child's birth? *See* the Uniform Putative and Unknown Fathers Act in the Appendix. What impact could HLA testing have on this rule?
7. Should Arin be required to demonstrate a commitment to Chastity in order to revoke the adoption? How would this be proven?
8. Review the Parental Kidnapping Prevention Act (PKPA). How does the PKPA apply in this case? In what ways does the PKPA differ from the UCCJA?
9. Does the PKPA prevent a party from attempting to exercise a remedy through a state's courts when another state of competent jurisdiction has reached a final decision in a custody dispute?

C. PSYCHOLOGICAL PARENTS

Problem 32

In re Adoption of T.L.C.

Tabatha Louise Clark was born on September 1, YR-4, to Emily Clark, currently a resident of New City, Michiana. Tabatha's father, Fred Firerock, is currently serving a seventeen-year sentence for a robbery he committed shortly before Tabatha's birth. Tabatha's mother, Emily, has been in and out of drug rehabilitation centers since a heroin possession conviction on December 14, YR-4.

Shortly before her mother's conviction, Tabatha was detained on grounds of neglect as a child in need of services (CHINS) by the Hoynes County Department of Public Welfare (DPW). A hearing on the CHINS petition was held on December 3, YR-4. The Hoynes Probate Court found Tabatha to be a CHINS and set the matter for a dispositional hearing. The dispositional order provided that Tabatha be placed with her maternal grandparents, John and Mona Clark. The dispositional order further required Emily to undergo treatment for her drug problem and to attend parenting classes at the New City Women's Center. The order also provided for supervised visitation by Emily in the presence of a caseworker.

At first, Emily attended the classes regularly, and her visitations showed a marked improvement in her attitude toward Tabatha. Over time, however, Emily's attendance at the parenting classes became erratic. She dropped out of the drug treatment program altogether. For a period of eight months, from October, YR-2, through June YR-1, Emily's parents and the caseworker lost all contact with her. When Emily finally turned up on June 23, YR-1, she was arrested for heroin possession.

On July 26, YR-1, the DPW filed a petition to terminate Emily's parental rights. Included in the petition was the DPW's permanency plan for Tabatha, which provided for her adoption by John and Mona Clark "or another qualified family." At the termination trial, Emily, represented by counsel, testified that she didn't want to give up her baby. During cross-examination, the DPW's attorney asked Emily how old Tabatha was, what was her birthday and when was the last time Emily attempted to see her. Emily could not answer any of the questions correctly. On August 31, YR-1, the court entered an order terminating Emily's parental rights and directed the DPW to pursue adoptive placement after the deadline for filing an appeal passed.

The DPW selected the grandparents for adoptive placement of Tabatha. The Clarks filed a petition for adoption of Tabatha on December 1, YR-1. On December 3, YR-1, George and Martha Clinton also filed a petition for adoption of Tabatha. The Clintons, married eighteen years, are fifteen years younger than the Clarks. George is a law professor and former attorney general of Michiana. Martha is a lawyer in the prestigious New City law firm of Carnation, Lily & Amaryllis. The Clintons have three times the financial resources of the Clarks, even if Martha quits her job, as planned. The DPW has directed weekend visitation for the Clintons, and has not taken a position on which couple should adopt Tabatha.

On February 4, YR-0, the DPW directed Tabatha to be interviewed by Dr. Joan Verdonk, a clinical psychologist who specializes in child placement issues. Dr. Verdonk's analysis may be found in the letter that follows this problem.

Questions

1. What is the "psychological parent" theory? How does it apply in this case?
2. Should psychological parents necessarily have a superior adoption claim over other parties?

Chapter Six. Adoption

3. What kinds of evidence can the court consider when deciding contested adoption questions? Under what theory of admissibility would the Clarks be able to introduce Dr. Verdonk's letter?
4. What factors should be considered in comparing competing adoption petitions? What factors should be most important?
5. How should the family placement preference apply in this case?
6. If the court decides in favor of the Clintons, can the Clarks' petition for visitation as Tabatha's natural grandparents?

MICHIANA CHILDREN'S WELLNESS CLINIC

105 East Jefferson Boulevard, Suite 512 *Southby, Michiana 47992*
Phone (218) 555-1212 *Fax (218) 555-1211*

February 8, YR-0

Jordan Angle
Department of Public Welfare
18 North County Building Road
Southby, Michiana 47994

Re: Tabatha Louise Clark DOB 9/1/YR-4

Dear Jordan:

Pursuant to your request, I met with Tabatha Louise Clark in my office at 10:30 a.m., on February 4, YR-0. Tabatha's grandparents, John and Mona Clark, accompanied her to my office. They waited in my lobby while I interviewed Tabatha.

Based on my interview with Tabatha, my professional opinion is that Tabatha has bonded so significantly with her grandparents that it would be against her psychological best interests to separate her from the Clarks.

Tabatha has lived with the Clarks for three years. She knows that her natural mother is Emily Clark, but her maternal bonding with Mona Clark is virtually complete. Tabatha refers to Mona as "Mother Mona" and to her grandfather as "Poppa John." Tabatha fully recognizes John's and Mona's parental authority.

Tabatha is a well-behaved child, with social development appropriate for her age. Her intelligence is average to below-average for her age. She is somewhat shy, but not beyond established norms for four-year-old girls. Given her current living situation, I predict she will thrive as a child.

I asked Tabatha about George and Martha Clinton. She showed affection for them, but not any significant parental bonding. She refers to the Clintons as "Uncle George" and "Aunt Martha," which is somewhat unusual; perhaps the names have been prompted by the Clintons.

Letter to Jordan Angle, DPW
February 8, YR-0
Page 2

Most important to Tabatha's social development is her emotional bonding with her grandparents. Psychologically, the Clarks *are* her parents. Because she has had a solid relationship with her grandparents and with no others, it is my professional opinion that it would be in Tabatha's best interests to be placed with John and Mona Clark.

Sincerely,

Joan Verdonk, Ph.D.

D. LESBIAN ADOPTION

Problem 33

In re Adoption of S.S. and W.S.

Gloria Fineman, formerly Mrs. Gloria Shuletock, met Nancy Milano in December, YR-4, while Ms. Fineman was going through her divorce. Ms. Fineman and Ms. Milano began living together in May, YR-3, one month before Ms. Fineman's divorce became final. At that time, Ms. Fineman's former husband maintained primary custody of their two children, Shelly and Wilberforce (Wil). Shelly had been born to a previous marriage of Mr. Shuletock, but her natural mother had died before Mr. Shuletock married Ms. Fineman. Gloria adopted Shelly shortly after the marriage, and gave birth to Wilberforce two years later. At the time of the divorce, Shelly was eight years old and and Wil was four.

On October 3, YR-3, Ms. Fineman and Ms. Milano were "married" in a private ceremony in their home. At that time, Ms. Fineman had only limited visitation rights with her two children. However, in June, YR-2, Mr. Shuletock was arrested and charged with six counts of child molestation. Three charges involved Shelly, and three involved Wilberforce. Ms. Fineman immediately took sole custody of the children and moved them into the home she shared with Ms. Milano. Upon his conviction on all six counts, Mr. Shuletock forfeited, by operation of Michiana law, all parental rights as to the two children.

On September 18, YR-1, Ms. Fineman and Ms. Milano jointly filed a petition in Hoynes County Family Court for the adoption of Shelly and Wil by Ms. Milano. In their petition, the couple noted that Michiana's adoption statute, which follows this problem, requires termination of a natural parent's rights in order to secure those of the adoptive parent. They requested that the court not give the statute a literal reading, which would tend to substitute Ms. Milano for Ms. Fineman rather than Mr. Shuletock. They further requested that the court declare that both Ms. Fineman and Ms. Milano are parents of the children. An affidavit filed by the Michiana Child Protection Services office states that "Adoption of the children by Ms. Milano might be in the children's best interests. The children need a stable home, and the home Ms. Milano and Ms. Fineman can provide for them is about as stable as the children can hope for, under the circumstances."

On September 28, YR-1, Mr. Shuletock moved to intervene in the adoption proceedings. His amended motion notes that his criminal conviction is currently on appeal and that a declaration of Ms. Milano's parenthood would, by the same Michiana adoption statute, effectively terminate his parental rights. He requests the court to deny Ms. Milano's petition. The facts are not in dispute.

Questions

1. How does adoption affect the rights of the following people: the natural mother; the natural father; the adoptive mother; the adoptive father; the natural grandparents; the adoptive grandparents; the natural siblings? (*See* the Uniform Adoption Act in the Appendix.)
2. If Nancy succesfully adopts Shelly and Wil, who is the children's mother? Who has parental rights regarding the children? Whose parental rights are terminated?
3. Should homosexual partners be allowed to adopt their partners' children?
4. Shelly is not Gloria's natural daughter. Can the adoption statute reasonably be read in such a manner as to allow Nancy to adopt Shelly while maintaining Gloria's rights as Shelly's adoptive mother?
5. How, legally, does an adoptive parent differ from a natural parent?
6. What role should child welfare officials play in adoption proceedings? *See* the Adoption Assistance and Child Welfare Act of 1980, 42 U.S.C. §§670 et seq.
7. What is the procedure for public placement adoption?
8. Suppose Nancy is allowed to adopt the children and Mr. Shuletock's rights are terminated. Later, his appeal is successful in obtaining a new trial, wherein it is proved that the children had alleged molestation based solely on coaching by Nancy and Gloria. What legal recourse does Mr. Shuletock have? What effects could this legal nightmare have on the children? Should the adoption proceeding be stayed pending the criminal appeal to avoid such difficulties?

ADOPTION — MICHIANA CODE

Section 8-1-3101: Who May Adopt

Any person may petition the court for a decree of adoption. A petition may not be considered by the court unless petitioner's spouse, if he or she has one, joins in the petition, except that if either is a natural parent of the prospective adoptee, the natural parent need not join in the petition, but must give his or her consent to the adoption.

Section 8-1-3110: Consent to Adoption

A petition may not be granted by the court unless there is a written statement of consent by the natural parents of the adoptee, if living, or unless a relinquishment of parental rights has been duly recorded.

Section 8-1-3130: Effects of Adoption

A final decree of adoption establishes the relationship of natural parent and natural child between adopter and adoptee for all purposes, including mutual rights of inheritance and succession as if adoptee were born to adopter. The adoptee takes from, through, and by the parent. All rights and duties including those of inheritance and succession between the adoptee, his or her natural parents, their issue, collateral relatives, and so forth, are cut off, except that when one of the natural parents is the spouse of the adopter, the rights and relations as between adoptee, the natural parent, and the collateral relatives are in no way altered. The family name of the adoptee shall be changed to that of the adopter unless the decree otherwise provides, and the given name of the adoptee may be fixed or changed at the same time.

E. INDIAN CHILD WELFARE ACT

Problem 34

In re Blackfoot

Snow Blackfoot is a member of the Illiniwek Indian tribe and lives on the tribe's reservation, located in the State of Michiana. In YR-2, Snow had a son she named John, and soon after his birth she became aware that she was not well equipped to be a mother and was not going to have the support of the child's father. Snow decided to put the child up for adoption. In YR-1, John was placed with a non-Indian foster family, and it was agreed by all parties that if the placement went well the foster family would adopt the child after one year. After one year, Snow voluntarily gave her consent for the termination of her parental rights.

In YR-1, John's father returned to Michiana, and he and Snow were reunited. He told Snow that he was ready and willing to settle down and have a family. Snow then decided that she would be able to raise John with help from his father, and therefore it was not necessary for her to allow John to be adopted. She consulted an attorney and has petitioned the court for the return of her child.

Questions

1. Does the Indian Child Welfare Act (ICWA) apply in this case? *See* the ICWA in the Appendix.
2. Will Snow be able to successfully petition for the return of her child even though he is presently in foster care? Does it matter that she has already signed a voluntary relinquishment of her parental rights?
3. Would there be a way for Snow to get John back even if her parental rights had already been terminated? What if John's father had not returned until two years after John had been adopted?

F. ADOPTION OF ADULTS

Problem 35

In re Adoption of Mollie Sue Sage

This is an appeal from an order of the Hoynes Superior Court affirming the denial by the Hoynes Probate Court of an adoption petition in which a thirty-year-old married man, Lincoln Lynn Fraser (Lincoln), seeks to adopt his twenty-year-old lover, Mollie Sue Sage (Mollie). In affirming the denial, the trial justice noted that Lincoln was "probably" the father of Mollie's child. Lincoln is married to another woman and is the father of the two children born of that marriage. Mollie is now married to someone other than Lincoln. However, notwithstanding her present marital status, Mollie continues to press her appeal, claiming that the trial justice's affirmance of the probate court's denial was totally erroneous.

Mollie's first claim of error relates to her lover's claim that there was no evidentiary support for the Superior Court's finding that she and Lincoln were "lovers." An easy answer to this contention is to be found in the trial court's written decision, in which the court noted:

> Although no evidence was taken in the case in Superior Court, it is conceded by the attorney for the appellants, who did not desire to present evidence, that the relationship of lovers existed between the proposed parties to this adoption.

This concession amounts to a judicial admission, which certainly takes the place of evidence.

Mollie's remaining contention is that a court that presides at an adult adoption proceeding has no discretion whatsoever but must grant the petition as a matter of course. In espousing this claim, Mollie points to two provisions of the Michiana adoption statutes.

The first provision vests jurisdiction to hear petitions for the adoption of an adult in the probate court of the city or town in which the petitioners may live. Section 15-7-5 speaks of the necessity of obtaining the consent of the natural parents to an adoption but specifically excludes the necessity of that consent where the potential adoptee has attained the age of majority. Thus Mollie claims that the probate court was foreclosed from considering in any manner, shape, or fashion her past adulterous association with Lincoln and its potentially incestuous impact.

When Lincoln and Mollie appeared before the superior court, their appeal was heard by the then-presiding judge. After referring to the tragedy of *Oedipus Rex* and the Michiana statutes regarding incest, the presiding justice then went on to observe:

> It may be that public morality in our community has reached a low ebb. However, it is the opinion of the Court that it has not yet descended to such a nadir as to require a probate or superior court judge to implement an adoption between persons whose relationship is essentially that of paramours. To suggest that the adoption statute requires such interpretation is to concede that the legislature of Michiana intended a sardonically ludicrous result. This Court cannot construe our adoption statutes in the light of any such intent.

Was the superior court's order affirming the probate court's denial of the adoption petition an abuse of discretion? Is this issue—seemingly governed by

Chapter Six. Adoption

statute—within the trial court's discretion? The presiding appellate judge, for whom you clerk, wants you to brief this issue and answer the following questions:

Questions

1. How do the legal requirements for adult adoption differ from those for infant adoption?
2. If Lincoln successfully adopts Mollie, does he become both the father and the grandfather of Mollie's child?
3. Should sexual relations between the parties to an adoption proceeding be good grounds for denying an adoption petition?
4. *See* the Uniform Adoption Act. If Lincoln wishes to adopt Mollie, who must be parties to the proceeding? How likely is it that all necessary parties would be willing to go through with the adoption?
5. Can a wife adopt her husband? Assume that a wife has an interest in land that divests if she dies without heirs, but she is infertile. Would the adoption of her husband be a proper solution to her problem?
6. What should be the court's position where an adult petitions to adopt his or her same-sex adult lover?

Chapter Seven

Family Torts

A. PARENTAL IMMUNITY

Problem 36

Freeman v. Jones

On May 3, YR-0, Hope Freeman filed suit in Hoynes Superior Court against her father, Julius Jones, alleging sexual battery. In her complaint, Mrs. Freeman alleged that for about a three-year period, starting in YR-17, Mr. Jones frequently came into her room at night and sexually molested her. Mrs. Freeman, now twenty-five, claims that she did not come forward with the claim at the time of the molestation because her parents were undergoing a divorce and she was afraid she would lose her father if she talked. Ultimately Mr. Jones was awarded custody of his daughter. Hope Freeman also claims that she was afraid he would harm her. She further alleges that after the molestation stopped, around YR-14, she suppressed her memory of the events until shortly before this claim was filed last year.

Mr. Jones filed a H.R.C.P. 12(b)(6) motion to dismiss the complaint for failure to state a claim upon which relief may be granted. Mr. Jones claimed that since the statute of limitations for sexual battery torts is two years from the transaction or occurrence, the statute bars liability. Judge Maria Lochraine denied the motion on its face. After discovery, Mr. Jones filed a motion for summary judgment, claiming that the statute of limitations has run on the alleged tort. In the alternative, Mr. Jones argues that parental immunity bars action against him.

Two additional facts have been determined during discovery. First, Julius Jones has been previously convicted of child abuse for repreatedly beating his son by another marriage. In the report filed by the Michiana Department of Social Services during his criminal trial, an MDSS social worker described Mr. Jones as "an incredibly strict disciplinarian who has trouble determining the scope of punishment for a child's misbehavior." Second, Hope Freeman has been treated for severe depression and schizophrenia. On January 3, YR-3, and again on June 4, YR-2, she was hospitalized for attempted suicide. Her medical reports state that the cause of her depression appears to be related to a childhood trauma, probably related to her parents' divorce.

Questions

1. Does a repressed memory allegation raise a question of fact such that summary judgment is unavailable?
2. When does the statute of limitations begin to run on normal torts? When does it start on normal torts against children? When does a child sexual abuse tort statute of limitations begin to run?
3. How does memory supression affect a statute of limitations? How should a legislature deal with memory suppression when drafting limitations statutes?
4. What is the parental immunity doctrine? Why does it exist? Do the reasons for the parental immunity doctrine apply in this case?
5. Similar to the parental immunity doctrine is the teacher immunity doctrine, which allows teachers to use corporal punishment to effect discipline in schools. The teacher immunity doctrine is dwindling in use. Should parental immunity dwindle as well?
6. What are the specifics under which a parent might be immune from tort? Are the acts involved in this case the kind that would make Julius immune?
7. How would evidence of Julius' previous child abuse likely affect the outcome of this action? Should such evidence be admitted? Under what theory of relevancy might such evidence be admissible during an evidentiary hearing?

B. DOMESTIC VIOLENCE

Problem 37

State v. Heldarco

Sitting at your dinner table one evening, you receive a telephone call from a former client, Julia Marie Heldarco. Julia is frantic. She tells you that her husband, Michael, is in the home, drunk, and that he has just beaten her up. Michael staggered upstairs, where he slapped their five-year-old son, Dominic, on the face. In the background, you can hear Dominic screaming, and Michael howling at him to "Shut up or so help you. . . ." "What do I do? Oh, God, what do I do?" Julia cries.

The applicable Michiana statute(s) follow this problem.

Questions

1. Without looking at the statute, what would you advise Julia to do?
2. What services must the police offer Julia? What steps can they take to prevent Michael from attacking her again? Of what rights must the police inform Julia?
3. Outline the specific procedures a police officer can take to obtain protection for a battered spouse. How do those procedures differ for a battered child?

4. What constitutes domestic violence? Who are the victims of domestic violence as opposed to other forms of violence?
5. Under what circumstances can a police officer arrest a domestic partner for domestic violence?
6. What due process requirements are there in domestic violence preliminary matters?
7. What civil action might Julia take to protect Dominic and herself? What are the disadvantages of a civil suit in this kind of case?
8. Who would best represent Dominic's interests in a domestic violence matter?
9. How would a subsequent divorce petition affect any protective order a court might issue on Julia's behalf?
10. What social services must the state provide for Julia and Dominic? For Michael?
11. What are the potential pitfalls of a state system to protect married people from each other while promoting their marriage?

MICHIANA PREVENTION OF DOMESTIC VIOLENCE ACT

Section 2C:25-1. Short title

This act shall be known and may be cited as the "Prevention of Domestic Violence Act."

Section 2C:25-4. Law enforcement officers; training; domestic crises teams; dispatch to scene of incident of domestic violence

The Public Training Commission in the Department of Law and Public Safety shall provide that all training for law enforcement officers on the handling of domestic violence complaints shall stress the enforcement of criminal laws in domestic situations, the protection of the victim, and the use of available community resources. Law enforcement agencies may establish domestic crises teams or individual officers may be trained in methods of dealing with domestic violence. The teams may include social workers, clergy, or other persons trained in counseling, crisis intervention, or in the treatment of domestic violence victims. When an alleged incident of domestic violence is reported, the agency shall dispatch a domestic crisis team or specially trained officer, if available, to the scene of the incident.

Section 2C:25-5. Arrests

A law enforcement officer may arrest a person:
   a. When the officer has probable cause to believe that a person has violated the terms of an order issued pursuant to section 10, 11, 13, or 14 of this act and that has been effective either in person or by substituted service. The officer may verify, if necessary, the existence of an order with the appropriate law enforcement agency; or
   b. A victim exhibits signs of injury or there is other probable cause to believe that an act of domestic violence has been committed.

Section 2C:25-7. Notice to victim; contents

A law enforcement officer shall disseminate to the victim the following notice, which shall be written in both English and Spanish:

"You have the right to go to the juvenile and domestic relations court and file a complaint requesting relief including but not limited to the following: an order restraining your attacker from abusing you or directing your attacker to leave your household. You may request that the clerk of the court assist you in applying for this order. You also have the right to go to court and file a criminal complaint.

On weekends, holidays, and other times when the courts are closed, you may go to the municipal court for an emergency order granting the relief set forth above."

Section 2C:25-8. Domestic violence offense report; completion by law enforcement officer; forwarding information; contents; annual report; information on orders in force or prior incidents

a. It shall be the duty of a law enforcement officer who responds to a domestic violence call to complete a domestic violence offense report. All information contained in the domestic violence offense report shall be forwarded to the State bureau of records and identification in the Division of State Police in the Department of Law and Public Safety.

b. The domestic violence offense report shall be on a form prescribed by the supervisor of the State bureau of records and identification, which shall include, but not be limited to, the following information:

(1) The relationship of the parties;
(2) The sex of the parties;
(3) The time and date of the incident;
(4) The number of domestic violence calls investigated;
(5) Whether children were involved, or whether the alleged act of domestic violence had been committed in the presence of children;
(6) The type and extent of abuse;
(7) The number and type of weapons involved;
(8) The action taken by the law enforcement officer;
(9) The existence of any prior court orders issued pursuant to sections 10, 11, 13 or 14 of this act concerning the parties; and
(10) Any other data that may be necessary for a complete analysis of all circumstances leading to the alleged incident of domestic violence.

c. It shall be the duty of the Superintendent of the State Police with the assistance of the Division of Systems and communications in the Department of Law and Public Safety to compile and report annually for a period of 5 years to the Governor, the Legislature and the Advisory Council on Shelters for Victims of Domestic Violence on the tabulated data from the domestic violence offense reports.

Section 2C:25-12. Complaint by victim; jurisdiction; filing

a. A victim may file a complaint alleging the commission of an act of domestic violence with the juvenile and domestic relations court in conformity with the rules of court. The court in domestic violence actions shall not dismiss any complaint or delay disposition of a case because the victim has left the residence to avoid further incidents of domestic violence. Filing a complaint pursuant to this section shall not prevent the filing of a criminal complaint for the same act.

b. The juvenile and domestic relations court shall waive any requirement that the petitioner's place of residence appear on the complaint.

c. The clerk of the court, or other person designated by the court, shall assist the parties in completing any forms necessary for the filing of a summons, complaint, answer, or other pleading.

d. Summons and complaint forms shall be readily available at the clerk's office and at the municipal courts.

Section 2C:25-13. Hearing; orders for relief; emergency relief

a. A hearing shall be held in juvenile and domestic relations court within 10 days of the filing of a complaint pursuant to section 12 of this act. A copy of the complaint shall be served on the defendant in conformity with the rules of court. If a criminal complaint arising out of the same incident which is the subject matter of a complaint brought under P.L. 1981, c. 426 (C.2C:25 et seq.) is filed, notice of any hearing on the complaint shall be given to the prosecuting attorney so that he may be heard with respect to a stay of the proceeding pending disposition of the criminal proceeding. At the hearing the standard for proving the allegations in the complaint shall be by a preponderance of the evidence. The court shall consider but not be limited to the following factors:

(1) The previous history of domestic violence between the cohabitants, including threats, harassment, and physical abuse;

(2) The existence of immediate danger to person or property;

(3) The financial circumstances of the cohabitants;

(4) The best interests of the victim and the child;

(5) In determining custody and visitation, the protection of the victim's safety; and

(6) Whether the application was made in a reasonable time after the alleged act of domestic violence occurred.

b. At the hearing the juvenile and domestic relations court may issue an order granting any or all of the following relief:

(1) An order prohibiting the defendant from having contact with the victim including, but not limited to, restraining the defendant from entering the plaintiff's residence, place of employment or business, or school. The court shall prohibit the defendant from harassing the plaintiff or plaintiff's relatives in any way;

(2) An order granting possession to the plaintiff of the residence to the exclusion of the defendant when the residence or household is jointly owned or leased by the parties provided that this issue has not been resolved nor is being litigated between the parties in another action. The court may amend its order at any time upon petition by either party;

(3) When the defendant has a duty to support the plaintiff or minor children living in the residence or household and the defendant is sole owner or lessee of the residence, an order granting possession to the plaintiff of the residence or household to the exclusion of the defendant may be issued or, upon consent of the parties, allowing the defendant to provide suitable, alternate housing provided that this issue has not been resolved nor is being litigated between the parties in another action;

(4) When the parties are married, sole ownership in the name of the defendant of the real property constituting the residence of the parties shall not bar the court from entering an order restraining the defendant from entering the marital residence. No order shall affect any interest in the residence held by either party;

(5) An order determining child support, child custody, or establishing visitation rights, provided that these issues have not been resolved nor are being litigated between the parties in another action. The court shall protect the safety of the plaintiff by specifying a place of visitation away from the plaintiff or take any other appropriate precaution necessary to protect the safety and well-being of the plaintiff and minor children;

(6) An order requiring the defendant to pay to the victim monetary compensation for losses suffered as a direct result of the act of domestic

violence. Compensatory losses shall include, but not be limited to, loss of earnings or support, out-of-pocket losses for injuries sustained, moving expenses, reasonable attorney's fees, and compensation for pain and suffering. Where appropriate, punitive damages may be awarded in addition to compensatory damages;

(7) An order requiring the defendant to receive professional counseling from either a private source or a source appointed by the court and, in that event, at the court's discretion requiring the defendant to provide the court at specified intervals with documentation of attendance at the professional counseling. The court may order the defendant to pay for the professional counseling.

c. In addition to the relief sought in subsection b. of this section, a plaintiff may seek emergency ex parte relief in the nature of a temporary restraining order. The juvenile and domestic relations court may enter ex parte orders when necessary to protect the life, health, or well-being of a victim on whose behalf the relief is sought. A hearing shall be held on an ex parte order within 10 days of the issuance thereof.

Whenever emergency relief is sought by the plaintiff, the clerk of the court or other person designated by the court shall immediately transmit the complaint to the presiding juvenile and domestic relations court judge regarding the emergency relief sought by the close of business on the day relief is sought. An order granting emergency relief shall immediately be forwarded to the sheriff for immediate service of the order for emergency relief upon the defendant.

d. An order for emergency relief shall be granted upon good cause shown.

e. Emergency relief may constitute all relief available under this act together with any other appropriate relief. A temporary restraining order shall remain in effect until further action by the court.

f. Notice of orders issued pursuant to this section shall be sent by the clerk of the juvenile and domestic relations court or other person designated by the court to the appropriate chiefs of police, members of the State Police, and any other appropriate law enforcement agency.

g. All pleadings, process, and other orders filed pursuant to this act shall be served upon the defendant in accordance with the rules of court. If personal service cannot be effected upon the defendant, the court may order other appropriate substituted service.

Section 2C:25-14. Temporary restraining order; jurisdiction; duration

a. On weekends, holidays, and other times when the court is closed, a juvenile and domestic relations court judge or a municipal court judge shall be assigned to issue a temporary restraining order pursuant to this act. The order shall be made by the judge of the jurisdiction where the alleged domestic violence occurred or the jurisdiction where the plaintiff resides, using the same procedure now available on other emergency applications.

b. If it appears that the plaintiff is in danger of domestic violence, the municipal court judge shall, upon consideration of the plaintiff's domestic violence complaint, order emergency relief, including ex parte relief, in the nature of a temporary restraining order. A decision shall be made by the judge regarding the emergency relief forthwith. An order granting emergency relief, together with all pleadings, process, and other orders, shall immediately be forwarded to the sheriff for immediate service of the order for emergency relief upon the defendant.

c. An order for emergency relief shall be granted upon good cause shown and shall remain in effect until the juvenile and domestic relations court issues a final order. The juvenile and domestic relations court shall hold a hearing on an emergency order within 10 days. Any order hereunder may be dissolved or modified on 24 hours' notice or immediately appealable for a plenary hearing de novo not on the record before the juvenile and domestic relations court of the county in which the plaintiff resides.

d. Emergency relief may include forbidding the defendant from returning to the scene of the domestic violence together with any other appropriate relief.

e. The judge may permit the defendant to return to the scene of the domestic violence to pick up personal belongings and effects but may by order restrict the time and duration and provide for police supervision of such visit.

f. Notice of temporary restraining orders issued pursuant to this section shall be sent by the clerk of the court or other person designated by the court to the appropriate chiefs of police, members of the State Police, and any other appropriate law enforcement agency.

g. An application for a temporary restraining order pursuant to this section shall, upon filing and issuance, be immediately forwarded to the clerk of the juvenile and domestic relations court of the plaintiff's county of residence for a final order.

Section 2C:25-15. Accompaniment to residence for removal of personal belongings; violation of orders; contempt

a. Upon the issuance of an order pursuant to section 10, 11, 13, or 14 of this act, the court may order law enforcement officer to accompany either party to the residence to supervise the removal of personal belongings in order to insure the personal safety of the plaintiff.

b. Violation of an order issued pursuant to section 10, 11, 13, or 14 of this act shall constitute contempt and each order shall so state.

Section 2C:25-16. Uniform record of requests for orders; annual report; confidentiality

The Administrative Office of the Courts shall maintain a uniform record of all requests for orders issued pursuant to section 10, 11, 13, or 14 of this act. The record shall include the following information:

a. The number of complaints filed by the parties;

b. The sex of the parties;

c. The relationship of the parties;

d. (Deleted by amendment, P.L. 1982, C. 82.)

e. The relief sought;

f. The nature of the relief granted, including but not limited to custody and child support;

g. The effective date and terms of each order issued; and

h. The number of orders issued.

It shall be the duty of the Director of the Administrative Office of the Courts to compile and report annually to the Governor, the Legislature and the Advisory Council on Shelters for Victims of Domestic Violence on the data tabulated from the records on these orders for a period of 5 years. The Advisory Council on Shelters for Victims of Domestic Violence may request the Legislature continue the reports for another 5 years.

All records maintained pursuant to this act shall be confidential and shall not be made available to any individual or institution except as otherwise provided by law.

C. VIOLENCE AGAINST WOMEN ACT

Problem 38

Murphy v. Murphy

Josie and Shamus Murphy married in YR-2. Soon after, Shamus began to physically abuse Josie. Shamus was also verbally abusive, often calling Josie a "slut" and a "whore." Two weeks ago, after a particularly violent episode, Shamus forced Josie to have intercourse with him against her will.

Josie has come to you seeking a divorce. She would like to charge Shamus with rape, as he has threatened to come after Josie if she leaves him. Josie believes she would be safer if Shamus were convicted of rape and put in jail. In Michiana, however, there is interspousal tort immunity, and spouses and cohabitants are exempt from rape laws. Also, after reviewing Josie and Shamus's financial information, you find that the parties executed a prenuptial agreement and that Shamus has been very careful about maintaining his assets as separate property (and therefore Josie is unlikely to receive much in the way of assets upon divorce).

Questions

1. Does Josie have a federal cause of action against Shamus? *See* the Violence Against Women Act, 42 U.S.C. §13981 (1994). Do the remedies under this statute apply to Josie? What two elements will Josie have to prove in order to come under the Act?
2. Is there any provision under the Act that could provide Josie with protection from Shamus despite the interspousal tort and rape immunity in Michiana?
3. Are there remedies provided under the Act that could improve Josie's financial situation?
4. What purpose does this statute serve that is not already provided for under state criminal law?

D. WIRETAPPING

Problem 39

In re Marriage of Rodriguez

Marie and Joseph Rodriguez were married in YR-3. In YR-1, Marie told Joseph that she was having an affair and was considering a divorce. Despite this problem, Marie and Joseph decided to attempt to salvage their marriage. They began going to counseling, and Marie ended her affair.

Two months ago, while Marie was cleaning, she found hidden under their bed a tape recorder that Joseph had been using to tape all of Marie's phone calls. Joseph claims that he put the wiretap on the phone because he feared that Marie was still having an affair. Marie immediately moved out of the home and filed a divorce action. As part of her divorce petition, Marie alleged that Joseph violated federal wiretapping law under Title III of the Omnibus Crime Control and Safe Streets Act of 1968, 18 U.S.C. §2511, and prayed for various civil remedies under §2520 of the Act.

Questions

1. *See* 18 U.S.C. §2511. Is there any language in the statute that could be construed as excluding spouses from liability under the Act?
2. Should a spouse be civilly liable for secretly wiretapping the conversations if his or her spouse? Consider other areas of the law that provide spousal immunity for acts for which one would otherwise be liable.
3. What policy considerations make such interspousal immunity necessary? Are the same policy concerns involved in wiretapping cases?

E. PASSIVE PARENT ACTION

Problem 40

Jackson v. Jackson

Sara Jackson is an eighteen-year-old girl who has just moved out of the house where she lived with her mother and father in Southby, Michiana. Sara alleges that, from the time she was thirteen until she moved out of the home, her father sexually abused her on a regular basis and that her mother was fully aware that the abuse was taking place. Sara has come to you to inquire as to whether or not she might have a civil suit against her father because she does not wish to criminally prosecute the case.

Your preliminary research discloses the following: First, there is no parental tort immunity in your jurisdiction, as it has been fully abrogated by an act of the legislature. Second, Sara's parents have few assets but do own a homeowners' insurance policy that covers negligent acts that take place in the home. The policy specifically excludes intentional torts from coverage.

Questions

1. Can Sara sue her father in tort and recover under the insurance policy?
2. Can Sara sue her mother in tort and recover under the insurance policy? Was Sara's mother negligent in not preventing the abuse? Did Sara's mother have an affirmative duty to prevent the abuse?
3. Assume that Michiana has only abrogated parental tort immunity in cases of intentional tort. Can Sara sue her mother in tort for negligence in not preventing an intentional tort?

Chapter Eight

Decisions About Children — The State's Role

A. CLAIMS AGAINST THE STATE—42 U.S.C. SECTION 1983

Problem 41

Lightfinger v. Michiana DROP

The state of Michiana passed a new juvenile crime statute in YR-8 as part of its continuing war against drugs. Under the law, first-time drug offenders who are of school age are given the choice between voluntarily admitting themselves into the Drug Rehabilitation Options Program (DROP) or being incarcerated in the state youth reformatory. Under DROP, the offenders attend special schools during the week to learn career skills, such as computer programming, typing, and auto mechanics, and on weekends attend a boot camp. Since the program's inception, only 17 percent of first-time youthful offenders have been adjudicated or convicted of subsequent drug-related crimes.

Leonard (Leo) Lightfinger, a sixteen-year-old from Dome City, Michiana, was stopped by police at 2:03 A.M. on January 30, YR-1, and questioned about violating the city's 1:30 A.M. curfew. The police searched Leo and found eight vials of crack cocaine. Leo confessed that he was carrying the crack for his older brother, Luther, a known drug addict. The police arrested Leo and the state charged him with an act of delinquency, to-wit: possession of a controlled substance with intent to distribute.

At trial, on April 19, YR-1, Leo repeated his story concerning his possession of the crack cocaine. The court convinced Leo to plead guilty to a lesser possession charge and to enter DROP. Leo's public defender persuaded the court to amend the terms of Leo's participation in DROP so that Leo could stay at home overnight during the school week. Defense counsel argued that since the Lightfinger residence was across the street from the school that Leo was to attend, it would be in the state's economic interest and Leo's best interest that he not be kept in the school with the rest of the offenders. When the court explained to Leo that he could either volunteer to take part in DROP for one school year under the terms described or go to the Michiana Youth Reformatory for eight months, Leo enthusiastically chose DROP. Leo pled guilty, and the judge suspended his eight-month sentence in return for Leo's volunteering for DROP.

Leo enrolled in DROP on August 28, YR-1. Over the course of the school year, he went to school each day at 7:00 A.M. and returned home after the school's dinner program began. On Saturdays Leo went with the other DROP participants to boot camp, returning Sunday night by 7:00 P.M.

Things started out fine for Leo in DROP. Leo had been an honor student in high school, so he excelled in DROP's school. Problems developed after October 10, YR-1, however, when Leo caught another student, Tommy Tuffasnails (Tommy) cheating on a test. Leo reported the incident to his teacher, who told him to mind his own business. The teacher failed Tommy on the test and wrote on Tommy's paper, "Don't think you can get away with cheating in any class Lightfinger's in." That same evening, Tommy found Leo alone as Leo was leaving for his home and physically beat him. In fact, Tommy beat Leo up every day for the next week, except when they were at weekend boot camp. The beatings always occurred as Leo was leaving the DROP school to go home for dinner.

On October 18, YR-1, when Leo's father informed the school of Leo being beaten by Tommy, the assistant principal, Mr. Sheepish, explained that "These are tough kids. Your son broke a code and now he's paying for it. Tommy will simmer down in a few days." Mr. Sheepish assured Mr. Lightfinger that he would prevent any further beatings. He also suggested that if Mr. Lightfinger was unhappy, he should transfer Leo to another DROP school. Mr. Lightfinger declined.

The beatings became sporadic but more severe. On December 12, YR-1, Leo returned home from DROP school with a broken nose and several bruises on his upper body. His father immediately took Leo to the hospital, where doctors found serious internal injuries caused by repeated beatings. Leo was checked into the hospital, where he remained until March 15, YR-0. Medical bills totaled $115,000.

On April 19, YR-0, the prosecutor filed a delinquency petition for criminal assault against Tommy and a motion to waive juvenile court jurisdiction. On the same day, Leo filed a 42 U.S.C. Section 1983 action against DROP and Mr. Sheepish in the U.S. District Court for the Northern District of Michiana. Leo claims that the actions of DROP and Mr. Sheepish violated his liberty interest in bodily integrity guaranteed by the Due Process Clause of the Fourteenth Amendment. Leo alleges medical expenses of $115,000, plus pain and suffering, and punitive damages against DROP and Mr. Sheepish for failure to prevent harm to him after being informed of the danger. On April 29, YR-0, DROP filed a F.R.C.P. 12(b)(6) motion to dismiss for failure to state a claim upon which relief can be granted. DROP and Mr. Sheepish argue that, even though Leo was on school property when the beatings took place, he was there voluntarily and had ample opportunity to avoid the harm he suffered. DROP argues that this situation does not give rise to the kind of substantive due process claim envisioned by Section 1983.

Questions

1. Read The Civil Rights Act of 1964 at 42 U.S.C. Section 1983. What are the requirements for a Section 1983 action?
2. Who has standing to bring this claim?
3. Was Leo in state custody in the DROP Program? If so, at what time?
4. *See DeShaney v. Winnebago County Dept. of Social Services*, 489 U.S. 189 (1989). In the *DeShaney* case, why did the Supreme Court hold that the state had no liability for its knowing failure to protect a child's interests? How does the *DeShaney* rule apply to Leo's lawsuit?
5. How should the court rule on the Rule 12(b)(6) motion filed by DROP and Mr. Sheepish?

Chapter Eight. Decisions About Children—The State's Role

6. Is Leo's liberty sufficiently restrained in the DROP Program to place an affirmative duty on the State of Michiana to protect Leo from harm?
7. What liability should the state have for wards of the state, whether these children are placed in residential care or foster family home care?
8. Should the state be held accountable under Section 1983 for a failure to prevent harm when it could do so more easily than any other party?
9. Is this case similar to *Estelle v. Gamble*, 429 U.S. 97 (1976), or *Youngberg v. Romeo*, 457 U.S. 307 (1982)?

B. PHYSICAL ABUSE

Problem 42

In re Ruth Ann Collins, A Child Alleged to Be a Child in Need of Services

Ruth Ann Collins, age seven, is alleged to be a child in need of services (CHINS), pursuant to Michiana Code 31-6-4-3. The CHINS petition, filed by the Hoynes County Department of Public Welfare, alleges that Ruth Ann's mental or physical health is seriously endangered as a result of being beaten by her father, Carl A. Collins, on the evening of May 4, YR-0. A guardian ad litem (GAL) has been appointed by the court to represent the best interests of Ruth Ann.

CHINS proceedings consist of an initial hearing, a factfinding hearing and a dispositional hearing. Michiana statutes describing the substantive requirements for CHINS, the CHINS hearings, along with the investigative reports, court documents, and other exhibits follow this Problem.

Questions

1. Who are the parties in this case? Who represents the interests of the parties?
2. What (constitutional) justification does the state have to remove a child from his or her home?
3. What is the nature of due process that is required in CHINS proceedings?
4. What determinations are made by the court in each of the three CHINS hearings?
5. What are the possible outcomes for Ruth Ann and her parents in each hearing?
6. What effect will these proceedings have on Carl's parental rights?
7. Read the police report and the statement by Carl Collins. Is the report admissible evidence in this case? Under what theories of relevancy might the report be admissible? How might it be kept out of evidence?
8. On the facts of this case, what outcome at the factfinding hearing would be in Ruth Ann's best interests?
9. Is coercive intervention of the court required in this case?
10. What rulings should the court make at the dispositional hearing?
11. Review the Adoption Assistance and Child Welfare Act of 1980. What are meant by the concepts of reunification and permanency plan?

Hoynes County Police Southby, Michiana	**REPORT**	Case No. 301565 Disp. No.

Classification of incident _____ Child Abuse _____ Date _5/4/YR-0_

Location of incident _1438 Cedar Street, Miller, Michiana_ Time _7:30 pm_

Complainant _Judith Jacobsen_ Occupation _caseworker, DPW_

Address _711 W. Randolph St., Southby, Michiana_ Res. phone _____ Bus. phone _239-6111_

Person involved (victim, etc.) _listed below_ Age _____

Address _____ Phone _____

Property attacked _____

Address _____ Phone _____

Report received by _Sgt. Lindbergh_ Date _5/5/YR-0_ Time _3:15 pm_

How received _in person_ Assisting personnel _Judith Jacobsen_ Weather _mild_

Report completed by _Sarah Hoffman_ Date _5/10/YR-0_ Time _11:00 am_

Further assignment to _____ Date _____ Time _____

NARRATIVE: (Give details of incident as received, remembering WHO, WHAT, WHERE, WHEN, WHY, HOW. Describe any action taken. Explain any suggestions or theories in separate paragraphs.)

```
        VICTIM:  Ruth Ann Collins
                 F/W/7
                 South Grade School
                 Father, Carl A. Collins
                 M/W/30  DOB 2-5-30
                 Mother, Traci M. Collins
                 F/W/30  DOB 4-15-30
                 1438 Cedar Street
                 Miller, Michiana 46355 (219-586-7024)
```

On 5/5/YR-0 around 3:15 p.m. undersigned officer received a phone call from the complainant who stated that she was at South Grade School investigating a child abuse case, and she would like to have me take pictures of the victim. She stated that the marks left on the child were severe and that she was going to detain the child, and would like for me to meet her at the welfare department. This officer did meet with Judith Jacobsen at her office at 4:00 p.m., where I did take photographs of the victim, Ruth Ann Collins, who did have numerous marks on her body from her head to her feet. Also at this time Judith Jacobsen did advise me that she had served detention papers on Mrs. Collins and that she and her husband were enroute to her office for an interview.

Prior to the parents' arrival we did talk with Ruth Ann, who stated that she had received a beating from her father the night before because of an incident involving her wearing an old hat and dress. She also stated that her father did use a belt to inflict the marks that had been left

HOYNES COUNTY POLICE DEPARTMENT

SUPPLEMENTARY

COMPLAINANT:
ADDRESS:
CITY AND STATE:

CASE NO. 301565
DATE:
TIME:

on her body. She also advised us that this was not the first beating she had received from her father. Judith Jacobsen also advised me in talking with the mother that she had also received information about one previous beating. Ruth Ann had also made a comment about being "a little bit afraid of her father," because he "sometimes screams at me," but Ruth Ann did state that she wanted to return to her home.

At 4:30 p.m. the parents did arrive at the D.P.W. office for the interview. At that time I did read the Warning and Waiver of Rights to Carl Collins, who stated that he did understand the rights and would be willing to talk to us about the alleged incident. He did sign the Waiver, which was witnessed by this officer and Judith Jacobsen. Carl Collins stated that around 7:15 p.m., 5/4/YR-0, his daughter Ruth Ann was wearing an old junky hat and dress belonging to her mother, which he had repeatedly told her to throw away. He states this was an act of defiance on Ruth Ann's part and that she only wore the hat and dress to spite him. He claims in the recent past she has been deliberately disobeying him as if she were testing his authority. He states he gave her the beating to teach her obedience, and that he never intentionally meant to hurt her. Mr. Collins stated, "As Rev. Tiller tells us at church, 'If you spare the rod you spoil the child.' And I believe that with all my heart." Mr. Collins readily admitted using a belt to administer the punishment on this occasion. He also admitted to using a belt on Ruth Ann one other time in the past, but stated it was only on her bottom and that he had never beaten her like this before. He stated that he was extremely mad on this occasion. When we asked Mr. Collins how many times he had struck Ruth Ann, he stated he believed it was around six or seven times. However, he also stated it took him around five minutes to administer the punishment. He advised us that he did not consider himself an abusive parent and child abuse had only been a term he had heard up to this point. Mr. Collins expressed resentment that the authorities were meddling in his right to discipline his own child. He said that the force used was not excessive and it was for Ruth Ann's own good. According to Mr. Collins, he never did see any marks left on Ruth Ann. We asked Mrs. Collins if she had observed any marks on Ruth Ann before she went to school this day, and she stated no because Ruth Ann had gotten herself dressed and she was not looking for any marks. Mrs. Collins was in her bedroom when her husband did start the beating the night before and she did come into the living room to see what was going on but states she did not interfere or ask him to stop because "it is his place to administer the punishment in the family, and he has only hit her one other time -- when she talks back or doesn't obey."

At this time Judith Jacobsen did explain to the parents what would take place at the detention hearing to be held in Hoynes Probate Court at 1:30 p.m. on 5/8/YR-0.

Case Pending

Sgt. R. Lindbergh

HOYNES COUNTY POLICE DEPARTMENT

Southby, Michiana

WARNING AND WAIVER

CASE NO. 301565

WARNING AS TO RIGHTS

Before we ask you any questions, it is our duty as police officers to advise you of your rights and to warn you of the consequence of waiving your rights.

You have the absolute right to remain silent.

Anything you say to us can be used against you in court.

You have the right to talk to an attorney before answering any questions and to have an attorney present with you during questioning.

You have this same right to the advice and presence of an attorney whether you can afford to hire one or not. We have no way of furnishing you with an attorney, but one will be appointed for you, if you wish.

If you decide to answer questions now without an attorney present, you will still have the right to stop answering at any time. You also have the right to stop answering at any time until you talk to an attorney.

WAIVER

I have read the above statement of my rights, and it has been read to me. I understand what my rights are. I wish to make a voluntary statement, and I do not want an attorney. No force, threats, or promises of any kind or neature have been used by anyone in any way to influence me to waive my rights. I am signing this statement after having been advised of my rights before any questions have been asked of me by the police.

Carl Collins
(Signature)

CERTIFICATION

I hereby certify that the foregoing warning and waiver were read by me to the person who has affixed his (her) signature above, and that he (she) also read it and signed it in my presence this __5th__ day of __May__, YR-0, at __10:15__ o'clock __P.M.__ at __Southby__, Michiana.

Sgt. R. Lindbergh
(Signature - Police Officer)

Sarah Hoffman
(Witness)

HOYNES COUNTY POLICE DEPARTMENT

SUPPLEMENTARY   Child Abuse

COMPLAINANT:	Judith Jacobsen	**CASE NO.**	301565
ADDRESS:	711 W. Randolph St.	**DATE:**	5/4/YR-0
CITY AND STATE:	Southby, Michiana	**TIME:**	7:30 pm

On 5/8/YR-0, a detention hearing was held in Hoynes Probate Court and Mr. Collins was present with a minister from his church. Mr. Collins advised that his wife was unable to attend because of health reasons. Judith Jacobsen presented the case to the Court asking for continued detention of Ruth Ann Collins. The photographs were shown to the judge and the father during the hearing and the minister was also given the opportunity to view the photos. After a statement was given by Mr. Collins and his minister, the Court did find there was probable cause to believe Ruth Ann was a CHINS and to continue detention of Ruth Ann Collins and so ordered same.

On 5/9/YR-0, Carl Collins came to the county police station for a second interview with this officer. He was again read the Warning and Waiver of Rights, which he again signed before any questions were asked of him. Mr. Collins' story was basically the same as before. He stated he believed that he committed the act out of self-justification. Mr. Collins felt that he was right and that disobedience had to be corrected and talking to the girl did not work. He also stated that he had not realized how much damage he had done until he had seen the photos during the detention hearing on 5/8/YR-0. At this time I asked Mr. Collins to give me some actual facts involved in the incident on 5-4-YR-0 and he stated the beating did occur in the living room of their home and that he did use a belt, which he had to get from another room because he was wearing suspenders at that time. The only clothing Ruth Ann was wearing was a T-shirt, which he states he now believes was too small because of the location of the marks that were on her body. Ruth Ann was on the couch during this time and she did offer resistance to the beating and also asked her father to stop. Mr. Collins states that one other time he gave Ruth Ann a spanking in the bathroom area where it would be private and she would be confined to this area and would not be free to move about, thus accounting for prior hand spankings being confined to her bottom side. Mr. Collins stated that Mrs. Collins never objects to him spanking Ruth Ann and was usually present when he does it. Collins stated that Rev. Tiller warns them at church about a wife who does not support her husband in these matters.

At this time I asked Mr. Collins if he would be willing to give a voluntary statement in regards to this incident. He agreed to give a statement, which was taken and notarized by Sarah Hoffman and witnessed by this officer at 10:35 a.m., 5/9/YR-0.

5/10/YR-0
Case Closed
Referred to prosecutor   *Sgt. R. Lindbergh*

HOYNES COUNTY POLICE DEPARTMENT

Southby, Michiana

WARNING AND WAIVER

CASE NO._____

WARNING AS TO RIGHTS

Before we ask you any questions, it is our duty as police officers to advise you of your rights and to warn you of the consequence of waiving your rights.

You have the absolute right to remain silent.

Anything you say to us can be used against you in court.

You have the right to talk to an attorney before answering any questions and to have an attorney present with you during questioning.

You have this same right to the advice and presence of an attorney whether you can afford to hir one or not. We have no way of furnishing you with an attorney, but one will be appointed for you, if you wish.

If you decide to answer questions now without an attorney present, you will still have the right to stop answering at any time. You also have the right to stop answering at any time until you talk to an attorney.

WAIVER

I have read the above statement of my rights, and it has been read to me. I understand what my rights are. I wish to make a voluntary statement, and I do not want an attorney. No force, threats, or promises of any kind or neature have been used by anyone in any way to influence me to waive my rights. I am signing this statement after having been advised of my rights before any questions have been asked of me by the police.

Carl Collins
(Signature)

CERTIFICATION

I hereby certify that the foregoing warning and waiver were read by me to the person who has affixed his (her) signature above, and that he (she) also read it and signed it in my presence this _____ day of ____May____, YR-0, at __4:30__ o'clock __P.M.__ at __Southby__, Michiana.

Sgt. R. Lindbergh
(Signature - Police Officer)

Judith Jacobsen
(Witness)

STATE OF MICHIANA   )   IN THE HOYNES PROBATE COURT
) SS:
HOYNES COUNTY   )   CAUSE NUMBER _____

IN THE MATTER OF   )
RUTH ANN COLLINS   )
)   ORDER ON DETENTION HEARING
)
A CHILD ALLEGED TO BE A CHILD)
IN NEED OF SERVICES   )

There having been conducted this date a timely Detention Hearing with respect to said child, the REFEREE (JUDGE) now FINDS and RECOMMENDS (ORDERS) as follows:

A. That actual notice of the time, place and purpose of hearing has been given to the child and __Mr. and Mrs. Carl A. Collins__.
   (parent/guardian/custodian)

B. That those present and appearing for the hearing are as listed in the Court's minute entry this date.

C. That the detention and removal of said child (was/was not) authorized and necessary under MC 31-6-4-4(c) to protect said child and that the following efforts were made by Hoynes County Department of Public Welfare to eliminate or prevent the need to remove the child/reunify the child and family:

   1. The safety of the child precluded (preplacement preventive services) (reunification services) (Please specify): __child, Ann Collins, age 7, reported present beating (several marks) by father and one prior beating__

   2. (Preplacement of preventive services) (Reunification services) were provided or offered and included: (Check all that apply):

      _____ twenty-four (24) hour emergency caretaker and homemaker services;
      _____ day care;
      _____ crisis counseling;
      _____ individual and family counseling;
      _____ emergency shelter;
      _____ procedures and arrangements for access to available emergency financial assistance;
      _____ arrangements for the provision of temporary child care to provide respite to the family for a brief period, as part of a plan for preventing children's removal from home;
      _____ home-based family services;
      _____ self-helf groups;
      _____ mental health counseling;
      _____ drug and alcohol abuse counseling;
      _____ vocational counseling or vocational rehabilitation;
      _____ post adoption services;
      _____ transportation;
      _____ visitation;
      _____ other services which the agency identifies as necessary and appropriate:_____
      _____

      _____ other information:_____
      _____

3. The efforts made to prevent the removal of the child(ren) (were/were not) reasonable.

    a. That there is no probable cause to believe that said child(ren) is (are) a Child in Need of Services and hence said child(ren) should be released to the custody of _____.
        (parent/guardian/custodian)

    b. That probable cause exists to believe that said child(ren) is (are) a Child in Need of Services but that said child(ren) is (are) not in need of further detention, and that said child(ren) should be released to _____
        (parent/guardian/custodian)
upon the following conditions:

    c. That probable cause exists to believe that said child(ren) is (are) a Child in Need of Services and that said child(ren) is (are) in need of removal because:

        ( ) the child(ren) is (are) unlikely to appear for subsequent proceedings;
        ( ) detention is necessary to protect the child(ren);
        ( ) the parent, guardian, or custodian cannot be located or is unable or unwilling to take custody of the child(ren);
        ( ) the child(ren) has (have) a reasonable basis for requesting that he (she) (they) not be released; or
        ( ) consideration for the safety of the child(ren) precludes the use of family services to prevent removal of the child(ren).

and hence a judicial determination has been made that the child(ren) is (are) to be removed from his (her) (their) home because continuation in his (her) (their) home would be contrary to his (her) (their) welfare; and that any foster care costs incurred in such removal are to be advanced by the County Welfare Department beginning on the __8__ day of ____May____, YR-0 until further order of the Court.

The appointment of a special advocate for the child(ren) is/is not appropriate.

Dated the date filed marked hereon.

_____
REFEREE, (JUDGE)

The Court having considered the findings and recommendation of the Referee, the Court now approves same and adopts them as the FINDINGS and ORDER of the Court on the date file marked hereon.

_____
JUDGE
HOYNES PROBATE COURT

VOLUNTARY STATEMENT

Case # 301565

DATE 5-9-YR-0   PLACE Hoynes County Police Department

Time Statement Started 10:00   A.M.   P.M.

I, the undersigned, Carl Collins, of 1438 Cedar St. Miller, Michiana, being 30 years of age, born at Plymouth, Michiana on 2-5-YR-0, do hereby make the following statement to Sgt. R. Lindbergh, he having first identified himself as a Hoynes County police officer.

This statement is voluntarily made by me without any threats, coercion or promises of any kind or nature. Before making any statement to the police, I was advised that I had the absolute right to remain silent and that anything I might say could be used against me in a criminal proceeding. I was advised also of my right to have an attorney present before answering any questions and that if I was unable to afford one, an attorney would be provided before questioning. I have freely and voluntarily waived my right to remain silent and my right to consult with an attorney before answering questions.

Carl Collins, being duly sworn and upon his oath, says:

Q. Carl, have you been advised of your rights and understand what your rights are?

A. Yeah.

Q. Have you been promised anything in return for making this statement, or have you been threatened in any way if you do not make this statement?

A. No.

Q. Carl, what can you tell me about an incident that occurred around 7:30 p.m., 5/4/YR-0, at your home between yourself and your daughter Ruth Ann?

A. I guess it all started when Ruth Ann disobeyed me by wearing some clothes that I asked her not to for the third time. It's not the first time that she disobeyed me in a direct manner. I decided to teach her a lesson concerning obedience. What started out to be a lesson turned into a beating. I was sorry when I saw the pictures in the courtroom. I might have gone overboard. I can only look back and think that I had taken my own frustrations out on Ruth Ann. I don't know how many times I hit her, it was more than six times. I made my little girl take her pants down with the intention of hitting her on the rear. She was clothed in a T-shirt that was too small for her I imagine. I hit her in the back, I hit her in the legs, the arms. If she hadn't tried to resist, she wouldn't have been hit all over. That's about all I have to say about the whole thing, I hate rehashing it.

Q. Carl, what did you use to strike Ruth Ann?

A. I used a belt.

Q. Was you wife present at this time or anytime during the incident?

A. Not to my knowledge.

Q. At any time during the incident did Ruth Ann offer resistance or ask you to stop?

A. She offered resistance, and that's why I missed her rear end. I didn't intentionally beat her on the back and arms. Had she not moved around so much, she wouldn't have welts on her back and arms.

85

VOLUNTARY STATEMENT

Case # 301565

DATE 5-9-YR-0   PLACE Hoynes County Police Department

Q. Carl, have you ever beaten Ruth Ann in this manner in the past?

A. No, not that bad, never.

Q. Carl, during this incident did you notice any blood and if so where did it come from?

A. A more descriptive word would have to be raw, Ruth Ann was raw. I didn't strike her in the nose, I've never stood on an even basis with her as a person would stand with a man. I never fisticuffed her.

Q. Carl, what would be your normal form of punishment with Ruth Ann?

A. I have used a strap one other time, but never as bad as I saw in the pictures in the courtroom. I always hit her in the rear end with my hand. I never missed her butt. There's nothing wrong with giving the child a good smack in the butt when they misbehave. That's what Rev. Tiller tells us. You know, spare the rod and spoil the child. I believe that.

Q. Carl, again, have any promises or considerations been given to you for giving this statement?

A. No, this is of my own free will, I hope for Ruth Ann's good.

Q. Is there anything you care to add to this statement at this time?

A. Yeah, I am her father, I do care about her. It doesn't look like it, but I want it on the record, I don't know what's going to happen now, but I'm sorry the whole thing happened.

Q. If you were asked the same questions at a later time and date, what would your answers be and why?

A. Basically the same, what I volunteered here is to the best of my knowledge. All things considered, our family does pretty well. Ruth Ann will be safe at home with us. We love her very much.

Subscribed and sworn to before me a Notary Public in and for Hoynes County, State of Michiana:

My Commission Expires: Sarah Hoffman /s/

3-10-YR+1

I have read this statement consisting of _____ page(s) and the facts contained therein are true and correct.

WITNESSES:

Carl Collins
Signature of Person giving voluntary statement

Page 2 of 2 Pages

DATE 5-9-YR-0

TIME STATEMENT FINISHED 10:35 A.M. _____ P.M.

reddish abrasion

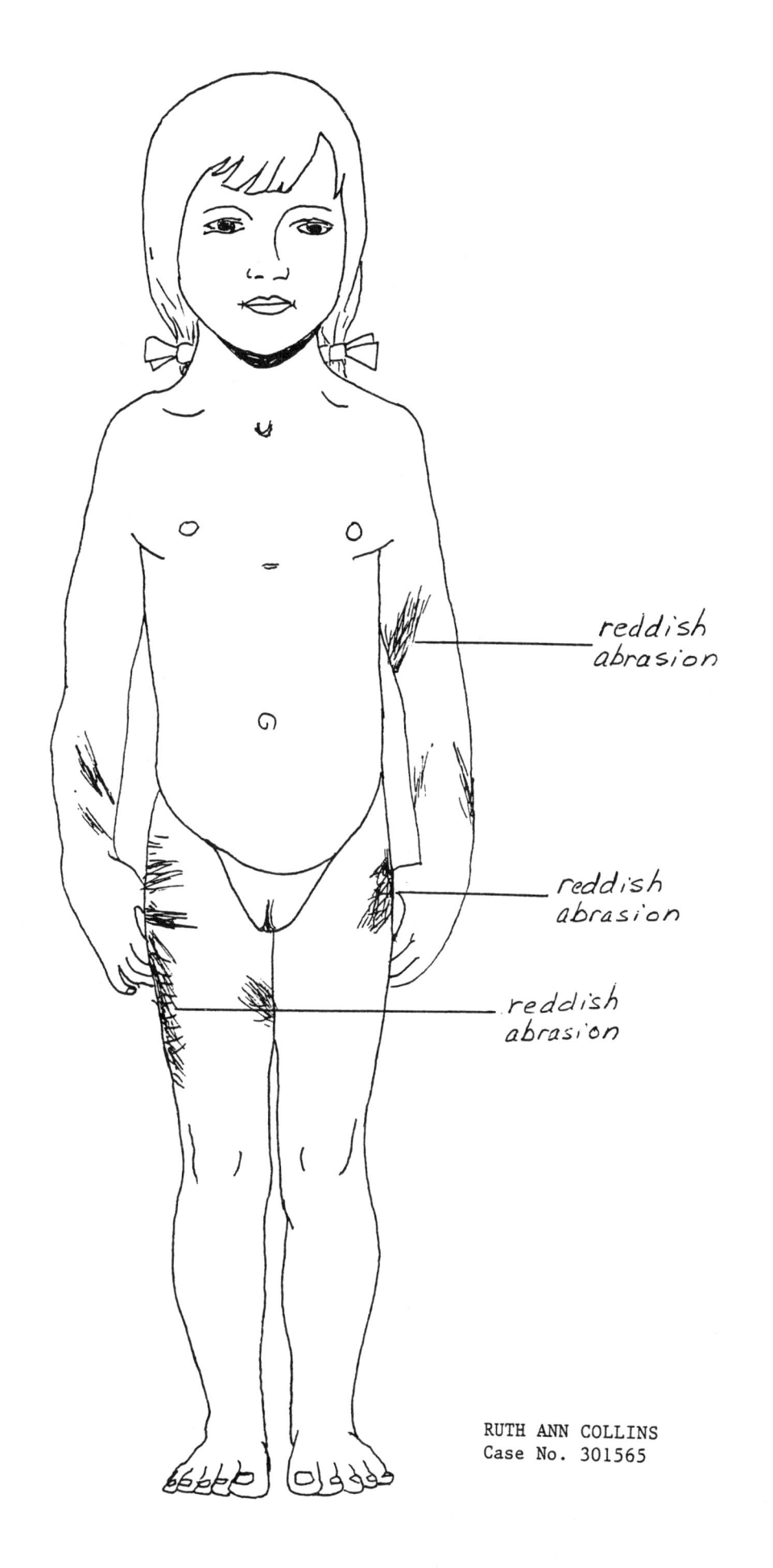

reddish abrasion

reddish abrasion

RUTH ANN COLLINS
Case No. 301565

reddish abrasions

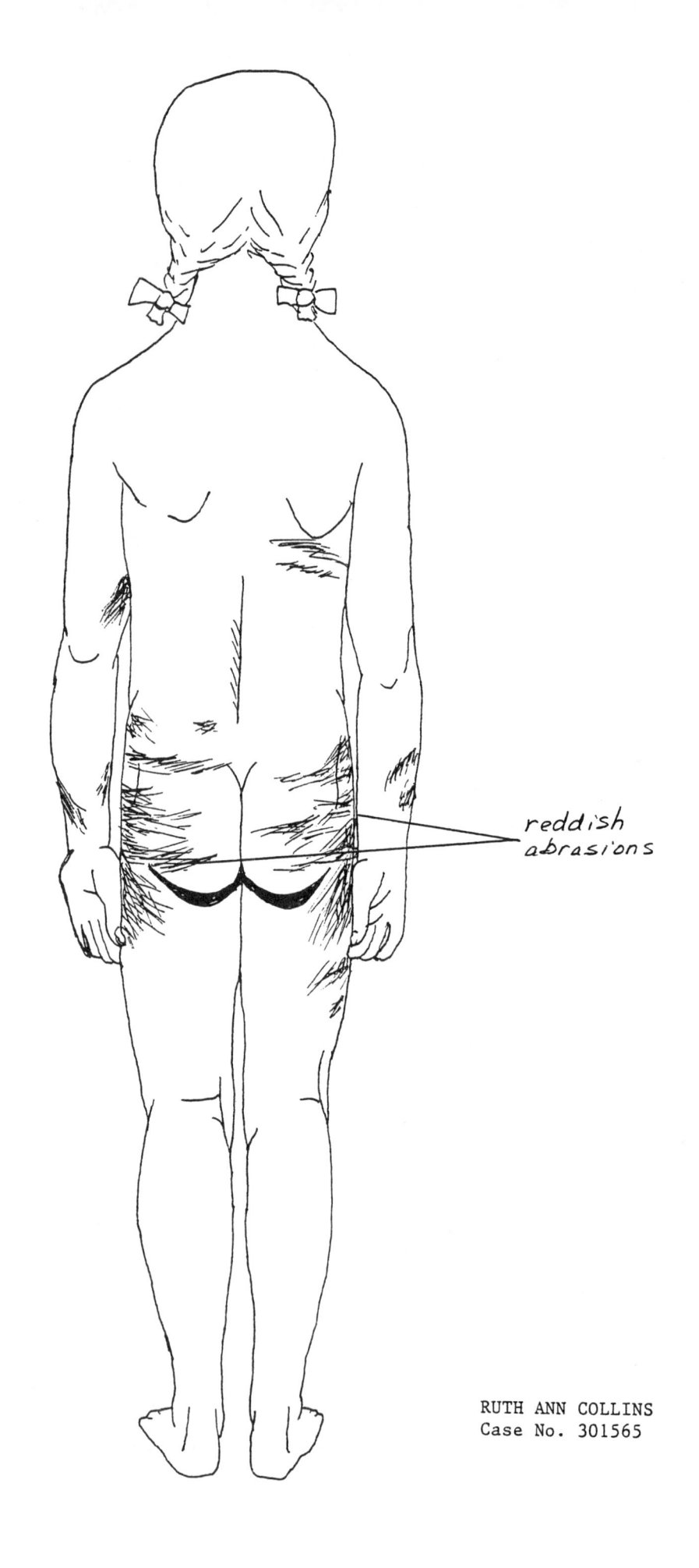

RUTH ANN COLLINS
Case No. 301565

M.C. 31-6-3-4 Appointment of Guardian ad litem or special advocate or both; duties; liabilities

Section 4. (a) The juvenile court may appoint a guardian ad litem or a court appointed special advocate, or both, for the child at any time. A guardian ad litem or court appointed special advocate need not be an attorney, but the attorney representing the child may be appointed his guardian ad litem or court appointed special advocate.

(b) A guardian ad litem or court appointed special advocate shall represent and protect the best interests of the child.

(c) If any fees arise, payment shall be made under MC 31-6-4-18.

(d) The guardian ad litem or the court appointed special advocate may be represented by an attorney. If necessary to protect the child's interests, the court may appoint an attorney to represent the guardian ad litem or the court appointed special advocate. The court may only appoint one (1) attorney under this subsection.

(e) The guardian ad litem or the court appointed special advocate, or both, shall be considered officers of the court for the purpose of representing the child's interests.

(f) Except for gross misconduct, if the guardian ad litem or court appointed special advocate performs his duties in good faith, he is immune from any civil liability that may occur as a result of his performance.

(g) A court may not appoint a party to the proceedings, that party's employee, or that party's representative as the guardian ad litem or as the court appointed special advocate for a child who is involved in the proceedings.

M.C. 31-6-4-3 Child in need of services

Section 3. (a) A child is a child in need of services if before his eighteenth birthday:

(1) his physical or mental condition is seriously impaired or seriously endangered as a result of the inability, refusal or neglect of his parent, guardian, or custodian to supply the child with necessary food, clothing, shelter, medical care, education, or supervision;

(2) his physical or mental health is seriously endangered due to injury by the act or omission of his parent, guardian, or custodian;

(3) he is the victim of a sex offense under MC 35-42-4-1, MC 35-42-4-2, MC 35-42-4-3(a) or MC 35-42-4-3(b), MC-35-42-4-3(c) or MC 35-42-4-3(d) if the offense was committed by the child's parent guardian, or custodian, MC 35-42-4-4, MC 35-45-4-1, MC 35-45-4-2, or MC 35-46-1-3;

(4) his parent, guardian, or custodian allows him to participate in an obscene performance, defined by MC 35-49-2-2 or MC 35-49-3-2;

(5) his parent, guardian, or custodian allows him to commit a sex offense prohibited by MC 35-45-4;

(6) he substantially endangers his own health or the health of another; or

(7) his parent, guardian, or custodian fails to participate in a disciplinary proceeding in connection with the student's improper behavior, as provided for by MC 20-8.1-5-7, where the behavior of the student has been repeatedly disruptive in the school;

and needs care, treatment, or rehabilitation that he is not receiving, and that is unlikely to be provided or accepted without the coercive intervention of the court.

(b) An omission under subdivision (a)(2) is an occurrence in which the parent, guardian, or custodian allowed his child to receive any injury that he had a reasonable opportunity to prevent or mitigate.

(c) A custodian under subsection (a) includes any person responsible for the child's welfare who is employed by a public or private residential school or foster care facility.

(d) When a parent, guardian or custodian fails to provide specific medical treatment for a child because of the legitimate and genuine practice of his religious beliefs, a rebuttable presumption arises that the child is not a child in need of services because of such failure. However, this presumption does not prevent a juvenile court from ordering, when the health of a child requires, medical services from a physician licensed to practice medicine in Michiana. This presumption does not apply to situations in which the life or health of a child is in serious danger.

(e) Nothing in this chapter limits the right of a person to use reasonable corporal punishment when disciplining a child if the person is the parent, guardian, or custodian of the child. In addition, nothing in this chapter limits the lawful practice or teaching of religious beliefs.

(f) A child in need of services under subsection (a) includes a handicapped child who is deprived of nutrition that is necessary to sustain life, or who is deprived of medical or surgical intervention that is necessary to remedy or ameliorate a life threatening medical condition, if the nutrition or medical or surgical intervention is generally provided to similarly situated handicapped or nonhandicapped children.

(g) A handicapped child under subsection (f) is an individual under eighteen (18) years of age who has a handicap as defined in MC 22-9-1-3(q).

M.C. 31-6-4-6 Child in need of services; custody; detention; hearings; findings; order

Section 6. (a) This section applies only to a child alleged to be a child in need of services.

(b) If a child is taken into custody under an order of the court, the law enforcement officer shall take him to a place designated in the order to await a detention hearing.

(c) If a child is taken into custody without an order of the court, the person taking him into custody may release the child or may deliver him to a place designated by the juvenile court and, if the child is detained, shall promptly notify the child's parent, guardian, or custodian, and an intake officer that the child is being held and of the reasons for his detention.

(d) If the child was not taken into custody under an order of the court, the intake officer shall investigate the reasons for his detention. He shall release the child to his parent, guardian, or custodian upon that person's written promise to bring the child before the juvenile court at a time specified; however, the intake officer may place the child in detention if he reasonably believes that the child is a child in need of services and that:

(1) detention is necessary to protect the child;

(2) the child is unlikely to appear before the juvenile court for subsequent proceedings;

(3) the child has a reasonable basis for requesting that he not be released; or

(4) the parent, guardian, or custodian cannot be located or is unable or unwilling to take custody of the child.

(e) If the child is not released, a detention hearing must be held within seventy-two (72) hours (excluding Saturdays, Sundays, and legal holidays) after he is taken into custody; otherwise he shall be released. Notice of the time, place, and purpose of the detention hearing shall be given to the child. Notice shall also be given to his parent, guardian, or custodian if he can be located. If a child has been removed from his parent, guardian, or custodian under section 4(c) of this chapter then, in accordance with federal law, at the detention hearing the court shall make written findings and conclusions that state:

(1) whether removal of the child, authorized under section 4(c) of this chapter, was necessary to protect the child;

(2) a description of the family services available before removal of the child;

(3) efforts made to provide family services before removal of the child;

(4) why the efforts made to provide family services did not prevent removal of the child; and

(5) whether the efforts made to prevent removal of the child were reasonable.

(f) The juvenile court shall release the child to his parent, guardian, or custodian; however, the court may order the child detained if it makes written findings of fact upon the record of probable cause to believe that the child is a child in need of services and that:

(1) detention is necessary to protect the child;

(2) the child is unlikely to appear before the juvenile court for subsequent proceedings;

(3) the child has a reasonable basis for requesting that he not be released;

(4) the parent, guardian, or custodian cannot be located or is unable or unwilling to take custody of the child; or

(5) consideration for the safety of the child precludes the use of family services to prevent removal of the child.

(g) Upon the juvenile court's own motion or upon the motion of the person representing the interests of the state, the parent, guardian, or custodian of a child who has been released may be ordered to appear with the child for an additional detention hearing.

(h) A child detained under subsection (f) or (g), or his parent, guardian, or custodian, may petition the juvenile court for additional detention hearings.

M.C. 31-6-4-10 Petition alleging child in need of services; request for authorization to file; probable cause determination; verification; contents; detention

Section 10. (a) The prosecutor or the attorney for the county department may request the juvenile court to authorize the filing of a petition alleging that a child is a child in need of services; that person shall represent the interests of the state at this proceeding and at all subsequent proceedings on the petition.

(b) The juvenile court shall consider the preliminary inquiry and the evidence of probable cause as contained in either the report of the preliminary inquiry or an affidavit of probable cause. The court shall authorize the filing of a petition if it finds probable cause to believe that the child is a child in need of services.

(c) The petition shall be verified and be entitled "In the Matter of _____, a Child Alleged to be a Child in Need of Services," must be signed and filed by the person representing the interests of the state, and must contain the following information:

(1) A citation to the section of this article that gives the juvenile court jurisdiction in the proceeding.

(2) A citation to the section of this article that defines a child in need of services.

(3) A concise statement of the facts upon which the allegations are based, including the date and location at which the alleged facts occurred.

(4) The child's name, birth date, and residence address, if known.

(5) The name and residence address of the child's parent, guardian, or custodian, if known.

(6) The name and title of the person signing the petition.

(7) A statement indicating whether the child has been removed from his parent, guardian, or custodian, and, if so, a description of:

(A) efforts made to provide the child or his parent, guardian, or custodian with family services before the removal; and

(B) reasons why family services were not provided before the removal of the child, if they were not provided.

(d) Error in a citation or its omission is ground for dismissal of the petition or for reversal of the adjudication only if the error or omission misleads the child or his parent, guardian, or custodian to his prejudice.

(e) If the petition is authorized, the person filing may request in writing that the child be taken into custody. He shall support this request with sworn testimony or affidavit. The court may grant the request if it makes written findings of fact upon the record that a ground for detention exists under section 6(f) of this chapter.

(f) If the juvenile court grants the request to have the child taken into custody, it shall proceed under section 6(e) of this chapter.

M.C. 31-6-4-13.5 Child in need of services; initial hearing; appointment of guardian ad litem or special advocate or both; warnings; informing parent or guardian: admission or denial of allegations; dispositional or factfinding hearings

Section 13.5. (a) This section applies only to a child alleged to be a child in need of services.

(b) The juvenile court shall hold an initial hearing on each petition.

(c) The juvenile court shall first determine whether it is appropriate to appoint a guardian ad litem or a court appointed special advocate, or both, for the child. If the child is alleged to be a victim of child abuse or neglect under MC 31-6-11, the court shall make and enter a finding as to the appointment for the child of a guardian ad litem or a court appointed special advocate, or both.

(d) The court shall next inform the child, if he is at an age of understanding, and his parent, guardian, or custodian, if that person is present, of:

(1) the nature of the allegations in the petition; and

(2) the dispositional alternatives available to the court if the child is adjudicated a child in need of services.

(e) The juvenile court shall inform the parent or guardian of the estate that if the child is adjudicated a child in need of services:

(1) he or the custodian of the child may be required to participate in a program of care, treatment, or rehabilitation for the child;

(2) he may be held financially responsible for any services provided for himself or the child; and

(3) he or the custodian of the child may controvert any allegations made at the child's dispositional or other hearing concerning his participation, or he may controvert any allegations concerning his financial responsibility for any services that would be provided.

(f) Except when the petition is filed under section 3(a)(6) of this chapter, the juvenile court shall then determine whether the parent, guardian, or custodian admits or denies the allegations of the petition. A failure to respond constitutes a denial.

(g) If the petition alleges that the child is a child in need of services under section 3(a)(6) of this chapter, the juvenile court shall determine whether the child admits or denies the allegations. A failure to respond constitutes a denial.

(h) If the parent, guardian, or custodian admits the allegations under subsection (f), the juvenile court shall enter judgment accordingly and schedule a dispositional hearing.

(i) If the allegations of the petition have been admitted, the juvenile court may hold a dispositional hearing immediately after the initial hearing. If the allegations have been denied, the juvenile court may hold the factfinding hearing immediately after the initial hearing. In each case:

(1) the child, if competent to do so;

(2) the child's counsel, guardian ad litem, court appointed special advocate, parent, guardian, or custodian; and

(3) the person representing the interests of the state;

must first give their consent.

M.C. 31-6-4-14 Factfinding hearing; continuance; judgment

Section 14 (a). Unless the allegations of the petition have been admitted, the juvenile court shall hold a factfinding hearing.

(b) If the court finds that the child is a delinquent child or a child in need of services, it shall enter judgment accordingly, order a predisposition report, and schedule a dispositional hearing.

(c) If the court finds that the child is not a delinquent child or is not a child in need of services, it shall discharge him.

(d) If the court finds that the allegations in the petition to terminate the parent-child relationship are true, it shall terminate the parent-child relationship; otherwise it shall dismiss the petition.

(e) At the close of all the evidence and before judgment is entered, the court may continue the case for not more than twelve (12) months unless the child or his parent, guardian, or custodian requests that judgment be entered, in which case the judgment shall be entered within thirty (30) days. However, if the child is in secure detention, he shall be released within seventy-two (72) hours (excluding Saturdays, Sundays, and legal holidays) pending the entry of judgment. A child released from secure detention pending the entry of judgment may be detained in a shelter care facility.

(f) In all cases where a finding of delinquency is based on a delinquent act that would be a felony if committed by an adult, the juvenile court shall state in the findings the specific statute that was violated and the class of the felony had it been committed by an adult.

M.C. 31-6-4-15 Predispositional reports; financial report; recommendations; examinations; disclosure

Section 15. (a) Upon finding that a child is a delinquent child or that he is a child in need of services, the juvenile court shall order a probation officer or a caseworker to prepare a predispositional report that contains a recommendation for the care, treatment, or rehabilitation of the child. Alternative reports may be prepared by the child or his parent, guardian, guardian ad litem, court appointed special advocate, or custodian for consideration by the court.

(b) In addition to providing the court with a recommendation for the care, treatment, or rehabilitation of the child, the person preparing the report shall consider the necessity, nature, and extent of the participation by a parent, guardian, or custodian in a program of care, treatment, or rehabilitation for the child.

(c) The probation officer or caseworker shall also prepare a financial report on the parent or the estate of the child to assist the juvenile court in determining that person's financial responsibility for any services provided for the child or himself.

(d) When consistent with the safety and welfare of the child and the community, the person preparing the report shall recommend care, treatment, or rehabilitation that:

(1) least interferes with family autonomy;
(2) is least disruptive of family life;
(3) imposes the least restraint on the freedom of the child and his parent, guardian, or custodian; and
(4) provides a reasonable opportunity for participation by the child's parent, guardian, or custodian.

(e) The juvenile court may authorize any examination of the child under MC 31-6-7-12, and may make provision for similar examination of the parent, guardian, or custodian if that person gives his consent.

(f) Predispositional reports shall be made available within a reasonable time before the dispositional hearing, unless the juvenile court determines on the record that they contain information that should not be released to the child or his parent, guardian, or custodian. The court shall provide a copy of the report to any attorney, guardian, ad litem, or court appointed special advocate representing the child or any attorney representing his parent, guardian, or custodian. It may also provide a factual summary of the report to the child or his parent, guardian, or custodian.

M.C. 31-6-4-15.3 Dispositional hearing; admissibility of reports; decree; findings and conclusions

Section 15.3. (a) The juvenile court shall hold a dispositional hearing to consider:

(1) alternatives for the care, treatment, or rehabilitation for the child;
(2) the necessity, nature, and extent of the participation by a parent, guardian, or custodian in the program of care, treatment, or rehabilitation for the child; and
(3) the financial responsibility of the parent or guardian of the estate for any services provided for himself or the child.

(b) Any predispositional report may be admitted into evidence to the extent that it contains evidence of probative value even if it would otherwise be excluded. If a report contains information that should not be released to the child or his parent, guardian, or custodian, a factual summary of the report may be admitted. The child, his parent, guardian, or custodian, and the person representing the interests of the state shall be given a fair opportunity to controvert any parts of the report admitted into evidence.

(c) If it appears to the juvenile court that a child is mentally ill, it may refer the matter to the court having probate jurisdiction for civil commitment proceedings under MC 16-14-9.1. If so referred, the juvenile court shall either discharge the child or continue its proceedings pending the outcome of the proceedings under MC 16-14-9.1.

(d) When consistent with the safety of the community and the welfare of the child, the juvenile court shall enter a dispositional decree that:

(1) least interferes with family autonomy;
(2) is least disruptive of family life;
(3) imposes the least restraint on the freedom of the child and his parent, guardian, or custodian; and

(4) provides a reasonable opportunity for participation by the child's parent, guardian, or custodian.

(e) The juvenile court shall send a copy of the dispositional report, which is described in subsection (g), to any person who receives placement or wardship of the child.

(f) The juvenile court shall advise the child and his parent, guardian, or custodian of the procedures under MC 31-6-7-16.

(g) The juvenile court shall accompany its dispositional decree with written findings and conclusions upon the record concerning:

(1) the needs of the child for care, treatment, or rehabilitation;

(2) the need for participation by the parent, guardian, or custodian in the plan of care for the child;

(3) efforts made, if the child is a child in need of services, to prevent the child's removal from or to reunite the child with his parent, guardian, or custodian in accordance with federal law;

(4) family services that were offered and provided to a child in need of services or his parent, guardian, or custodian in accordance with federal law; and

(5) the court's reasons for the disposition.

C. FETAL ABUSE

Problem 43

State v. Fitzgerald and In re Baby John, A Child Alleged to Be a Child in Need of Services

Colleen Fitzgerald gave birth to Baby John in State Hospital in Southby, Michiana. Shortly after Baby John was born, he began to exhibit the symptoms of withdrawal from narcotics. A urine screen test was positive for crack cocaine. Michiana law mandates that any sign of physical abuse or neglect of a child must be reported to the Department of Public Welfare and to the police. The attending nurse was unsure if exposing an unborn child to a controlled substance is child abuse, but it is hospital policy to report questionable cases.

Part I

The police were notified of Baby John's positive drug screen, and a police officer came to the hospital and verified Baby John was born addicted to cocaine. The officer is unsure of the charge on which to arrest Colleen, as he has never handled a case like this before. He narrows it down to either "Distribution or Delivery of a Controlled Substance" or "Criminal Child Abuse."

Part II

The Department of Public Welfare was also notified that Baby John was born addicted to cocaine, and a caseworker came to the hospital to investigate. The caseworker verified that both Baby John and Colleen are addicted to cocaine. Michiana law states that if an infant tests positive for certain controlled substances, it is prima facie evidence of neglect, and therefore Baby John is likely to be adjudicated a "child in need of services" (CHINS). The caseworker began to investigate the case further to determine whether or not the Department of Public Welfare should seek a court order for immediate removal of Baby John from Colleen's custody.

Questions

Part I

1. What obstacles will the State of Michiana face in prosecuting Colleen for either of these crimes (where the "victim" of the criminal activity is an unborn child)?
2. Does the application of either of these statutes to this case violate Colleen's constitutional right to privacy? What about her right to equal protection? What about Colleen's right to be protected against cruel and unusual punishment under the Eighth Amendment?
3. Would it be a better case for the state if there was a statute making it a felony to give birth to a child who is born addicted to a controlled substance? Are there policy arguments against having such a statute? Would such a law deter a mother who is addicted to drugs from seeking prenatal care?
4. Is criminalizing the mother's conduct the most effective way to deal with this problem? What are some alternatives?

Part II

1. Is the Michiana law, which allows a finding of abuse or neglect based solely on the mother's pre-natal conduct, contrary to the holding in *Roe v. Wade*? Does the statute violate the mother's right to privacy?
2. What factors should the case worker investigate and consider when determining whether or not she will petition to remove the child from the mother's care?

Problem 44

In re Mary Jones

Mary Jones is five months pregnant and is addicted to cocaine. Her mother, Cecily Jones, has attempted several times to help Mary get treatment for her addiction, but her efforts have been in vain, and Mary continues to use drugs. Cecily fears for the well-being of her unborn grandchild and wants to do something to stop Mary's drug use. Cecily is convinced that Mary is incapable of stopping drug use on her own and Mary is unwilling to participate in a voluntary treatment program. Cecily comes to you for advice. Cecily wants to know if she can have Mary arrested and kept in jail until the baby is born, or if there is any way to hold Mary in a treatment program against her will.

Questions

1. Could Mary be arrested for "delivery or distribution of a controlled substance" or "criminal child abuse or endangerment"? (*See* Problem

43.) In light of *Roe v. Wade*, is an unborn child a "person" or "child" within the meaning of these statutes? Does the state have a compelling interest that justifies interfering in Mary's pregnancy? Does it matter that Mary is only five months pregnant?
2. The following is an excerpt from the Michiana involuntary civil commitment statute:

   1. The standard for involuntary civil commitment shall be as follows:
      a. an individual may be involuntarily committed for medical treatment if they are mentally ill, *and*
      b. dangerous, *or*
      c. gravely disabled.
   2. Definitions:
      a. "mentally ill" means a psychiatric disorder that substantially disturbs an individual's thinking, feeling, or behavior and impairs the individual's ability to function. The term includes any mental retardation, alcoholism, or addiction to narcotics or dangerous drugs.
      b. "dangerous" means a condition in which an individual as a result of mental illness presents a substantive risk that the individual will harm the individual or others.
      c. "gravely disabled" means a condition in which an individual is unable to provide basic life sustaining care to himself and/or is unable to function independently.

   Could Cecily, as an interested party, petition the court to have Mary involuntarily committed? Does potential harm to others include harm to an unborn child?
3. Does Mary's unborn child have any rights? If the child is born with disabilities due to Mary's drug use, could he or she sue Mary in tort?

D. CHILD NEGLECT

Problem 45

> ### In re Leonard R. Bowman, a Child Alleged to Be a Child in Need of Services

Clyde and Bonnie Bowman were married in YR-3. In YR-2, Clyde adopted Bonnie's son, Leonard, who had been born out of wedlock in YR-4. Bonnie and Clyde are both employed in Southby, Michiana—Bonnie as a hair stylist at Ben's Den and Clyde as part owner of an auto body shop, with his brother-in-law, Austin Carl Hall. Clyde is a professional race car driver (midgets and stock cars), and his racing has required much travel outside of Michiana. Bonnie and Clyde frequently take race trips lasting several days and leave Leonard with friends in Southby. Bonnie's brother, Austin, and his wife, Fuchsia, often take care of Leonard during his parents' absence. In November of YR-1, after returning from a race in Pensacola, Florida, Leonard told Bonnie and Clyde that while they were gone Uncle Austin had removed Leonard's trousers and touched Leonard's "private parts" with his mouth. Bonnie and Clyde told

Leonard that everything would be okay and asked him no further questions. Austin had been convicted of sodomy of a four-year-old boy in YR-2. He had served six months in the county jail and was on probation at this time. Bonnie and Clyde state that they knew only that Austin Hall had been convicted of "a sexual offense." When Clyde questioned Austin about touching Leonard, Austin replied, "Hey, man; Leonard is my nephew. He must be imagining things." Bonnie and Clyde took no further action.

On January 5, YR-0, Bonnie and Clyde left Leonard with Austin and Fuchsia before traveling to Columbia, South Carolina, for a race. When Bonnie and Clyde returned to Southby and picked up Leonard at Austin and Fuchsia's apartment, they noticed that Leonard has suffered several abrasions over his body. After returning home and talking to Leonard, Bonnie called the police to report Leonard's condition.

Following a detention hearing on January 11, YR-0, Leonard Bowman was placed in a foster home, where he presently resides. Leonard, age three, is alleged to be a child in need of services (CHINS) pursuant to Michiana Code 31-6-4-3. The CHINS petition, filed by the Hoynes County Department of Public Welfare, alleges that Leonard's physical or mental condition is seriously impaired or endangered as a result of the neglect of his parents to supply the child with necessary supervision. The State of Michiana has also charged Austin Carl Hall in a two-count criminal information with battery and neglect of a dependent, both felonies, as a result of the injuries suffered by Leonard Bowman from January 5th to 10th, YR-0, while the child was in his uncle's physical custody. A court-appointed special advocate (CASA) has been appointed by the court to represent the best interests of Leonard in the CHINS proceedings.

The Michiana statutes that govern CHINS proceedings, along with the court documents, investigative reports, exhibits, and information filed in the pending criminal prosecution against Austin Carl Hall follow this Problem.

Questions

1. What procedure is required for removing Leonard from Bonnie and Clyde's home? Should Leonard be removed from his parents' home?
2. Can the state hold Bonnie and Clyde responsible for the acts of Austin, a third party?
3. Should Austin be a party to the CHINS proceedings? What legal sanctions can be brought against Austin in the CHINS case?
4. Can criminal prosecution be brought against Bonnie and Clyde? If so, what effect would the filing of criminal actions against them have on the CHINS proceedings? What effect would a criminal conviction have?
5. What result at the fact-finding hearing is in Leonard's best interests?
6. What is the meaning of "wardship"?
7. What arguments should Bonnie and Clyde make at the dispositional hearing to support returning Leonard to their home?
8. What result at the dispositional hearing is in Leonard's best interests?

Chapter Eight. Decisions About Children—The State's Role

STATE OF MICHIANA) IN THE HOYNES SUPERIOR COURT
) SS:
HOYNES COUNTY) CAUSE NO. _____

STATE OF MICHIANA)
) INFORMATION IN TWO COUNTS:
vs.) COUNT I. BATTERY, CLASS C FELONY
) COUNT II. NEGLECT OF A DEPENDENT,
AUSTIN CARL HALL) CLASS B FELONY

COUNT I

ROBERT DAWSON, upon information and belief, after being duly sworn upon his oath, says that:

From on or about January 5, YR-0, through January 10, YR-0, AUSTIN CARL HALL, being twenty-one (21) years of age, did knowingly touch LEONARD R. BOWMAN, a child three (3) years of age, in a rude, insolent or angry manner, to wit: by striking the body of LEONARD R. BOWMAN, by grabbing the neck of LEONARD R. BOWMAN, and by pinching the penis of LEONARD R. BOWMAN, resulting in serious bodily injury to LEONARD R. BOWMAN, to wit: bruises and scratches behind both the ears and on the neck area, bruises on the left shoulder, abdomen, back, and buttocks, and inflamed and enlarged rectum, and bruises on the penis of LEONARD R. BOWMAN, which injuries, separately and as a whole, caused LEONARD R. BOWMAN to suffer great pain.

All of which is contrary to the form of the statute in such cases made and provided, to wit: Michiana Code 35-42-2-1(3), and against the peace and dignity of the State of Michiana.

COUNT II

ROBERT DAWSON, upon information and belief, after being duly sworn upon his oath, says that:

From on or about January 5, YR-0, through January 10, YR-0, AUSTIN CARL HALL, having the care, custody and control of LEONARD R. BOWMAN, a child of three (3) years of age, a dependent, did knowingly place LEONARD R. BOWMAN, his dependent, in a situation endangering the life and health of LEONARD R. BOWMAN, to wit: by causing LEONARD R. BOWMAN to be beaten and tortured, resulting in burns to his face, injuries to his penis and rectum, and other serious injuries.

All of which is contrary to the form of the statute in such cases made and provided, to-wit: Michiana Code 35-46-1-4, and against the peace of dignity of the State of Michiana.

Robert Dawson
ROBERT DAWSON

Subscribed and sworn to before me, this _____ day of February, YR-0.

Jacqueline Weiler
NOTARY PUBLIC, A Resident
of Hoynes County, Michiana.

Approved by me this _____ day of February, YR-0.

DEPUTY PROSECUTING
ATTORNEY

Warrant ordered issued; corporate surety bond set at $_____ or cash in lieu thereof $_____.

JUDGE, HOYNES SUPERIOR
COURT

WITNESSES:
Sgt. Robert Dawson

Chapter Eight. Decisions About Children—The State's Role

STATE OF MICHIANA	)	IN THE HOYNES SUPERIOR COURT
	) SS:	
HOYNES COUNTY	)	CAUSE NO. _____
STATE OF MICHIANA	)	
	)	
vs.	)	SUPPLEMENTAL AFFIDAVIT IN
	)	SUPPORT OF PROBABLE CAUSE
AUSTIN CARL HALL	)	

ROBERT DAWSON, being duly sworn upon his oath, says that:

I am a police officer with the Hoynes County Police Department.

On January 10, YR-0, Clyde Bowman and Bonnie Bowman reported that their son Leonard R. Bowman had been abused. They stated that they dropped their son off at the home of Austin and Fuchsia Hall, 801 Beech Street, Southby, Michiana, on January 5, YR-0. They stated that Austin Hall is the brother of Bonnie Bowman. They stated that they made arrangements for the Halls to babysit for their son Leonard until they returned from South Carolina to pick him up. Mr. and Mrs. Bowman stated that they went to the Hall's apartment twice on January 9, YR-0, to pick up their son Leonard, but they found no one home. They stated that they went to the apartment again on January 10, YR-0, but again found no one home. They stated that when they went to the Hall's apartment on January 10, YR-0, no one answered the door. They made several attempts that day to find their son, and Austin Hall finally answered the door.

Clyde Bowman stated that when he came into the home, Austin Hall said that they had a problem. Clyde Bowman stated that Austin Hall said that Leonard had burned his face while taking a bath. Clyde Bowman said that when Bonnie Bowman brought Leonard downstairs, he noticed a large burn on the right side of Leonard's face. He also had bruises and abrasions over his body.

Clyde Bowman and Bonnie Bowman made a police report, and Leonard R. Bowman, who is three years of age, his date of birth being October 17, YR-4, was taken to St. Vincent's Hospital in Southby, Michiana.

Leonard R. Bowman was examined at St. Vincent's Hospital by Dr. Elsa Kiley. Dr. Kiley reported that her examination revealed that Leonard R. Bowman had definite signs of battery. She stated that both of his ears were reddened and he had bruises, scratches, and petechia minute hemorrhagic purplish spots behind both ears and on the neck area. Dr. Kiley stated that they were pressure injuries. She stated that he also had a bruise on his left shoulder, bruises on his abdomen and back area, and multiple bruises on his buttocks. Dr. Kiley stated that Leonard's rectum was red, inflamed, and enlarged. She stated that Leonard Bowman's penis had bruises and had an abrasion on it. There was a large second-degree burn on Leonard's face.

On January 15, YR-0, I spoke with Austin Carl Hall, after first advising him of his constitutional rights and after he waived his constitutional rights. Austin Carl Hall stated that he is twenty-one years old, his date of birth being March 18, YR-22. Austin Carl Hall admitted "whipping" Leonard R. Bowman on the "butt," grabbing him on the neck, and grabbing and pinching Leonard Bowman on his penis. A copy of this statement is attached hereto, made a part hereof, and marked as "Exhibit A."

Further your affiant sayeth not.

Robert Dawson
ROBERT DAWSON

Subscribed and sworn to before me, a Notary Public, this _____ day of February, YR-0.

NOTARY PUBLIC, A Resident
of Hoynes County, Michiana

HOYNES COUNTY POLICE DEPARTMENT

Southby, Michiana

WARNING AND WAIVER

CASE NO._____

WARNING AS TO RIGHTS

Before we ask you any questions, it is our duty as police officers to advise you of your rights and to warn you of the consequence of waiving your rights.

You have the absolute right to remain silent.

Anything you say to us can be used against you in court.

You have the right to talk to an attorney before answering any questions and to have an attorney present with you during questioning.

You have this same right to the advice and presence of an attorney whether you can afford to hir one or not. We have no way of furnishing you with an attorney, but one will be appointed for you, if you wish.

If you decide to answer questions now without an attorney present, you will still have the right to stop answering at any time. You also have the right to stop answering at any time until you talk to an attorney.

WAIVER

I have read the above statement of my rights, and it has been read to me. I understand what my rights are. I wish to make a voluntary statement, and I do not want an attorney. No force, threats, or promises of any kind or neature have been used by anyone in any way to influence me to waive my rights. I am signing this statement after having been advised of my rights before any questions have been asked of me by the police.

Austin Carl Hall

(Signature)

CERTIFICATION

I hereby certify that the foregoing warning and waiver were read by me to the person who has affixed his (her) signature above, and that he (she) also read it and signed it in my presence this __15__ day of __January__, YR-0, at __11:45__ o'clock __A.__ M. at __Southby__, Michiana.

Robert Dawson
(Signature - Police Officer)

_____
(Witness)

VOLUNTARY STATEMENT

No. Lib. #580-200

Case # _____

DATE __January 15, YR-0__ PLACE __Hoynes County Police__

Time Statement Started __11:45__ A.M. _____ P.M.

I, the undersigned, __Austin Carl Hall__, of __801 Beech St., Southby, Michiana__, being __21__ years of age, born at __Howard__ __Michiana__ on __3/28/YR-22__, do hereby make the following statement to __Sgt. Robert Dawson__, he having first identified himself as a __Hoynes County__ police officer.

This statement is voluntarily made by me without any threats, coercion or promises of any kind or nature. Before making any statement to the police, I was advised that I had the absolute right to remain silent and that anything I might say could be used against me in a criminal proceeding. I was advised also of my right to have an attorney present before answering any questions and that if I was unable to afford one, an attorney would be provided before questioning. I have freely and voluntarily waived my right to remain silent and my right to consult with an attorney before answering questions.

Austin Carl Hall, being duly sworn and upon his oath, says:

Q. Austin, were you read the warning and waiver of your rights before being asked any questions, and do you understand your rights?

A. Yes.

Q. Are you aware of an investigation we are currently conducting involving Leonard R. Bowman?

A. Yeah.

Q. Austin, what can you tell us about any marks or injuries to Leonard which would have occurred between 1-5-YR-0 and 1-10-YR-0?

A. I guess it would be Sunday, we was messing, well wrestling, that's how he got the marks on his ear. Then Monday, he got the mark on his butt from peeing on the bed, right after we took him off the toilet. Then on Tuesday, he got the mark on his thing, by being pinched. I guess, for the same reason that he got his butt whipped.

Q. In regards to the marks on his neck and ears, how were these caused?

A. I was wrestling around, just grabbing him real hard on the neck, and all that.

Q. In regards to the bruises and swelling on his penis, did these events occur more than once?

A. Maybe on the butt, but that's it. It all happened on the same night, well the whippings on the butt happened the same night, and the other thing happened the other night.

Q. Austin, there is a second degree burn on the right cheek and forehead of Leonard, which are unaccounted for. Do you know how he received these?

A. Just from what my wife told me, he was taking a bath, and she was taking care of the kid, and she came back over and he had a burn mark on his face.

VOLUNTARY STATEMENT

No. Lib. #580-200

Case # 0-91

DATE January 15, YR-0   PLACE Hoynes County Police Dept.

Q. Austin, what led to the incident where he received an injury to his penis and how did he get the injury?

A. I guess he was just laying on the floor, had pissy pants, so I just grabbed him, that's all I guess I can say.

Q. Is there anything you care to add to this statement at this time?

A. No.

Q. Have any promises or considerations been given to you for giving this statement?

A. No.

Q. If you were asked these same questions at a later date and time, what would your answers be and why?

A. The same as they are now. Why should I change them? I guess it's the truth.

I have read this statement consisting of __2__ page(s) and the facts contained therein are true and correct.

WITNESSES: *Sgt. R. Dawson*   *Austin Carl Hall*
Signature of Person giving voluntary statement

Page __2__ of __2__ Pages

DATE _____

TIME STATEMENT FINISHED _____ A.M. __12:05__ P.M.

INITIAL CASE REPORT

This Agency is requesting your Social Security No. only to expedite the processing of this form. You are not required to provide this information and cannot be penalized for declining to provide it.	Control No (Cent. Rec. Only)	1 Page 1 Of 3	2 Case No 0-91

3 Offense: Child Abuse
4 Supervisory Correction No 2 or 3:

5 Victim Name: Leonard R. Bowman
5a Responsible Party:

6 Victim's Address: 1101 Linden Rd., Southby, Michiana 46617
7 Home Phone: None
8 Business Phone:

9 Victim's Sex	10 Race	11 DOB	12 Age	13 SSN	14 Describe Injury	15 Place of Treatment
M	W	10-15-YR-4	3	None	Bruises over body/burned face	St. Vincent's

16 Month of Occurrence	17 Day	18 Year	19 Military Time	20 Month Reported	21 Day	22 Year	23 Military Time	24 How Reported?	25
01	9	YR-0	1830	01	09	YR-0	2040	Person	X Rural / ☐ Urban

26 Received by	27 Reported By (Name)	28 Address of Reporter
PE 73	Clyde Bowman	#6

29 Home Phone / 30 Business Phone: None
31 Exact Location of Offense: 801 Beech Street

32 City	33 Township	34 County	35 State
Southby	Center	Hoynes	Michiana

36 Was there a witness to the crime? ☒ No

37 Witness/Neighborhood Check	38 Address	39 Home Phone / 40 Business Phone	41 ☐ Interviewed ☐ Statement
37a.	38a. Address	39a. / 40a.	41a. ☐ Interviewed ☐ Statement

42 Suspect? ☒ Named ☐ Known ☒ Known Location ☒ Identified ☐ Previously Seen ☒ Description ☐ No ☒ Yes

43 Suspect (Alias)	44 DOB	43a Suspect (Alias)	44a DOB
Austin Carl Hall	Unkn		

45 Location/Address	46 SSN	45a Location/Address	46a SSN
801 Beech Street	Unkn		

47 Description: M/W/21, 6" 215 lbs, Dk Brn, Jody - 1 arm
47a Description:

48 Identified By	48a Identified By

49 Arrested?	50 ID No.	51	52 CR Check	49a Arrested?	50a ID No.	51a	52a CR Check
☐ Yes ☒ No		☐ Mug ☐ Print	☐ Yes ☐ No	☐ Yes ☐ No		☐ Mug ☐ Print	☐ Yes ☐ No

53 Vehicle Identified? ☐ Suspect ☐ Stolen ☐ Recovered ☐ Other ☒ No

54 Veh. Make	55 Color	56 Yr	57 Model	58 Body S	59 Lic Yr	60 Lic St	61 Lic No	62 Where Held	63 VIN

64 ☐ Significant M.O. or ☒ Limited Opportunity to Commit the Crime? ☐ No

65 Describe: Suspect was babysitting victim for last five days
66 Motive: Gratification/Sexual Other

67 Was there? ☐ Traceable Property ☒ Significant Physical Evidence? ☐ No

68 Scene Processing	69 Scene Tech.	70 PE No. Tech.	71 Property Form No.	Recovered/Collected Evidence	72 Instrument, Force, Weapon
☒ Photo ☐ Fingerprint ☐ Other	☒ Yes ☐ No	40			Hand & Other Unknown

73 Property Stolen/Property Recovered	74 Identification No.	75 Value
73a	74a Identification No.	75a Value
73b	74b Identification No.	75b Value

BLOCK SPACE — NARRATIVE
76 ☐ IDACS Entry ☐ NCIC Entry
77 Total Value Recovered/Stolen:
78 Total Value Stolen:

See Supplemental

Investigating Officer	PN	Unit No.	Supervisory Officer	PN
Sgt. Robert Dawson	#106			
Date-Time/Disp.	Loc. Disp. To	Date/Time Arrived	Date/Time Report Comp 1/9/YR-0	D N

WHITE - Records/Data CANARY - Investigative PINK - Crime Analysis

HOYNES COUNTY POLICE DEPARTMENT
SUPPLEMENTAL CASE REPORT

Page 2 of 3 Pages
Case No. 0-91

Offense: Child Abuse

Victim Name (or if Business list Incorporated Name): Leonard R. Bowman

NARRATIVE:

Clyde Bowman reports that he and his wife, Bonnie Bowman, F/W/20, DOB/11-21-YR-21, went to Columbia, South Carolina from 1-5-YR-0 to 1-9-YR-0. Austin Hall and his wife, Fuchsia, were going to babysit for Leonard while they were gone. Austin Hall is the brother of Bonnie Bowman and the uncle to the reported victim. When the parents went for their son, on Monday, around 1000 hrs., no one one was home. They tried a second time that date, again no one was there. They tried to get their son again on Tuesday, 1-10-YR-0, and as they arrived, Bonnie noticed the lights being turned off. They kept knocking until Austin finally answered the door.

When Clyde went into the house, Austin told him that they had a problem. He told Clyde that Leonard had burned his face while taking a bath. This information was told to Clyde before he saw his son. When the boy came downstains, the father noticed a large red blister on the right side of his face. The parents left with Leonard at that time and returned home. Other marks were found at this time and the boy was taken to St. Vincents' Hospital for an exam.

This investigator was sent to the hospital to help with an investigation, and take photographs. Several bruises and marks were found on the boy's face, neck and body. He also had a red penis, which was swollen, and black and blue. His rectum was also red, and had small

HOYNES COUNTY POLICE DEPARTMENT
SUPPLEMENTAL CASE REPORT

Page 3 of 3 Pages
Case No. 0-91

Offense: Child Abuse

Victim Name (or if Business list Incorporated Name): Leonard R. Bowman

NARRATIVE:

cuts around it. Photographs were taken of the boy by this officer.

The only thing the boy had told his parents was that Austin hurt him. He was upset in the hospital and was not questioned at this time. He did say again that Austin hurt him. The boy was admitted to the hospital at this time.

The parents were advised that a case worker from the Child Protection Service of the Department of Public Welfare would be contacted, and that the boy would then be interviewed. They were also advised that Austin and Fuchsia would also be interviewed.

Investigating Officer: Sgt. Robert Dawson   P.N. #106
Date/Time Report Comp. 1/9/YR-0

WHITE - Records/Data   CANARY - Investigative   PINK - Crime Analysis

HOYNES COUNTY POLICE DEPARTMENT
SUPPLEMENTAL CASE REPORT

Case No. 0-91

Offense: Child Abuse

Victim Name (or if Business list Incorporated Name): Leonard R. Bowman

NARRATIVE:

On 1-12-YR-0, at 1200 hrs., this officer and caseworker, Clara McGill, of Child Protection Service, interviewed Fuchsia M. Hall, F/W/18, DOB/8-13-YR-18, at the Hoynes County Police Station. Fuchsia is the wife of the suspect, Austin Carl Hall. Fuchsia also had her five-month old son with her at the time of the interview, so we could check him for any injuries.

Fuchsia was advised as to why we needed to talk with her, and see if she could tell us what had happened to Leonard Bowman. She stated that Clyde had been dropped off on Sunday, 1-5-YR-0, and nothing had been said about when he was to be picked up by his parents. Her husband was at work, Monday through Wednesday, during the day and had no contact with Leonard. Fuchsia was shown the photographs of Leonard Bowman and was asked how any of the injuries could have occurred. At first, she stated that she had no idea, except for the burn on the face, which she claims happened on Monday, when Leonard Bowman burned himself in the shower. Each time we asked about a certain mark or injury, she would explain it, and then later give a different reason for the same injury. She did not see what had happened to Leonard's bottom but thought it got bruised when he and her husband were playing on the stairway. This also would have occurred on Monday. On Monday,

Investigating Officer: Sgt. Robert Dawson   P.N. #106

Date/Time Report Comp.: 1/14/YR-0

HOYNES COUNTY POLICE DEPARTMENT
SUPPLEMENTAL CASE REPORT

Page 2 of 3 Pages
Case No. 0-91

Offense: Child Abuse

Victim Name (or if Business list Incorporated Name): Leonard R. Bowman

NARRATIVE:

while Leonard was taking a bath, she noticed a razor on the edge of the tub, and she feels that Leonard used it to cut himself on the penis. She was advised that these injuries did not appear to be cuts, and she informed us that she did not know what happened, but she remembered that it did bleed.

Fuchsia advised us that no one except her or her husband was with Leonard, but that neither of them hurt the boy. She also stated that the boy did get into a lot of trouble and maybe he hurt himself.

We informed Fuchsia that the young boy had told us that Austin hurt him and he also told us that he did not like Austin. She still stated that she did not think Austin had caused any of the marks, even after she admitted that he had hit her in the past. We asked her if she was afraid to tell us what happened, because her husband might then hurt her, and she stated no. We also advised that we felt her own son might be in danger, because of what happened to Leonard. Neither she nor Austin hurt Leonard, or at least they were not able to keep him from getting hurt. Fuchsia's father also came to the police station and tried to talk with her, but she claimed that she still did not know what had occurred.

Fuchsia was advised several times that the burn on Leonard's face could not have occurred from hot water coming down on him from a

Investigating Officer	P.N.	Unit No.	Supervisory Officer	P.N.	
Date-Time/Disp.	Loc. Disp. To		Date/Time Arrived	Date/Time Report Comp.	D.N

WHITE - Records/Data   CANARY - Investigative   PINK - Crime Analysis

HOYNES COUNTY POLICE DEPARTMENT
SUPPLEMENTAL CASE REPORT

Page 3 of 3 Pages
Case No. O-91

Offense: Child Abuse

Victim Name (or if Business list Incorporated Name): Leonard R. Bowman

NARRATIVE:

shower, but she still stated that was how it happened. She left the bathroom to check on her own son, and when she returned, Leonard was crying from the injury. The shower was running when she left and was still running when she returned.

Due to the fact that she could not explain when or how the injuries occurred, and our fear that her young son could be in danger, Austin Hall Jr. was taken into our custody. A detention hearing was scheduled for 1-14-YR-0 in Probate Court at 1:30 p.m. Fuchsia was also advised to have her husband come to the county police station at 10:00 a.m. this same date for an interview regarding this case.

Investigating Officer: Sgt. Robert Dawson   P.N. #106   Date/Time Report Comp.: 1/14/YR-0

HOYNES COUNTY POLICE DEPARTMENT
SUPPLEMENTAL CASE REPORT

Case No. 0-91

Offense: Child Abuse

Victim Name (or if Business list Incorporated Name): Leonard R. Bowman

NARRATIVE:

Austin Carl Hall   M/W/21

DOB/3-28-YR-21   SSN 311-78-3187

On 1-14-85, at 1020 hrs, Austin Carl Hall did come to the county police station where an interview was conducted, with this officer and the caseworker, Clara McGill. A warning and waiver was read to Austin before any questions were asked. He stated that he did understand these rights and signed the waiver.

Austin was advised that we wanted to talk to him about all of the injuries on Leonard, and just how they occurred. At first he stated that he did not know how the boy received any of the injuries and that the burned face occurred on either Monday or Tuesday, while he was at work, and that his wife told him the same story about the shower. I asked Austin if any arrangements had been made as to how long Leonard would be in their care, and he advised that Clyde and Bonnie were to pick up their son when they got back from South Carolina, just as we had been advised by them.

We talked with Austin for approximately one hour, and he changed the story several times. He at one time stated that he has seen the parents kick and hit the young boy and maybe they caused the marks before they left Leonard in their care. He also made the statement

Investigating Officer: Sgt. Robert Dawson   P.N. #106

Date/Time Report Comp. 1/28-YR-0

HOYNES COUNTY POLICE DEPARTMENT
SUPPLEMENTAL CASE REPORT

Case No. 0-91

Offense: Child Abuse

Victim Name (or if Business list Incorporated Name): Leonard R. Bowman

NARRATIVE:

that Leonard did not like him, and maybe he was making up the story. As we talked, Austin said that the marks around the boy's neck were caused by him, and he was wrestling with Leonard. He also received the marks on his ears at this time. When we talked about the bruises on Leonard's bottom, Austin stated he spanked the boy because he pissed in his pants, even after going to the bathroom. At that time I asked if that was how the boy got hurt in the area of his penis. Austin stated "yes." On a different occasion the boy was on the floor when he went in his pants and Austin pinched or grabbed him by his penis. Austin admitted to causing all of the injuries, except for the burn on Leonard's face. We also got a written statement in regards to his actions.

We again talked with Fuchsia, but she again stated that she did not know about the marks, and again said the burn was from a shower. She was given every opportunity to tell us what happened, but still claimed no knowledge of any of the incidents.

At this time, we cannot say for sure how Leonard received the burn on his face, but it could not have been caused from hot water falling on his body while in the shower. One adult arrest will be referred to the Prosecutor's Office. Will discuss possible CHINS action with D.P.W.

Investigating Officer: Sgt. Robert Dawson   P.N. #106   Date/Time Report Comp. 1/28/YR-0

CASE NO.   O-91   DATE   1/12/YR-0

COMPLAINANT   BOWMAN, Clyde T.

ADDRESS   1101 Linden Rd., Southby, Michiana

Narrative:

On the above date at approximately 7:45 a.m., the undersigned reporting officer went to apartment 832 Beech Street to interview the the neighbors of Austin and Fuchsia HALL.

The neighbors interviewed were:

    Robert L. Jones   Julie M. Jones
    DOB 7/02/YR-29   DOB 8/22/YR-28
    SSN 315-25-1576   SSN 306-71-7218

    PHONE: 656-8313

Mr. and Mrs. Jones have the apartment directly south and connected by a common wall with the Halls. According to the Joneses, "sometime during the last few days," (Julie Jones thought it might have been Sunday, but was not sure) they heard a small child, but not the baby, "crying and run up the steps." According to the Joneses, the child was "not screaming, but was crying loudly."

Julie Jones further stated that "someone went up the stairs after the child, not right away, but shortly afterwards."

According to the Joneses, they have heard the baby crying at times, but have never heard anything to indicate that the baby was being abused.

No further information could be obtained at this time. This case will be considered pending further investigation.

Robert Dawson (signature)
Robert Dawson #106
Hoynes County Police Department

Attach to Original Report Upon Completion

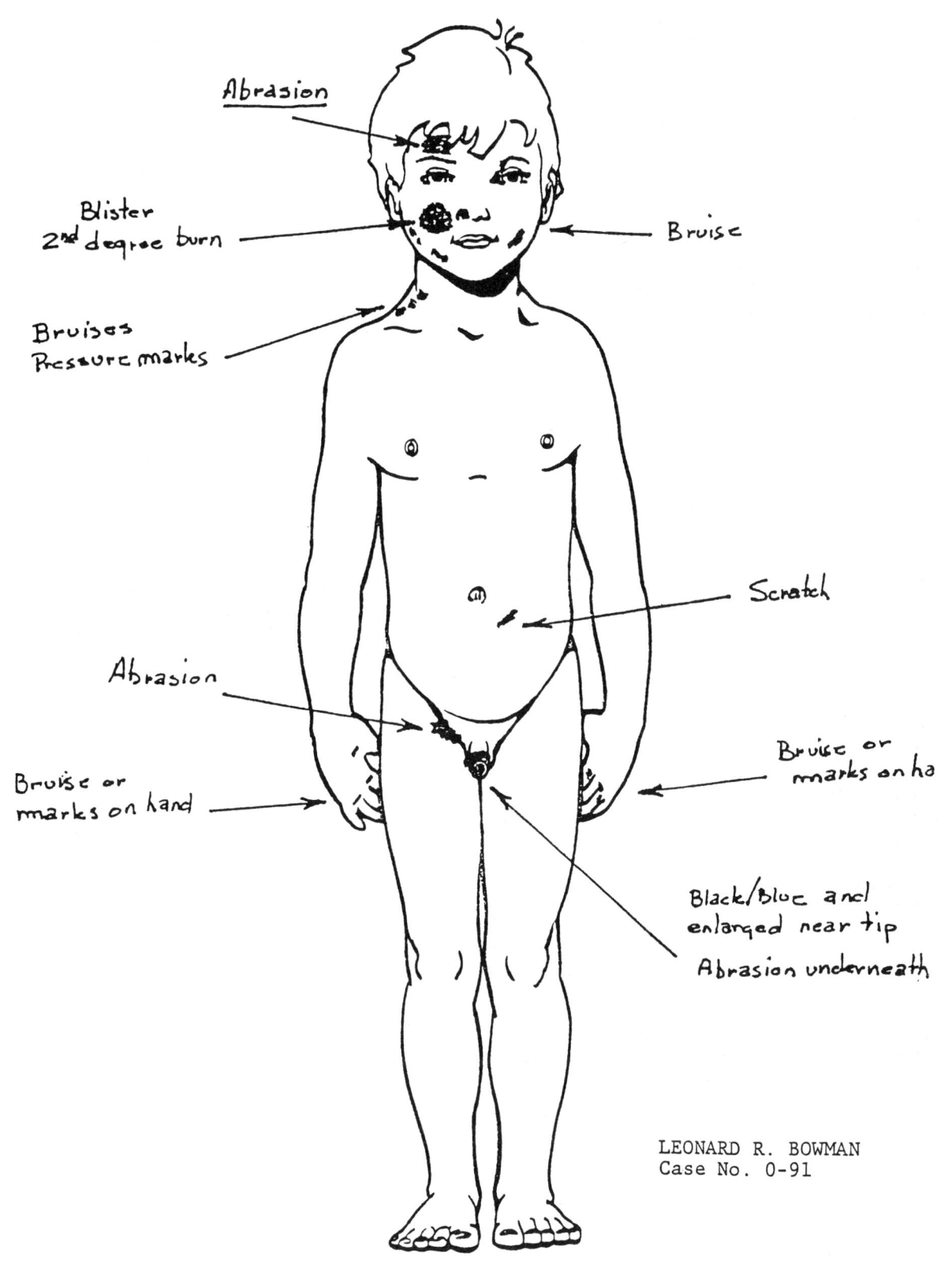

Figure 5: White, pre-school, male child (front view)

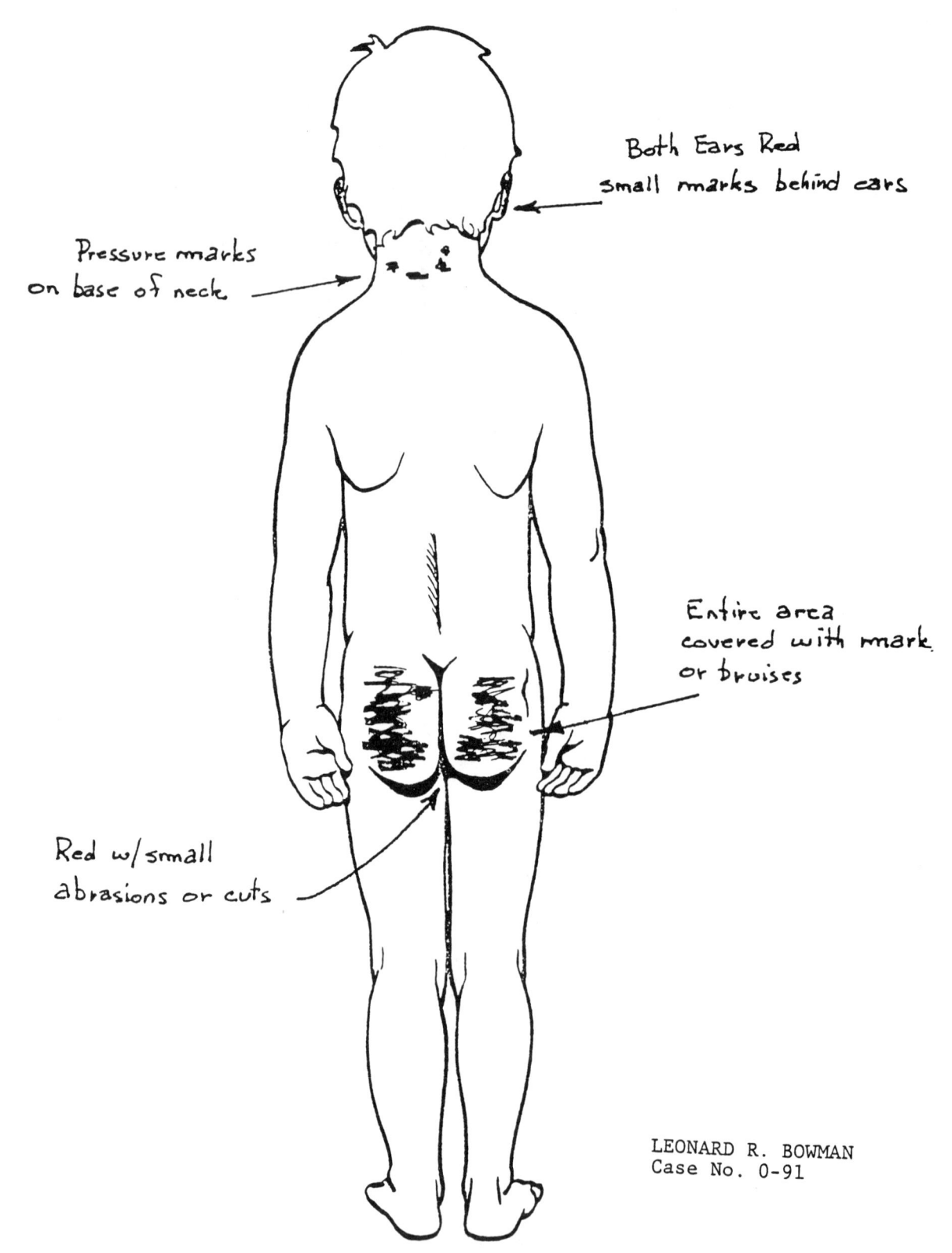

Figure 6: White, pre-school, male child (back view)

STATE OF MICHIANA)
) SS:
HOYNES COUNTY)

IN THE HOYNES PROBATE COURT

CAUSE NUMBER _____

IN THE MATTER OF   )
LEONARD R. BOWMAN   )
)
)
A CHILD ALLEGED TO BE A CHILD)
IN NEED OF SERVICES   )

ORDER ON DETENTION HEARING

  There having been conducted this date a timely Detention Hearing with respect to said child, the REFEREE (JUDGE) now FINDS and RECOMMENDS (ORDERS) as follows:

  A. That actual notice of the time, place and purpose of hearing has been given to the child and   Mr. and Mrs. Clyde Bowman .
                  (parent/guardian/custodian)

  B. That those present and appearing for the hearing are as listed in the Court's minute entry this date.

  C. That the detention and removal of said child (was/was not) authorized and necessary under MC 31-6-4-4(c) to protect said child and that the following efforts were made by Hoynes County Department of Public Welfare to eliminate or prevent the need to remove the child/reunify the child and family:

    1. The safety of the child precluded (preplacement preventive services) (reunification services) (Please specify):_____
      Leonard R. Bowman, age 3, suffered severe facial burns, bruising, and abrasions over his body and physical evidence of sexual abuse by uncle

    2. (Preplacement of preventive services) (Reunification services) were provided or offered and included: (Check all that apply):

     _____ twenty-four (24) hour emergency caretaker and homemaker services;
     _____ day care;
     _____ crisis counseling;
     _____ individual and family counseling;
     _____ emergency shelter;
     _____ procedures and arrangements for access to available emergency financial assistance;
     _____ arrangements for the provision of temporary child care to provide respite to the family for a brief period, as part of a plan for preventing children's removal from home;
     _____ home-based family services;
     _____ self-help groups;
     _____ mental health counseling;
     _____ drug and alcohol abuse counseling;
     _____ vocational counseling or vocational rehabilitation;
     _____ post adoption services;
     _____ transportation;
     _____ visitation;
     _____ other services which the agency identifies as necessary and appropriate:_____

     _____ other information:_____

3. The efforts made to prevent the removal of the child(ren) (were/were not) reasonable.

   a. That there is no probable cause to believe that said child(ren) is (are) a Child in Need of Services and hence said child(ren) should be released to the custody of _____.
   (parent/guardian/custodian)

   b. That probable cause exists to believe that said child(ren) is (are) a Child in Need of Services but that said child(ren) is (are) not in need of further detention, and that said child(ren) should be released to _____
   _____.
   (parent/guardian/custodian)
   upon the following conditions:

   c. That probable cause exists to believe that said child(ren) is (are) a Child in Need of Services and that said child(ren) is (are) in need of removal because:

   ( ) the child(ren) is (are) unlikely to appear for subsequent proceedings;
   ( ) detention is necessary to protect the child(ren);
   ( ) the parent, guardian, or custodian cannot be located or is unable or unwilling to take custody of the child(ren);
   ( ) the child(ren) has (have) a reasonable basis for requesting that he (she) (they) not be released; or
   ( ) consideration for the safety of the child(ren) precludes the use of family services to prevent removal of the child(ren).

and hence a judicial determination has been made that the child(ren) is (are) to be removed from his (her) (their) home because continuation in his (her) (their) home would be contrary to his (her) (their) welfare; and that any foster care costs incurred in such removal are to be advanced by the County Welfare Department beginning on the __8__ day of ____May____, YR-0 until further order of the Court.

The appointment of a special advocate for the child(ren) is/is not appropriate.

Dated the date filed marked hereon.

_____
REFEREE, (JUDGE)

The Court having considered the findings and recommendation of the Referee, the Court now approves same and adopts them as the FINDINGS and ORDER of the Court on the date file marked hereon.

_____
JUDGE
HOYNES PROBATE COURT

Chapter Eight. Decisions About Children—The State's Role

M.C. 31-6-3-4 Appointment of Guardian ad litem or special advocate or both; duties; liabilities

Section 4. (a) The juvenile court may appoint a guardian ad litem or a court appointed special advocate, or both, for the child at any time. A guardian ad litem or court appointed special advocate need not be an attorney, but the attorney representing the child may be appointed his guardian ad litem or court appointed special advocate.

(b) A guardian ad litem or court appointed special advocate shall represent and protect the best interests of the child.

(c) If any fees arise, payment shall be made under MC 31-6-4-18.

(d) The guardian ad litem or the court appointed special advocate may be represented by an attorney. If necessary to protect the child's interests, the court may appoint an attorney to represent the guardian ad litem or the court appointed special advocate. The court may only appoint one (1) attorney under this subsection.

(e) The guardian ad litem or the court appointed special advocate, or both, shall be considered officers of the court for the purpose of representing the child's interests.

(f) Except for gross misconduct, if the guardian ad litem or court appointed special advocate performs his duties in good faith, he is immune from any civil liability that may occur as a result of his performance.

(g) A court may not appoint a party to the proceedings, that party's employee, or that party's representative as the guardian ad litem or as the court appointed special advocate for a child who is involved in the proceedings.

M.C. 31-6-4-3 Child in need of services

Section 3. (a) A child is a child in need of services if before his eighteenth birthday:

(1) his physical or mental condition is seriously impaired or seriously endangered as a result of the inability, refusal or neglect of his parent, guardian, or custodian to supply the child with necessary food, clothing, shelter, medical care, education, or supervision;

(2) his physical or mental health is seriously endangered due to injury by the act or omission of his parent, guardian, or custodian;

(3) he is the victim of a sex offense under MC 35-42-4-1, MC 35-42-4-2, MC 35-42-4-3(a) or MC 35-42-4-3(b), MC-35-42-4-3(c) or MC 35-42-4-3(d) if the offense was committed by the child's parent guardian, or custodian, MC 35-42-4-4, MC 35-45-4-1, MC 35-45-4-2, or MC 35-46-1-3;

(4) his parent, guardian, or custodian allows him to participate in an obscene performance, defined by MC 35-49-2-2 or MC 35-49-3-2;

(5) his parent, guardian, or custodian allows him to commit a sex offense prohibited by MC 35-45-4;

(6) he substantially endangers his own health or the health of another; or

(7) his parent, guardian, or custodian fails to participate in a disciplinary proceeding in connection with the student's improper behavior, as provided for by MC 20-8.1-5-7, where the behavior of the student has been repeatedly disruptive in the school;

and needs care, treatment, or rehabilitation that he is not receiving, and that is unlikely to be provided or accepted without the coercive intervention of the court.

(b) An omission under subdivision (a)(2) is an occurrence in which the parent, guardian, or custodian allowed his child to receive any injury that he had a reasonable opportunity to prevent or mitigate.

(c) A custodian under subsection (a) includes any person responsible for the child's welfare who is employed by a public or private residential school or foster care facility.

(d) When a parent, guardian or custodian fails to provide specific medical treatment for a child because of the legitimate and genuine practice of his religious beliefs, a rebuttable presumption arises that the child is not a child in need of services because of such failure. However, this presumption does not prevent a juvenile court from ordering, when the health of a child requires, medical services from a physician licensed to practice medicine in Michiana. This presumption does not apply to situations in which the life or health of a child is in serious danger.

(e) Nothing in this chapter limits the right of a person to use reasonable corporal punishment when disciplining a child if the person is the parent, guardian, or custodian of the child. In addition, nothing in this chapter limits the lawful practice or teaching of religious beliefs.

(f) A child in need of services under subsection (a) includes a handicapped child who is deprived of nutrition that is necessary to sustain life, or who is deprived of medical or surgical intervention that is necessary to remedy or ameliorate a life threatening medical condition, if the nutrition or medical or surgical intervention is generally provided to similarly situated handicapped or nonhandicapped children.

(g) A handicapped child under subsection (f) is an individual under eighteen (18) years of age who has a handicap as defined in MC 22-9-1-3(q).

M.C. 31-6-4-6 Child in need of services; custody; detention; hearings; findings; order

Section 6. (a) This section applies only to a child alleged to be a child in need of services.

(b) If a child is taken into custody under an order of the court, the law enforcement officer shall take him to a place designated in the order to await a detention hearing.

(c) If a child is taken into custody without an order of the court, the person taking him into custody may release the child or may deliver him to a place designated by the juvenile court and, if the child is detained, shall promptly notify the child's parent, guardian, or custodian, and an intake officer that the child is being held and of the reasons for his detention.

(d) If the child was not taken into custody under an order of the court, the intake officer shall investigate the reasons for his detention. He shall release the child to his parent, guardian, or custodian upon that person's written promise to bring the child before the juvenile court at a time specified; however, the intake officer may place the child in detention if he reasonably believes that the child is a child in need of services and that:

(1) detention is necessary to protect the child;

(2) the child is unlikely to appear before the juvenile court for subsequent proceedings;

(3) the child has a reasonable basis for requesting that he not be released; or

(4) the parent, guardian, or custodian cannot be located or is unable or unwilling to take custody of the child.

(e) If the child is not released, a detention hearing must be held within seventy-two (72) hours (excluding Saturdays, Sundays, and legal holidays) after he is taken into custody; otherwise he shall be released. Notice of the time, place, and purpose of the detention hearing shall be given to the child. Notice shall also be given to his parent, guardian, or custodian if he can be located. If a child has been removed from his parent, guardian, or custodian under section 4(c) of this chapter then, in accordance with federal law, at the detention hearing the court shall make written findings and conclusions that state:

(1) whether removal of the child, authorized under section 4(c) of this chapter, was necessary to protect the child;

(2) a description of the family services available before removal of the child;

(3) efforts made to provide family services before removal of the child;

(4) why the efforts made to provide family services did not prevent removal of the child; and

(5) whether the efforts made to prevent removal of the child were reasonable.

(f) The juvenile court shall release the child to his parent, guardian, or custodian; however, the court may order the child detained if it makes written findings of fact upon the record of probable cause to believe that the child is a child in need of services and that:

(1) detention is necessary to protect the child;

(2) the child is unlikely to appear before the juvenile court for subsequent proceedings;

(3) the child has a reasonable basis for requesting that he not be released;

(4) the parent, guardian, or custodian cannot be located or is unable or unwilling to take custody of the child; or

(5) consideration for the safety of the child precludes the use of family services to prevent removal of the child.

(g) Upon the juvenile court's own motion or upon the motion of the person representing the interests of the state, the parent, guardian, or custodian of a child who has been released may be ordered to appear with the child for an additional detention hearing.

(h) A child detained under subsection (f) or (g), or his parent, guardian, or custodian, may petition the juvenile court for additional detention hearings.

M.C. 31-6-4-10 Petition alleging child in need of services; request for authorization to file; probable cause determination; verification; contents; detention

Section 10. (a) The prosecutor or the attorney for the county department may request the juvenile court to authorize the filing of a petition alleging that a child is a child in need of services; that person shall represent the interests of the state at this proceeding and at all subsequent proceedings on the petition.

(b) The juvenile court shall consider the preliminary inquiry and the evidence of probable cause as contained in either the report of the preliminary inquiry or an affidavit of probable cause. The court shall authorize the filing of a petition if it finds probable cause to believe that the child is a child in need of services.

(c) The petition shall be verified and be entitled "In the Matter of _____, a Child Alleged to be a Child in Need of Services," must be signed and filed by the person representing the interests of the state, and must contain the following information:

(1) A citation to the section of this article that gives the juvenile court jurisdiction in the proceeding.

(2) A citation to the section of this article that defines a child in need of services.

(3) A concise statement of the facts upon which the allegations are based, including the date and location at which the alleged facts occurred.

(4) The child's name, birth date, and residence address, if known.

(5) The name and residence address of the child's parent, guardian, or custodian, if known.

(6) The name and title of the person signing the petition.

(7) A statement indicating whether the child has been removed from his parent, guardian, or custodian, and, if so, a description of:

(A) efforts made to provide the child or his parent, guardian, or custodian with family services before the removal; and

(B) reasons why family services were not provided before the removal of the child, if they were not provided.

(d) Error in a citation or its omission is ground for dismissal of the petition or for reversal of the adjudication only if the error or omission misleads the child or his parent, guardian, or custodian to his prejudice.

(e) If the petition is authorized, the person filing may request in writing that the child be taken into custody. He shall support this request with sworn testimony or affidavit. The court may grant the request if it makes written findings of fact upon the record that a ground for detention exists under section 6(f) of this chapter.

(f) If the juvenile court grants the request to have the child taken into custody, it shall proceed under section 6(e) of this chapter.

M.C. 31-6-4-13.5 Child in need of services; initial hearing; appointment of guardian ad litem or special advocate or both; warnings; informing parent or guardian: admission or denial of allegations; dispositional or factfinding hearings

Section 13.5. (a) This section applies only to a child alleged to be a child in need of services.

(b) The juvenile court shall hold an initial hearing on each petition.

(c) The juvenile court shall first determine whether it is appropriate to appoint a guardian ad litem or a court appointed special advocate, or both, for the child. If the child is alleged to be a victim of child abuse or neglect under MC 31-6-11, the court shall make and enter a finding as to the appointment for the child of a guardian ad litem or a court appointed special advocate, or both.

(d) The court shall next inform the child, if he is at an age of understanding, and his parent, guardian, or custodian, if that person is present, of:

(1) the nature of the allegations in the petition; and

(2) the dispositional alternatives available to the court if the child is adjudicated a child in need of services.

(e) The juvenile court shall inform the parent or guardian of the estate that if the child is adjudicated a child in need of services:

(1) he or the custodian of the child may be required to participate in a program of care, treatment, or rehabilitation for the child;

(2) he may be held financially responsible for any services provided for himself or the child; and

(3) he or the custodian of the child may controvert any allegations made at the child's dispositional or other hearing concerning his participation, or he may controvert any allegations concerning his financial responsibility for any services that would be provided.

(f) Except when the petition is filed under section 3(a)(6) of this chapter, the juvenile court shall then determine whether the parent, guardian, or custodian admits or denies the allegations of the petition. A failure to respond constitutes a denial.

(g) If the petition alleges that the child is a child in need of services under section 3(a)(6) of this chapter, the juvenile court shall determine whether the child admits or denies the allegations. A failure to respond constitutes a denial.

(h) If the parent, guardian, or custodian admits the allegations under subsection (f), the juvenile court shall enter judgment accordingly and schedule a dispositional hearing.

(i) If the allegations of the petition have been admitted, the juvenile court may hold a dispositional hearing immediately after the initial hearing. If the allegations have been denied, the juvenile court may hold the factfinding hearing immediately after the initial hearing. In each case:

(1) the child, if competent to do so;

(2) the child's counsel, guardian ad litem, court appointed special advocate, parent, guardian, or custodian; and

(3) the person representing the interests of the state;

must first give their consent.

M.C. 31-6-4-14   Factfinding hearing; continuance; judgment

Section 14 (a). Unless the allegations of the petition have been admitted, the juvenile court shall hold a factfinding hearing.

(b) If the court finds that the child is a delinquent child or a child in need of services, it shall enter judgment accordingly, order a predisposition report, and schedule a dispositional hearing.

(c) If the court finds that the child is not a delinquent child or is not a child in need of services, it shall discharge him.

(d) If the court finds that the allegations in the petition to terminate the parent-child relationship are true, it shall terminate the parent-child relationship; otherwise it shall dismiss the petition.

(e) At the close of all the evidence and before judgment is entered, the court may continue the case for not more than twelve (12) months unless the child or his parent, guardian, or custodian requests that judgment be entered, in which case the judgment shall be entered within thirty (30) days. However, if the child is in secure detention, he shall be released within seventy-two (72) hours (excluding Saturdays, Sundays, and legal holidays) pending the entry of judgment. A child released from secure detention pending the entry of judgment may be detained in a shelter care facility.

(f) In all cases where a finding of delinquency is based on a delinquent act that would be a felony if committed by an adult, the juvenile court shall state in the findings the specific statute that was violated and the class of the felony had it been committed by an adult.

M.C. 31-6-4-15   Predispositional reports; financial report; recommendations; examinations; disclosure

Section 15. (a) Upon finding that a child is a delinquent child or that he is a child in need of services, the juvenile court shall order a probation officer or a caseworker to prepare a predispositional report that contains a recommendation for the care, treatment, or rehabilitation of the child. Alternative reports may be prepared by the child or his parent, guardian, guardian ad litem, court appointed special advocate, or custodian for consideration by the court.

(b) In addition to providing the court with a recommendation for the care, treatment, or rehabilitation of the child, the person preparing the report shall consider the necessity, nature, and extent of the participation by a parent, guardian, or custodian in a program of care, treatment, or rehabilitation for the child.

(c) The probation officer or caseworker shall also prepare a financial report on the parent or the estate of the child to assist the juvenile court in determining that person's financial responsibility for any services provided for the child or himself.

(d) When consistent with the safety and welfare of the child and the community, the person preparing the report shall recommend care, treatment, or rehabilitation that:

(1) least interferes with family autonomy;

(2) is least disruptive of family life;

(3) imposes the least restraint on the freedom of the child and his parent, guardian, or custodian; and

(4) provides a reasonable opportunity for participation by the child's parent, guardian, or custodian.

(e) The juvenile court may authorize any examination of the child under MC 31-6-7-12, and may make provision for similar examination of the parent, guardian, or custodian if that person gives his consent.

(f) Predispositional reports shall be made available within a reasonable time before the dispositional hearing, unless the juvenile court determines on the record that they contain information that should not be released to the child or his parent, guardian, or custodian. The court shall provide a copy of the report to any attorney, guardian, ad litem, or court appointed special advocate representing the child or any attorney representing his parent, guardian, or custodian. It may also provide a factual summary of the report to the child or his parent, guardian, or custodian.

M.C. 31-6-4-15.3 Dispositional hearing; admissibility of reports; decree; findings and conclusions

Section 15.3. (a) The juvenile court shall hold a dispositional hearing to consider:

(1) alternatives for the care, treatment, or rehabilitation for the child;

(2) the necessity, nature, and extent of the participation by a parent, guardian, or custodian in the program of care, treatment, or rehabilitation for the child; and

(3) the financial responsibility of the parent or guardian of the estate for any services provided for himself or the child.

(b) Any predispositional report may be admitted into evidence to the extent that it contains evidence of probative value even if it would otherwise be excluded. If a report contains information that should not be released to the child or his parent, guardian, or custodian, a factual summary of the report may be admitted. The child, his parent, guardian, or custodian, and the person representing the interests of the state shall be given a fair opportunity to controvert any parts of the report admitted into evidence.

(c) If it appears to the juvenile court that a child is mentally ill, it may refer the matter to the court having probate jurisdiction for civil commitment proceedings under MC 16-14-9.1. If so referred, the juvenile court shall either discharge the child or continue its proceedings pending the outcome of the proceedings under MC 16-14-9.1.

(d) When consistent with the safety of the community and the welfare of the child, the juvenile court shall enter a dispositional decree that:

(1) least interferes with family autonomy;

(2) is least disruptive of family life;

(3) imposes the least restraint on the freedom of the child and his parent, guardian, or custodian; and

(4) provides a reasonable opportunity for participation by the child's parent, guardian, or custodian.

(e) The juvenile court shall send a copy of the dispositional report, which is described in subsection (g), to any person who receives placement or wardship of the child.

(f) The juvenile court shall advise the child and his parent, guardian, or custodian of the procedures under MC 31-6-7-16.

(g) The juvenile court shall accompany its dispositional decree with written findings and conclusions upon the record concerning:

(1) the needs of the child for care, treatment, or rehabilitation;

(2) the need for participation by the parent, guardian, or custodian in the plan of care for the child;

(3) efforts made, if the child is a child in need of services, to prevent the child's removal from or to reunite the child with his parent, guardian, or custodian in accordance with federal law;

(4) family services that were offered and provided to a child in need of services or his parent, guardian, or custodian in accordance with federal law; and

(5) the court's reasons for the disposition.

STATE OF MICHIANA)
) SS:
HOYNES COUNTY)

HOYNES PROBATE COURT

CAUSE NUMBER _____

IN THE MATTER OF

_____
A CHILD ALLEGED TO BE A CHILD
IN NEED OF SERVICES

PREDISPOSITIONAL REPORT IN ACCORDANCE
WITH MC 31-6-4-15

Current status of child's condition: _____
_____
_____
_____

Recommendation for care, treatment or rehabilitation of child: _____
_____
_____
_____

Necessity, nature and extent of the participation by a parent, guardian, or
custodian in a program of care, treatment or rehabilitation for the child:
_____
_____
_____

Financial responsibility of the parent or guardian of the estate for any services
provided for himself or the child. (Financial Sheet attached.)
_____
_____

Family history, including economic and living conditions, medical, psychological
history, and any other information pertinent to this case:
_____
_____
_____
_____
_____

_____
Caseworker

Dated: _____

CW Form 35

CW Form 36

STATE OF MICHIANA)
) SS:
HOYNES COUNTY   )

HOYNES PROBATE COURT

CAUSE NUMBER _____

IN RE THE MATTER OF

_____

_____   ORDER ON DISPOSITIONAL HEARING

_____

_____

A CHILD ALLEGED TO BE A CHILD
IN NEED OF SERVICES

      Comes now _____, Attorney for the County Department of Public Welfare of Hoynes County, Michiana, and shows that on the _____ day of _____, 19___, he filed his Verified Petition alleging that the above child(ren) is (are) in need of services: (H.I.)

      Present at the hearing are those listed on the docket.

      Said dispositional hearing concerning said Verified Petition is now held.

      The juvenile, parent, guardian, or custodian having entered an admission of CHINS (having been found to be a CHINS) alleged in said Verified Petition, the child(ren) is (are) now adjudicated a CHINS. The Court, after reviewing the predispositional report and having heard the evidence regarding the disposition of this matter, now finds that:

      1. The needs of the child(ren) for care, treatment, and rehabilitation are: _____
_____
_____

      2. Participation by the parent, guardian, or custodian in the plan of care for the child is necessary because: _____
_____
_____
_____

      3. The following efforts were made to (prevent the child's removal from) or (to reunite the child) with his parent, guardian, or custodian: _____
_____
_____
_____

4. The following family services were offered and provided to the child(ren) or his parent, guardian, or custodian: _____
_____
_____

5. The Court's reasons for the above described disposition are: _____
_____
_____
_____
_____
_____

6. The Court finds that efforts to prevent the child's removal from his/her/their home or to reunify the child/children with his/her/their family were/were not reasonable.

The Court now ORDERS:

1. Supervision by the County Department of Public Welfare of Hoynes County, Michiana, of the child(ren) found to be in need of services.

2. The child(ren) removed from his (her) (their) home and placed by said Department in a suitable place.

3. Said Department to obtain all medical, psychiatric and counseling services appropriate for said child(ren).

4. The appointment of a special advocate for the child(ren) is/is not appropriate.

Dated the date filed marked hereon.

_____
JUDGE, HOYNES PROBATE COURT

Rev. 7/87

CASE PLAN

State Form 2956

County Name
Case No.

1) Name of Child	2) Name of Child	3) Name of Child
Wardship Date	Wardship Date	Wardship Date

A. TERMS OF WARDSHIP ORDER

1)	Has the court ordered removal of child from his home? ☐ Yes ☐ No
2)	Has the court ordered removal of child from his home? ☐ Yes ☐ No
3)	Has the court ordered removal of child from his home? ☐ Yes ☐ No

B. PLACEMENT INFORMATION

Type (i.e., own home, foster or adoptive home, name of institution)	Date of Placement
1)	
2)	
3)	

Has any child(ren) been placed in a county or state other than that of the parents' residence? ☐ Yes ☐ No (If yes, give reason for such placement and specify children.)

If any child has been placed in an institution/group home, describe the child's special needs for such a placement. (Specify child)

C. PERMANENT PLAN

Remain in Own Home	Return to Own Home (Indicate estimated date)	Alternate Permanent Placement (Specify type and indicate estimated date)
1)		
2)		
3)		

D. ASSESSED NEEDS AND SERVICES

Identify family/child needs and problems. (Individualize when necessary. Relate child's needs to current placement.)

Identify preventive/reunification services necessary to meet family/child's needs and problems. (Include an evaluation of the appropriateness of past preventive/reunification services received by the child.)

Parents'/child's responsibilities. (Include parental visitation arrangements. Individualize when necessary.)

County Department responsibilities in relation to service delivery and in arranging parental visitation. (Include services to foster parents. Asterisk any items that are terms of a court order.)

E. TIME LIMITATION

Effective dates to	The case plan will be in effect during the dates shown at left. It should be revised when significant changes occur.

If the terms of the plan have been met, the following may occur:

If the terms of the plan have not been met, the following may occur:

F. AGREEMENT OF ALL PARTIES

We are/I am aware of the reason for wardship and/or placement of the above named child(ren) and agree to the terms set forth above. Signatures indicate agreement. (Parental signatures are not required, but are strongly recommended.)

Signature/name of parent, guardian, or custodian	Date	Signature/name of parent, guardian, or custodian	Date
Signature/name of other agreeing party	Date	Signature/title CDPW Representative	Date

Case review of above to be held on	Parents notified of case review on	Copy of case plan given to parent(s) on	Caseworker's name

CW Form 38

STATE OF MICHIANA)
) SS:
HOYNES COUNTY)

HOYNES PROBATE COURT

CAUSE NUMBER _____

IN THE MATTER OF

6 MONTH REVIEW OR 18 MONTH DISPOSITIONAL HEARING IN ACCORDANCE WITH MC 31-6-4-19(a) (b) or (c) OR WITH MC 31-6-7-16

_____
A CHILD IN NEED OF SERVICES

    Comes now the County Department of Public Welfare of Hoynes County, Michiana, and reports to the Court as follows:

1. That on the _____ day of _____, 19___, in the above-entitled cause, the Court entered a dispositional decree pursuant to MC 31-6-4-16, wherein: (include any modification and dates thereof)

2. Present placement of child and reason for said placement.

3. Present physical and psychological condition of child.

4. Case plan has been completed per PL-96-272 and offered to the parent, guardian or custodian for services to facilitate a reunion.

5. The extent to which the parent, guardian or custodian has enhanced his ability to fulfill his/her parental obligations.

6. The extent to which the parent, guardian or custodian has visited the child, including the reasons for infrequent visitation.

7. The extent to which the parent, guardian or custodian has cooperated with the county department.

8. The child's recovery from any injuries suffered before removal.

9. Additional services that may be required for the child or the parent, guardian or custodian and the exact nature and extent of said services.

10. The extent to which the child has been rehabilitated psychologically or socially.

11. The County Department of Public Welfare of Hoynes County, Michiana, recommends the following case plan and projected date for child's return home or alternate permanent plan.

County Department of Public Welfare
of Hoynes County, Michiana, by

_____   _____
Date

CW Form 40

STATE OF MICHIANA)
) SS:
HOYNES COUNTY   )

HOYNES PROBATE COURT

CAUSE NUMBER _____

IN THE MATTER OF

_____
_____
_____
_____

ORDER ON 6 MONTH REVIEW OR
18 MONTH HEARING IN ACCORD
WITH MC 31-6-4-19(a) (b) or (c)
OR WITH MC 31-6-7-16

A CHILD IN NEED OF SERVICES

      Comes now _____, Attorney for the County Department of Public Welfare of Hoynes County, Michiana and shows that on the _____ day of _____, 19___ he filed his Verified Petition alleging that the above child is a CHILD IN NEED OF SERVICES: (H.I.)

      Present at the hearing are those listed on the docket.

      The court having heard evidence in this matter: (H.I.)

now accepts the report of the County Department of Public Welfare as presented and finds that:

    1. The child's case plan attached hereto, services heretofore provided, and the child's present placement meet the special needs and best interests of the child.

    2. The County Department of Public Welfare has made reasonable efforts to provide the family with the following preplacement preventive (reunification services):

        ____24 hour emergency caretaker and/or homemaker services;
        ____day care;
        ____crisis counseling;
        ____individual and family counseling;
        ____emergency shelters;
        ____procedures and arrangements for access to available emergency financial assistance;
        ____arrangement for the provision of temporary child care to provide respite to the family for a brief period, as a part of a plan for preventing children's removal from home;
        ____home-based family services;
        ____self-help groups
        ____mental health counseling;
        ____drug and alcohol abuse counseling;
        ____focational counseling or vocational rehabilitation;
        ____post adoption services;
        ____transportation;
        ____other services which the agency identifies as necessary and appropriate.

                _____.

-2-

    3. _____ is the projected date for the child's return home, adoptive placement, or emancipation.

    4. The appointment of a guardian ad litem is (is not) necessary for the child.

    The Court now ORDERS:

1. The supervision by the County Department of Public Welfare to continue for the child previously found to be a Child in Need of Services.

2. The child to remain in his present placement; if placement is not with parent, guardian or custodian, suggested date of return _____.

3. The Department of Public Welfare shall obtain all such medical, psychiatric or counseling services as may be appropriate for the child.

4. The parent, guardian or custodian is to cooperate with additional services as listed in the most current case plan on file with the court.

    Dated the date file marked hereon.

                                                                          Judge, Hoynes Probate Court

MC-31-6-4-19

E. INDIAN CHILD WELFARE ACT

Problem 46

> **In re Blackstone**

Robert Blackstone is a member of the Cherokee tribe and resides on the Cherokee reservation in the state of Michiana. In YR-4, his girlfriend, Dawn Morning, died while giving birth to Robert's son, Hill. Overwhelmed by Dawn's death, and by becoming a father at the same time, Robert, who was also an alcoholic, voluntarily agreed to have Hill placed in foster care until Robert could get "back on his feet."

It is now YR-0 and Robert feels as though his life is back on track. He is employed and has successfully completed an alcohol rehabilitation program. Robert has decided to petition for the return of Hill from foster care. Robert filed his petition with the Cherokee Tribal Court, but the foster parents and the Hoynes County Department of Public Welfare (DPW) objected, claiming that under the Michiana law the child is not a resident or a domiciliary of the reservation. The DPW and the foster parents argue that the proper forum for the petition is the state court because that is the court through which foster placement was made. Robert argues that under federal law Hill is a domiciliary of the reservation, and the tribal court is thus the proper forum in which to bring the petition. Robert also argues that even if the child is not a domiciliary of the reservation, the state must transfer the case to the tribal court at Robert's request unless the foster parents can show "good cause" why the transfer should not take place.

> **Questions**

1. Does the Indian Child Welfare Act (ICWA) determine what law the court will use in determining whether or not the child is a domiciliary of the reservation? (*See* Appendix.)
2. Does the ICWA define "good cause" or how that standard should be applied?
3. Why is it likely that Robert would want the case to be heard in the tribal court?

F. MEDICAL TREATMENT OF CHILDREN

Problem 47

> **State v. Anderson**

On January 3, YR-0, Kimberly Anderson, age seven, went into her parents' bedroom and informed them that she was not feeling well. She said her tummy hurt. Her parents, Bob and Phyllis Anderson, sat her down on their bed and told her to pray about her sickness. Together the three prayed for Kimberly to get better. During the prayer, Kimberly cried out in pain at least four times.

On January 4, YR-0, Kimberly's parents sent her to school, advising her that although she was not feeling well, Jesus would heal her pain and take away her tummy ache very soon. When Kimberly boarded the school bus, Joan Janson, the bus driver, noted that the little girl had tears in her eyes.

During Kimberly's first hour at school on January 4, her teacher noticed something was very wrong. Kimberly continually held her stomach as if someone had just punched her. Afraid that Kimberly might have been the victim of child abuse, the teacher sent Kimberly from class to see the school social worker.

The social worker immediately recognized that Kimberly's problem was sickness, not physical abuse. She walked Kimberly to the school nurse's office. When the school nurse talked with Kimberly about her problem, Kimberly responded, "I'll be okay. Mommy and Daddy told me Jesus would make me feel better if I prayed hard enough." Not appreciating Kimberly's answer, the nurse asked further questions and ascertained that Kimberly was having serious abdominal pain, possibly arising from acute appendicitis. The school nurse called 911.

By the time the ambulance arrived, Kimberly was doubled over in pain and screaming constantly. The ambulance crew sedated her and placed her on an intravenous saline solution. They drove her to the Southby Mercy Hospital emergency room, where Kimberly was admitted in critical condition. Southby Mercy is a state-run hospital.

Meanwhile, the school nurse contacted both of Kimberly's parents and informed them that Kimberly had been taken to the hospital for appendicitis. Both Bob and Phyllis were outraged that they had not been consulted first. The school nurse expressed her anger in return that the parents had let their child's condition worsen while telling her prayer would cure her.

Bob and Phyllis arrived at the hospital at 11:00 A.M., just as Kimberly's condition was beginning to stabilize enough for her to undergo emergency surgery. The parents demanded to see the treating physician. When Dr. Mary Tudor came to speak with them, they informed her that they are Christian Scientists and that they do not believe in earthly medicine as a proper method of treating their child's illness. Dr. Tudor, a born-again Christian herself, said she empathized with their religious beliefs, but in this case there was no question but that Kimberly would die without proper medical treatment, that this treatment was relatively routine, and that they had nothing to fear from her taking care of Kimberly. In fact, Dr. Tudor said, "Your daughter is in the hands of some good Christian people. You have nothing to worry about."

The Andersons adamantly refused to allow Dr. Tudor to treat Kimberly and demanded that she return Kimberly to their care so that they could take her home. Dr. Tudor refused to release Kimberly as her patient. Bob then shoved Dr. Tudor out of his way and ran to Kimberly's hospital bed. Before he could remove the needles in her arms, an orderly grabbed and subdued him. Hospital security escorted the Andersons from the premises.

Michiana has a statute dating back to 1924 that makes it a felony for any doctor to perform surgery on any patient (who could consent) without that patient's consent. Longstanding case law under this statute requires parental consent for operations on children. Fearing the loss of her medical license and the possibility of jail, Dr. Tudor does not want to go forward with the surgery until she has the legal clearance to do so.

Assume that Bob and Phyllis Anderson will not budge on their consent to surgery. You represent Southby Mercy Hospital. It's 8:51 A.M. on January 5,

YR-0. Dr. Tudor has informed you that she must perform the surgery by noon or Kimberly's appendix will likely burst, causing peritonitis and maybe causing the child's death. Dr. Bryan Benson, brought in for a second opinion, tells you that although Dr. Tudor's analysis might be somewhat exaggerated, Kimberly's life probably is in some danger, but her appendicitis does not pose an immediate danger to her life. You have already scheduled a hearing on your emergency motion in front of the Hoynes Circuit Court. For this Problem, you should thus allow yourself only two hours of work.

Questions

1. What kind of motion should you file with the court? Who should be the named parties? Quickly draft the appropriate motion (remembering that you have less that two hours before the court will hear your motion), including a brief memorandum citing relevant California (or the state of your choice) case law on the issues presented.
2. What significance should the Andersons' religious convictions have on the court's determination?
3. Should a special advocate for the child's best interests be appointed? Should an attorney be appointed to represent Kimberly?
4. Assume that Bob and Phyllis have never done anything else to cause any danger to Kimberly and that they are model members of the community. How do you argue that they are not acting in Kimberly's best interests? How should the parents argue? How can you respond legally to the parents' freedom of their religious convictions without arguing the merits of those convictions?
5. Assume the court refuses to let Dr. Tudor operate on Kimberly, and that as a result Kimberly dies at Mercy Hospital at 3:15 P.M. on January 5. What legal actions, if any, might be brought against the Andersons? Does their freedom of religion stand in the way of any prosecution?
6. How should a legislature deal with the question of religious freedom when drafting statutes providing emergency medical care for children?
7. Should the statute requiring consent before surgery be allowed to bar Dr. Tudor from caring for Kimberly? Should Dr. Tudor have to risk jail to care for her patient? What public policy stands behind the consent statute? How would that policy best be applied in Kimberly's case?

G. TERMINATION OF PARENTAL RIGHTS

Problem 48

In re Termination of the Parent-Child Relationship Between Leonard R. Bowman and Bonnie and Clyde Bowman

For this Problem, assume that on the eighth day of July, YR-0, the Hoynes Probate Court, based on the record contained in Problem 45, found Leonard R. Bowman to be a child in need of services (CHINS). At the dispositional hearing, the court ordered that Leonard be placed in a foster home for six months, subject to monitoring by the Department of Public Welfare (DPW) and review by the court as necessary. On August 12, YR-0, the court conducted a review hearing and determined that Leonard should be returned to the custody of his parents, Bonnie and Clyde Bowman, the home placement to be monitored by the DPW and subject to periodic review by the court.

On September 15, YR-0, Bonnie and Clyde left Leonard with their neighbor, Maxine Walker, and drove to Florida, where Clyde hoped to find a better job. On September 16, Maxine became concerned about Leonard's health and took him to see Dr. Nolan Hibner. Dr. Hibner diagnosed Leonard as suffering from malnutrition and pneumonia, treated him for head lice, and ordered that Leonard be hospitalized. In his report, Dr. Hibner made the following statement: "The combination of severe malnutrition and pneumonia constitute a life-threatening situation for the child." Following Dr. Hibner's report to the DPW, a DPW caseworker went to the hospital and formally detained Leonard (leaving him in the hospital). Following a detention hearing on September 19, YR-0, the court ordered that Leonard be detained pending further proceedings and that upon release from the hospital, Leonard be placed in foster family home care. The court also designated a court-appointed special advocate (CASA) to represent Leonard's best interests.

Bonnie and Clyde returned from Florida on October 10 and learned that Leonard had been hospitalized and had been placed in foster care on October 3. Bonnie will testify that she called Maxine Walker's residence without success on September 19 and 25. As part of the disposition in the CHINS proceedings, Bonnie and Clyde had agreed to attend counseling and parent-training classes. Clyde failed to attend any of the sessions, and Bonnie attended only the first two parent-training meetings. In a letter to the DPW of July 12, YR-0, Bonnie stated, "We have done nothing wrong. We are good parents and we want Leonard back home with us. You official people have ruined our family." Bonnie's brother, Austin, who was convicted and imprisoned for battery for his assault on Leonard, will be released on parole in thirty days. He intends to return to Southby and work with Clyde in their auto body shop business.

The DPW will file a petition for involuntary termination of the parent-child relationship between Bonnie and Clyde and Leonard. The applicable Michiana termination of parental rights statutes follow this problem. The student should also refer to the exhibits that follow Problem 45. Assume further that the DPW has identified prospective adoptive parents for Leonard R. Bowman.

Questions

1. What does termination of parental rights mean? What legal effect would termination have on Bonnie and Clyde and Leonard?
2. How are Leonard's best interests served by a termination order?
3. What is the nature of due process at termination proceedings?
4. Does the DPW continue to have an obligation to reunify the family after the termination petition is filed?
5. What effect should the parents' refusal to complete counseling and parenting classes have on this case?
6. Suppose the reason for Leonard's medical neglect is that Bonnie and Clyde are both mildly mentally retarded (both have I.Q.s in the 70s). Both Bonnie and Clyde show willingness to learn how to care for Leonard, but the services arranged by DPW are moving so slowly that the DPW caseworker has concluded that they will not learn adequate

parenting skills before Leonard turns eighteen. The DPW caseworker further concludes that, despite their best intentions, Bonnie and Clyde will pose a continual danger to Leonard until they develop the necessary parenting skills. Should DPW recommend termination (or should the court order termination) merely because services for the parents will take many years, with no reasonable likelihood of success?

7. At the termination trial, may the court take judicial notice of court records from the CHINS proceedings?

M.C. 31-6-5-4 Petition for termination of rights; delinquent child or child in need of services

Section 4. (a) A verified petition to terminate the parent-child relationship involving a delinquent child or a child in need of services may be signed and filed with the juvenile or probate court by:

(1) the attorney for the county department;
(2) the prosecutor;
(3) the child's court appointed special advocate; or
(4) the child's guardian ad litem.

(b) Upon the filing of a petition under this section, the attorney for the county department or the prosecutor shall represent the interests of the state in all subsequent proceedings on the petition. The probate court has concurrent original jurisdiction with the juvenile court in proceedings on the petition.

(c) The petition shall be entitled "In the Matter of the Termination of the Parent-Child Relationship of _____, a child, and _____, the child's parent (or parents)" and must allege that:

(1) the child has been removed from the parent for at least six (6) months under a dispositional decree;
(2) there is a reasonable probability that:
   (A) the conditions that resulted in the child's removal will not be remedied; or
   (B) the continuance of the parent-child relationship poses a threat to the well-being of the child;
(3) termination is in the best interests of the child; and
(4) there is a satisfactory plan for the care and treatment of the child.

M.C. 31-6-5-5 Disposition upon termination of parental rights

Section 5. When the juvenile or probate court terminates the parent-child relationship, it may:

(1) refer the matter to the court having probate jurisdiction for adoption proceedings; or
(2) order any dispositional alternative specified by MC 31-6-4-15.4.

M.C. 31-6-5-6 Rights, privileges and obligations of parent and child upon termination of relationship

Section 6. (a) When the juvenile or probate court terminates the parent-child relationship, all rights, powers, privileges, immunities, duties, and obligations (including any rights to custody, control, visitation, or support) pertaining to that relationship are permanently terminated, and the parent's consent to the child's adoption is not required.

(b) Any support obligations that accrued before the termination are not affected except that the support payments shall be made under the juvenile or probate court's order.

Chapter Nine

Dissolution of Marriage

A. SUBJECT MATTER JURISDICTION

Problem 49

Fisher v. Fisher

Stanley and Michelle Fisher were married in Southby, Michiana, in June of YR-18, following Michelle's freshman year and Stanley's graduation from Michiana University. In September of YR-18, the couple moved to Cambridge, Massachusetts, where Stanley began medical school at Harvard University. Michelle obtained a baccalaureate degree from Boston University, and Stanley graduated from medical school in June of YR-14. Following two years of residency in cardiovascular surgery at Boston General Hospital, Stanley and Michelle moved to Pittsburgh, Pennsylvania, in August of YR-12, where Stanley was employed at the world-famous Kruger Clinic. Stanley served on a team of heart surgeons headed by Dr. Seymour Bunton, inventor of the Bunton VIII artificial heart. A daughter, Desiree, was born on January 7, YR-11, followed by two sons, Jeremy, born on June 30, YR-8, and Joshua, born on November 21, YR-5. During the period of YR-12 to YR-3, Michelle assumed the homemaking duties and was not employed outside the home.

In YR-2, Michelle enrolled as a part-time student at the University of Pittsburgh School of Law. Michelle and Stanley hired a nanny to take care of the children and a housekeeper to clean the house and prepare meals. A great deal of tension developed between Michelle and Stanley over Michelle's desire to pursue law study and not confine her energies to being a homemaker. Stanley began drinking at home, which he had never done before, and physically assaulted Michelle on several occasions.

In January of YR-1, Michelle left Stanley and the children in Pittsburgh and moved to Harwood, Michiana, where she enrolled in law school at Michiana University, paying out-of-state tuition for the YR-1 spring term. In May of YR-1, Michelle canceled her apartment lease in Harwood, and left a forwarding address of her parents' home at 1170 Winding Way, Shaker Heights, Michiana 31710. In early June of YR-1, Michelle moved to New York City to stay with Stanley, who was directing a series of seminars for the Metropolitan Institute of Health during mid-June and July of YR-1. The children remained at home in Pittsburgh in the care of their nanny, Mrs. Morris.

Michelle and Stanley returned to Pittsburgh at the end of July, YR-1, where Stanley continued to physically and verbally abuse Michelle. Michelle told Stanley that she wanted a divorce, and in late August of YR-1, she moved back to Harwood, Michiana. Michelle attended law school at Michiana University from August to December of YR-1.

Michelle states that her intention in August of YR-1 was to become a Michiana resident, because she knew that the marriage was over and her only reason for returning to Pennsylvania was to get the children and return to Michiana. Michelle admits, however, that from September through December of YR-1 she made frequent weekend trips from Harwood to Pittsburgh at Stanley's request. Michelle told Stanley several times that she was going to stay in Michiana. Stanley agreed that it was "probably best" for the children to return to Michiana with Michelle. After a loud and heated argument at Thanksgiving dinner, during which Stanley physically struck Michelle in the presence of the children, Michelle screamed, "This marriage is over, God damn you! Over! Over! Over!"

In late November, YR-1, Michelle filled out an application to Southby State University School of Law for the YR-0 spring term and asked her parents to contact a realtor concerning houses available for occupancy in January of YR-0. In December of YR-1, Stanley leased a condominium in Pittsburgh and suggested that Michelle stay there with the children until they "patch things up." On December 20, YR-1, Michelle vacated her apartment in Harwood, again leaving her forwarding address as 1170 Winding Way, Shaker Heights, Michiana 31710.

Michelle returned to Pittsburgh on December 21. Stanley said to Michelle, "Honey, please stay with us in Pittsburgh. We are a family. Desiree, Jeremy, and Joshua need their mother here, and I need their mother here too. I've thought it over and maybe it's a good idea for you to finish law school. I've talked to Dean Lawless at the University of Pittsburgh and he says you're welcome to return for the spring term." Stanley handed Michelle a signed check made out to the University of Pittsburgh with the notation "YR-0 spring term law tuition" and said, "How 'bout it, Michelle?" Michelle replied, "One more try, Stanley." Michelle told Stanley that she had registered for classes at Pittsburgh Law School. She attended law school classes on January 5 and filled out an application for the oldest child, Desiree, to attend a prestigious private school in Pittsburgh for the Spring YR-0 term. On January 5, Michelle also stated to her close friend, Beatrice, "It's good to be back in Pittsburgh where we belong." On January 9, YR-0, Stanley lost his temper during dinner and physically assaulted Michelle and Desiree, who had tried to intervene. On the morning of January 10, YR-0, Michelle telephoned Southby State Law School and was told that she had been admitted for the YR-0 spring term. Michelle and the children packed their suitcases, took a taxi to the airport and caught a flight to Southby, where they were met by Michelle's parents. On January 12, YR-0, Michelle sent the uncashed tuition check to Stanley with a note stating, "Here's your check back. Did you really believe I was serious about staying in Pittsburgh? I was merely buying time until I heard from Southby State Law School. I start classes tomorrow. I'll see you in court in Southby." Michelle rented a house in Southby on January 13, YR-0.

Michelle consults an attorney in order to initiate divorce proceedings in Michiana. Michelle files her complaint for divorce, along with petitions for temporary custody and support, temporary alimony, a temporary restraining order without notice, and attorney fees in the Hoynes Circuit Court on March 7, YR-0. Stanley retains local counsel in Southby and files a motion for summary disposition pursuant to the following Michiana statute:

Chapter Nine. Dissolution of Marriage

101.1 Divorce, residence of parties

Section 1. A judgment of divorce shall not be granted by a court in this state in an action for divorce unless the complainant or defendant has resided in this state for 180 days immediately preceding the filing of the complaint and the complainant or defendant has resided in the county in which the complaint is filed for 10 days immediately preceding the filing of the complaint.

Plaintiff's and defendant's exhibits follow this Problem.

Questions

1. What are the policy reasons behind durational residency requirements to establish subject matter jurisdiction in divorce proceedings? Why should the court be concerned about jurisdiction in this case?
2. What are the different legal meanings for the terms "residence," "resident," and "domicile"?
3. In which state was Michelle domiciled on the following dates: January 30, YR-1; July 1, YR-1; September 1, YR-1; December 22, YR-1; January 10, YR-0; January 14, YR-0; March 7, YR-0?
4. What is the appropriate state in which to bring this divorce proceeding on March 7, YR-0?
5. How should the court rule on Stanley's motion?
6. What if the following additional facts were added to the *Fisher* case:
   a. While attending law school at Michiana University, Michelle wrote checks on her Pittsburgh checking account.
   b. Michelle was registered to vote in Pennsylvania and in fact did vote in Pennsylvania in November of YR-1.
   c. Michelle continues to rent a safety deposit box at a Pittsburgh bank.
7. Are the parties' exhibits admissible in evidence?
8. Suppose the Michiana court dismisses Michelle's complaint for lack of subject matter jurisdiction. Must Michelle wait to file for divorce? Does dismissal of the complaint violate Michelle's constitutional rights?
9. What are the differences among durational residency requirements for the following: qualification for public assistance benefits (welfare payments) (*see Shapiro v. Thompson*, 394 U.S. 618 (1969)); voting (*see Dunn v. Blumstein*, 405 U.S. 330 (1972)); medical care (*see Memorial Hospital v. Maricopa County*, 415 U.S. 250 (1974)); and divorce (*see Sosna v. Iowa*, 419 U.S. 393 (1975))?
10. Does the Michiana durational residency statute unconstitutionally deny Michelle access to court in Michiana?

STATE OF MICHIANA   )   IN THE HOYNES CIRCUIT COURT
) SS:
COUNTY OF HOYNES   )   YR-0 CALENDAR TERM

MICHELLE FISHER,   )
       Plaintiff,   )   CAUSE NO. _____
   vs.   )
STANLEY FISHER,   )
       Defendant.)

AFFIDAVIT

STANLEY FISHER, being first duly sworn before me a Notary Public, deposes and says as follows:

1. That he is the Defendant in the above entitled cause pending in the Circuit Court for the County of Hoynes and State of Michiana.

2. That this Affidavit is given in support of Defendant's Motion filed herewith.

3. That Affiant states that the Plaintiff has not resided in the State of Michiana for 180 days prior to March 7, YR-0, being the date of filing of her Complaint.

4. That the Exhibits attached to Defendant's motion are true and accurate copies of said supporting documents.

Further, affiant saith not.

                                                    _____
                                                         Stanley Fisher

Subscribed and sworn to before me this 20th day of April, YR-0.

_____
Notary Public
Hoynes County, Michiana

My Commission Expires: December 10, YR-0

STATE OF MICHIANA	)	IN THE HOYNES CIRCUIT COURT
	) SS:	
COUNTY OF HOYNES	)	YR-0 CALENDAR TERM
MICHELLE FISHER,	)	
Plaintiff,	)	CAUSE NO. _____
vs.	)	
STANLEY FISHER,	)	MOTION FOR SUMMARY DISPOSITION
Defendant.	)	

NOW COMES the above-named Defendant, STANLEY FISHER, by his Attorney and by way of Motion for Summary Disposition, pursuant to Michiana D.C. 101.1, and says as follows:

1. That the Plaintiff in this matter filed a Summons and Complaint in the Hoynes County Circuit Court on March 7, YR-0.

2. That Court II of said Complaint specifically states that the Plaintiff has resided in the County of Hoynes for more than 10 days and in the State of Michiana for a period in excess of 180 days immediately preceding the filing of this Complaint.

3. The Defendant states that for the purposes of this Motion that the Plaintiff has not resided within the State of Michiana for at least 180 days prior to filing her Complaint for divorce as required under Michiana D.C. 101.1

   A. Exhibit 1, being correspondence received from the Department of Health and Human Services, dated December 14, YR-1, to your Plaintiff regarding possible employment, which specifically states Plaintiff's address as being 52790 Tiffany Trace, Pittsburgh, Pennsylvania;
   B. Exhibit 2, being a letter to Quincy Elementary School, signed by Plaintiff, postmarked Harwood, Michiana, and dated December 10, YR-1, which requests an application form, and indicates that your Plaintiff's residence is 52790 Tiffany Trace, Pittsburgh, Pennsylvania;
   C. Exhibit 3, being "Basic Enrollment Information," dated January 5, YR-0, which had been completed by your Plaintiff, and which indicates that your Plaintiff's residence is 52790 Tiffany Trace, Pittsburgh, Pennsylvania, and that Plaintiff is enrolled at the University of Pittsburgh Law School in Pittsburgh, Pennsylvania.

4. That Plaintiff did not have an abode, property ownership or other contacts with the State of Michiana for at least 180 days prior to the commencement of this action which could be considered in making the determination as to Plaintiff's residency.

WHEREFORE, Defendant prays that the Complaint for Divorce, Summons, Interim Order of Support, Temporary Restraining Order Without Notice, Ex-Parte Order Regarding Disposition of Marital Assets and Ex-Parte Custody Order be dismissed together with all pending Petitions for the reason that Plaintiff does not satisfy the residency requirement as set forth in Michiana D.C. 101.1.

_____
Stanley Fisher

_____
Attorney for Defendant

STATE OF MICHIANA)
) SS:
COUNTY OF HOYNES   )

On this _____ day of _____, YR-0, before me personally came the above-named Defendant, and made oath that he has read the foregoing Motion by him subscribed, that he knows the contents thereof and that the same is true of his own knowledge excepting as to those matters alleged to be upon his information and belief and as to those matters he believes the same to be true.

                                                      _____
                                                            Notary Public
                                                      Hoynes County, Michiana

My Commission Expires:
    ___September 15, YR+2___

DEPARTMENT OF HEALTH & HUMAN SERVICES

Office of the General Counsel
Pittsburgh, PA 21405

December 14, YR-1

Ms. Michelle Fisher
52790 Tiffany Trace
Pittsburgh, Pennsylvania 21410

Dear Ms. Fisher:

Thank you for your recent letter regarding possible employment with the Public Health Division of the Office of the General Counsel. At the present time there are no vacancies in this Division, but I am sending your letter and resume to the Office of the General Counsel's central personnel office in Washington, D.C. for their retention and use in the event there are any openings in other OGC divisions.

Sincerely yours,

Lawson J. Clarke
Assistant General Counsel
   for the Public Health

DEFENDANT'S EXHIBIT 1

52790 Tiffany Trace
Pittsburgh, Pennsylvania 21410

December 10, YR-1

Quincy Elementary School
8810 Donowald Avenue
Pittsburgh, Pennsylvania 21405

TO WHOM IT MAY CONCERN:

My husband, Dr. Stanley Fisher, and I are interested in having our oldest child, Desiree, age 10, transfer to Quincy Elementary School.

This letter is to request application documents for Desiree to attend Quincy beginning the Spring term YR-0.

I look forward to hearing from you at your earliest convenience.

Sincerely,

Michelle Fisher

DEFENDANT'S EXHIBIT 2

QUINCY ELEMENTARY SCHOOL
8810 Donowald Avenue
Pittsburgh, Pennsylvania 21405

BASIC ENROLLMENT INFORMATION

INFORMATION ABOUT PUPIL   Date 1-5-YR-0

Legal Name: __Fisher__   __Desiree__   __M.__   __Desi__
                Last   First   Middle   Nickname

Address: __52790 Tiffany Trace__
          __Pittsburgh, PA__   __21410__   Phone No. __216-936-2197__
                                       Zip

Date of Birth: __1-7-YR-11__ Evidence of Birth _____ Birthplace __Pittsburgh__

Sex: __F__ Citizenship Status __U.S.__ Primary Language __English__

RACE/ETHNIC GROUP

_____ AMERICAN INDIAN OR ALASKAN NATIVE - A person having origins in any of the original peoples of North America, and who maintains cultural identification through tribal affiliation or community recognition.

_____ Asian/Pacific Islander - A person having origins in any of the original peoples of the Far East, Southeast Asia, the Indian sub-continent, or the Pacific Islands. This area includes for example, China, India, Japan, Korea, the Philippine Islands and Samoa.

_____ BLACK (NOT OF HISPANIC ORIGIN) - A person having origins in any of the Black racial groups of Africa.

__X__ WHITE (NOT OF HISPANIC ORIGIN) - A person having origins in any of the original peoples of Europe, North Africa or the Middle East.

_____ HISPANIC - A person of Mexican, Puerto Rican, Cuban, Central or South American or other Spanish culture or origin, regardless of race.

Tuition Status: Mellon County Resident ___X___ Non-Resident _____

Brothers and Sisters:

Name	Birthdate	Residence at Birth	Age
Jeremy Fisher	6-30-YR-8	Pittsburgh, PA	7
Joshua Fisher	11-21-YR-5	Pittsburgh, PA	4

DEFENDANT'S EXHIBIT 3

BASIC ENROLLMENT INFORMATION

INFORMATION ABOUT MALE HEAD OF HOUSEHOLD:

Name: __Fisher__ __Stanley__ __J.__ __father__
           Last   First   Middle   Relationship to Child

Citizenship: __U.S.__ Years of Education: __M.D.__ Primary Lang.: __English__

Employer's Name: __Kruger Clinic__ Address: __101 Burgess Avenue__

Telephone No. __214-933-8905__ Job Title: __physician-surgeon__

Name and address of father if other than head of household: _____

INFORMATION ABOUT FEMALE HEAD OF HOUSEHOLD:

Name: __Fisher__ __Michelle__ __M.__ __mother__
           Last   First   Middle   Relationship to Child

Citizenship: __U.S.__ Years of Education: __B.A.__ Primary Lang.: __English__

Employer's Name: _____ Address: _____

Telephone No. _____ Job Title: _____

Name and address of mother if other than head of household: _____

Emergency Person: __Mrs. Grace Tillman__ __103 Everest, Pittsburgh, PA 21415__ __214-932-9687__
                          Name   Address   Tel. No.

Person Responsible for
Child After School: __Michelle Fisher__ __52790 Tiffany Trace, Pittsburgh, PA 21410__ __214-936-2197__
                      Name   Address   Tel. No.

Physician: __Nolan Cantwell__ __214-933-6659__
              Name   Tel. No.

Dentist: __R. Everett Sheer__ __214-933-4214__
          Name   Tel. No.

Hospital Preference: __St. Joseph__

Wishing You A Joyful Thanksgiving

11-23-YR-1

Dear Michelle,

So good to speak over the telephone with you yesterday. This morning, I spoke with the realtor, Mr. Peacock, and he says that he has a few nice rental properties which will be available in early January. Your father and I love you and look forward to having you and the grandchildren back in Southby Poon. We know that your decision to leave Stanley was not easy, but had to be done. Look forward to hearing from you.

Wishing you
all those special joys
that make
your Thanksgiving
just right!

Love,
Mother & Father

PLAINTIFF'S EXHIBIT A

APPLICATION FOR ADMISSION TO THE SOUTHBY STATE LAW SCHOOL

Please read the instructions on the previous pages before completing this application.

1. Last name (print or type)   First   Middle
   Fisher   Michelle   M.
2. Social Security number
   317-44-5550
3. Date of birth
   11-21-YR-37
4. City, state and country of birth
   Southby, Michiana   USA
5. Sex
   F
6. Marital Status
   Married
7. Present mailing address
   315 S. Hawthorne
   Harwood, Michiana   34101
                                      zip code
8. Present telephone and area code
   212-239-7324
9. Permanent mailing address
   1170 Winding Way
   Shaker Heights, Michiana 31710
                                      zip code
10. Permanent telephone and area code
11. After what date should permanent address be used?
    December 10, YR-1
12. To whom should statement of your tuition, fees, etc., be sent? (give name and address)
    Michelle Fisher
    1170 Winding Way
    Shaker Heights, Michiana 31710
                                       zip code
13. State your citizenship and, if you wish, your predominant ethnic background.
    U.S. citizen
14. When do you wish to enter law school? (August of what year?) January, YR-0
    Have you previously applied to C.S.U. Law School? If yes, when? no
15. Are you applying as a transfer student? yes

    If so, see requirements in this bulletin and indicate each law school and dates of attendance.

16. LSDAS Registration No. P3837
17. Have you taken or are you scheduled to take the LSAT? If so, list dates and scores received. If not, when do you plan to take it? 2-10-YR-2
    score of 42
18. Do you plan to repeat the LSAT? If so, when?
    Date: no
19. List below (in order of attendance) all colleges, universities and professional schools which you have attended.
    a. Name of institution
       Michiana University
       Major   Minor
       Freshman Studies
       Dates of attendance   Class rank
       8-YR-19 to 6-YR-18
       Degree and date awarded

    b. Name of institution
       Boston University
       Major   Minor
       Psychology
       Dates of attendance   Class rank
       8-YR-18 to 6-YR-14
       Degree and date awarded
       B.A. Arts and Letters

    c. Name of institution
       University of Pittsburgh
       Major   Minor
       Law
       Dates of attendance   Class rank
       1-YR-2 to 12-YR-2
       Degree and date awarded

    d. Name of institution
       Michiana University
       Major   Minor
       Law
       Dates of attendance   Class rank
       1-YR-1 to 12-YR-1
       Degree and date awarded

PLAINTIFF'S EXHIBIT B

20. List scholastic, honorary or professional societies of which you are or were a member.

    Phi Eta Sigma freshman honorary
    at
    6-YR-18

21. List any significant academic accomplishments not reflected in the LSDAS report or otherwise included on this form.

22. List any volunteer social service work in which you are or have been involved, and the amount of time devoted to it.

23. List other extracurricular activities.

    Pittsburgh Opera Guild

24. Were you employed during school terms while attending any college or university? If so, what was the nature of your employment and approximately how much time did you devote to it per week?

25. If you are not now attending an educational institution, describe the positions which you have held since your last attendance, indicating the length of your employment in each position.

26. Have you ever served in the armed forces of the United States? If so, indicate branch and dates of service.

    No

27. If the answer to any of the following questions is "yes" you must submit with this application a full explanation of circumstances for each question so answered.

    a. Were you ever requested to withdraw from any school, college or university?

       No

    b. Have you ever been suspended, dismissed, expelled or placed on probation for scholastic, disciplinary or other reasons by any school, college or university?

    c. Were you discharged or dismissed from the armed forces with other than an honorable discharge?

28. Have you ever been convicted of a crime? If so, describe the circumstances.

    No

29. Two letters of recommendation are required. These should be from persons who know you well enough to comment substantively as to your scholastic ability, your extracurricular activities, your character in the community and your work experiences. No specific form is required. List the names of people submitting your recommendations.

    1. _____

    2. _____

    Note: You may, if you wish, include your recommendations in sealed envelopes with your application.

30. A personal statement is required. Please append to application.

31. In order for the Law School to receive your LSDAS report, it will be necessary for you to include your Law School Matching Form with this application. Please check to be sure you have affixed your registration number to the form.

32. Application Checklist:

    _____ $35 Application Fee
    _____ LSDAS Matching Form (for current year)
    _____ Personal Statement
    _____ Recommendations enclosed
    _____ Recommendations will be sent separately

33. I hereby certify that the information I have provided on this application form and in any attached materials is true and complete.

    _____
    Signature

    Date   November 21, YR-1

B. PERSONAL JURISDICTION

Problem 50

Fisher v. Fisher

Please review the facts of Problem 49. In addition to those facts, assume that Michelle is approximately six months pregnant at this time. Michelle and Stanley agree that conception of the unborn child occurred during Stanley's October 2-3, YR-1, weekend stay at Michelle's apartment in Harwood, Michiana.

Assume that Stanley files a special appearance in Hoynes Circuit Court, and in addition to the motion filed in Problem 49, Stanley files a motion to dismiss Michelle's petition for temporary custody and support, temporary alimony, a temporary restraining order without notice and attorney fees, based on the Michiana court's lack of in personam jurisdiction, under *International Shoe Co. v. Washington*, 326 U.S. 310 (1945).

Questions

1. What is in personam jurisdiction?
2. What would be the impact on Stanley's in personam jurisdiction defense if his lawyer had filed a general appearance in this case? See *Kulko v. Superior Court of California*, 436 U.S. 84 (1978).
3. What effect does the fetus's conception in Michiana have on the court's personal jurisdiction over Stanley? What if the baby had been conceived while Stanley and Michelle were on vacation in Michiana?

C. DEATH AND LOSS OF JURISDICTION

Problem 51

In re Marriage of Crosby

Pentacost (Pen) and Fara Crosby were married in Southby, Michiana, in YR-5. In November of YR-2, Pen filed a petition for dissolution of marriage with the Hoynes County Circuit Court in Southby. The final hearing was concluded on August 10, YR-1, and the court took the matter under advisement. On September 12, YR-1, Pen died of a massive heart attack. Fara immediately filed a motion to dismiss the divorce proceedings, claiming that Pen's death dissolved the marriage before the court entered a decree of dissolution. In response, Pen's attorney filed an objection to the motion to dismiss, claiming that Pen's estate is entitled to a nunc pro tunc decree of dissolution because the divorce had taken place but for the entering of the final decree by the court.

Chapter Nine. Dissolution of Marriage

Questions

1. What would Fara's motivation be for wanting the divorce proceedings dismissed?
2. In many jurisidictions, the general rule is that the trial court loses jurisdiction of a divorce when one of the parties dies unless certain narrow exceptions exist. What is the policy behind this rule?
3. Is the policy behind the general rule served in this case? Is the result fair if the general rule applies?
4. Consider the impact that not allowing the divorce might have on Pen's other heirs. Would it still be fair if Pen had not yet changed his will, which left everything to Fara, and Pen had three small children from a previous marriage?

D. GROUNDS AND DEFENSES: THE FADING OF FAULT

1. Fault Divorce

Problem 52

Kilmer v. Kilmer

Marna Kilmer, age thirty-four, and Conrad Kilmer, age forty-two, were married on May 21, YR-9. Conrad is employed as a clerk in the men's department of Bastin's, a large department store in Southby, Michiana. Marna is an English teacher at Johnson Middle School in Southby. Marna and Conrad have no children. They have occasionally engaged in sexual intercourse during the marriage, but Conrad has told Marna several times that he does not want children. In early March of YR-1, Marna arrived home and saw Conrad on the front porch kissing his friend, Clint, who works in the kitchenware department of Bastin's. Marna confronted Conrad and said, "What you do away from home is your business, but I'm still your wife inside this house." The next day, Marna confided in her best friend, Jewel, who said to her, "Marna, honey, I can't believe it has taken so long for you to find out that Conrad is gay. I was shocked when I saw Con holding hands and kissing Clint outside the Tea Leaf Restaurant downtown last year." Marna has attended weekly therapy sessions with Dr. Wilhelm, a psychiatrist, since March 28, YR-1. Conrad states that he is not homosexual or bisexual and that Marna has approved of his close friendship with Clint since she met him in YR-3. Conrad does not want a divorce.

Marna consults you and states that she wants a divorce. The applicable Michiana law is contained in the statutes that follow this Problem.

Questions

1. What are the fault grounds for divorce in this case?
2. What defense(s) may Conrad plead?

3. Assume Marna has filed a petition for divorce on the grounds of Conrad's infidelity and mental cruelty and that Conrad has cross-petitioned for no-fault dissolution. If grounds exist for Conrad's petition, can the court consider Marna's grounds for divorce? Should it? Why or why not?

MICHIANA CODE

Section 3.01. Insupportability

On the petition of either party to a marriage, a divorce may be decreed without regard to fault if the marriage has become insupportable because of discord or conflict of personalities that destroys the legitimate ends of the marriage relationship and prevents any reasonable expectation of reconciliation.

Section 3.02. Cruelty

A divorce may be decreed in favor of one spouse if the other spouse is guilty of cruel treatment toward the complaining spouse of a nature that renders further living together insupportable.

Section 3.03. Adultery

A divorce may be decreed in favor of one spouse if the other spouse has committed adultery.

Section 3.04. Conviction of Felony

(a) A divorce may be decreed in favor of one spouse if since the marriage the other spouse:

(1) has been convicted of a felony; and
(2) has been imprisoned for at least one year in the state penitentiary, a federal penitentiary, or the penitentiary of another state; and
(3) has not been pardoned.

(b) A divorce may not be decreed under this section against a spouse who was convicted on the testimony of the other spouse.

Section 3.05. Abandonment

A divorce may be decreed in favor of one spouse if the other spouse left the complaining spouse with the intention of abandonment and remained away for at least one year.

Section 3.06. Living Apart

A divorce may be decreed in favor of either spouse if the spouses have lived apart without cohabitation for at least three years.

Section 3.07. Confinement in Mental Hospital

A divorce may be decreed in favor of one spouse if at the time the suit is filed:

(1) the other spouse has been confined in a mental hospital, a state mental hospital, or private mental hospital, as defined in Section 571.002,

Health and Safety Code, in this state or another state for at least three years; and

(2) it appears that the spouse's mental disorder is of such a degree and nature that he is not likely to adjust, or that if he adjusts it is probable that he will suffer a relapse.

2. No-Fault Divorce

Problem 53

In re Marriage of Barton

Alan and Jeanette Barton were married on June 15, YR-4, one week following their graduation from Southby Central High School. Alan works as an optical supplies salesman, earning $40,000 a year, and Jeanette is employed as a receptionist and typist with a Southby law firm, earning $20,000 a year. From the outset of their marriage, in addition to her full-time job, Jeanette assumed responsibility for preparing meals, cleaning house, shopping, and paying the bills. On most days, Alan came home from work, watched the evening news, and drank a few beers before dinner. Jeanette states that during nearly four years of marriage, Alan never once offered to help her wash or dry the dishes. Alan does, however, take out the trash each Sunday evening for Monday morning pickup. The law firm recently rewarded Jeanette's job performance with a salary increase and paid for her to take a night course at Southby Business College twice a week on the use of word processing equipment. Alan wants Jeanette to stay home each evening and has suggested that she drop the night course.

Jeanette consults an attorney and states that she's tired of being a "house slave" and wants a divorce. There are no children born of the marriage, and Jeanette is not pregnant. Alan and Jeanette own certain real and personal property. Alan states that the marriage can be salvaged and that he does not want a divorce, but he refuses to attend marriage counseling. Assume that the applicable Michiana law is identical to the Uniform Marriage and Divorce Act (UMDA). (*See* Appendix.)

Questions

1. Jeanette is obviously overworked and frustrated, but is divorce the appropriate step for her at this time? The student is reminded here that clients often come into a lawyer's office convinced of what they want but are unaware of other issues underlying their problems—issues that if known could change their minds. What is the lawyer's role in such a situation?
2. What are the requirements for no-fault divorce under the UMDA?
3. Why would a state allow no-fault divorce when it has a standing public policy against divorce? Does no-fault divorce encourage divorce?
4. Assume Jeanette goes forward with her divorce petition. Under the facts in this case, can she obtain a divorce?
5. What defenses, if any, to the no-fault divorce petition are available to Alan? Will any of them prevail in this case?

3. Jewish Divorce

Problem 54

Rubin v. Rubin

Joshua and Evelyn Rubin were married in YR-10, in both a civil ceremony and a Jewish ceremony. Two children were born of the marriage. Evelyn, having been unhappy in the marriage for several years, decided to divorce Joshua. Under Jewish law, divorce is a private act between the two parties and is overseen by a rabbinical tribunal. Jewish divorce can only be accomplished once the wife procures a bill of divorcement, or "get" from the husband. In order for Evelyn to divorce Joshua and be able to remarry under Jewish faith, she must follow Jewish law and also obtain a civil divorce under the law of the State of Michiana.

Evelyn recently filed a civil divorce action in the Hoynes Circuit Court and, as required by Michiana law, she participated in mediation with Joshua (because there were custody issues in the marriage). During mediation, Joshua made it clear the he would not grant Evelyn a get under Jewish law unless she waived her right to support and gave him custody of the children.

Precisely because of this type of situation, the Michiana legislature passed an amendment to its domestic relations law that provides that if a couple is married in a religious ceremony and then later files for divorce, both parties must submit an affidavit declaring that they have removed all barriers, including religious ones, to remarriage after the divorce. The court therefore informed Joshua that if he refused to grant Evelyn a get unless she meets his demands, he and Evelyn cannot be civilly divorced.

Joshua has filed an interlocutory appeal based on the court's instructions. Joshua claims, first, that the Michiana statute is a violation of the principle of separation of church and state; and, second, that as the get must be voluntary under Jewish law, if Joshua grants it to Evelyn at the urging of the court it is invalid anyway.

Questions

1. Does the Michiana law that requires the parties to remove any religious barriers to remarriage (that are within their power to remove) before they can get a civil divorce constitute a violation of the principle of separation of church and state?
2. If the involuntary get is invalid and therefore a marriage can still not be obtained under Jewish law, what more can the state do to protect Evelyn from Joshua's unfair tactics?

E. ATTORNEY—CLIENT RELATIONS IN DIVORCE CASES

(The professor may at this point wish to consider Problem 100—*In re Marriage of Constant.*)

F. RIGHT TO DIVORCE

Problem 55

Manilow v. Pension Board

Mandy and Loretta Manilow were married in Honolulu, Hawaii, on June 15, YR-30, after a three-week courtship while Mandy was on leave from military service. Mandy's furlough expired one week after their wedding, and he returned to active duty to complete another three years' service before joining his wife in Sacramento, California, in May, YR-27. Upon returning to the United States and receiving an honorable discharge from the Army, Mandy applied for positions with the Sacramento Police Department and the California State Highway Patrol.

Mandy could not find work in California, so the couple moved to Michiana in January, YR-26. Loretta's father, chief of the New City Police Department, got Mandy admitted to the Michiana Regional Police Academy, Hoynes County, starting in August, YR-26. Mandy, who is now fifty-eight, has been a police officer with the New City Police Department since that time. He is currently captain of the fourth precinct, covering the posh Sterling Heights neighborhood and the dangerous Neumann Green neighborhood. Because Mandy's job pays well, the family home is located in the heart of Sterling Heights.

When Mandy and Loretta moved to New City, Loretta took a job as a teacher in Mother of Hope School for Adolescent Girls. Mother of Hope, run by the Little Sisters of the Poor, is a school for daughters from abusive households. Loretta has taught at Mother of Hope continuously since January, YR-26.

Mandy and Loretta have two children, Phil (currently age twenty-five and a construction worker in Chicago) and Geraldo (age twenty-three and a graduate student in journalism). Both children are emancipated. In the current dispute, which is described below, Phil sides with his father's view of the facts, while Geraldo maintains that his mother is telling the truth.

On January 10, YR-0, Loretta filed a petition for permanent separation from Mandy. In her petition, Loretta states that Mandy has beaten her continually throughout their marriage, and that he has used family funds for his use on secret trips with various lovers. Loretta's petition specifically requests the court not to grant a petition for divorce because Mandy's police pension will divest her of all her rights if she is divorced from her husband. The applicable portions of the Michiana Police Pension Code follow this problem.

The Michiana statute provides that no-fault divorce must be granted where the circumstances permit it.

On January 18, YR-0, Mandy filed an answer and counter-petition for divorce based on the no-fault statute. In Mandy's counter-petition, he alleges that he has not lived with his wife for thirteen months and that, as of December 15, YR-0, the couple will be separated for the statutory two-year period. In his responsive pleading, Mandy stated that he never raised a hand against Loretta except in her defense, that he never misappropriated any of the marital assets, and that Loretta is suffering from paranoia and jealousy. Mandy admits that he has been living with Heather A. Arthur, his longtime girlfriend, since he moved out.

Mandy has been diagnosed with lung cancer, allegedly stemming from his exposure to harmful chemicals when he was in military service, but his prognosis is currently good. Mandy wants to divorce Loretta as soon as possible so he can marry Heather, retire with his pension, and make sure that Heather, rather than Loretta, gets the survivor's benefit when he dies.

Loretta, of course, would like nothing more than to see Mandy die shortly before the divorce is finalized. Because they made a marital decision to fund Mandy's pension fully, Mandy and Loretta never planned for Loretta's retirement. Under the Michiana Police Pension Code, which follows this Problem, if Mandy and Loretta are divorced, for whatever reason, Loretta is entitled to nothing from Mandy's pension.

Finally, Michiana has a statute that provides that police pensions are contractual in nature, and that the right to a police pension may not be attached by any creditor.

Loretta has filed a declaratory judgment action in Hoynes County Superior Court seeking a determination that the Michiana Police Pension Code is unconstitutional, based on equal protection and substantive due process grounds. Loretta's complaint states that the pension code makes a classification based on marital status, that this classification is suspect, and that since there is no compelling state interest to which the pension code is strictly drawn, the statute is unconstitutional. Loretta also argues that the pension code interferes with her fundamental right to divorce because it penalizes divorced spouses by terminating their pension rights.

Questions

1. May a state court in a pure no-fault jurisdiction deny a divorce petition?
2. Is there a fundamental right to a divorce? If there is a fundamental right to divorce, does a statute that penalizes married people for divorcing violate due process?
3. Does the Michiana Police Pension Code violate equal protection? If there is no suspect classification involved, does the pension code still pass a rational basis test?
4. Would Loretta's case against the pension board be any different if she had filed for a divorce rather than permanent separation?
5. How would this case be decided if the dispute was over Mandy's military pension? *See* the Uniformed Services Former Spouses Protection Act.
6. Does Loretta have standing to sue the pension board, given that she will soon be divorced from the pensioner? Can the pension board successfully argue that the pension code does not deny Loretta the right to divorce but rather merely penalizes her for doing so?
7. The state has an interest in promoting marriage and an interest in making sure that marriage occurs only between parties who have the capacity to marry. What is the state's role in a divorce proceeding where no children are involved? What about where child custody is an issue?

MICHIANA POLICE PENSION CODE

Section 5. Pension and Retirement Rights

Membership in any pension or retirement system of the State, any unit of local government or school district, or any agency or instrumentality thereof, shall be an enforceable contractual relationship, the benefits of which shall not be diminished or impaired.

5/5-133. Widow's prior service annuity

Section 5-133. Widow's prior service annuity. "Widow's Prior Service Annuity" shall be credited for the widow of a male present employee for service prior to the effective date, in accordance with the "Policemen's Annuity and Benefit Fund Act of the Michiana Municipal Code" and this Article.

The amounts so credited shall be improved by interest at 4% per annum during the employee's service subsequent to the effective date until he attains age 57.

5/5-134. Widow's annuity

Section 5-134. Widow's annuity. "Widow's Annuity" shall be provided for the widows of policemen for service after the effective date.

5/5-135. Amount of present employee's widow's annuity on effective date

Section 5-135. Amount of present employee's widow's annuity on effective date. The amount of the annuity for the wife of a present employee who attains age 57 or more on or before the effective date shall be fixed on the effective date as of the wife's age at the time the employee attained age 57. The widow shall receive the annuity, from the date of the employee's death, of such amount as can be provided from the employee's credit for such annuity on the effective date.

G. SPOUSAL SUPPORT: ALIMONY OR MAINTENANCE

1. At Dissolution

Problem 56

In re Marriage of Farrell

Blake and Rose Farrell were married on December 28, YR-10, during Blake's senior year at Michiana University at Harwood and Rose's sophomore year at Southby State University. In the spring semester of YR-9, Rose moved to Harwood and worked full time while Blake finished work on his baccalaureate degree. In August of YR-9, Blake began his first year of study at Michiana University School of Law. On September 15, YR-9, Rose gave birth to a son, Blair. In November of YR-9, Rose arranged day care for Blair and returned to work part-time at Reliable Title Insurance Company in Harwood. Rose developed extensive knowledge of real estate and title work and was often consulted by lawyers in Harwood. During YR-9 and YR-8, Rose frequently expressed to family and friends her interest in some day attending law school. In January of YR-7, Rose enrolled in a paralegal studies program. In June of YR-6, Blake graduated from law school. After passing the bar exam, Blake went to work for a large law firm in Dolton, Michiana, in the fall of YR-6, earning a salary of $75,000. Rose received her paralegal certificate in June of YR-6 and was offered several jobs in the $25,000 to $30,000 salary range with law firms, abstract companies and title insurance companies in Harwood and nearby Dolton. Blake and Rose, being seven months pregnant in June of YR-6, agreed that Rose would quit her job with Reliable Title Company. In August of YR-6, Rose gave birth to a second child, Angel. Rose stayed home with the children and continued to be responsible for all of the homemaking duties. Blake's late nights at the office, six and seven-day work weeks, and very little communication between Blake and Rose took their toll on the marriage, and in February of YR-1, Blake announced, "The Rose petals have wilted. I'm boltin' from Dolton." Rose responded, "I've been having an affair with Irv for the past year, and it's the first time in years that I've felt loved and needed." A few months later, Blake moved to Chicago and joined the city's largest law firm, earning an annual salary of $150,000. In June of YR-1, Rose hired Irma to take care of the two children five days a week and returned to work as a paralegal in a Dolton law firm, at a salary of $30,000. Rose was hired on the condition that she become proficient with the office computer equipment within six months of her hiring. The firm agreed to pay for one-half of Rose's tuition to take the necessary training courses at Dolton Business College. Rose would like to finish her baccalaureate degree and attend law school in a few years, but she doesn't have enough money to cover tuition and other necessary expenses.

In August of YR-1, Rose filed a petition for dissolution of marriage, along with requests for provisional relief—temporary alimony, temporary custody, child support, and attorney fees. The court granted the requested relief and also ruled that Blake's law degree was not marital property subject to equitable distribution. At the final dissolution hearing, Rose requests an order for alimony, the only issue in dispute.

Questions

1. What is alimony? Why is it granted to a party in a divorce?
2. What policy reasons exist for granting spousal support to a party?
3. Under the Uniform Marriage and Divorce Act (UMDA), what factors are considered when the court makes an award of alimony? What other factors should be considered?
4. What reasons does Rose have for obtaining alimony?
5. What is temporary alimony? Does it differ from temporary spousal maintenance? If so, in what ways?
6. Assume the Michiana court grants Rose alimony in this case and the court's order states that Rose deserves alimony sufficient for her to earn a law degree and embark on a legal career. Should the alimony be terminated when Rose graduates from law school? What if Rose takes five years to finish law school? How long should Rose get alimony?
7. What is permanent alimony? Under what circumstances is it applicable? Should Rose be awarded permanent alimony in this case?
8. What effect should Rose's affair with Irv have on her receiving the alimony? Suppose that immediately after Blake moves out Irv, a cardiologist, moves in with Rose. Is Rose's cohabitation with Irv relevant on the issue of spousal support?
9. What effect does the court's determination that Blake's law degree is not marital property have on the alimony calculation?

Chapter Nine. Dissolution of Marriage

2. Modification of Alimony Order

Problem 57

> **In re Marriage of Perry**

The marriage of Pamela and Merlin Perry was dissolved by decree of the Hoynes Superior Court on July 1, YR-4. The court's decree included a property settlement and an alimony agreement (which follows this Problem). In July of YR-1, Merlin sold his 49 percent of Merco Industries, Inc. for $50,000 worth of equipment used in the manufacture of sheet metal products and $15,000 cash. Merlin transferred the equipment to his new company, Midwest Sheet Metal, Inc., located in Southby, Michiana. Merlin used the $15,000 to remodel and purchase inventory for his new tavern business, The Boathouse, which opened in late July of YR-1.

Merlin made payments pursuant to the alimony agreement through December 1, YR-1. On December 24, YR-1, Merlin sent the following letter to Pamela:

Dear Pamela,

I'm sorry to inform you that I can no longer make alimony payments. The Boathouse is about to sink and the sheet metal market is flat. We're just not getting the orders. At the time of the divorce, I had the mortgage and my car payment and that's all. Now I have less income and the following other debts:

IRS—unpaid taxes	$3,000
Michiana Department of Revenue—unpaid taxes	$ 500
Workmen's Compensation, Boathouse—unpaid	$2,500
Frontier Savings—second mortgage	$ 350/mo.
National Bank—third mortgage	$ 320/mo.
First Source Bank—car payment	$ 400/mo.

I know you understand that things are different now. I hope to make it up to you.

Merlin

Pamela is unmarried and earns $20,000 per year at her job as a hair stylist. Pamela states that without the alimony payments, she can't make ends meet.

Questions

1. What legal action should Merlin take to reduce his court-ordered obligation to pay alimony to Pamela?
2. How much discretion does the court have to modify alimony under Section 316 of the Uniform Marriage and Divorce Act?
4. What must be proved before a court can modify an alimony order? Who has the burden of proof?
5. Assume Michiana allows for modification of alimony under a "substantial change of circumstances" test. Read the Property Settlement

and Alimony Agreement that follows this Problem. How should the court rule?

6. Will a mere decrease in income, without more, result in a reduction in alimony? If not, how do people who lose their jobs pay alimony? If mere monetary loss is enough, can't someone merely quit his or her job to get out of paying alimony or at best have it reduced?

7. Review the facts of Problem 56. What effect will there be on Rose's alimony if in YR+3 Rose marries Charlie, a grocery store clerk, who makes $17,500 per year? If Rose stands to lose alimony, doesn't that discourage her marriage to a poorer person? If Rose can keep her alimony (either permanently or until the end of her alimony term), doesn't she get a windfall (and doesn't Charlie get one too) at Blake's expense?

STATE OF MICHIANA)	IN THE HOYNES SUPERIOR COURT
)	
HOYNES COUNTY)	CAUSE NO. SC 81-49
IN RE THE MARRIAGE OF)	
)	
PAMELA A. PERRY,)	
Petitioner,)	
Cross-Respondent)	
)	
vs.)	
)	
MERLIN V. PERRY,)	PROPERTY SETTLEMENT
Respondent,)	AND ALIMONY AGREEMENT
Cross-Petitioner)	

THIS AGREEMENT made and entered into this 1st day of July, YR-4, by and between MERLIN V. PERRY, hereinafter "Husband," and PAMELA A. PERRY, hereinafter "Wife."

WITNESSETH:

WHEREAS, the parties were heretofore married on December 5, YR-26, and separated on March 9, YR-4; and

WHEREAS, the Wife has filed her Verified Petition for Dissolution of Marriage in the Hoynes Superior Court under Cause Number SC 81-49, and Husband, in the same Court and under the same Cause Number, has filed a Verified Counter-Petition for Dissolution of Marriage; and

WHEREAS, the parties, in order to avoid the rigors and expense of protracted litigation in regard to the disposition of their property and all rights of support of the Wife by the Husband, together with any and all other rights existing between the parties, without agreeing to a dissolution of marriage, have entered into an agreement to settle and adjust their property and marital rights, including alimony due the Wife.

NOW, THEREFORE, for and in return for the mutual promises and obligations hereinafter contained, the parties do hereby agree as follows:

1. That there are two (2) children born of the marriage: Merlin Michael Perry and Lisa Ann Dodge, both of whom are emancipated and therefore neither party shall pay any sums to the other for the support of said children.

2. The Wife shall have and own as her property, free of any claims of the Husband, the following items of personal property:

   a. YR-5 Chevrolet Citation;
   b. household furnishings and personal property listed on Exhibit 1, which is attached hereto and incorporated by reference herein;
   c. all funds in savings account numbered 54-736280-2 at the First Bank and Trust Company of Southby;
   d. all funds in checking account numbered 017 31402 010 501 2, at the Hoynes County Bank and Trust Company of Hoynes County, Michiana;
   e. all personal effects, clothing and jewelry.

3. The Husband shall have his own property free of any claim of the Wife with the following items of personal and real property:

   a. the following described real estate located in Hoynes County, Michiana, more particularly described as: (see Exhibit 2) and commonly known as Route 7, Box 216, Southby, Michiana. The Wife has this date tendered to the Husband a quitclaim deed relinquishing all right, title and interest she may have in said real estate, a copy of which quitclaim deed is attached hereto, incorporated by reference herein and marked Exhibit 2;

b. YR-19 Chevrolet Corvette;
c. forty-nine (49) shares of common stock of Merco Industries, Inc.
d. all funds in checking account numbered 82103663 at the First Bank and Trust Company of Southby, Michiana;
e. all funds in savings account numbered 45523530 at the Pacesetter Bank and Trust Company of Michiana;
f. all funds in the Merco Profit Sharing Trust held at the Pacesetter Bank and Trust Company of Michiana;
g. all clothing, personal effects and jewelry;
h. the personal property and household furnishings listed on Exhibit 3, which is attached hereto and incorporated by reference herein.

4. The Husband shall assume and agree to pay the following outstanding obligations of the parties:

a. loan from the Hoynes County Bank and Trust Company, the proceeds of which were used to purchase the real estate described in Exhibit 2; which loan is secured by a real estate mortgage on said real estate, and which loan has an outstanding balance of approximately $28,000.00;
b. loan from Pacesetter Bank and Trust Company of Michiana, the proceeds of which were used to purchase the YR-19 Chevrolet Corvette, and which loan has an approximate unpaid balance of $4,906.77.

5. The Wife represents that she has caused a certain loan from the Pacesetter Bank and Trust, the proceeds of which were used to buy the YR-5 Chevrolet Citation, which shall become the absolute property of the Wife, to be transferred to her name solely, and that, further, she has caused the Husband to be released from any liability for the payment of said loan.

6. Each of the parties does hereby agree to defend, indemnify and hold harmless the other from any damage or liability as a result of the failure of either to repay any obligation assumed by either party.

7. In addition to the division of property set out above, Husband further agrees to the entry of an order providing for continuing alimony and maintenance payments to the Wife for a period of one-hundred twenty-one (121) consecutive months, commencing on July 1, YR-4. Said alimony and maintenance shall be paid as follows:

a. one (1) monthly payment of Fifteen Thousand ($15,000.00) Dollars due on July 1, YR-4; then
b. One hundred twenty (120) monthly payments of $1,717.96, commencing August 1, YR-4, in accordance with the amortization schedule which is attached hereto and incorporated by reference herein and marked Exhibit 4.

Such order shall be entered by the Court having jurisdiction in this cause. The parties agree that the alimony and the payments due thereunder shall constitute a non-dischargeable obligation of the Husband in any bankruptcy proceedings which he might hereinafter file or which may be filed involuntarily by any other person against him. Said alimony order due from the Husband to the Wife shall be due and payable regardless of the remarriage of the Wife.

To secure the payment of the aforementioned alimony order, the Husband agrees that he will, if possible, purchase and, once purchased, will maintain, an insurance policy having a death benefit of not less than the unpaid principal balance of the alimony order. Within thirty (30) days from the date of this Agreement, the Husband shall create a trust to be the recipient of the death benefits of said insurance policy, and said trust will be compelled to pay the alimony and maintenance payments described above in the amounts and according to the schedule set out in Paragraph 7(a) and (b) above. Said insurance policy shall name said trust as primary beneficiary of said policy.

To further secure the payment of the alimony order, the Husband grants to the Wife a security interest in forty-nine (49) shares of common stock of Merco Industries, Inc., which he owns, and which are represented by stock certificate numbered 9, a copy of which is attached hereto and incorporated by reference herein and marked Exhibit 5. Wife agrees that said security interest shall be released at the rate of .000221564 shares for every dollar paid by the Husband pursuant to the terms of the alimony order. The Husband shall have the right at all times to vote said shares, to receive all dividends, and to exercise all other rights of ownership of said stock, and to receive all benefits therefrom.

The Husband and Wife intend that said monthly alimony payments shall be deductible by the Husband and taxable to the Wife on their Federal and State income tax returns.

8. The Husband shall pay to the law firm of Park and Jacobs on or before the date of the entry of a decree of dissolution, the total sum of Two Thousand ($2,000.00) Dollars for attorney's fees incurred by the Wife. The Two Thousand ($2,000.00) Dollar payment shall be composed of the Eight Hundred ($800.00) Dollars previously ordered by the Court to be paid plus One Thousand Two Hundred ($1,200.00) Dollars additional fees incurred since then. The payment of said Two Thousand ($2,000.00) Dollars shall discharge any obligation the Husband may have of the payment of attorney's fees incurred by the Wife.

9. The parties hereto agree to sign and execute all necessary deeds, documents, automobile titles, and stock certificates and other documents needed to carry out the terms of this Agreement and to deliver all necessary papers to show title in accordance with this Agreement.

10. Both parties hereunder understand that this Agreement shall be binding only in the event a dissolution of marriage is granted herein, and further, that this Agreement may be approved by the Judge of the Court having jurisdiction of this case. This Agreement is not entered into for the purpose of inducing either party to procure or consent to a dissolution of marriage, but only as an instrument thereto and for the purpose of resolving any and all matters of alimony, maintenance, and property between them.

11. Each of the parties hereto expressly certifies that each of them has entered into this Agreement upon mature consideration and upon advice of his or her respective counsel, and that the consent to the execution of this Agreement has not been obtained by duress, fraud, or undue influence of any person, and that the Husband has delivered to the Wife accurate and complete information concerning his business affairs and the valuations thereof, and income tax records therefor. Further, the parties agree that this Agreement is therefore fair and equitable and reasonable to both parties.

12. The parties hereto have read the foregoing Agreement and feel that it is fair and equitable and subject only to the approval of the Court having jurisdiction of the action for dissolution of marriage, and they further agree that the Judge of the Hoynes Superior Court shall retain jurisdiction to enforce the terms of this Agreement after the same is approved by the Court. This Agreement shall be binding upon the parties, their heirs, personal representatives, successors, and assigns.

13. The parties shall separately compute and file their state and federal tax returns for the taxable year YR-0 and for all subsequent taxable years.

14. In consideration of all the promises contained in this Agreement, Husband and Wife hereby release all claims and rights which either ever had, now has, or might hereafter have against the other by reason of their former relationship as Husband and Wife, or otherwise, excepting all of the claims and rights of each party created and outstanding against the other pursuant to the terms of this Agreement. It is the intent hereof that each party accepts the provisions of this Agreement in full

release and settlement of any and all claims and rights against the other. It is the further agreement of the parties that the provisions of this Agreement shall inure to the benefit of and be binding upon the parties, their heirs, administrators, successors, and assigns.

15. Each party hereto acknowledges that no representations of any kind have been made by him or her as an inducement to enter into this Settlement Agreement other than the representations set forth herein, and that this Agreement constitutes all of the terms of the contract between the parties.

16. A modification or waiver of any of the provisions of this Settlement Agreement shall be effective only if made in writing and executed with the same formality as this Agreement. Failure of either party to insist upon the strict performance of any of the provisions of this Agreement shall not be construed as a waiver of any subsequent default of the same or a similar nature.

17. If either of the parties shall default in the performance of any of the obligations incumbent upon him or her by virtue of this Agreement, then the non-defaulting party shall be entitled to recover from the defaulting party all court costs, reasonable attorney's fees, and other expenses incurred by the non-defaulting party in the enforcement of his or her rights hereunder.

18. Not later than August 1, YR-4, the Wife shall vacate the family residence at Route 7, Box 216, Southby, Michiana, and shall remove therefrom all of the personal property to which she is entitled by virtue of this Agreement.

IN WITNESS WHEREOF, the parties have executed this Agreement on the day first written above.

_____
Merlin V. Perry, Husband

Witness:

_____
Counsel for Respondent,
Cross-Petitioner

_____
Pamela A. Perry, Wife

Witness:

_____
Counsel for Petitioner,
Cross-Respondent

The Court having examined the aforementioned Property Settlement and Alimony Agreement now specifically approves its terms, orders the parties to carry them out, and makes this Agreement a part of the Decree of Dissolution entered in this cause.

DATED this 1st day of July, YR-4.

_____
Judge, Hoynes Superior Court

EXHIBIT 1
ITEMS OF PERSONAL PROPERTY TO BE TAKEN BY WIFE

1. Bedroom
    a. full-size bedroom suite (bed, chest of drawers & dresser)
    b. straight chair with red seat
    c. chifforobe
    d. all bedding
    e. desk
    f. typewriter
    g. trunk
    h. all pictures and photos
    i. hanging lamp in hall
    j. red phones
    k. old silver coins
2. Living Room
    a. couch
    b. two green chairs
    c. stereo
    d. two tables and two lamps
    e. portable TV
    f. all wall items
    g. all knick-knack items
3. Dining Room
    a. table and chairs
    b. wash stand
    c. dehumidifier
    d. items on walls
4. Kitchen
    a. all kitchen dishes and pots and pans
    b. all wall items, including spice box
    c. electrical items: toaster, can opener, etc.
5. Family Room
    a. brown couch
    b. hutch
    c. round table
    d. school desk
    e. hanging lamp
    f. wall pictures
    g. fan
6. Beauty Shop
    a. wet sink
    b. chair
    c. dryer
    d. small TV
    e. corner stand and cabinet for supplies
7. Front Porch
    a. two twin beds
    b. piano
    c. Christmas decorations
    d. rocking chair
    e. boxes of glass and books
8. Outside
    a. two lawn chairs

   b. push lawn mower
   c. plant stand
 9. Personal Items
   a. clothes
   b. gold jewelry
   c. diamond ring
   d. 22 pistol

EXHIBIT 2

MAIL DEED TO: MAIL TAX BILLS TO:

AUDITOR'S RECORD
Transfer No. _____
Taxing Unit _____
Date _____

QUIT-CLAIM DEED

PAMELA A. PERRY   *the Grantor*

Release and Quit-Claim to   MERLIN V. PERRY

the Grantee

for and in consideration of $1.00 and other valuable consideration,

the receipt of which is hereby acknowledged, Real Estate in Hoynes *County, in the State of* Michiana*, described as follows:*

> The East Thirty-two and one-half (E32½) Acres of the South Half (S½) of the Southwest Quarter (SW¼) of Section Nineteen (19), Township Thirty-four (34) North, Range One (1) East, excepting therefrom a tract of land One Hundred Twenty-six (126) yards North and South by Seventy-seven (77) yards East and West of approximately Two (2) Acres, the South line of which is the center line of an East and West public road in the Southeast (SE) corner of the East Thirty-two and one-half (E32½) acres of said South Half (S½) of the Southwest Quarter (SW¼) of said Section Nineteen (19) Township Thirty-four (34) North, Range One (1) East, total being conveyed is 30½ acres, more or less. Situate in Polk Township, Hoynes County, State of Michiana, as it now is, subject to recorded restrictions, easements of record and zoning ordinances.
>
> This conveyance is made in compliance with the terms of a judgment made for dissolution of marriage granted on the _____ day of _____, YR-4, in Cause Number SC 81-49 on the dockets of the Hoynes Superior Court.

Signed and dated on _____, YR-4.

State of MICHIANA, HOYNES County, ss:

Before me, the undersigned, a Notary Public in and for said County and State, personally appeared:

Pamela A. Perry

and acknowledged the execution of the foregoing deed on

_____, YR-4.

_____, *Notary Public*
Signature

_____
Typed or printed name

My commission expires _____

Prepared by _____
        Attorney at Law

Signature
Pamela A. Perry
Typed or printed name

Signature
_____
Typed or printed name

Signature
_____
Typed or printed name

Signature
_____
Typed or printed name

EXHIBIT 3
ITEMS OF PERSONAL PROPERTY TO BE TAKEN BY HUSBAND

1. Master Bedroom
    a. king-size bed
    b. dresser
    c. chest
2. Living Room
    a. mantel clock
    b. one chair (not green)
3. Dining Room
    a. collection of plates and glass
4. Kitchen
    a. stove
    b. refrigerator
    c. dishwasher
    d. microwave oven
5. Utility Room
    a. washer
    b. dryer
    c. freezer
6. Family Room
    a. 24" color TV
    b. chair
    c. antique stove
7. Lawn Equipment
    a. riding lawnmower
    b. tractor
    c. miscellaneous tools, lawn hose, shovels, rakes, etc.
    d. ax
8. Machine Shed
    a. refrigerator
    b. miscellaneous lumber
9. Barn
    a. hand tools
    b. torch
    c. welder
    d. chain saw
    e. extension ladders
10. Front Porch
    a. window air conditioner
11. Man's gold ring with five (5) diamonds
12. Luggage
13. All other items of personal property of the parties not listed on Exhibit 1 (Items of Personal Property to Be Taken by Wife) or not removed by Wife pursuant to Paragraph 2(e).

EXHIBIT 4

LOAN AMORTIZATION SCHEDULE

ROMAN AND DOUGLAS   TO: ATTORNEY FOR PETITIONER

LOAN AMOUNT	ANNUAL RATE	PAYMENTS/YEAR	MONTHLY/PAYMENT	START DATE
130,000.00	10.0 %	12	1,717.96	08/01/YR-4

PMT NBR	DUE DATE	PAYMENT ON INTEREST	PAYMENT ON PRINCIPLE	LOAN BALANCE	DATE PD	CHECK NBR
1	08/01/YR-4	1,083.33	634.63	129,365.37	[/ /]	[ ]
2	09/01/YR-4	1,078.04	639.92	128,725.45	[/ /]	[ ]
3	10/01/YR-4	1,072.71	645.25	128,080.20	[/ /]	[ ]
4	11/01/YR-4	1,067.33	650.63	127,429.57	[/ /]	[ ]
5	12/01/YR-4	1,061.91	656.05	126,773.52	[/ /]	[ ]
**YR-4 TOTALS		5,363.32	3,226.48	126,773.52	**	
6	01/01/YR-3	1,056.45	661.51	126,112.01	[/ /]	[ ]
7	02/01/YR-3	1,050.93	667.03	125,444.98	[/ /]	[ ]
8	03/01/YR-3	1,045.37	672.59	124,772.39	[/ /]	[ ]
9	04/01/YR-3	1,039.77	678.19	124,094.20	[/ /]	[ ]
10	05/01/YR-3	1,034.12	683.84	123,410.36	[/ /]	[ ]
11	06/01/YR-3	1,028.42	689.54	122,720.82	[/ /]	[ ]
12	07/01/YR-3	1,022.67	695.29	122,025.53	[/ /]	[ ]
13	08/01/YR-3	1,016.88	701.08	121,324.45	[/ /]	[ ]
14	09/01/YR-3	1,011.04	706.92	120,617.53	[/ /]	[ ]
15	10/01/YR-3	1,005.15	712.81	119,904.72	[/ /]	[ ]
16	11/01/YR-3	999.21	718.75	119,185.97	[/ /]	[ ]
17	12/01/YR-3	993.22	724.74	118,461.23	[/ /]	[ ]
**YR-3 TOTALS		12,303.23	8,312.29	118,461.23	**	
18	01/01/YR-2	987.18	730.78	117,730.45	[/ /]	[ ]
19	02/01/YR-2	981.09	736.87	116,993.58	[/ /]	[ ]
20	03/01/YR-2	974.95	743.01	116,250.57	[/ /]	[ ]
21	04/01/YR-2	968.75	749.21	115,501.36	[/ /]	[ ]
22	05/01/YR-2	962.51	755.45	114,745.91	[/ /]	[ ]
23	06/01/YR-2	956.22	761.74	113,984.17	[/ /]	[ ]
24	07/01/YR-2	949.87	768.09	113,216.08	[/ /]	[ ]
25	08/01/YR-2	943.47	774.49	112,441.59	[/ /]	[ ]
26	09/01/YR-2	937.01	780.95	111,660.64	[/ /]	[ ]
27	10/01/YR-2	930.51	787.45	110,873.19	[/ /]	[ ]
28	11/01/YR-2	923.94	794.02	110,079.17	[/ /]	[ ]
29	12/01/YR-2	917.33	800.63	109,278.54	[/ /]	[ ]
**YR-2 TOTALS		11,432.83	9,182.69	109,278.54	**	
30	01/01/YR-1	910.65	807.31	108,471.23	[/ /]	[ ]
31	02/01/YR-1	903.93	814.03	107,657.20	[/ /]	[ ]
32	03/01/YR-1	897.14	820.82	106,836.38	[/ /]	[ ]
33	04/01/YR-1	890.30	827.66	106,008.72	[/ /]	[ ]
34	05/01/YR-1	883.41	834.55	105,174.17	[/ /]	[ ]

LOAN AMORTIZATION SCHEDULE

LOAN AMOUNT	ANNUAL RATE	PAYMENTS/YEAR	MONTHLY/PAYMENT	START DATE
130,000.00	10.0 %	12	1,717.96	08/01/YR-4

PMT NBR	DUE DATE	INTEREST	PRINCIPLE	LOAN BALANCE	DATE PD	CHECK NBR
35	06/01/YR-1	876.45	841.51	104,332.66	[/ /]	[ ]
36	07/01/YR-1	869.44	848.52	103,484.14	[/ /]	[ ]
37	08/01/YR-1	862.37	855.59	102,628.55	[/ /]	[ ]
38	09/01/YR-1	855.24	862.72	101,765.83	[/ /]	[ ]
39	10/01/YR-1	848.05	869.91	100,895.92	[/ /]	[ ]
40	11/01/YR-1	840.80	877.16	100,018.76	[/ /]	[ ]
41	12/01/YR-1	833.49	884.47	99,134.29	[/ /]	[ ]
**YR-1 TOTALS		10,471.27	10,144.25	99,134.29	**	
42	01/01/YR-0	826.12	891.84	98,242.45	[/ /]	[ ]
43	02/01/YR-0	818.69	899.27	97,343.18	[/ /]	[ ]
44	03/01/YR-0	811.19	906.77	96,436.41	[/ /]	[ ]
45	04/01/YR-0	803.64	914.32	95,522.09	[/ /]	[ ]
46	05/01/YR-0	796.02	921.94	94,600.15	[/ /]	[ ]
47	06/01/YR-0	788.33	929.63	93,670.52	[/ /]	[ ]
48	07/01/YR-0	780.59	937.37	92,733.15	[/ /]	[ ]
49	08/01/YR-0	772.78	945.18	91,787.97	[/ /]	[ ]
50	09/01/YR-0	764.90	953.06	90,834.91	[/ /]	[ ]
51	10/01/YR-0	756.96	961.00	89,873.91	[/ /]	[ ]
52	11/01/YR-0	748.95	969.01	88,904.90	[/ /]	[ ]
53	12/01/YR-0	740.87	977.09	87,927.71	[/ /]	[ ]
**YR-0 TOTALS		9,409.04	11,206.48	87,927.81	**	
54	01/01/YR+1	732.73	985.23	86,942.58	[/ /]	[ ]
55	02/01/YR+1	724.52	993.44	85,949.14	[/ /]	[ ]
56	03/01/YR+1	716.24	1,001.72	84,947.42	[/ /]	[ ]
57	04/01/YR+1	707.90	1,010.06	83,937.36	[/ /]	[ ]
58	05/01/YR+1	699.48	1,018.48	82,918.88	[/ /]	[ ]
59	06/01/YR+1	690.99	1,026.97	81,891.91	[/ /]	[ ]
60	07/01/YR+1	682.43	1,035.53	80,856.38	[/ /]	[ ]
61	08/01/YR+1	673.80	1,044.16	79,812.22	[/ /]	[ ]
62	09/01/YR+1	665.10	1,052.86	78,759.36	[/ /]	[ ]
63	10/01/YR+1	656.33	1,061.63	77,697.73	[/ /]	[ ]
64	11/01/YR+1	647.48	1,070.48	76,627.25	[/ /]	[ ]
65	12/01/YR+1	638.56	1,079.40	75,547.85	[/ /]	[ ]
**YR+1 TOTALS		8,235.56	12,379.96	75,547.85	**	
66	01/01/YR+2	629.57	1,088.39	74,459.46	[/ /]	[ ]
67	02/01/YR+2	620.50	1,097.46	73,362.00	[/ /]	[ ]
68	03/01/YR+2	611.35	1,106.61	72,255.39	[/ /]	[ ]
69	04/01/YR+2	602.13	1,115.83	71,139.56	[/ /]	[ ]
70	05/01/YR+2	592.83	1,125.13	70,014.43	[/ /]	[ ]
71	06/01/YR+2	583.45	1,134.51	68,879.92	[/ /]	[ ]

LOAN AMORTIZATION SCHEDULE

LOAN AMOUNT	ANNUAL RATE	PAYMENTS/YEAR	MONTHLY/PAYMENT	START DATE
130,000.00	10.0 %	12	1,717.96	08/01/YR-4

PMT NBR	DUE DATE	---PAYMENT ON--- INTEREST	PRINCIPLE	LOAN BALANCE	DATE PD	CHECK NBR
72	07/01/YR+2	574.00	1,143.96	67,735.96	[/ /]	[ ]
73	08/01/YR+2	564.47	1,153.49	66,582.47	[/ /]	[ ]
74	09/01/YR+2	554.85	1,163.11	65,419.36	[/ /]	[ ]
75	10/01/YR+2	545.16	1,172.80	64,246.56	[/ /]	[ ]
76	11/01/YR+2	535.39	1,182.57	63,063.99	[/ /]	[ ]
77	12/01/YR+2	525.53	1,192.43	61,871.56	[/ /]	[ ]
**YEAR+2 TOTALS		6,939.23	13,676.29	61,871.56	**	
78	01/01/YR+3	515.60	1,202.36	60,699.20	[/ /]	[ ]
79	02/01/YR+3	505.58	1,212.38	59,456.82	[/ /]	[ ]
80	03/01/YR+3	495.47	1,222.49	58,234.33	[/ /]	[ ]
81	04/01/YR+3	485.29	1,232.67	57,001.66	[/ /]	[ ]
82	05/01/YR+3	475.01	1,242.95	55,758.71	[/ /]	[ ]
83	06/01/YR+3	464.66	1,253.30	54,505.41	[/ /]	[ ]
84	07/01/YR+3	454.21	1,263.75	53,241.66	[/ /]	[ ]
85	08/01/YR+3	443.68	1,274.28	51,967.38	[/ /]	[ ]
86	09/01/YR+3	433.06	1,284.90	50,682.48	[/ /]	[ ]
87	10/01/YR+3	422.35	1,295.61	49,386.87	[/ /]	[ ]
88	11/01/YR+3	411.56	1,306.40	48,080.47	[/ /]	[ ]
89	12/01/YR+3	400.67	1,317.29	46,763.18	[/ /]	[ ]
**YEAR+3 TOTALS		5,507.14	15,108.38	46,763.18	**	
90	01/01/YR+4	389.69	1,328.27	45,434.91	[/ /]	[ ]
91	02/01/YR+4	378.62	1,339.34	44,095.57	[/ /]	[ ]
92	03/01/YR+4	367.46	1,350.50	42,745.07	[/ /]	[ ]
93	04/01/YR+4	356.21	1,361.75	41,383.32	[/ /]	[ ]
94	05/01/YR+4	344.86	1,373.10	40,010.22	[/ /]	[ ]
95	06/01/YR+4	333.42	1,384.54	38,625.68	[/ /]	[ ]
96	07/01/YR+4	321.88	1,396.08	37,229.60	[/ /]	[ ]
97	08/01/YR+4	310.25	1,407.71	35,821.89	[/ /]	[ ]
98	09/01/YR+4	298.52	1,419.44	34,402.45	[/ /]	[ ]
99	10/01/YR+4	286.69	1,431.27	32,971.18	[/ /]	[ ]
100	11/01/YR+4	274.76	1,443.20	31,527.98	[/ /]	[ ]
101	12/01/YR+4	262.73	1,455.23	30,072.75	[/ /]	[ ]
**YEAR+4 TOTALS		3,925.09	16,690.43	30,072.75	**	
102	01/01/YR+5	250.61	1,467.35	28,605.40	[/ /]	[ ]
103	02/01/YR+5	238.38	1,479.58	27,125.82	[/ /]	[ ]
104	03/01/YR+5	226.05	1,491.91	25,633.91	[/ /]	[ ]
105	04/01/YR+5	213.62	1,504.34	24,129.57	[/ /]	[ ]
106	05/01/YR+5	201.08	1,516.88	22,612.69	[/ /]	[ ]
107	06/01/YR+5	188.44	1,529.52	21,083.17	[/ /]	[ ]
108	07/01/YR+5	175.69	1,542.27	19,540.90	[/ /]	[ ]

LOAN AMORTIZATION SCHEDULE

```
LOAN AMOUNT        ANNUAL RATE      PAYMENTS/YEAR   MONTHLY/PAYMENT    START DATE
130,000.00         10.0 %                12            1,717.96        08/01/YR-4

PMT                        ---PAYMENT ON---    LOAN
NBR   DUE DATE             INTEREST  PRINCIPLE  BALANCE      DATE PD      CHECK NBR
109   08/01/YR+5            162.84   1,555.12   17,985.78    [ / / ]      [           ]
110   09/01/YR+5            149.88   1,568.08   16,417.70    [ / / ]      [           ]
110   10/01/YR+5            136.81   1,581.15   14,836.55    [ / / ]      [           ]
111   11/01/YR+5            123.64   1,594.32   13,242.23    [ / / ]      [           ]
112   12/01/YR+5            110.35   1,607.61   11,634.62    [ / / ]      [           ]

**YEAR+5 TOTALS           2,177.39  18,438.13   11,634.62       **

114   01/01/YR+6             96.96   1,621.00   10,013.62    [ / / ]      [           ]
115   02/01/YR+6             83.45   1,634.51    8,379.11    [ / / ]      [           ]
116   03/01/YR+6             69.83   1,648.13    6,730.98    [ / / ]      [           ]
117   04/01/YR+6             56.09   1,661.87    5,069.11    [ / / ]      [           ]
118   05/01/YR+6             42.24   1,675.72    3,393.39    [ / / ]      [           ]
119   06/01/YR+6             28.28   1,689.68    1,703.71    [ / / ]      [           ]
120   07/01/YR+6             14.20   1,703.71        0.00    [ / / ]      [           ]

**YEAR+6 TOTALS             391.05  11,634.62        0.00       **

------------------------------------------------------------------------------

TOTAL INTEREST  :    76,155.15      LAST PAYMENT:   1,717.91
TOTAL PRINCIPAL:    130,000.00
TOTAL PAID      :   206,155.15
```

INCORPORATED UNDER THE LAWS OF

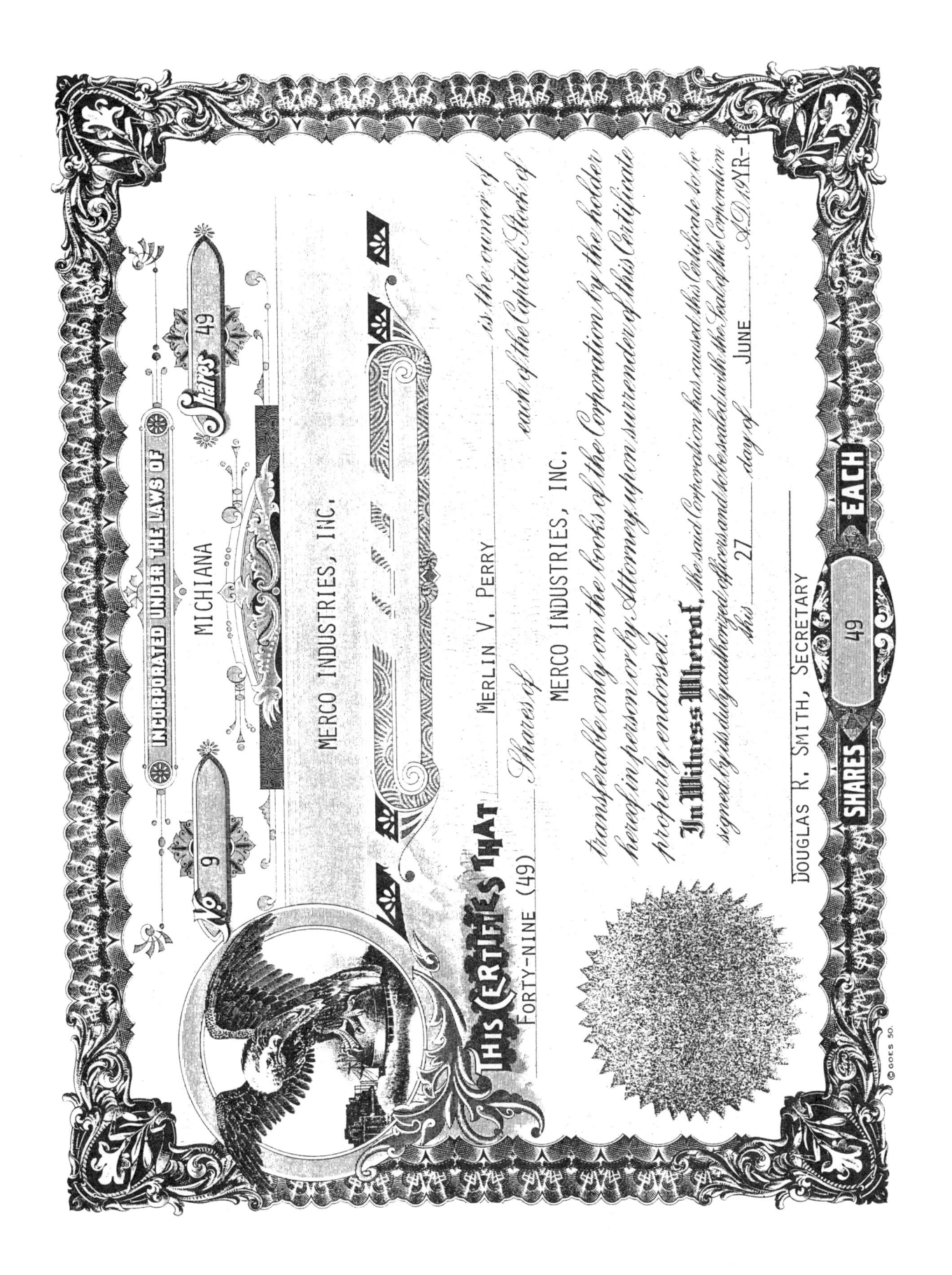

MICHIANA

No. 9

Shares 49

MERCO INDUSTRIES, INC.

THIS CERTIFIES THAT MERLIN V. PERRY is the owner of FORTY-NINE (49) Shares of each of the Capital Stock of

MERCO INDUSTRIES, INC.

transferable only on the books of the Corporation by the holder hereof in person or by Attorney upon surrender of this Certificate properly endorsed.

In Witness Whereof, the said Corporation has caused this Certificate to be signed by its duly authorized officers and to be sealed with the Seal of the Corporation this 27 day of JUNE A.D. 19 YR-1

DOUGLAS R. SMITH, SECRETARY

49 SHARES EACH

3. Necessaries Rule

Problem 58

Southby Community Hospital v. Sherer

After a long bout with cancer, Paul Sherer died in YR-1. Before his death, Paul incurred in his name alone several thousand dollars in expenses at Southby Community Hospital in Southby, Michiana. The assets in Paul's estate are insufficient to discharge his entire debt. When Paul's widow, Valerie, refused to pay the remainder of his debt from her own funds, Southby Community Hospital filed suit against her, claiming that Valerie is liable under the necessaries rule for the necessary expenses incurred by her husband, even though the debt was not in her name and she did not agree to jointly assume the debt. Valerie argues that the common law necessaries doctrine applies only to a husband's liability for his wife's necessary expenses and there is no precedent for making a wife liable for her husband's expenses.

Questions

1. What is the common law necessaries rule?
2. Analyze Valerie's argument in terms of relevant law and public policy.

H. BANKRUPTCY: DISCHARGE OF MARITAL OBLIGATIONS

1. Property Division or Support of Spouse or Child?

Problem 59

In re Marriage of Perry

Review the facts of Problem 57. Assume that another year has gone by and Merlin Perry's financial condition has deteriorated. Both of his corporations are insolvent and he is personally liable for his business loans. Merlin files bankruptcy and lists Pamela as a creditor for the unpaid past and future payments due under the property settlement agreement. He asks his attorney whether he will be successful in discharging the "maintenance" debt.

For purposes of this Problem, assume that the agreement between the parties is the agreement that follows this Problem (captioned "Property Settlement Agreement"), rather than the agreement that follows Problem 57.

The relevant bankruptcy statute is 11 U.S.C. Section 523(a)(5):

> A discharge under . . . this title does not discharge a debtor from any debt . . . to a spouse, former spouse, or child of the debtor, for alimony to, maintenance for, support of such spouse or child, in connection with a separation agreement, divorce decree . . . or property settlement agreement.

Chapter Nine. Dissolution of Marriage

The applicable Michiana statutes follow this Problem. Assume for this Problem that Pamela A. Perry was employed at the time of the divorce at a salary of $18,000 per year. She is presently employed part-time, earning an annual gross salary of $15,000 and is remarried. Her new husband is an executive at AM General Corporation and earns a gross salary of $85,000 per year.

Questions

1. What are the legal tests for determining non-dischargeability of marital obligations in bankruptcy?
2. Which payments to Pamela are alimony? Which payments are property division? Which payments are dischargeable in bankruptcy?
3. Is the federal bankruptcy court bound by the labels of the parties' agreement and state law in determining whether the liability is in the nature of alimony, maintenance, or support? Explain why or why not.
4. Can Merlin use bankruptcy to be relieved from his obligation to purchase life insurance for Pamela's benefit?
5. Assume the debt is assigned to another entity (e.g., the Department of Public Welfare). Is the debt, based on the right of support, dischargeable in bankruptcy?
6. What is the purpose of property division and alimony? What is the purpose of bankruptcy? How do these conflicting purposes combine for a divorce-related bankruptcy policy?
7. Pamela's alimony was secured by Merlin's shares of Merco Industries (*see* Section 7 of the property settlement agreement). Merlin has sold those shares. Is Pamela's alimony right still secured?
8. Assume Merlin has not paid Pamela's attorney fees, as he is required to do under Section 8 of the property settlement agreement. Is this obligation dischargeable under Section 523 of the Bankruptcy Code?
9. Review the property settlement agreement. Is its tenor one of equalizing property or one of providing monetary support? If the latter, should Pamela's remarriage be considered in the dischargeability decision?

STATE OF MICHIANA	)	IN THE HOYNES SUPERIOR COURT
	) SS:	
HOYNES COUNTY	)	CAUSE NO. SC 81-49

IN RE THE MARRIAGE OF)	
PAMELA A. PERRY,)	
Petitioner,)	
Cross-Respondent)	
)	
vs.)	
)	
MERLIN V. PERRY,)	
Respondent,)	PROPERTY SETTLEMENT AGREEMENT
Cross-Petitioner)	

THIS AGREEMENT made and entered into this 1st day of July, YR-4, by and between MERLIN V. PERRY, hereinafter "Husband," and PAMELA A. PERRY, hereinafter "Wife."

WITNESSETH;

WHEREAS, the parties were heretofore married on December 5, YR-26, and separated on March 9, YR-4; and

WHEREAS, the Wife has filed her Verified Petition for Dissolution of Marriage in the Hoynes Superior Court under Cause Number SC 81-49, and Husband, in the same Court and under the same Cause Number, has filed a Verified Counter-Petition for Dissolution of Marriage; and

WHEREAS, the parties, in order to avoid the rigors and expense of protracted litigation in regard to the disposition of their property and all rights of support of the Wife by the Husband, together with any and all other rights existing between the parties, without agreeing to a dissolution of marriage, have entered into an agreement to settle and adjust their property and marital rights.

NOW, THEREFORE, for and in return for the mutual promises and obligations hereinafter contained, the parties do hereby agree as follows:

1. That there are two (2) children born of the marriage: Merlin Michael Perry and Lisa Ann Dodge, both of whom are emancipated and therefore neither party shall pay any sums to the other for the support of said children.

2. The Wife shall have and own as her property, free of any claims of the Husband, the following items of personal property:

   a. YR-5 Chevrolet Citation;
   b. household furnishings and personal property listed on Exhibit 1, which is attached hereto and incorporated by reference herein;
   c. all funds in savings account numbered 54-736280-2 at the First Bank and Trust Company of Southby;
   d. all funds in checking account numbered 017 31402 010 501 2, at the Hoynes County Bank and Trust Company of Hoynes County, Michiana;
   e. all personal effects, clothing and jewelry.

3. The Husband shall have his own property free of any claim of the Wife the following items of personal and real property:

   a. the following described real estate located in Hoynes County, Michiana, more particularly described as: (see Exhibit 2) and commonly known as Route 7, Box 216, Southby, Michiana. The Wife has this date tendered to the Husband a quitclaim deed relinquishing all right, title and interest she

may have in said real estate, a copy of which quitclaim deed is attached hereto, incorporated by reference herein and marked Exhibit 2;
b. YR-19 Chevrolet Corvette;
c. forty-nine (49) shares (representing 50% of the outstanding shares) of common stock of Merco Industries, Inc., Merco Industries, Inc., having a value of $60,000;
d. all funds in checking account numbered 82103663 at the First Bank and Trust Company of Southby, Michiana;
e. all funds in savings account numbered 45523530 at the Pacesetter Bank and Trust Company of Michiana;
f. all funds in the Merco Profit Sharing Trust held at the Pacesetter Bank and Trust Company of Michiana;
g. all clothing, personal effects, and jewelry;
h. the personal property and household furnishings listed on Exhibit 3, which is attached hereto and incorporated by reference herein.

4. The Husband shall assume and agree to pay the following outstanding obligations of the parties:

a. loan from the Hoynes County Bank and Trust Company, the proceeds of which were used to purchase the real estate described in Exhibit 2; which loan is secured by a real estate mortgage on said real estate, and which loan has an outstanding balance of approximately $28,000.00;
b. loan from Pacesetter Bank and Trust Company of Michiana, the proceeds of which were used to purchase the YR-19 Chevrolet Corvette, and which loan has an approximate unpaid balance of $4,906.77.

5. The Wife represents that she has caused a certain loan from the Pacesetter Bank and Trust, the proceeds of which were used to buy the YR-5 Chevrolet Citation, which shall become the absolute property of the Wife, to be transferred to her name solely and that further, she has caused the Husband to be released from any liability for the payment of said loan.

6. Each of the parties does hereby agree to defend, indemnify, and hold harmless the other from any damage or liability as a result of the failure of either to repay any obligation assumed by either party.

7. In addition to the foregoing division of property, Husband further agrees to the entry of an order providing for periodic payments to the Wife for a term of one-hundred twenty-one (121) consecutive months, commencing on July 1, YR-4. Said payments shall be made as follows:

a. one (1) monthly payment of Fifteen Thousand ($15,000.00) Dollars due on July 1, YR-4; then
b. One hundred twenty (120) monthly payments of $1,717.96 commencing August 1, YR-4, in accordance with the amortization schedule which is attached hereto and incorporated by reference herein and marked Exhibit 4.

Such order shall be entered by the Court having jurisdiction in this cause. Said payments from the Husband to the Wife shall be due and payable regardless of the remarriage of the Wife.

To secure the payments, the Husband agrees that he will, if possible, purchase, and once purchased, will maintain an insurance policy having a death benefit of not less than the unpaid principal balance of the alimony order. Within thirty (30) days from the date of this Agreement, the Husband shall create a trust to be the recipient of the death benefits of said insurance policy, and said trust will be compelled to pay the payments above in the amounts and according to the schedule set out in Paragraph 7(a) and (b) above. Said insurance policy shall name said trust as primary beneficiary of said policy.

To further secure the foregoing payments, the Husband grants to the Wife a security interest in forty-nine (49) shares of common stock of Merco Industries, Inc. which he owns, and which are represented by stock certificate numbered 9, a copy of which is attached hereto and incorporated by reference herein and marked Exhibit 5. Wife agrees that said security interest shall be released at the rate of .000221564 shares for every dollar paid by the Husband pursuant to the terms of the maintenance order. The Husband shall have the right at all times to vote said shares, to receive all dividends and to exercise all other rights of ownership of said stock, and to receive all benefits therefrom.

The Husband and Wife intend that said monthly maintenance payments shall be deductible by the Husband and taxable to the Wife on their Federal and State income tax returns.

8. The Husband shall pay to the law firm of Park and Jacobson on or before the date of the entry of a decree of dissolution the total sum of Two Thousand ($2,000.00) Dollars for attorney's fees incurred by the Wife. The Two Thousand ($2,000.00) Dollar payment shall be composed of the Eight Hundred ($800.00) Dollars previously ordered by the Court to be paid plus One Thousand Two Hundred ($1,200.00) Dollars additional fees incurred since then. The payment of said Two Thousand ($2,000.00) Dollars shall discharge any obligation the Husband may have of the payment of attorney's fees incurred by the Wife.

9. The parties hereto agree to sign and execute all necessary deeds, documents, automobile titles, and stock certificates and other documents needed to carry out the terms of this Agreement and to deliver all necessary papers to show title in accordance with this Agreement.

10. Both parties hereunder understand that this Agreement shall be binding only in the event a dissolution of marriage is granted herein and, further, that this Agreement may be approved by the Judge of the Court having jurisdiction of this case. This Agreement is not entered into for the purpose of inducing either party to procure or consent to a dissolution of marriage, but only as an instrument thereto and for the purpose of resolving any and all matters between them.

11. Each of the parties hereto expressly certifies that each of them has entered into this Agreement upon mature consideration and upon advice of his or her respective counsel, and that the consent to the execution of this Agreement has not been obtained by duress, fraud, or undue influence of any person, and that the Husband has delivered to the Wife accurate and complete information concerning his business affairs and the valuations thereof, and income tax records therefor. Further, the parties agree that this Agreement is therefore fair and equitable and reasonable to both parties.

12. The parties hereto have read the foregoing Agreement and feel that it is fair and equitable and subject only to the approval of the Court having jurisdiction of the action for dissolution of marriage, and they further agree that the Judge of the Hoynes Superior Court shall retain jurisdiction to enforce the terms of this Agreement after the same is approved by the Court. This agreement shall be binding upon the parties, their heirs, personal representatives, successors, and assigns.

13. The parties shall separately compute and file their state and federal tax returns for the taxable year YR-0 and for all subsequent taxable years.

14. In consideration of all the promises contained in this Agreement, Husband and Wife hereby release all claims and rights which either ever had, now has, or might hereafter have against the other by reason of their former relationship as Husband and Wife, or otherwise, excepting all of the claims and rights of each party created and outstanding against the other pursuant to the terms of this Agreement. It is the intent hereof that each party accepts the provisions of this Agreement

Chapter Nine. Dissolution of Marriage

in full release and settlement of any and all claims and rights against the other. It is the further agreement of the parties that the provisions of this Agreement shall inure to the benefit of and be binding upon the parties, their heirs, administrators, successors, and assigns.

15. Each party hereto acknowledges that no representations of any kind have been made by him or her as an inducement to enter into this Settlement Agreement other than the representations set forth herein, and that this Agreement constitutes all of the terms of the contract between the parties.

16. A modification or waiver of any of the provisions of this Settlement Agreement shall be effective only if made in writing and executed with the same formality as this Agreement. Failure of either party to insist upon the strict performance of any of the provisions of this Agreement shall not be construed as a waiver of any subsequent default of the same or a similar nature.

17. If either of the parties shall default in the performance of any of the obligations incumbent upon him or her by virtue of this Agreement, then the non-defaulting party shall be entitled to recover from the defaulting party all court costs, reasonable attorney's fees and other expenses incurred by the non-defaulting party in the enforcement of his or her rights hereunder.

18. Not later than August 1, YR-4, the Wife shall vacate the family residence at Route 7, Box 216, Southby, Michiana, and shall remove therefrom all of the personal property to which she is entitled by virtue of this Agreement.

IN WITNESS WHEREOF, the parties have executed this Agreement on the day first written above.

_____
Merlin V. Perry, Husband

Witness:

_____
Counsel for Respondent,
Cross-Petitioner

_____
Pamela A. Perry, Wife

Witness:

_____
Counsel for Petitioner,
Cross-Respondent

The Court having examined the aforementioned Property Settlement Agreement now specifically approves its terms, orders the parties to carry them out, and makes this Agreement a part of the Decree of Dissolution entered in this cause.
DATED this 1st day of July, YR-4.

_____
Judge, Hoynes Superior Court

M.C. 31-1-11.5-9 Dissolution decree; finality; support; maintenance; legal separation decree

Section 9. (a) In an action pursuant to section 3(a) of this chapter, when the court has made the findings required by section 8(a) of this chapter, the court shall enter a dissolution decree. The decree may include orders as provided for in this chapter. A dissolution decree shall become final when entered, subject to the right of appeal. An appeal from the provisions of a dissolution decree that does not challenge the findings as to the dissolution of the marriage shall not delay the finality of that provision of the decree which dissolves the marriage, so that the parties may remarry pending appeal.

(b) In an action pursuant to section 3(b) of this chapter, when the court has made the findings required by section 8(b) of this chapter, the court may enter a decree. The decree may include orders as provided for in this chapter.

(c) The court may order maintenance in final decrees entered under subsections (a) and (b) after making the findings required under section 11(e) of this chapter.

(d) In an action under section 3(c) of this chapter, when the court has made findings required by section 8(c) of this chapter, the court may enter a legal separation decree. The decree may include orders as provided in this chapter. A decree under this subsection may not include a maintenance provision that extends beyond the period of legal separation.

M.C. 31-1-11.5-11 Disposition of property; maintenance

Section 11. (a) For purposes of this section, "final separation" means the date of filing of the petition for dissolution of marriage under section 3 of this chapter.

(b) In an action pursuant to section 3(a) of this chapter, the court shall divide the property of the parties, whether owned by either spouse prior to the marriage, acquired by either spouse in his or her own right after the marriage and prior to final separation of the parties, or acquired by their joint efforts, in a just and reasonable manner, by:

(1) division of the property in kind;

(2) setting the property or parts of it over to one (1) of the spouses and requiring either spouse to pay such sum, either in gross or in installments, as may be just and proper;

(3) ordering the sale of the property under such conditions as the court may prescribe and dividing the proceeds of the sale; or

(4) ordering the distribution of any benefits described in section 2(d)(2) or 2(d)(3) of this chapter that are payable after the dissolution of marriage, by setting aside to either of the parties a percentage of those payments either by assignment or in kind at the time of receipt.

(c) In determining what is just and reasonable, the court shall consider the following factors:

(1) The contribution of each spouse to the acquisition of the property, including the contribution of a spouse as homemaker.

(2) The extent to which the property was acquired by each spouse prior to the marriage or through inheritance or gift.

(3) The economic circumstances of each spouse at the time the disposition of the property is to become effective, including the desirability of awarding the family residence or the right to dwell in that residence for such periods as the court may deem just to the spouse having custody of any children.

(4) The conduct of the parties during the marriage as related to the disposition or dissipation of their property.

(5) The earnings or earning ability of the parties as related to a final division of property and final determination of the property rights of the parties.

(d) When the court finds there is little or no marital property, it may award either spouse a money judgment not limited to the property existing at the time of final separation. However, this award may be made only for the financial contribution of one (1) spouse toward tuition, books, and laboratory fees for the higher education of the other spouse.

(e) A court may make the following findings concerning maintenance:

(1) If the court finds a spouse to be physically or mentally incapacitated to the extent that the ability of the incapacitated spouse to support himself is materially affected, the court may find that maintenance for that spouse is necessary during the period of incapacity, subject to further order of the court.

(2) If the court finds a spouse lacks sufficient property, including marital property apportioned to that spouse, to provide for that spouse's needs and that spouse is the custodian of a child whose physical or mental incapacity requires the custodian to forgo employment, the court may find that maintenance is necessary for that spouse in an amount and for a period of time as the court deems appropriate.

(3) After considering:

(A) the educational level of each spouse at the time of marriage and at the time the action is commenced;

(B) whether an interruption in the education, training, or employment of a spouse who is seeking maintenance occurred during the marriage as a result of homemaking or child care responsibilities, or both;

(C) the earning capacity of each spouse, including educational background, training, employment skills, work experience, and length of presence in or absence from job market; and

(D) the time and expense necessary to acquire sufficient education or training to enable the spouse who is seeking maintenance to find appropriate employment;

a court may find that rehabilitative maintenance for the spouse seeking maintenance is necessary in an amount and for a period of time that the court considers appropriate, but not to exceed two (2) years from the date of the final decree.

2. Dischargeability of Attorney Fees

Problem 60

In re Howard W. Ganglinger, Debtor

On August 8, YR-3, the debtor, Howard Ganglinger, filed a divorce action against his wife, Mary Alice Ganglinger, in the Hoynes Superior Court, Cause No. D-454. On September 17, YR-3, the debtor was ordered to pay support of $60.00 per week for the parties' son, Dwight, and "all monthly bills and taxes on the marital residence." The court preliminarily granted Mary Alice Ganglinger's motion that she be allowed to occupy and maintain the marital residence while her husband lived in the family's recently purchased lakeside cabin. On October 18, YR-2, due to delinquencies on the home bills, Howard

Ganglinger was ordered to pay the fixed sum of $200.00 per week to his wife, beginning October 21, YR-2, as "support and maintenance." Mary Alice was to pay the "mortgage and utilities for the residence of the parties," the record being silent on taxes. By October 18, YR-2, when Howard's support obligation was changed to a fixed amount, the home mortgage was in default, in violation of Howard's prior obligation, causing Mary Alice to pay $6,500.00, which was never reimbursed to her.

On March 27, YR-1, trial on Howard's petition for dissolution of marriage was conducted; exhibits were received and testimony taken. Howard was found on that date to be "in contempt of court as to the support payments which have not been made for many weeks herein." (Docket sheet; entry 3/17/YR-1.) At the time of the final hearing, Mary Alice was employed as a private duty nurse, working fifty-six hours per week for annual gross pay of $11,500, which was used in large part for the private school education of the parties' son. Mary Alice had nothing remaining from income for extra or incidental expenses. Howard's YR-3 W-2 earnings were $53,000; his YR-2 W-2 earnings were $43,000, and at the time of the final hearing, he had base pay of $3,500 per month, plus overtime, which in February, YR-1, was $525. At the final hearing, real estate taxes that had accrued and that were unpaid on the marital residence were $1,600, which Mary Alice paid at a later date out of funds borrowed from relatives. On April 16, YR-1, the court entered its decree of dissolution, which provided in pertinent part as follows:

1. Howard W. Ganglinger shall pay Mary Alice Ganglinger's reasonable attorney fees in the amount of $5,000, within 180 days, said order enforceable in the name of Guy L. Drewpup. JUDGMENT.
2. As under prior orders of this Court, Howard W. Ganglinger is ordered to pay YR-2 real estate taxes due in YR-1, in the sum of $1,600, and utilities, due up to the date of this hearing, in the sum of $3,700. JUDGMENT.
3. Howard W. Ganglinger shall pay Mary Alice Ganglinger as property settlement the sum of $28,342.75, representing one-half of the undistributed assets of the marital estate. In lieu of such payment, Mary Alice Ganglinger shall have a lien against the property referenced above as the lakeside cabin for the said amount. JUDGMENT.

On December 10, YR-1, Howard filed a Chapter 7 bankruptcy petition under 11 U.S.C. Section 301, in the U.S. Bankruptcy Court for the Northern District of Michiana. Howard listed Mary Alice as a lien holder on his personal residence, for which he claimed a homestead exemption. Assume for this problem that the applicable Michiana family law is that of Arkansas. Michiana is in the Fifteenth Federal Judicial Circuit.

Questions

1. Can Howard obtain discharge of (a) the attorney fees; (b) the delinquent real estate taxes; and (c) the property settlement amount?
2. Assume Mary Alice promptly recorded her lien against the lakeside cabin on April 17, YR-1. Even if Howard can obtain discharge of the property settlement award, can't Mary Alice use her status as a secured creditor to enforce the lien? How does the homestead exemption work against the lien? What other bankruptcy practice provisions might Howard employ to get out from under Mary Alice's lien?

3. Can Guy L. Drewpup, Mary Alice's divorce attorney, represent her in the bankruptcy proceedings?
4. Howard's duty to pay bills on the family house stems primarily from the separation agreement, not from the divorce proceedings. The divorce court deemed the bills "support and maintenance" when it ordered Howard to pay the bills. What effect does this determination have on the dischargeability of Howard's obligation to pay that debt?
5. Assume the divorce court held Howard in contempt for his failure to pay support. What effect will this determination have on Mary Alice's objections to discharge of divorce debts? What about Guy L. Drewpup's objections?
6. Should any divorce debts be dischargeable?

I. CUSTODY OF MINOR CHILDREN

1. At Dissolution

Problem 61

In re Marriage of Gardner

Glenn Gardner, age thirty-seven, and Loretta Gardner, age thirty-four, were married in YR-14. At the time of their marriage, Glenn had just received his B.A. degree from Michiana University. Loretta had completed her second year at Michiana University, but she dropped out of school to work in an insurance office while Glenn attended dental school. Glenn graduated from the Michiana University School of Dentistry in YR-11, and shortly thereafter he and Loretta purchased a home in the suburban Seneca Gardens district of Southby, Michiana. Glenn worked at University Hospital and later joined a group of oral surgeons in a Southby clinic. In YR-11, their first child, Lyle, was born. In YR-8, Glenn opened his own dental office in Southby. That same year, their daughter, Sissy, was born.

From YR-11 until YR-5, Loretta cared for the children and was not employed outside the home. In YR-5, she took a real estate course and obtained a broker's license. Since YR-5, Loretta has sold real estate on a part-time basis. As a part of that business, she holds open houses on two Sundays each month. The children sometimes accompany her to the open houses. Loretta occasionally has appointments to show other homes on the weekends as well, and the children often go with her when she shows these houses. Loretta also attends aerobic exercise classes two nights a week. She has become a vegetarian, and the children have often complained that they are hungry, feel tired and don't want to eat herbs and drink vegetable juices for each meal. Since YR-3, Loretta has been romantically involved with a twenty-seven-year-old law student, Stacy Teal, whom she met in connection with her work.

Glenn's dental practice is growing each year. He has won the respect of his professional peers in the Southby area and is now practicing oral surgery on a referral basis only. His office employs a receptionist, a secretary-bookkeeper, and two dental assistants. Glenn's receptionist has informed Loretta that Glenn and one of his dental assistants, Sheila, have been having an affair since early YR-2.

After Glenn and Loretta separated in February of YR-1, Glenn hired a private detective, who followed Loretta on several evenings during a two-week period. On two of those evenings, Loretta left the house at 5:30 P.M., went to Stacy's apartment, and returned home at 11:00 P.M. While she was out, the children were watched by Blanche Carter, a retired neighbor lady who has cared for the children on a regular basis over the years. Stacy is a member of the Michiana Magpies semiprofessional basketball team. Glenn's investigator has spotted Loretta seated in the front row at several Magpie home games in YR-1. Also, the guard at the apartment complex where Stacy lives has seen Loretta enter Stacy's apartment on several afternoons during the past three months. On these occasions, the children were in school, but once Loretta did not return home until after 5:00 P.M. The children let themselves into the house through the garage and then telephoned Glenn. Glenn left his office and came to the home to watch the children. When Loretta returned home, she and Glenn had a heated argument, and Glenn physically struck Loretta, causing facial abrasions and bruises. Glenn thereafter amended his petition for dissolution of marriage and requested sole custody of Lyle and Sissy or, in the alternative, joint physical custody.

When Glenn and Loretta separated in February of YR-1, Glenn moved into a two-bedroom apartment at Colonial Crest Village, approximately three miles from the parties' residence. Soon thereafter, Glenn traded his Toyota Cressida for a YR-1 Lamborghini. He has been dating several women since the separation, including his dental assistant, Sheila. Glenn recently spent one week at a dental conference in Nassau, Bahamas accompanied by Sheila.

Glenn took the children to Epcot Center in Orlando, Florida, over the YR-1 Christmas break. Also, Glenn recently gave Lyle a ten-speed bicycle, a personal computer, and a portable color television set. Glenn has made other promises of gifts to the children recently. Glenn works four days a week and generally plays golf and gin rummy at the country club after he leaves the office. Glenn states that if Loretta is awarded sole custody of the children he will be ordered to make substantial weekly payments under the Michiana Child Support guidelines. Glenn claims that the children would be better served if he were awarded custody and after paying for child care he would have more funds left over to spend on the children's needs.

The children's teachers at St. Matthew's School indicate that Glenn has never attended a parent-teacher conference but has made a few telephone calls concerning the children. Loretta has attended only one parent-teacher conference, with Lyle's teacher, Mrs. Sheen. Mrs. Sheen states that Lyle has become frequently disruptive in the classroom in the last three months. She describes Lyle throwing chalk and erasers and his assaultive behavior toward other students. Lyle's work habits have deteriorated, and his homework is often incomplete. Sissy's teacher, Mrs. Cowger, says that she has noticed changes in Sissy's personality since her parents' separation. Mrs. Cowger states that Sissy has lost a lot of weight and seems depressed, distant, and lonely. Ms. Sandra Hood, the school social worker, states that Lyle is desirous of attention and has indicated to her that he wants to live with his father. Sissy did not express to the social worker a preference for either parent. Ms. Hood states that she has discussed the children and their feelings with Mrs. Sheen and Mrs. Cowger.

Blanche Carter states that Loretta is a kind, warm person who loves her children very much and keeps a spotless home. Blanche indicates that Dr. Gardner is friendly and apparently "plays golf quite a bit." Blanche states that before the separation "Dr. Gardner appeared to be intoxicated, loud and obnoxious on several occasions when the parties returned home from an evening out."

Prior to the separation in YR-1, Loretta was primarily responsible for the care of the children; however, Glenn has always helped the children with their homework, and after Loretta started working in YR-5, Glenn took on some ad-

Chapter Nine. Dissolution of Marriage

ditional chores around the house to help out. Since the separation, Glenn has increased the amount of his caretaking of the children and has taken an active role in Lyle's youth rugby program.

Glenn has had three automobile accidents since YR-14, all of which followed drinking and card-playing at the country club. All of these accidents involved property damage but no personal injuries. Loretta has undergone psychotherapy since YR-3 and has been admonished by her therapist that she is taking too many tranquilizers to deal appropriately with her problems.

The children have resided with Loretta since the parties separated ten months ago. Glenn has met all of his obligations in the provisional order and has exercised regular and frequent visitation. There have been several occasions, however, when the children weren't ready for visitation when Glenn arrived to pick them up. A neighbor, Marie O'Brien, states that she recently witnessed a loud argument at the Gardner home when Glenn came for visitation with the children. Marie described the children as crying uncontrollably where Loretta called Glenn "an alcoholic Disneyland asshole," and Glenn replied, "You're nothing but a self-indulgent, neurotic feminist bitch." Glenn has often brought the children back late from visitation or kept them an extra day against Loretta's wishes.

Loretta follows a schedule (which she has posted on the refrigerator door) for the children's meals, kitchen and household duties, homework, and bedtime. She objects to Glenn's "laissez faire" ways with the children. The children state that they have no rules whatsoever when they are at Glenn's apartment, and that there are a lot of women in and out of Glenn's apartment, some of whom spend the night with Glenn. Loretta requests that the provisional order granting Loretta sole custody be continued at the final hearing.

Following this Problem is some relevant information on the Gardner family and a letter and resumé submitted by Mr. Joseph B. Holmes, a social worker retained by Glenn.

Questions

1. It is important to understand which facts are relevant to a custody decision. The student should review the facts of this Problem, including the attached letter from Mr. Holmes, marking those sentences that favor Glen with a G and those that favor Loretta with an L. Then review the marked facts, circling those that should be included in a memorandum concerning custody. Next, prepare a written memorandum and proposed form of order, including findings of fact and conclusions of law concerning the custody issues in this case. Assume that Michiana law is identical to Section 402 of the Uniform Marriage and Divorce Act (UMDA) (*See* Appendix.).
2. Aside from the facts presented in this Problem, what other important factors should be considered in custody determinations?
3. Who is the children's primary caretaker? How might this concept be applied under Section 402 of the UMDA?
4. Who is best suited to determine the child's best interests in a child custody proceeding?
5. What problems are there with the "best interests of the child" standard for custody determinations?
6. Should the court, *sua sponte*, appoint an expert to investigate and report on the custody issues in this case?

INFORMATION

	Husband	**Wife**
Name:	Glenn Gardner, D.D.S.	Loretta Gardner
Address:	Colonial Crest Village #9	2553 Dell Road, Seneca Gardens
Age:	37	34
Health:	Good	Good
Education and Training:	M.U. Graduate YR-14 M.U. School of Denistry YR-11	2 yrs. M.U. School of Business R. Estate Brokers License YR-5
Present Employer and Compensation:	Self Employed Dentist $125,000	Century 21 Real Estate $16,000
Employment History:	YR-11 - Staff Univ. Hosp YR-10/YR-8 - Oral Surgery YR-8 - Self Employed	Has only worked part time since the parties separated in November, YR-1
Employability:	Good	Current Market Conditions Are Unfavorable
Income for past 5 years:	YR-1 - $125,000 YR-2 - 80,000 YR-3 - 72,500 YR-4 - 67,000 YR-5 - 60,000	YR-1 - $17,000 YR-2 - 16,000 YR-3 - 27,000 YR-4 - 11,000 YR-5 - -0-

Length of Marriage:	14 years
Children's birthdays, names, special factors:	Lyle, age 10, 5th grade at St. Matthew's School, and very bright student, but work and grades have declined since parties' separation. Sissy, age 7, 2nd grade, exceptional student currently in class for gifted, also piano, violin, and dance lessons; marked personality change since separation, withdrawn, prefers isolation, often goes without meals, experiencing weight loss
Prior Marriages and Children:	None

Significant assets and liabilities:

Assets: House: 2553 Dell Road, Seneca Gardens, Southby, Michiana

                   FMV #375,000.00 (JTWRS)

Cash/CD's, etc.:   4 CDs ($25,000 @) Society Bank, Southby, Michiana
Stocks/Bonds: H: 500 sh Sears; 500 sh Allstate;
                    200 sh Dean Witter; 200 sh Michiana Natural Gas

Other Real Estate: NA
Retirement Plan:
Auto: YR-2 Volvo (H); YR-9 Toyota Cressida (W)

Liabilities:

    House Mortgage: N/A

    Bank Loans: N/A

Contributions by Husband to Property: N/A

Contributions by Wife to Property: N/A

Dissipation of Assets: N/A

Inheritance and Gifts: N/A

Other Facts: Both parties desire custody of the two minor children. Lyle has expressed a strong preference to reside with his father. Sissy has not indicated any preference.

Restraining Order Needed? Parties are bickering over visitation and using the children to get at each other.

Custody Dispute? Both parties desire custody. Lyle desires to live with Father, and Sissy refuses to indicate.

Fee Arrangements

GOOD MARRIAGES, INC.
1470 Bardstown Road
Southby, Michiana 46601

Vincent R. Dana, Ph.D.
Carolyn B. Byrnes, MSW
Joseph B. Holmes, MSW

Dear Attorney Shysto:

I understand that the permanent custody of Lyle Gardner, age eleven, and Sissy Gardner, age eight, is in dispute. Both parents have selected family therapists to consider and evaluate the issue of custody. Although I have been asked by Dr. Gardner to perform this task, I believe my opinion is objective and unbiased, being based upon interviews with Dr. Gardner, Mrs. Loretta Gardner and the children, Lyle and Sissy Gardner.

Loretta Gardner is a thin, attractive woman who has had difficulty adjusting to the separation from Dr. Gardner. She attributes the breakdown of the marriage to her fading looks and her lack of an impressive career. She has responded to these feelings by an almost fanatic interest in self-improvement. She attends aerobic classes regularly, feeling despondent if she misses a class and she has turned to absolute vegetarianism, imposing her newly discovered nutrition views upon the children. She has also become extremely zealous and aggressive in her career, frequently taking the reluctant children to home showings and open houses.

Mrs. Gardner admits to being "in love" with a much younger man, although she apparently has been discreet about keeping her relationship with him away from the children. The relationship itself, however, is consistent with her intense feeling of rejection and need for approval of her physical attractiveness and worth.

Dr. Gardner is comparatively a more stable, emotionally mature individual, well satisfied with his career advancement and lifestyle. While he admits to enjoying "a drink at the club," he is decidedly not an alcoholic. His drinking is confined to social settings; Mrs. Gardner could not recall her husband ever drinking at home. Moreover, Dr. Gardner's extreme concern for his children would prevent him from appearing even mildly intoxicated in their presence.

Lyle definitely wants to stay with his father. He is proud of his father's career and that his father is a caring, concerned parent. Lyle's academic record has declined dramatically since his parents' separation, evidencing the child's depression and confusion over the unresolved status of his custody. Although a child of eleven should not have a determinative choice in custody, such a child is old enough to have a significant voice in this decision. It is also true that to the extent possible, siblings close in age should not be separated. It is significant that little Sissy has not stated a preference for either parent. Often children of this age, especially females, have a preference for their mother.

Because neither child is flourishing in Mrs. Gardner's care, and indeed, both seem to be experiencing significant trauma, it is my opinion that custody of these children would be best reposed in Dr. Gardner's care, with substantial, liberal visitation to Mrs. Gardner. At this time, at least, Mrs. Gardner is removed and distant from her children, apparently directing her energies toward self-improvement. Moreover, Dr. Gardner's home is more comfortable and secure. During the marriage, Dr. Gardner showed a more active interest in the schoolwork of both children; both could benefit from such interest at this time.

Attached is a statement for my professional services to date. If I can provide you with further information, please contact me.

Sincerely,

Joseph B. Holmes, MSW

JBH/mjh
Encl.

RESUME

JOSEPH B. HOLMES

2035 Breeze Wood Drive
Southby, Michiana 46350
Home: 219-491-7097
Office: 219-488-6913

Personal:	Birthdate: 7-29-YR-34 Marital Status: Single Health: Excellent
Education:	B.S. (cum laude) University of Michiana (YR-13) Clinical Psychology M.S.W. University of Kansas (YR-10)
Professional Membership:	Academy of Certified Social Workers (A.C.S.W.) eligible Northern Michiana Chapter of Hospital Social Workers Association
Professional Experience:	

	YR-13/YR-7	The Arc Runaway Shelter, Chicago, Illinois live-in worker, case management team leader, shift supervisor
	YR-7/YR-4	Salvation Army social worker, family counselor
	YR-4/Present	Community Hospital of Southby Oncology Department Patient Services worker Pediatrics Department Department Head
	YR-2/Present	Good Marriages, Inc. part-time consulting and family therapy

Publications:	Community Hospital Newsletter monthly columns on various social services topics
References:	Available upon request.

Chapter Nine. Dissolution of Marriage

2. Homosexual Parent

Problem 62

Ginger v. Ginger

In YR-4, Jennifer Ginger married Greg Greeway. On November 1, YR-3, Greg moved out of the family home, two weeks before Jennifer gave birth to their son, Bobby. Greg has never contacted Jennifer, and her attempts to locate him were unsuccessful. Jennifer has filed a divorce petition and served Greg with summons by publication.

In the past three years Jennifer has been involved in several romantic relationships and has maintained three different residences. After Greg left her, Jennifer dated and eventually moved in with a man she met at work. When that relationship ended, she moved into a house with a lesbian couple. Soon after, she began dating Laura Ford and has lived with Ms. Ford for the past year.

Since Bobby's birth in YR-3, Jennifer's mother, Sara Ginger, has played a significant role in the care and custody of Bobby. Jennifer often left Bobby with Sara for long periods of time at the home Sara shared with her live-in male companion, Tom. On several occasions, Jennifer failed to leave information with Sara as to where Jennifer could be reached.

Recently, Jennifer informed Sara that she would not be leaving Bobby with her overnight any longer, because Jennifer and Laura where settling down and would be able to provide a more stable home life for Bobby, and because of Tom's presence in Sara's home. Jennifer recently informed her mother that Tom had sexually abused her when she was a young girl, and therefore Jennifer did not feel comfortable leaving Bobby at Sara and Tom's home.

Sara was so shocked and upset by the realization that her daughter was a lesbian and by the accusation that Tom had abused Jennifer that she filed in the Hoynes Circuit Court a motion to intervene in Jennifer's divorce action and a further motion seeking custody of Bobby. Sara's motion for custody alleges that Jennifer is not a fit parent and states that Bobby's mental, physical and moral welfare are in danger when the child is in Jennifer's care. Sara alleges that Jennifer's current lifestyle shows that she is irresponsible, immoral, and sexually promiscuous, and that this behavior puts Bobby at risk.

In Jennifer's answer to Sara's motion for custody, Jennifer acknowledges that she is a lesbian and that she lives with her lover, Laura. She admits that she and Laura share the same bed and engage in consensual sexual acts in the privacy of their home and that they also show affection for one another in front of Bobby. However, Jennifer maintains that she and Laura never engage in any type of sexual conduct in front of Bobby.

The only contested issue at the final divorce hearing on January 3, YR-0, is the custody of Bobby. Bobby is presently in Jennifer's care, and Jennifer continues to live with Laura. Sara, on the advice of counsel, requested that Tom move out, and she is now living alone. Greg fails to appear at the final hearing and is defaulted.

Questions

1. Should Jennifer's homosexuality be an issue in determining whether she or Sara receive custody of Bobby? Should it be? Does Jennifer's sexual orientation make her an unfit parent?

2. How should the court rule on the custody issue under Section 402 of the Uniform Marriage and Divorce Act (UMDA)? (*See* Appendix.)
3. If Michiana recognizes the tender-years presumption (maternal preference rule), should it apply in this case?
4. Assume that Jennifer based her responsive pleading on the facts that Tom is an African-American, who is also an officer in the Michiana Chapter of the Black Panther Party, and Tom remains in Sara's home. Would this be a permissible basis to deny Sara custody of Bobby?
5. Assume, in addition to the facts in 4, above, that Tom was convicted in YR-10 of armed robbery and served two years in prison.

3. *Joint Custody*

Problem 63

In re Marriage of Morgan

Peter and Barbara Morgan were married on May 11, YR-16, following a very brief courtship. Peter and Barbara have four minor children: Brian, age eighteen (Barbara's son by a previous marriage), who was adopted by Peter in YR-9, and three daughters born of the marriage—Jennifer, fifteen, Erika, fourteen, and Jessica, four. Barbara filed a petition for legal separation in July of YR-0. Peter filed a petition for dissolution of marriage on September 11, YR-0. Peter and Barbara both desire sole custody of the children. Peter alternatively requests an order of joint legal and physical custody. The Domestic Relations Counseling Bureau (DRCB) filed its report, which follows this Problem.

Questions

1. What is joint legal custody? What is joint physical custody? Can there be one without the other?
2. Why would a court grant sole custody over joint custody?
3. Is there a preference in the law for one form of custody over another?
4. List a number of factors that should be present before a court orders joint physical custody.
5. When should the court order a DCRB report? If the DRCB report is dispositive in the court's decision, is the court not abdicating its authority over family issues to a social service agency? If it is not dispositive, in what ways can the report be considered relevant?
6. Read the DRCB report in this case. What recommendation does it make? What response should counsel for Peter and Barbara make to the DRCB report?
7. In addition to the DRCB report, what other third-party reports could aid the court in its child custody determination? Strategically, should either party attempt to supply the court with such additional information? Which party?
8. Assuming that Michiana law is identical to the Uniform Marriage and Divorce Act (UMDA), what should the court's custody ruling be in this case? What facts from the DRCB report support this result?

Domestic Relations Counseling Bureau
121 County City Building
Southby, Michiana 46601
219-236-5094

DATE: October 24, YR-0

TO: Honorable Albert B. Simpson, Judge
               Hoynes Circuit Court

FROM: Susan Sheehan, Chief Counselor
               Domestic Relations Counseling Bureau

IN RE: The Marriage of Peter R. Morgan—Husband
               and Barbara S. Morgan—Wife

CAUSE NO.   R-7138

CUSTODY STUDY

On 8/27/YR-0, Mr. Peter R. Morgan and Mrs. Barbara S. Morgan were referred to DRCB by the Honorable Albert B. Simpson, Judge of the Hoynes Circuit Court, for assistance in the matters of temporary and permanent support as well as permanent custody determination for their four minor children, who are 18, 15, 14, and 4 years of age.

On 9/14/YR-0, a Temporary Support Study was submitted to the Court by DRCB. Each of the parents was interviewed prior to submission of that report.

On 10/9/YR-0, Mr. Morgan was seen in this office for 1 1/2 hours.

On 10/11/YR-0, Mrs. Morgan was seen in this office for 2 hours.

On 10/18/YR-0, three of the four children: Jennifer, 15, Erika, 14, and Jessica, 4, were seen in the family home. Brian, 18, was not included in the one hour visit since he is now working full-time at Von Tobel Lumber Company.

One collateral contact was made with Ronald Randell, Ph.D., psychologist, who has seen Mr. and Mrs. Morgan and the four children. This contact was made with the written consent of Mrs. Morgan.

A copy of this original report is on file in DRCB. Two additional copies are attached for distribution to the respective attorneys for the parties.

Situation and Background

The parties were married on 5/11/YR-16, after an extremely brief courtship. At the time of their marriage, Peter was 24 and Barbara was 23 years of age.

Mrs. Morgan had been married previously and brought into the marriage her two-year-old son, Brian, date of birth 6/26/YR-18. Mr. Morgan adopted Brian, now 18, in Reno, Nevada, in YR-9. Three children were born of the marriage: Jennifer, 15, date of birth 7/2/YR-15, Erika, 14, date of birth 7/14/YR-14, and Jessica, 4, date of birth 4/21/YR-4.

On 8/7/YR-0, at the first hearing in the matter of the wife's Petition for Legal Separation, Mrs. Morgan was granted the right to exclusive, but temporary, occupance of the family dwelling. She was granted temporary care, charge, and custody of the minor son and three minor daughters, while Mr. Morgan was afforded reasonable visitation with the children. Mr. Morgan was ordered to pay the sum of $500 per week beginning 8/31/YR-0 as supplemental support of the wife and child support for the four minor children. The issues of temporary and permanent support were referred to DRCB, with the request that the temporary support study be expedited. As Mr. Morgan represented to the Court that he was requesting sole custody or alternatively joint legal and physical custody, the issue of permanent custody was also referred to DRCB.

On 9/11/YR-0, Mr. Morgan filed a Petition for Dissolution of the Marriage.

Father

Mr. Morgan, 40, date of birth 4/24/YR-40, was the eldest of three sons born to his parents. His father was an executive for Washoe County Bank and Trust Company in Reno, Nevada, where Mr. Morgan completed high school and college. His youngest brother, Marvin, was working as a "pit boss" at Harold's Club in Reno when he died of a self-inflicted gunshot wound in YR-19. His parents moved to California in YR-14 and his father died there at age 52. His mother had not worked outside the home until YR-12. She presently lives in California and is terminally ill with lung cancer. Mr. Morgan states that his family was a close, "regular" group. There were no drinking problems or financial difficulties in the home as he grew up.

Mr. Morgan graduated from high school in Reno, Nevada, in YR-22. He described himself as a good student who was interested in soccer and track. He graduated with a B.A. degree in history from the University of Nevada-Reno in YR-18. Mr. Morgan was elected President of the Student Body during his senior year at UNR. Presently, he is enrolled part-time in the Southby State Law School from which he hopes to graduate in the spring of next year. He enjoys his schooling because it brings him in touch with stimulating personalities and "bright people."

After his graduation from the University of Nevada-Reno, Mr. Morgan worked from the Summer of YR-18 to the Summer of YR-17 for a private foundation in Chicago, Illinois. Mr. Morgan monitored grants for the foundation, traveling extensively in the United States with his employer. During the Summer of YR-17, he was on active duty in the U.S. Army Reserve. In the fall of YR-17, he began employment at the YMCA in Peoria, Illinois, where he met and married Mrs. Morgan. In December of YR-15, Mr. Morgan took employment in the Development Office of Central College in Madison, Wisconsin. When he left that employment in YR-5, he became Assistant to the President at Central College. In YR-5, he came to Ripley College in Southby, Michiana as Vice President for Public Relations. He describes himself as an holistic planner for the College. He states that his duties at Ripley do not require his being gone more than three to five overnight days a month.

When Mr. Morgan first took employment with Ripley College in YR-5, his yearly salary was $40,000 gross. In YR-0, he states that he will be earning about $75,000 gross.

Since about 8/27/YR-0, when he was required to leave the family home, Mr. Morgan has lived in a one bedroom apartment at 301 S. Illinois Street in Southby, Michiana.

Mother

Mrs. Morgan, 39, date of birth 3/3/YR-39, has two younger brothers. Her father, who died in YR-4, was retired after thirty years in the U.S. Marines at the time of his death. Mrs. Morgan remembered that in her earlier years, her father might be gone for three to six months but that later he was gone for extended periods. Her mother, Mrs. Rosalyn Twilley, did not work outside of the home until she, Mrs. Twilley, was 40. Mrs. Morgan recalled that the family moved about until she was about 15 years of age, living in California, North Carolina, Virginia, and finally Illinois. She spoke of her childhood home as financially comfortable and one in which there were close relationships between her two brothers, her mother and her father. Mrs. Morgan describes her mother, who lived in the Morgan home for the past four years, as a "jewel."

Because her family moved around a lot, she attended four grade schools and two high schools. She did not complete her high school education in a formal setting in Illinois but did take her G.E.D. in YR-20. She has accumulated 21 hours of college credit from courses taken in Madison, Wisconsin and then at Ripley College. The emphasis of her college work was on elementary education and child psychology. Now, however, she expresses an interest in paralegal training.

Marital History/Relationship

The couple met at a citizens action meeting in Peoria, Illinois. Mrs. Morgan had been working with a group of parents relative to racial confrontations in Peoria in YR-16. Mr. Morgan was at the meeting as a YMCA employee. Mr. Morgan, who reported that he was "ready to get married," was married to Mrs. Morgan three weeks after they met. The couple lived in Peoria for about a year and a half with her son, Brian, who was about twenty-three months of age when they married. Their first daughter, Jennifer, was born in Peoria before they moved on to Madison, where Mr. Morgan took employment with Central College. In YR-14, their second daughter, Erika, was born and in YR-9, Mr. Morgan adopted Brian, then about 11 years of age. Their third daughter, Jessica, was born in YR-4.

Mrs. Morgan indicated that early in their marriage, she and Mr. Morgan had a "beautiful relationship". Their home, she said, was in a "lovely, close-knit neighborhood" in Madison. Mrs. Morgan indicated that she interacted with her neighbors in block parties, child care and chauffeuring children. Mr. Morgan, she said, was not that much involved with neighborhood activities, preferring to work or read in his room.

Their life in Madison, as described by Mrs. Morgan, was "comfortable and interesting". They did share an interest in political matters; both ran for public office and she worked for Mrs. Pat Souza, now a Congresswoman from Wisconsin.

In YR-5, Mr. Morgan was approached by the President of Ripley College, where he took employment that year. The Morgans purchased a $90,000 home in Sugar Acres for their family unit, which was joined about a year later by Mrs. Morgan's mother, Mrs. Dahlia Twilley.

After the arrival of Mrs. Twilley in YR-4, Mrs. Morgan traveled with Mr. Morgan on occasion; this gave them some free time together. Mr. Morgan admitted, however, that he has not spent any time with the children. Mrs. Morgan stated that this was the main cause of friction between them. Mr. Morgan also reported that his wife loved the children dearly, and that without her help, Brian, now 18, would not have completed high school. The couple gives the impression that the lives of the children have revolved mainly around the mother. It was she who took the children on vacation to Kansas, where Mrs. Morgan's sisters and their families lived. In YR-2, there was a family vacation in Boston, Massachusetts, during which Mr. Morgan worked and the mother and children went sightseeing. Mrs. Morgan reports that Mr. Morgan generally takes his vacation periods to go off with his friends fishing for two- to three-week periods.

Mr. Morgan entered law school at Southby State University in YR-3. He is critical of Mrs. Morgan that she has failed to take the opportunity for tuition-free courses at Ripley College. Mrs. Morgan simply states that the interruptions of running a family and the home, as well as assisting Brian, the eldest child, with some personal and academic problems, did not give her free time to commit herself to college study.

In addition to friction over the time Mr. Morgan had for the children, there have been problems in the home over money management. Mr. Morgan states that Mrs. Morgan cannot manage money. He said that when he attempted to take over the family finances, he was frustrated by the short-term as opposed to long-term planning they were able to do with their finances. Mr. Morgan had indicated to DRCB on 9/11/YR-0 that among the bills owing were an $11,000 loan from the Southby Credit Union and a $2,000 loan from Ripley College. On or about 9/9/YR-0, Mrs. Morgan informed this office that she had learned quite by accident that Mr. Morgan had borrowed almost five thousand dollars from the Southby Credit Union on 9/12/YR-0.

Children

Brian, 18, was not seen at the time of the visit to the Morgan home on 10/18/YR-0, inasmuch as he is now working full-time at Von Tobel Lumber Company. Brian, who in June of YR-0 graduated from Millard Filmore High School, is scheduled to go into the Navy in January of next year. Reference has been made above to Mrs. Morgan's investment in getting Brian through high school. This was related to his having a learning disability. He came from a private school in Madison,

Wisconsin, into Filmore High School at age 13. Mr. Morgan states that it was because of his wife's efforts that Brian was able to finish school.

Jennifer, age 15, is a sophomore at Filmore High School. Jennifer is described by her mother as an independent young lady who is bright, aware and growing socially.

Her sister, Erika, age 14, is a freshman at Filmore. Erika is described by her mother as being flighty and restless. She is a creative child who is interested in writing and art. Erika underwent surgery in Milwaukee about a year ago for a condition described by Mrs. Morgan as a "blocked bowel." In August of this year, Erika was to return to Milwaukee for a yearly check-up. This was not possible because of the financial situation of the family. Jennifer and Erika are attractive adolescents. During our discussion, they touched upon school, friends and their extra-curricular interests.

Jessica, age 4, attends Montessori preschool and is described as a "very bright, precocious child" by the school's director, Ms. Eva Ring. Jessica stated that "Mommy shouldn't be doing that," to describe her feelings about Mrs. Morgan's seeing another man, Mr. Juan Avila, while still married to Mr. Morgan. Jennifer and Erika were openly hostile toward their mother for seeing Mr. Avila, and stated that on a few occasions Mr. Avila had stayed overnight in their mother's bedroom.

The three girls are going through much stress related to the divorce of their parents. Their questions regarding support and joint custody indicated that they have done a great deal of thinking about both subjects. We talked about the financial problems that divorce does bring to both parents and to the children. Their anger with their mother for seeking the separation is evident. They distrust their mother and blame her for "driving their father away." They do acknowledge, however, that in the past their mother, rather than their father, was the one who was "always there when we needed help." The girls did not wish to express a preference for either parent. When asked how they felt about living with both parents, Jennifer said, "That might not be too bad," and Erika responded, "I'll do it if Jennifer does."

Collateral Contact

On 10/12/YR-0, Dr. Ronald Randell, Ph.D., who had been working with this family or individual members for about four years, talked briefly with DRCB about the parenting positions and skills of Mr. Peter Morgan and Mrs. Barbara Morgan. Dr. Randell believes that Mr. Morgan was education and status-oriented and that in the past he had "abdicated his role as father." Dr. Randell feels, however, that Mr. Morgan is now quite serious about his role as a parent and is capable of fulfilling the role of custodial parent.

Dr. Randell talked about Mrs. Morgan's hypoglycemic condition, which dictates she must take good care of her diet and the depression related to the divorce. Dr. Randell talked of the remarkable job she had done in assisting Brian, the eldest child, with social and academic problems. He feels that Mrs. Morgan's relationship with Mr.

Avila is creating a great deal of resentment and stress which is harmful to the children.

Support

On 8/31/YR-0, Mr. Morgan was to begin to pay $500 weekly in spousal maintenance and child support for the three minor children. As this report is being dictated on 10/30/YR-0, Mr. Morgan has been 100% responsible for his obligation.

Assessment

The docket sheet reflects the following entry on 8/27/YR-0:

> "On representation of husband that he will request sole custody, or alternatively joint legal and physical custody, the issue of permanent custody is referred to DRCB."

Giving cognizance to the docket entry, DRCB focused upon Sections (f) and (g) in being guided by MC 31-3-11.5.21.

Section (f) states "The Court may award legal custody of a child jointly if the Court finds that an award of joint legal custody would be in the best interest of the child." Section (f) goes on to explain that "joint legal custody" means that the persons awarded joint custody will share authority and responsibility for the major decisions concerning the child's upbringing, including the child's education, health care, and religious training. Further, that section notes that an award of joint legal custody does not require an equal division of the physical custody of the child.

Section (g) goes on to state that in determining whether an award of joint legal custody would be in the best interest of the child, the Court shall consider it a matter of primary, but not determinative importance, that the persons awarded joint custody have agreed to an award of joint custody. The Court shall also consider:

1) The fitness and suitability of each of the persons awarded joint custody:

    Both Mr. and Mrs. Morgan could be considered fit and suitable persons to act as custodial or joint custodial parent to the children.

2) Whether the persons awarded joint custody are willing and able to communicate and cooperate in advancing the child's welfare:

    Mrs. Morgan indicated that when their son, Brian, was in trouble socially and academically, Mr. Morgan wanted the child out of their home. She further indicated that when Jennifer and Erika are doing well academically, it pleases Mr. Morgan. When they are not doing well academically, Mr. Morgan is critical and non-supportive of the children. During the course of the investigation, Mr. Morgan cut off lines of communication from Mrs. Morgan and began to give the impression that he was not as interested in the children as he was in his own feelings and welfare.

3) The wishes of the child and whether the child(ren) has established a close and beneficial relationship with both of the persons awarded joint custody:

Next year, when he enters the Navy, Brian Morgan, 18, will be an emancipated child. He was not available for interview, and his wishes were not sought because he is approaching emancipation. Jennifer, 15, and Erika, 14, have indicated to this office and to Robert Randell, Ph.D., psychologist, that they would like to be with both parents. Mrs. Morgan states that Mr. Morgan has made himself available to the children on "about half the weekends since we split up." While his work may have kept him from his family when they lived in Madison and then in Southby, he is described by Mrs. Morgan as remaining aloof from neighborhood-family activities and as taking his fishing vacations with his friends rather than with the family. The grief and anger of Jennifer, Erika and Jessica at this time seems related to a change in lifestyle and their mother's liaison with another man, with whom she has already planned to share the Thanksgiving and Christmas holidays this year.

4) Whether the persons awarded joint custody live in close proximity to each other and plan to continue to do so:

During the course of the investigation, Mrs. Morgan spoke of her plan to return to Peoria, Illinois, where her two brothers and their families and other relatives reside. It was presumed that her mother, Mrs. Rosalyn Twilley, would also return to Peoria. On 10/20/YR-0, Mrs. Morgan reported to DRCB that she has now reconsidered her move after the sale of the family home here, and is willing to remain in Southby if the Court orders joint custody. Mr. Morgan plans to continue with his position at Ripley College. If awarded custody of the parties' three minor children, he states that he will purchase a home in Southby.

5) The nature of the physical and emotional environment in the home of each of the persons awarded joint custody:

Mr. Morgan is presently living in an one bedroom apartment. The family home in which Mrs. Morgan, the children, and her mother presently reside is for sale. There is nothing to suggest that following the sale of their large home that each of the parents could not establish a suitable living situation for the children. In the course of this study, however, Mrs. Morgan emerges as the parent to whom the children were bonded emotionally until she initiated separation proceedings and began spending time with Mr. Avila.

Jennifer and Erika recognize the important part that she has played in their lives as homemaker, chauffeur, nurse and mother, but are bitter at her for "breaking up our home." Mrs. Morgan's emotional investment in the children is clear, while the past and present emotional bond of Mr. Morgan to the children has little depth despite his financial provisions for them.

Recommendations

That the Court review and assign financial obligations, regarding the medical needs of the children.

That the Court order support for Jennifer, Erika and Jessica according to its Guidelines (with the information regarding income provided in the DRCB report of 9/14/YR-0).

That the Court consider an order of joint physical custody only if both parties maintain their residences in the Southby, Michiana area. The Court should consider ordering joint legal custody even if the parties do not maintain their residences in Southby. Otherwise, it is recommended that either Mr. or Mrs. Morgan is a fit and proper person to have custody of the three minor children.

_____
Susan Sheehan, Chief Counselor
Domestic Relations Counseling Bureau

_____
John R. Connell, Director
Domestic Relations Bureau

Copies to: Counsel for Peter R. Morgan and Barbara S. Morgan

4. Non-Marital Relationships

Problem 64

Fontes v. MacNamara

This case is at the summary judgment stage. Ellen Fontes moved for summary judgment in her custody action to remove all visitation and custody rights from Joan MacNamara. The Hoynes Circuit Court has issued a temporary restraining order forbidding Joan from visiting or taking custody of Samuel and Dwayne Fontes.

In November, YR-15, Ellen and Joan met in a bar in New City, Michiana. They immediately became friends, and eventually lovers. After signing a domestic partnership agreement by which Ellen was to maintain their home, in June, YR-14, they moved in together. In return, Joan was to use her well-paying job to provide for all expenses. After several happy years of living together, Ellen and Joan decided that they would like to have children. Ellen signed an artificial insemination contract with a Southby, Michiana, fertility clinic, listing Joan on the contract as the potential legal father. The artificial insemination process was a success, and on April 6, YR-10, Samuel Fontes was born.

In YR-7, on the advice of counsel, Joan formally adopted Samuel so she could name him in her will without any contest from her family. Joan and Ellen decided that they would like another child, so Ellen signed up again for artificial insemination. The second time it took nearly three years before Ellen became pregnant. During that time, partially because of Ellen's fertility problem, the couple's relationship began to deteriorate. Dwayne Fontes was born on December 4, YR-3. Both Samuel and eventually Dwayne called Joan "Mom." Although Joan had planned to adopt Dwayne on his third birthday, she never formally adopted him.

In January, YR-1, Ellen and Joan ended their relationship. Pursuant to their domestic partnership agreement, Joan provided Ellen with payments to support her and the two boys. Joan had partial custody of the boys, keeping them on weekends and on any holiday she didn't work. When Joan's job reduced her number of working days each week from five to four, she attempted to increase the amount of time she spent with the boys. Ellen, however, refused to agree to a change in the custody arrangement.

After both parties sought legal counsel and resolution of their dispute became impossible, Ellen filed suit in Hoynes Circuit Court seeking temporary and permanent injunctive relief to prevent Joan from visiting with the children. Joan cross-claimed for a declaratory judgment, stating that she is a parent of both Samuel and Dwayne, under the alternative theories of de facto parenthood, in loco parentis, equitable estoppel, and equitable parentage. In the alternative, Joan requested that the court adjudge her a parent of Dwayne under a functional definition of "parenthood." Assume that the applicable Michiana law is identical to the Uniform Parentage Act.

The Hoynes Circuit Court has granted a temporary restraining order, over objection, refusing Joan any custody or visitation until the matter is disputed. There is no dispute between the parties as to the facts of the case. Ellen has filed a motion for summary judgment, claiming that she is entitled to sole custody of both Samuel and Dwayne as a matter of law.

> **Questions**
>
> 1. Read the Uniform Parentage Act. (*See* Appendix.) How can Joan successfully bring an action for visitation based on the terms of the UPA?
> 2. How would Section 2 of the Uniform Status of Children of Assisted Conception Act affect the determination of custody in this case?
> 3. Define each of the following terms: (a) de facto parenthood; (b) in loco parentis; (c) equitable estoppel; (d) equitable parent. How would each of these terms apply to the custody dispute in this case?
> 4. Should Joan have any special visitation rights regarding either Dwayne or Samuel? What effect does Joan's adoption of Samuel have on her rights? On Ellen's rights?
> 5. Should the visitation question in this case be decided, like typical parental visitation questions, as a consequence of the custody issue?
> 6. How should courts approach custody disputes among unmarried cohabitants when one party clearly is not a natural parent? How should adoption be considered in such cases?

5. *Parental Alienation Syndrome*

Problem 65

In re Marriage of Wallace

Alice and Chester Wallace were married on August 23, YR-8. Their marriage produced one child, Lorena, who was born on October 10, YR-6, in Southby Memorial Hospital.

Since the birth of Lorena, the relationship between Alice and Chester became strained, and by late YR-2 the marriage was beyond repair. On January 3, YR-1, Alice filed for a divorce in Hoynes Superior Court. The couple has had joint physical custody of Lorena since that time. Lorena stays with Alice on weekdays and with her father on weekends.

One Monday morning, November 7, YR-1, when Alice picked Lorena up from Chester's condo, Lorena was in tears. Alice asked Lorena what was wrong. Lorena responded by describing in great detail that over the weekend her father had touched her "private place" three times. Shocked and angered, Alice immediately drove Lorena to the family physician, Dr. Conner. During the examination of Lorena, Dr. Conner found no physical evidence to support Lorena's account of what happened. He then referred Lorena to Dr. Wilma Rubble, a child psychologist specializing in child sexual abuse.

Dr. Rubble interviewed Lorena on the afternoon of November 7 and again two days later. Dr. Rubble concluded that Lorena had been molested the prior weekend. Based on Dr. Rubble's conclusions, Alice filed a petition for a temporary restraining order without notice to prevent Chester from having contact with Lorena. The court granted Alice's motion but set the matter for a hearing on the preliminary injunction to be held that Friday.

At the hearing, Chester's lawyer convinced the judge to require Lorena to be interviewed by a different child psychologist. During that interview the fol-

Chapter Nine. Dissolution of Marriage

lowing week, Lorena recanted her story and told the psychologist, Dr. Benjamin Stone, that she was just joking. When asked who told her to joke, Lorena said "I don't know." Dr. Stone concluded that Lorena had not been molested and, in fact, that she was exhibiting the characteristics of parental alienation syndrome (PAS). Under the circumstances, Dr. Stone suspects that Alice has coached Lorena and recommends that Lorena be removed from Alice's custody immediately in order to put the child on neutral ground.

Questions

1. What is the parental alienation syndrome (PAS)? What bearing does PAS have on child custody cases?
2. Should testimony by an expert on PAS be admissable as scientific evidence? If so, how should Chester's lawyer introduce PAS, and how should Alice's lawyer challenge it?
3. What effect should Lorena's recanting her story have on Dr. Rubble's testimony? Outline a direct and a cross-examination of Dr. Rubble.
4. What effect should the lack of physical evidence have in this case?
5. Assume that Lorena's allegations are incorrect but that Alice never coached Lorena to make them. Is joint legal or physical custody an option in this case any longer?

6. Modification of Custody Order

Problem 66

In re Marriage of Goddard

The marriage of Joe and Mary Goddard was dissolved by the Hoynes Circuit Court in June of YR-6. The decree awarded custody of their five children (Robert, 17, John, 16, Renee, 15, Lucy, 12, and Dwight, 11) to Mary with visitation rights and weekly support payments for Joe. Also, the family home was awarded to Mary, while Joe was given a mortgage for $10,000.00, payable upon the occurrence of any of the following conditions:

(1) Mary's remarriage;
(2) The sale of the home; or
(3) The emancipation of the last child.

Neither party has remarried; however, Mary has lived almost continuously with one Norman Lust since May of YR-3. And, while Mary has been regularly employed and Joe has regularly supported the children, without Norman's financial assistance, she would have been "in the hole." Norman also has extensively remodeled the home. He and the children, particularly the youngest, enjoy a good relationship. Mary and Norman love one another but have not married, according to their statements, because substantial college grants for the two oldest children would be lost. Mary is a Catholic, sees to her children's religious training, and does not deem her conduct immoral. Acknowledging the learning process at home to be important, she nevertheless states, "These are difficult times, and I'm simply trying to do my best and, anyway, the children see it done elsewhere and on television."

Joe resides with his parents but is prepared to move to larger quarters if granted custody. Joe is presently employed full time at a tool-and-die shop in Southby, Michiana. In YR-7, because of the marital problems, Joe attempted suicide. After receiving counseling at a VA hospital, however, he has had no further emotional problems. Joe visits the children on a rather regular basis. The two oldest boys, 17 and 16, have had occasional drug-related problems, and about a year ago the oldest attempted suicide. At the present time, however, none of the children has any emotional or physical problems, and each regularly attends school.

Questions

1. Joe wishes to obtain custody of the two oldest children because he is concerned about their drug problems and Robert's attempted suicide. In fact, Joe would like custody of all five children, but he reasonably expects only the two oldest would want to live with him. What steps, both personally and legally, should Joe take to achieve his goal?
2. What legal arguments can Joe use for modifying the court's child support order?
3. Read Section 409 of the Uniform Marriage and Divorce Act in the Appendix. Under what circumstances can Joe obtain modification of custody? What consideration for the children's best interests is given by the UMDA? Should a best interests analysis be applied in addition to (or to supplant) the UMDA's strict "unknown facts" test? Why or why not?
4. The traditional rule in many states is a change in circumstances test. *See Starke v. Starke*, 458 N.W.2d 758 (N.D. App. 1990). How substantially have circumstances changed for the children since YR-6? Since YR-3? Should Joe have brought his modification petition immediately in YR-3? Does a change in Joe's ability to care for the children matter?
5. How should a court evaluate Norman's presence as an unwed sexual partner when determining custody issues?
6. Suppose Norman beats May regularly. What result in custody modification?
7. Assume that, rather than Norman Lust, Noreen Love moved in with Mary. Should sexual orientation make a difference in custody modification? *See* Problem 62, *supra*.

Problem 67

In re Marriage of Porter

The marriage of Steven and Louise Porter was dissolved by decree of the Hoynes Circuit Court on March 4, YR-6. The parties' one child, Bonnie Sue, age one at that time, was awarded, pursuant to agreement between the parties, to Louise's permanent care and custody.

Chapter Nine.   Dissolution of Marriage

Louise, a native of Southby, Michiana, who did not graduate from high school and has an I.Q. of 73, has been employed continuously from the date of her dissolution until a few weeks ago. In the past three years, Louise was employed as a waitress at the Truckers Oasis Restaurant in nearby Adams County. During this period, Louise married three additional times and lived in nine different places, not including the time she lived with her mother. Her last marriage to Raymond "Dutch" Altman occurred on March 10, YR-0. Louise was laid off at the Truckers Oasis, and she and Dutch moved to Monticello, Michiana, where Dutch found employment in a welding shop earning $400.00 per week.

In the six years following the dissolution, Louise often left Bonnie Sue with older boys as baby-sitters. Two of these boys, who were foster children of Louise's mother, were adjudicated juvenile delinquents for their admitted involvement in a burglary in YR-1. The places in which Louise lived with Bonnie Sue were substandard, consisting of one bedroom apartments, trailers, and homes that were also occupied by stepfathers and boyfriends from time to time. Louise admits to drinking "more than I should" and a lack of modesty. (She sometimes appeared in the doorway nude or semi-nude when Steven arrived for visitation with Bonnie Sue.)

Raymond Altman, Louise's fourth husband, is a heavy drinker, and during periods of drinking he has physically assaulted Louise. Dutch also beat his previous wife, and in YR-9 he shot a man. Regarding the shooting incident, he was tried on a criminal charge and acquitted by a jury. The victim of the shooting testified at trial that Dutch, for undisclosed reasons, was called to the scene of a drunken fight at a party. Dutch appeared with a double-barreled shotgun and, as one of the participants fled, Dutch leveled the shotgun at him but was prevented from shooting by the intervention of the victim, who was wounded in the struggle. Dutch has also been expelled from the East Side Little League ball park in Southby during the past year for drunkenness and boisterous conduct at games in which his son played.

Bonnie Sue's school teacher, June Street, describes Bonnie Sue as fearful, lacking in confidence, not well-adjusted, and given to crying spells. As a result of standardized tests at school, Bonnie Sue was placed in special education classes for learning-disabled students. Mrs. Street states that Bonnie Sue, like other children her age, needs love and reassurance that she is a "good kid."

Steven is a graduate of Michiana Vocational Technical College in Southby. He is currently employed full time as a draftsman at Stahley Machinery, Inc. in Southby. Steven has remarried to Linda May, who is employed full time as a receptionist at the Eagle Life Insurance Company in Southby. The couple recently purchased a $85,000 home. Steven suffered serious bouts of depression, accompanied by excessive drinking, following his divorce from Louise. He admits that he has been drinking excessively "off and on" during the past year. Steven's employer suspects him of drinking on the job, has warned him of excessive lateness to work, and has suggested to Steven that he consider obtaining professional help for his problem through the company alcohol abuse program. Steven refuses to receive any type of counseling for his drinking, stating, "I don't have a problem."

Steven's employer also suspects that Steven is homosexual. Ray Zmarley, the plant manager, reports seeing Steven often holding hands and embracing Clay, also a draftsman at Stahley, during the past few months. Steven states that he has romantic feelings for Clay and admits to having several sexual encounters with Clay within the past six months. Steven and Linda have not had sexual intercourse for several months; however, Steven states that he loves and is devoted to her. Steven has discussed his feelings for Clay with Linda, who, although angered and hurt, is willing to attend counseling if necessary. Steven does not wish to attend therapy at this time. He states, "This is something Linda and I have to work out. Bonnie Sue doesn't know and won't know about any of my problems."

Linda and Bonnie Sue have developed a warm, loving relationship.

Steven consults an attorney for the purpose of gaining custody of Bonnie Sue.

Questions

1. In what ways does this Problem differ from Problem 66? Which differences are significant?
2. What legal and personal (if any) advice should Steven's lawyer give him?
3. Read Section 410 of the Uniform Marriage and Divorce Act (UMDA). (*See* Appendix.) What facts should Steven state in his affidavit?
4. Who, under these facts, is likely to be the better custodian for Bonnie Sue?
5. What is the legal significance of the fact that Bonnie Sue's initial custody was arranged by agreement, rather than as the result of a contested petition?
6. Under circumstances such as these, would a guardian ad litem (GAL) or a court-appointed special advocate (CASA) be useful in determining custody?
7. Suppose Bonnie Sue is twelve rather than seven. Should she have standing to represent herself before the court concerning her custody?
8. How should the court rule on Steven's motion to modify the March 4, YR-6, custody order? Assume that the applicable Michiana law is identical to Section 409 of the UMDA.

7. *Petition by the Child*

Problem 68

In re Sammy H.

Rebecca and Tom H. were divorced in YR-3. The court found that Tom was emotionally and mentally abusive to his wife and son, Sammy, and granted Rebecca sole custody of Sammy. A few months ago, Rebecca died. Tom recently told Sammy, age fourteen, that he was going to file a court petition for sole custody of Sammy, who has been living with his twenty-four-year-old half-sister since his mother's death.

Sammy, convinced that he could not bear to live with his father again, sought the advice of an attorney. The attorney thought that it might be possible for Sammy to file a petition on his own behalf to have his custody changed from his mother to his sister. The Michiana custody statute states that a petition for the change of custody of a child can be filed by a non-parent if it is shown that the child is no longer living in a parent's home. There is no language in the statute expressly excluding a child's standing to petition for a change of his or her own custody.

Chapter Nine. Dissolution of Marriage

Questions

1. What are the policy arguments for and against allowing a minor child the right to petition to change his or her own custody?
2. Is Sammy's petition essentially a request to terminate Tom's parental rights?
3. Notwithstanding the presumption that parents' rights to custody are superior to non-parents', are there situations where a non-parent should be awarded custody over the parents' wishes?

J. VISITATION

1. Rights of Custodial and Non-Custodial Parents

Problem 69

In re Marriage of Rockaway

Philip (Phil) and Ruth Rockaway were married in YR-20. Five children, Will, age seventeen, Candace, age twelve, Mia, age six, Randall, age three, and Bruce, age two, were born of the marriage.

Phil graduated from Michiana University in YR-20 with a B.S. degree in business. In YR-18, Phil received his M.B.A. degree (with a major in accounting) from Michiana University. That same year, Phil passed the CPA examination and began private practice in the accounting firm of Rockaway and Hite in Southby, Michiana.

In YR-20, after Phil and Ruth were married, Ruth dropped out of Michiana University (during her junior year) in order to work and support herself and Phil during his graduate studies. Throughout the marriage, Ruth stayed at home and was solely responsible for rearing the children and doing household work. Other than being a homemaker, Ruth never acquired any job skills.

The two youngest children, Randall and Bruce, have been diagnosed with seizure disorders, and Randall also requires speech therapy twice a week. Randall is subject to unpredictable outbursts of violent behavior and continues to have bladder control problems.

In January of YR-1, Ruth observed Mia rubbing her vaginal area and concluded that either Phil or the parties' oldest son, Will, had sexually abused Mia. When Ruth asked Phil if he had molested Mia, Phil, who always believed that the parties had a good marriage, was shocked and furious. Phil demanded that Ruth seek immediate mental health treatment.

In February of YR-1, Ruth met with Dr. Raymond Ball, a clinical psychologist in Southby, Michiana. Ruth told Dr. Ball that she suspected either Phil or her son, Will, had sexually abused Mia. On the recommendation of Dr. Ball, Phil persuaded Will to take a polygraph examination. After reviewing the polygraph examiner's reports, Dr. Ball stated to Ruth, "Based upon my personal assessment and having examined the polygraph reports on Phil and Will, I'm absolutely certain that the abuse of Mia you've described did not occur." Dr. Ball repeated this statement in a letter addressed to Phil and Ruth. In the letter, Dr. Ball also wrote, "I trust that you and your family will put this matter behind you by participating in family counseling to restore the family trust and strength in your marriage."

After receipt of Dr. Ball's letter, during a follow-up session with Dr. Ball, Ruth revealed that she continued to believe that Mia was sexually abused. Ruth also told Dr. Ball that she feared that Phil desired to have her committed to a mental health facility. On March 10, YR-1, Phil moved out of the family home. Ruth told Dr. Ball that she continued to disagree with his opinion about the abuse, and she expressed fear for the safety of her three youngest children if they should have visitation with Phil. On March 25, YR-1, Ruth filed in the Hoynes County Circuit Court a petition for dissolution of marriage, together with a verified motion for temporary custody of the five children, temporary child support, spousal support, and attorney fees.

At the contested hearing on temporary custody of the parties' minor children, Dr. Ball testified that in his opinion Ruth suffered from a "fixated delusional disorder." The disorder was fixated because it was limited solely to the matter of Phil's alleged molestation of Mia and did not otherwise affect Ruth's behavior. Dr. Ball testified that both Phil and Ruth were devoted parents, but that Ruth tended to be somewhat more lenient and less rule-oriented with the children, and that Mia, Randall, and Bruce, in particular, might benefit from a more structured environment. Ruth testified that she continued to believe that Candace and her two younger brothers would be harmed if they were in the sole and unsupervised presence of Phil.

The court awarded temporary custody of the children to Phil. The court noted, "It is clear to the court that the children will enjoy better access to both parents if Mr. Rockaway is the custodial parent." The court made no order for Ruth's visitation and urged the parties to arrange visitation at reasonable times and places.

The parties agreed to a visitation arrangement whereby Ruth would have the children two mornings per week and would take Randall to his speech therapy sessions. Ruth would also have visitation one evening per week with all of the children. Will would have visitation with Ruth as determined by him. Ruth would also have alternate weekend visitation. Phil stated that he planned to hire Eunice as a nanny to care for the children while he was at work. Phil told Ruth that she would be best off trying to find a job, in order that she could become self-supporting and contribute to the support of the children. Phil's gross annual income is approximately $150,000.

After the court's temporary custody order, Ruth became very depressed. Ruth continued to see Dr. Warren Boze, a psychiatrist, who was recommended to Ruth by Dr. Ball. Ruth began taking medication, prescribed by Dr. Boze, to minimize the effects of her "fixated delusional disorder."

On March 1, YR-0, Ruth filed with the court a petition for visitation, requesting that she be permitted to care for the children while Phil is at work. Ruth claims that she is doing well in the care of Dr. Boze and that as the children's natural mother she, not Eunice, should have the right to care for the children while Phil works.

Dr. Boze will testify at the visitation hearing that Ruth has remained under his care for ten months and that he observed a significant difference in Ruth's attitude once prescription medication was initiated. Dr. Boze will describe Ruth's condition when he first met her as "analogous to a hippopotamus being in the middle of the living room and that Ruth was unable to see the living room without the hippopotamus." Her "delusion" presently is more akin to a speck of sand in the eye that distorts vision slightly but does not fully impair it. Dr. Boze believes that there is no reason why Ruth would be unable to watch the children while Phil is at work.

Other than Phil's opposition to Ruth's motion for visitation, there are no disputed issues between the parties in the pending dissolution action.

Questions

1. As the natural parent, is Ruth entitled to the relief she requests?
2. Conduct research on nonlegal authorities with respect to the issues raised by Ruth's motion. Does the social and behavioral science literature suggest a proper result in this situation?
3. Assume that Michiana law is identical to the Uniform Marriage and Divorce Act (UMDA). How should the court rule on Ruth's motion?

2. *The AIDS Issue*

Problem 70

Carson v. Carson

Kit and Annette Carson were married in YR-15. Two children were born of the marriage, Rebecca, born in YR-12, and John, born in YR-10. After Rebecca's birth, the Carson's happy marriage began to fall apart because, as Kit claims, "Annette is an ambitious corporate lawyer; she's never home and spends little time with the family." In YR-5, Kit and Annette decided to divorce. During the divorce proceedings, the court found that Kit was a medical doctor in private practice, with a flexible schedule, that Kit was the primary caretaker of the two children, and that Kit therefore should be granted custody of the two children. The court ordered that Annette have standard weekend and summer visitation rights.

Several months ago, when Annette went to pick up the children for weekend visitation, Kit sat Annette down and told her that he was leaving his practice because he had tested positive for the HIV virus. Kit explained that financially he would be fine, as he had professional insurance, but that it might be necessary for Annette to take the kids more often if the virus developed into AIDS before the kids went to college.

Annette, having little understanding of AIDS, was immediately concerned that the children were infected with the virus. She thought that if they weren't already infected, they soon would be if they continued to live in Kit's home. After meeting with her priest, on May 1, YR-0, Annette filed a motion for modification of the divorce decree, seeking full custody of Rebecca and John with no visitation for Kit.

Questions

1. Assuming that Michiana has enacted the Uniform Marriage and Divorce Act (UMDA), what standard will the court apply in determining if a modification of the divorce decree is appropriate? In applying this standard, is it likely that the court will grant custody to Annette?

2. If Annette is granted custody of the children, will she be able to prevent Steven from having visitation?
3. Would facts concerning the manner in which Kit was infected with the HIV virus be relevant evidence on the custody and visitation issues?

3. Grandparent Visitation

Problem 71

In re Marriage of Daley

Ralph and Alice Daley were divorced in YR-5. According to Ralph, he and Alice had irreconcilable differences over what Ralph described as excessive involvement of Alice's parents in Ralph and Alice's marriage and the children's upbringing. The divorce decree awarded custody of the parties' two minor children, Sanford, age eight, and Anna, age seven, to Alice, with reasonable visitation for Ralph. In January of YR-2, Alice was diagnosed as having ovarian cancer, and within a few weeks she began chemotherapy treatments. During YR-2, the children's maternal grandparents, Wilfred and Vivienne Walton, helped care for Alice and the children. The Waltons fixed meals, did housekeeping, shopping, and yard work, drove Alice to the hospital for her treatments, and took the children to school and other activities. Alice died on April 10, YR-1, and the children moved into the home of their grandparents in Southby, Michiana. Ralph, who works on an off-shore oil drilling project in the Gulf of Mexico, hasn't visited with his children since YR-3, and didn't learn of Alice's death until he received a FAX from a friend on October 4, YR-1. When Ralph telephoned the Waltons on October 12, YR-1, and told Vivienne that he was moving back to Southby and wanted to see his children, Vivienne replied, "Sanford and Anna consider us to be their parents now. We've supported them, and the lawyer says you owe $8,000 in child support. Had you stayed around to support the children, Alice might be here today. Please leave us alone, Ralph." In December of YR-1, Ralph returned to Southby and removed Sanford and Anna from their grandparents' home. The children presently reside with Ralph in Southby. The Waltons' attempts to arrange visitation with their grandchildren have been rejected by Ralph. Sanford states that he and Anna would like to visit their grandparents but "not if it will make Dad angry."

The Michiana Grandparent Visitation Act follows this problem.

Questions

1. What legal steps should the Waltons take to obtain visitation with the children?
2. What are the Waltons' prospects for success under the Michiana Grandparent Visitation Act?
3. Assume that Ralph claims that the Grandparent Visitation Act is an unconstitutional intrusion on his right to rear his children as he sees fit without state interference. What arguments should be presented by the Waltons? How should the court rule?

4. Would the Waltons have been able to obtain court-ordered visitation if Ralph and Alice had not been divorced? What if Ralph and Alice had both died and Bill, Ralph's brother, had adopted the children?
5. In addition to grandparents, to whom should visitation rights be granted? To aunts and uncles? To siblings? To foster parents? To close family friends?
6. What standard should be applied to grandparent visitation? Should visitation be a matter of right? Should there be a "best interests" analysis?
7. What role should the opinions of Sanford and Anna play in the Waltons' visitation petition?

MICHIANA CODE 31-6-7-1
GRANDPARENT VISITATION ACT

Section 1. Grandparents may file a visitation petition when one of the following threshold requirements has been met: the filing of a judgment of dissolution of marriage, legal separation, or the existence of a parent-child relationship pursuant to the Uniform Parentage Act; one or both parents are deceased; a child under six years resided with a grandparent at least three months; a child over six years resided with a grandparent at least six months; or adoption proceedings are involved.

Once one of the threshold requirements is met, the trial court must assess the best interests of the child, the prior interaction between the child and grandparent, the prior interaction and present relationship between the grandparent and each parent of the child, and the time-sharing or visitation arrangements that were in place prior to the filing of the petition.

4. *Visitation by Third Parties*

Problem 72

In re Marriage of Sherry (T.) B. and Gary T.

Please review the facts of Problem 24.

Next Monday at 9:00 A.M., the Hoynes Circuit Court will hold a hearing on Gary's Verified Information for Rule to Show Cause. Sherry's counsel plans to defend by calling Dr. Franklin Moses to testify. Dr. Moses will testify consistently with his letter, which accompanies Problem 24.

Questions

1. Prepare a direct and a cross-examination for Dr. Moses. What are the most important points of his testimony? Is his testimony relevant to a child custody enforcement matter?
2. What power does the court have to enforce the visitation order against Sherry? Assume Lucy is with Sherry's parents in Illinois. Can the court enforce the visitation order against them through Sherry?
3. Can the court reconsider its prior custody order at a contempt hearing? Why or why not?

5. *Termination of Visitation*

Problem 73

In re Marriage of Houser

Cindy Mayhill met Dale Houser in YR-6 at "The Loredo Corral," a singles night spot in Southby, Michiana. Dale was a truck driver and Cindy was a receptionist for a small insurance company in Southby. They were married six months later, when Cindy discovered she was pregnant. Cindy quit her job a few weeks before Tammy was born on March 25, YR-5.

Cindy and Dale's marriage was stormy from the start; their only common interests were hanging out at western bars, dancing, and watching soft porn movies. Having a baby and supporting a family of three was a shock to Dale's free and easy lifestyle. He stayed out on the road longer and came home less often, and when he was home Dale and Cindy fought bitterly. Occasionally, Dale and Cindy could recapture a bit of their earlier romance by watching porn films together. Tammy was one year old at the time and their movie-viewing included her.

Cindy whined and complained all the time that Dale was at home; she didn't enjoy being cooped up in a dingy little house and losing her youth. This made Dale all the more angry and irritable, and so he began hitting and slapping Cindy during their arguments.

Dale and Cindy separated in October of YR-4. Cindy filed a complaint for divorce on November 1, YR-4. Dale didn't bother to answer or appear at the final hearing, and the divorce was granted on February 16, YR-3. Cindy was awarded custody of Tammy, and Dale received reasonable visitation. Dale was ordered to pay $40.00 per week as support for Tammy.

Dale hadn't paid much attention to Tammy when she was a baby; she cried too much and the idea of dirty diapers repulsed him. But Tammy was a very cute toddler, with curly blonde hair and blue eyes, and she was full of smiles. She was much more of a "mommy's girl," but she was happy to see Dale when he came by to deliver his support check. For several months after the divorce, Cindy wouldn't allow Dale to be alone with Tammy and strictly limited the time he could see her at Cindy's apartment.

In YR-2, Cindy began dating Jim, who worked at a local factory. He was around much more than Dale had ever been, so Cindy renewed her passion for dancing and staying out late. She and Jim also watched soft porn films together, at his place and hers. Jim subscribed to *Penthouse* and *Gay Blade* magazines, and he and Cindy spent some evenings at the peep shows and adult bookstores on the "strip" near downtown Southby. During these times with Jim, Cindy's twelve-year-old sister, Sue, watched Tammy.

In March of YR-2, Dale asked to have visitation with Tammy every other weekend. Cindy hated Dale, but she figured that Jim could stay over at her place while Tammy was with Dale. Cindy permitted the alternate-weekend visitation to continue until May of YR-1, when Tammy was four years old. Tammy liked Jim well enough, and her dad too, but she was confused. Cindy made Tammy call Jim "Daddy Jim." Tammy didn't seem friendly toward men most of the time. Cindy has four sisters, three of whom were divorced, and Cindy's father died when she was twelve. Her mother never remarried.

By May of YR-1, Tammy became withdrawn. She wasn't as cheerful or affectionate as she had been. The change wasn't dramatic, but it worried Cindy.

Chapter Nine. Dissolution of Marriage

She wanted to marry Jim, and her parental relations with Dale were strained. Dale fell behind on support, claiming that he was laid off and swamped with debts. Cindy had nothing but bad words for Dale, and it never bothered her to let off steam in front of Tammy.

On May 5, YR-1, Dale came to take Tammy for weekend visitation while Tammy was with Cindy's sister Sue. Cindy told Dale there would be no more weekend visitation and that Tammy was acting strangely and it was all his fault. Dale was furious. He slammed the door and yelled at Cindy, "I'll see you in court; no one will take away my daughter!"

On May 17, YR-1, Dale filed a petition with the Hoynes Superior Court for an order of specific visitation with Tammy. Cindy didn't appear for the hearing, and Dale obtained a visitation order providing for extended alternate weekend visits from Friday evening at 5:30 P.M. through Sunday evening at 7:00 P.M., beginning June 1, YR-1, and for three continual weeks of summer visitation. The order was delivered to Cindy's house by a deputy sheriff. When Dale came to Cindy's home on Friday, June 1, at 5:30 P.M., nobody was home. Dale tried to call, but the phone was changed to an unpublished number. On June 15, Dale again went to Cindy's house and no one answered the doorbell.

Dale filed a petition for contempt of court against Cindy on June 25, YR-1, alleging that Cindy had deliberately violated the court's visitation order. Cindy again failed to appear in court, and a body attachment was issued for Cindy on July 3, YR-1. Cindy was picked up on July 6, YR-1, and a hearing took place. Cindy didn't have a lawyer, but she told the judge that Dale had molested their daughter and that his visitation with Tammy should be terminated. A lawyer was appointed to represent Cindy and the entire case was continued. On August 2, YR-1, Cindy's lawyer filed a counter-petition to terminate visitation, alleging that Dale's visitation with Tammy caused physical, mental, moral, and emotional harm to her and was against the child's best interests. The court ordered that all parties involved—Cindy, Dale, and Tammy—be examined by professional staff of the Crossroads Clinic. The reports follow this Problem.

Questions

1. Read the psychological evaluations following these questions. How would Cindy's counsel be able to present this evidence in a hearing on the issue of visitation? How might Dale's counsel keep this evidence from being admitted? Failing an attempt to suppress the psychological evaluations, how should Dale's counsel discredit the evidence?
2. Based on the facts of this case and the psychological evaluations, what visitation determination would be in Tammy's best interests?
3. Cindy alleged on July 6 that Dale had molested Tammy. The psychological evaluations confirmed her allegations on September 10. Assume the court will not hear arguments regarding Dale's visitation until November 18. Should the court have entered a preliminary order terminating Dale's visitation as of July 6? As of September 10? Remember that Dale had obtained rights to three weeks of uninterrupted visitation during the summer. Should at least that visitation be stopped? What legal action should Cindy's counsel take to prevent Dale's visitation? What response should Dale's counsel make?

4. Should Cindy be held in contempt of court if her fears were justified? What if her fears were not justified?
5. What standard is used for determining the amount of visitation? What factors should be considered? *See* Section 407 of the Uniform Marriage and Divorce Act (UMDA).
6. When Cindy interfered with Dale's visitation, was she frustrating the legislative purpose behind visitation?
7. Should the fact that Dale has fallen behind in his child support payments affect his visitation rights?
8. Assume that an expert witness testifies that Cindy exhibits the traits of the battered-wife syndrome. By one definition the four general stages of the syndrome are: (a) denial, (b) anger and vengeance, (c) reconciliation, and (d) return to battery. Often divorced wives will remain in the second phase of the syndrome for years after divorce. Assume this is the case for Cindy, and that her motivations for removing Tammy from Dale were purely vengeful. If Dale has not harmed Tammy, what custody and visitation order should the court issue?
9. Assuming no sexual misconduct is involved, how would Dale go about modifying his visitation?
10. Is it in Tammy's best interests to have Dale's visitations terminated completely?

CROSSROADS CLINIC

5711 Oxford Avenue
Southby, Michiana 46601
Telephone (219) 239-6676

STEPHEN M. HENLEY, M.D.

*Renee T. Summers, M.A.
Vernon A. Miles, M.H.T.
Wendall R. Walker, Ph.D.
Kate Dalton, M.A., N.C.C.
Christine M. Thacker, A.C.I.S.
Wilma J. Bates, R.N., M.A.*

PSYCHOLOGICAL EVALUATION

Dale Houser
Cindy Houser
Tammy Houser

10 September YR-0

Psychological evaluations were conducted with Dale Houser, Cindy Houser, and their five-year old daughter, Tammy Houser. The evaluations were ordered by the Hoynes Superior Court. Psychological interviews were conducted with each of the above individuals. In addition, Dale Houser and Cindy Houser completed the Minnesota Multiphasic Personality Inventory and Tammy Houser completed a projective drawing test referred to as the House-Tree-Person Test. Both Dale and Cindy were seen and interviewed by this writer in sessions lasting 1½ hours each. Tammy Houser was interviewed for 1½ hours alone and for ½ hour with her mother. Dale Houser did not wish to have a session with his daughter. He stated that her mother had poisoned her against him and that such a session would not be helpful to her or him.

In the interview with Tammy, the child stated that she was afraid to visit her father because of the things he was doing to her. She explained that on several occasions her father had taken off all her clothing and also his own clothing and then began kissing her between her legs. She also said that her father would lay on top of her rubbing against her, until some "white stuff" came out of his penis, and that he would clean up with a kleenex afterwards. She also said that her father would tell her to rub his penis with her hands until he would "see some white stuff" in her mouth. She said that her father had spanked her in order to teach her not to tell anyone of the activity.

Tammy was questioned at length about telling the truth. She specifically said that a lie is something that "is not right," and that "God doesn't like people who tell lies." When I asked whether it would be a lie to say she is in third grade, she said it was. She promised to tell the truth, and it is apparent that she is a fairly well balanced child, not prone to fantasy or story telling. Her account was stated in a straightforward matter-of-fact way, and she did not appear to have been programmed by her mother in what she said. Nor did she exhibit any signs of unusual animosity toward her father which might lead a child to create a story about a parent to hurt him or her or to avoid contact with that parent.

Tammy showed no confusion between her real father, Dale Houser, and her mother's boyfriend, Jimmy Reed, whom she referred to as "Daddy Jim." Her real father was always just "Dad."

PSYCHOLOGICAL EVALUATION (Continued)
Dale Houser
Cindy Houser
Tammy Houser
10 September YR-0

When asked if "Daddy Jim" or any other person besides her father had done the things to her she described, she said "No!" quite emphatically. Again, she was reminded of her promise to tell the truth, and she said she told me only the truth.

I asked if she had seen anything like she described with her father, and she said that it was "like the movies." Despite the fact that this child has apparently been exposed to adult love-making on film, which is highly unusual for a child of five, it is apparent that this was not a source for fanciful fiction about her father. Rather, the film exposure has caused her to be more matter-of-fact about her experience than would be a more sheltered five-year old.

From my interview with Tammy Houser, I conclude that Dale Houser has engaged in sexual conduct with this five year old daughter.

In the interview with Cindy Houser, she said that she refused to allow Dale Houser to visit his daughter after Tammy described actions on his part that she believed was sexual abuse. She said that she was concerned about her daughter's welfare and felt that she needed to protect Tammy from her father. From the interview, Cindy appeared to be a concerned and responsible parent. She was cooperative throughout the interview.

Cindy admitted that she had not always been most attentive to Tammy because she was so young when Tammy was born and felt cheated of her youth. She also admitted that she and Mr. Houser were extremely hostile. Because she was able to recognize these feelings maturely and with regret, it is clear that her strong belief that Tammy and Dale should not visit at all is based entirely on concern for Tammy, and not revenge and hostility toward Dale. When Tammy and Cindy were seen together, Cindy showed herself to be a patient mother. Tammy sat on her mother's lap most of the time and the two seemed very affectionate.

In the interview with Dale Houser, he reported that he did not know why Cindy refused to allow him to see his daughter. He was angry and not very cooperative in the interview. I asked him about his daughter's description of his having sexually abused her. He denied such activity. He stated that Cindy had not been a good mother, that she permitted Tammy to watch porn films, that her boyfriend practically lived with her and that the boyfriend might have been the abuser. He was angry that he had not seen his daughter in a long time, said that he loved her, and that he knew I was poisoned against him "like the rest of them." It was difficult to elicit any details from him about the marriage, his current feelings toward Cindy, and his own past. I explained that he might have a better chance of seeing Tammy under restricted conditions if he would admit to the sexual contact with her and agree to counseling. Again, he denied the conduct.

PSYCHOLOGICAL EVALUATION (Continued)
Dale Houser
Cindy Houser
Tammy Houser
10 September YR-0

Tammy's House-Tree-Person Test revealed that she has mixed feelings about her father. She both loves and fears him. The drawings also included sexual content that Tammy described as a time when she was rubbing her father's penis and both were breathing heavily. The drawings also indicated that Tammy felt hurt and unprotected. Finally there are indications of depression and a feeling of vulnerability in her relationship with her father.

The MMPI reports for Cindy Houser and Dale Houser are included with this report.

Conclusion

It is my opinion that the sexual activity between Tammy and Dale Houser, as described by Tammy, did occur. Dale Houser's denial was not convincingly made and a denial is expected in a person with Dale's personality profile.

Whether this should result in the total elimination of his visitation rights is a more difficult question. Had Dale recognized and taken responsibility for his conduct, then restricted visitation with counseling for father and daughter would be appropriate. This is because a child has a need for contact with a father, and Tammy is fortunately not severely scarred by what has happened. However, Dale's total denial and refusal to acknowledge his conduct leads me to recommend a termination of visitation until such time as Dale would agree to face responsibility and undergo counseling. His present hostility and denial might result in subtle psychological abuse to Tammy if he were permitted to continue seeing her even in a restricted atmosphere where no sexual activity could take place.

Renee T. Summers, M.A.
Clinical Psychologist

Stephen M. Henley, M.D.

SMH/mh

CROSSROADS CLINIC

5711 Oxford Avenue
Southby, Michiana 46601
Telephone (219) 239-6676

STEPHEN M. HENLEY, M.D.

Renee T. Summers, M.A.
Vernon A. Miles, M.H.T.
Wendall R. Walker, Ph.D.
Kate Dalton, M.A., N.C.C.
Christine M. Thacker, A.C.I.S.
Wilma J. Bates, R.N., M.A.

SUPPLEMENTAL SUMMARY
MMPI
Cindy Houser
1 October YR-0

This patient produces a valid MMPI profile which probably gives a good indication of her present level of personality functioning. The clinical profile is within normal limits, suggesting that this patient is experiencing no serious psychological problems at this time. She seems to have no unmanageable psychological conflicts or threatening stressors at this time, and her personal adjustment appears to be adequate. She seems to be dealing effectively with situational demands and is obtaining satisfaction out of life. Her personal manner appears to be stereotypically feminine. She tends to be quite passive and submissive in interpersonal relationships, and may lack autonomy and prefer to let others make decisions for her. She is rather non-competitive, generally easy going, and uncritical in interpersonal situations, as reported in the content of her responses. Interpersonally, she appears to be somewhat shy, with some social concerns and inhibitions. She may be a bit hypersensitive about what others think of her and is occasionally concerned over her relationships with others. None of the Welsh nor Wiggins Content Scales show significant elevation, and reviewing the "Extended Score Report," it is noted that none of the content scales here shows significant elevation.

SUGGESTED DIAGNOSIS: Axis I: No diagnosis
                                   Axis II: No diagnosis

_____
Wendall R. Walker, Ph.D.

WRS/mh

CROSSROADS CLINIC

5711 Oxford Avenue
Southby, Michiana 46601
Telephone (219) 239-6676

STEPHEN M. HENLEY, M.D.

Renee T. Summers, M.A.
Vernon A. Miles, M.H.T.
Wendall R. Walker, Ph.D.
Kate Dalton, M.A., N.C.C.
Christine M. Thacker, A.C.I.S.
Wilma J. Bates, R.N., M.A.

SUPPLEMENTAL SUMMARY
MMPI
Dale Houser
23 September YR-0

This patient produces a valid MMPI profile which is likely to give an adequate indication of his present level of personality functioning. The patient's clinical profile reflects a high degree of psychological distress at this time. An intense and somewhat mixed pattern of symptoms is indicated, the patient appearing rather tense and depressed, and feeling agitated over problems in his environment. He may be experiencing a great deal of stress following a period of acting-out behavior, including possibly an excessive use of alcohol or drugs. He shows a long standing pattern of poor impulse control and lack of acceptance of societal standards. He may also be angry over his present situation and tends to blame others for his problems. He may be somewhat uncomfortable in relationships with women. His response content also suggests that he feels somewhat estranged from people, somewhat alienated and concerned over the actions of others, and may blame others for his negative frame of mind. He tends to see the world as a threatening place, sees himself as having been unjustly blamed for others' problems, and feels that he is getting a raw deal out of life. His relationship with others may be somewhat superficial. It appears as though he tends to be manipulative in relationships and may use others for his own gratification. He appear to be rather introverted and has some difficulties meeting other people.

Reviewing the "Extended Score Report," it is noted that the patient's Dependency (DY) Scale approaches significant elevation, and the McAndrews Addiction Scale (MAS) is significantly elevated. The patient reports feelings of lassitude-malaise and endorses a high number of items dealing with narcissism-hypersensitivity. He may be reporting some persecutory ideas. The patient identifies an excessively high number of items dealing with feelings of inferiority which result in his personal discomfort and distrust of others.

The patient's Lithium Response Scale for Depression (male) is 7, which is significant.

SUGGESTED DIAGNOSES: Axis I: Dysthymic disorder (300.40)
Unspecified substance abuse (305.90)

Axis II: Mixed personality disorder consisting of dependent and narcissistic features (301.89)

Wendall R. Walker, Ph.D.
WRW/mh   9/24/YR-0

RESUME

RENEE T. SUMMERS

1781 Riverside Drive
Southby, Michiana 46615
Home: 219-284-3348

Personal:
    Birthdate: 11-21-YR-44
    Marital Status: Married (1 child)
    Health: Excellent

Education:
    B.A. Psychology
    Michiana University (YR-20)

    M.A. Clinical Psychology
    Southby State University (YR-17)

Professional Membership:
    American Psychological Association

    Secretary, Great Lakes Clinical Psychology Association

Professional Experience:

YR-16/YR-11   Central High School
                Southby, Michiana 46601
                    taught psychology and served as full time school psychologist

YR-11/YR-8   Supervisor, Counseling Services
                Woodlawn Residential Treatment Center
                Destiny, Michiana 46108
                    counseling youth on alcohol and drug abuse, pregnancy, etc.

YR-8/present   Crossroads Clinic
                Southby, Michiana 46601
                    private counseling clientele and court referred counseling services and reports

References:

Prof. Karling Schmoll   Mr. Avery Cramer
Chairman, Clinical Psychology   Director, Woodlawn Residential Treatment
   Department   Center
Southby State University   Destiny, Michiana 46108
Southby, Michiana 46556

K. DOMESTIC VIOLENCE

Problem 74

In re Marriage of Custer

Bob and Mary Custer were married on March 21, YR-6. They had three children, Barbara (born January 2, YR-9), Amos (born August 1, YR-6), and Eliza (born July 2, YR-5). Their ten-year relationship was rocky from the start. Their mutually volatile tempers often got the better of them, and the couple fought with regularity throughout their relationship.

After Amos was born, Bob began drinking excessively. Mary yelled abusively at Bob for his drunkenness. When Bob felt the abuse was too much, he would strike Mary. These batteries continued regularly throughout the course of the marriage. On January 13, YR-2, when Bob was beating on Mary because he had found out that she was cheating on him, Barbara stepped in the way, crying "No Daddy, don't! Don't hit her!" Bob threw Barbara out of his way and continued to beat Mary. Barbara struck her head on a coffee table. She suffered a concussion and a severe facial contusion that has caused a permanent scar.

Bob was convicted of domestic battery and sentenced to twelve months in prison on May 3, YR-2. Mary filed a divorce petition on September 18, YR-2. In her petition, Mary claims that Bob has beaten her and the children regularly. Bob admits to having beaten Mary, but denies having struck any of the children other than the one time he hit Barbara.

The issues of marital property and distribution of assets have already been settled in this case. The only remaining issues involve child custody and child support.

Both Bob and Mary desire to have sole custody of all three children. Mary makes her claim for custody based on Bob's battery of the children. She stated in deposition that Bob would not remember beating the children because he was usually drunk when he beat them. Bob, in return, states that Mary's affair with George DiGioni has placed the children at great risk.

In support of his statements regarding Mary's custody of the children, Bob refers to three police reports filed during YR-1. In each of those reports, the police were summoned to investigate child molestation based on allegations made by the children's day care provider. Those reports have led to George's indictment for child molestation. The criminal case goes to trial later this year. Mary, of course, denies that George has molested any of her children.

In the first police report, dated October 31, YR-1, the children's afterschool day care provider stated that she had seen Eliza playing with her Barbie doll in "an inappropriate manner." The provider immediately called the police. A subsequent police investigation showed that Eliza had had vaginal sexual contact on at least one occasion. Eliza was unable to discuss her molestation credibly, so the police did not arrest anyone.

The second report, based on the day care provider's call of November 24, YR-1, resulted in police discovery of further sexual contact between Eliza and an unknown male. Further investigation, including a third report of molestation entered by the day care provider (although the third report indicated molestation of Amos rather than Eliza), indicated that George had been molesting the two younger children for several months. The police immediately arrested

George, and upon his release on bail a protective order was issued to prevent him from coming into contact with the children.

Mary, not wanting to lose her paramour, has ignored the protective order and has let George stay with her frequently during the last few months. Bob claims that on January 22, YR-0, he received a telephone call from a frightened Barbara. "Daddy," she cried, "He's here! He's touching Amos again! Please, Daddy, make him stop!" Bob immediately called the police, but by the time they got to Mary's apartment, George was not there. Mary claimed that George had never been there, and that the children were unavailable. The police did not investigate the incident any further.

Mary and George continue to deny any molestation on George's part. Mary believes that any molestation of the children must somehow be Bob's doing. Bob admits that he was in contact with the children within two days of each complained incident but states that he has never done anything to harm any child.

In an interview with a court-appointed psychiatrist, Barbara indicated a marginal interest in living with her mother, but not unless she can stay with her two siblings. She stated that she was willing to live with her father if she could stay with and take care of her younger brother and sister. The younger children could not give the psychiatrist a cohesive answer regarding their wishes, although all of the children had expressed some fear of George. The social worker assigned to the three children has determined that their educational and peer environment would be about the same with either parent. Neither the social worker nor the psychiatrist was able to suggest one parent over the other for the court's consideration.

The child custody issue in this case is the only question before the court.

Questions

1. Who has a better claim to custody of the children? What further facts would be useful in this determination?
2. How should Bob's repeated batteries against Mary be considered during the custody proceeding?
3. Assume that if George is convicted of child molestation, he will be sentenced to two years in prison. He and Mary have already stated that, whatever happens, they plan to remain together. How should this information impact the court's custody decisions?
4. What effect should Mary's refusal to abide by the protective order have on the outcome of this case?
5. Assume that George has molested Amos and Eliza. Must a court find that Barbara is in a dangerous environment?
6. Assume that Amos had told the police that George molested him, but in a competency hearing Amos recanted his story. Is Amos's testimony admissible to prove George's danger to the children?
7. Does the court have the right to terminate the parental rights of both Mary and Bob? What factual determinations must the court make in order to terminate the interests of either parent?

L. BATTERED WOMEN'S SYNDROME

Problem 75

Dobbs v. Dobbs

Mike and Lesley Dobbs were married in YR-10. Throughout their marriage, Mike physically and mentally abused Lesley on a regular basis. As a result of the abuse, Lesley was unable to make basic decisions for herself, was barely capable of functioning independently, and had little self-confidence or feeling of self-worth. Although not formally diagnosed at that time, Lesley was probably suffering from battered women's syndrome (BWS).

In YR-2 Mike took a job as a long haul truck driver and was rarely home during the next two years. During that period of time, Lesley was able to go back to school and establish some independence. In YR-0, Lesley decided she would be better off on her own and decided to file for divorce. As part of her divorce petition, Lesley asserted claims for compensatory and punitive damages based on the years of abuse that Mike inflicted on her during their marriage.

The court, after reviewing her petition, dismissed most of Lesley's tort claim against Mike, because all but two of the alleged beatings that Lesley included in her complaint occurred more than two years prior to the filing of the petition (and thus were barred by the applicable Michiana statute of limitations).

Questions

1. How persuasive is Lesley's argument that the statute of limitations had not begun to run?
2. Does it make a difference that Lesley suffered from battered women's syndrome (BWS)? How would you prove to the court that Lesley was a victim of BWS?
3. What is a "continuous tort"? Does abuse that causes BWS constitute a continuous tort?

M. REMOVAL OF CHILD FROM JURISDICTION

Problem 76

In re Marriage of O'Neil

Terrence and Nora Mary O'Neil met while they were students in the dramatic arts program at Michiana University. They were both active onstage performers and dreamed of pursuing careers in New York or California. Following winter graduation, they married on St. Patrick's Day, YR-9. Both Terrence and Nora Mary had entered graduate school pursuing degrees in theater arts. Nora

Mary became pregnant and on February 7, YR-8, their son, Sean, was born. Being a responsible husband and father, Terrence left graduate school to support his family and opened an insurance agency with two of his brothers. As a native of Southby from a large extended family, Terrence watched the business grow and prosper. Three years later, on March 15, YR-4, Nora Mary gave birth to a daughter, Caitlin.

Although Terrence was busy expanding his business, Nora Mary maintained her contacts with the theater and was active in the local community acting group. As time passed, Terrence and Nora Mary drifted apart. Terrence's friends were business associates and clients. Nora Mary's friends and interests revolved around the theater league. She was working at the local civic theater, assuming responsibility for bookings and for entertaining visiting cast members. In YR-2, Terrence and Nora Mary decided it was better for them to part as friends, rather than maintain a marriage that was increasingly empty for both of them. They reached an amicable settlement agreement for dividing property between them and decided that joint legal custody would be in the best interests of both Sean and Caitlin. The children would live with Nora Mary, but Terrence would have visitation at reasonable times, to be arranged by the parties. Child support was established using the state guidelines. A decree of dissolution, which incorporated their agreements, was entered on September 19, YR-1.

Nora Mary and the children remained in the marital home. Terrence moved back into his old neighborhood, close to his mother and several of his brothers and sisters. Terrence had frequent visitation with the children during the week and on weekends. Sean and Caitlin had close relationships with their grandmother, aunts, uncles, and cousins. Both were enrolled in Our Lady of Sorrows Grade School, the school Terrence had attended as a child.

In May, YR-0, Nora Mary was contacted by Reggie Llewellyn, an agent she had met through her work. He suggested that the time was right for Nora Mary to make her move to New York for a career on Broadway. Reggie was able to line up auditions for Nora Mary with some of the best known directors in the business and was willing to represent her for a reasonable fee. New York is approximately 600 miles from Southby, Michiana. Pursuant to the dissolution decree, Nora Mary has notified the court of her intent to move out of Michiana with the children.

Questions

1. What should Terrence do to prevent Nora Mary from removing the children immediately from Michiana?
2. What policies underlie rules governing removal of minor children to another jurisdiction?
3. What should be the rule for modifying a child custody order when the custodial parent moves out of state? What about when the noncustodial parent moves?
4. Which party has the burden of proving the legal requirements for removal of a child from the jurisdiction?
5. On the facts of this case, with whom should the children stay when Nora Mary moves to New York? Who should have custody?
6. How should Nora Mary's decision to move out of state be analyzed under Sections 409-410 of the Uniform Marriage and Divorce Act (UMDA)? (*See* Appendix.)

Chapter Nine. Dissolution of Marriage

N. INTERSTATE CUSTODY DISPUTES

1. Uniform Child Custody Jurisdiction Act and Parental Kidnapping Prevention Act

Problem 77

In re Marriage of Tried

Medgar and Cecily Tried were married in Illinois and moved to Michiana in YR-4. In YR-1, Medgar took the parties' two minor children to Illinois for a two-week visit after agreeing that he would return with them and file for divorce in Michiana. At the end of the visitation, however, Medgar advised Cecily that he was staying in Illinois and filing for divorce and custody, which he did five days later. Two days after that, Cecily filed her own divorce action in Michiana. The Michiana court was not aware of prior Illinois court action when the court dissolved the marriage and awarded custody to Cecily. An Illinois court later awarded custody to Medgar, on the basis of the best interests of the children, a comparison of the home environments in Michiana and Illinois, and the fact that Medgar lived with paternal grandparents, who would care for the children while he worked. Cecily had to have a babysitter while she worked. The Illinois trial court did not find Medgar's conduct in retaining the children in Illinois as wrongful. Assume that Illinois and Michiana have statutory laws identical to the Uniform Child Custody Jurisdiction Act (UCCJA). Cecily claims that the Illinois order is invalid and that the Michiana order granting her custody should be upheld.

Questions

1. Where should Cecily file her claim regarding the invalidity of the Illinois order?
2. What is the purpose of the Uniform Child Custody Jurisdiction Act (UCCJA)? What procedural requirements, if any, does the UCCJA require of Medgar before he may file his divorce petition in Illinois? (*See* Appendix.)
3. What effect should Cecily's failure to inform the Michiana court of Medgar's petition have on the validity of her petition?
4. Under the UCCJA, assuming Cecily files her claim in the proper court, what should be the result regarding the validity of the Illinois custody order?
5. Why would Medgar have wanted to have the divorce action brought in Illinois?
6. What effect does the Parental Kidnapping Prevention Act (PKPA) have on this case? (*See* Appendix.)

O. INTERNATIONAL CUSTODY DISPUTES

1. *Hague Convention and International Child Abduction Remedies Act*

Problem 78

In re Application of Fiona Bindra

Jasjit Bindra and Fiona Wilkinson-Brown, both citizens of the United Kingdom, were married in London on October 25, YR-17. Two children were born of the marriage—a daughter, Harinder, born October 21, YR-16, and a son, Nigel, born November 17, YR-10. The family has resided in the north London suburb of Hampstead since YR-6. Jasjit is a lecturer in biochemistry at Central London Polytechnic. On May 30, YR-0, Jasjit told Fiona that he was taking the children to Southby, Michiana, in the United States, where he planned to work at Michiana University as a research associate in biochemistry during the summer of YR-0. Fiona stated, "It may be jolly good for all of us. I need a bit of space right now." On July 20, YR-0, Fiona filed a complaint for divorce in the Hampstead County Court. Because of the complexity of the issues, which involved the Hague Convention, the case was transferred to the Family Division of the High Court in London. Service by certified mail of the complaint for divorce and notice of hearing on Fiona's request for temporary custody was refused by Jasjit. On August 1, Jasjit informed Fiona over the telephone that he had accepted a faculty position at Michiana University beginning the fall of YR-0, and that he and the children would not be returning to England. Jasjit stated that the children were enrolled in school and it was their expressed wishes not to return to the U.K. Jasjit further stated to Fiona that he was advised by his attorney that under U.K. law "the father and mother of a child are equally entitled to custody of the child, subject to alteration by an order of court or separation agreement." Fiona demanded that Jasjit immediately return the children to London. On September 30, the Family Division entered a temporary order providing that Fiona have the care and custody of Harinder and Nigel, and fixing reasonable visitation for Jasjit along with his obligation to pay child support.

On October 19, YR-0, having made application to the U.S. Central Authority, Fiona's American counsel filed in the Hoynes County Circuit Court in Southby, Michiana, her petition for return of the children to her in London. A copy of Fiona's petition follows this Problem. On October 26, YR-0, Jasjit filed his responsive petition, which also follows this Problem. On October 20, YR-0, Fiona admitted herself to the Quiet Care Mental Health Unit of Middlesex Hospital in London for what she described as "depression and stress over the loss of my children." Fiona is presently an outpatient at Middlesex Hospital and attends weekly therapy sessions. Jasjit claims that Fiona is an alcoholic, mentally unstable, and that the children would be at grave risk of psychological harm if they were returned to their mother in the U.K.

Chapter Nine. Dissolution of Marriage

Questions

1. Do the Hague Convention and the International Child Abduction Remedies Act (ICARA) apply in this case? (*See* Appendix.)
2. Does this case involve a wrongful removal or retention pursuant to the Hague Convention and ICARA?
3. What is the significance of Fiona's consent for Jasjit to take the children with him to the United States?
4. Should the Hoynes Circuit Court dismiss the petition as to Harinder Bindra?
5. Are the children's wishes relevant?
6. Is it significant that on September 30, YR-0, the Family Division of the High Court in London did not address the issues of wrongful removal or retention or return of the children to Fiona?
7. What bearing should the Hoynes Circuit Court's opinion—that it is in the best interests of the children to remain with Jasjit—have on that court's ruling on Fiona's petition?
8. Would it be appropriate for the Hoynes Circuit Court to place the children in the care and custody of child welfare authorities in Hoynes County to assure their continued presence in the jurisdiction?
9. What are the parties' burdens of proof under the Convention and ICARA?
10. What ruling(s) should the Hoynes Circuit Court make on Fiona's petition and Jasjit's response?
11. Who is entitled to custody of the children?
12. May Fiona recover from Jasjit the costs for her mental health treatment? What about her attorney fees?

STATE OF MICHIANA   )   IN THE HOYNES CIRCUIT COURT
)
HOYNES COUNTY   )   CAUSE NO. DR-1992-112144

IN RE THE APPLICATION OF FIONA BINDRA

PETITIONER: FIONA BINDRA
AND
RESPONDENT: JASJIT BINDRA

PETITION FOR RETURN OF CHILDREN TO PETITIONER

Preamble

1. This petition is brought pursuant to The Convention on the Civil Aspects of International Child Abduction, done at the Hague on 25 October 1980 (Convention) and 42 U.S.C. Section 11603(b), the International Child Abduction Remedies Act (ICARA). The Convention went into effect on July 1, 1988.
2. The objectives of the Convention are:
    Article 1(a): To secure the prompt return of children wrongfully removed to or retained in any Contracting State; and
    Article 1(b): To ensure that rights of custody and of access under the law of one Contracting State are effectively respected in the other Contracting States.

Jurisdiction

3. This court has jurisdiction pursuant to 42 U.S.C. Section 11603 of ICARA.

Status of Petitioner and Child

4. Petitioner, Fiona Bindra (Fiona), has a right of custody of the children, Harinder Bindra, DOB 10-21-YR-16, and Nigel Bindra, DOB 11-17-YR-10, within the meaning of Articles Three and Five of the Convention, in that Fiona is the mother of the two children, and pursuant to the 9-30-YR-0 temporary order of the Family Division of the High Court of England and Wales, Fiona has the right of custody of the two minor children of the parties. Fiona at the time of the wrongful removal or retention was actually exercising custody within the meaning of Articles Three and Five of the Convention.
5. Fiona at the time of the application to the Central Authority of the United States was located in the United Kingdom, and continues to reside in the United Kingdom.
6. The children were habitually resident in London, U.K., within the meaning of Article Three of the Convention immediately before the removal of the children from the U.K. by Respondent, Jasjit Bindra (Jasjit). See the DECLARATION UNDER UNIFORM CHILD CUSTODY JURISDICTION ACT (DUUCCJA), attached as Exhibit A.

Removal and/or Retention of Children By Respondent

7. On or about August 1, YR-0, Respondent wrongfully removed the children from the United Kingdom within the meaning of Article Three of the Convention and continues to wrongfully retain the children in the United States despite efforts on the part of Fiona to have the children returned.

8. The children are presently in the State of Michiana, County of Hoynes.
9. The Respondent, at the time of application to the Central Authority of the United States, was a habitual resident of the United Kingdom.

Custody Proceedings in the United Kingdom

10. The status and/or pendency of custody proceedings in the United Kingdom are set forth in the DUUCCJA (Exhibit A).
11. The United Kingdom on 9-30-YR-0 issued an order for custody of the children in favor of Fiona.
12. The courts of this state are requested to stay any other proceedings concerning the custody of the child as required by Article 16 of the Convention.
13. Pending further hearing in this Court, it is requested that this Court issue its immediate order prohibiting the removal of the children, Harinder Bindra and Nigel Bindra, from the jurisdiction of this Court and requiring Jasjit to post a bond in the amount of $5,000.00, said bond to remain in effect until further order of the Court.

Relief Requested

14. Fiona requests the following relief: the two children, Harinder Bindra and Nigel Bindra, are to be returned to Fiona.

Notice of Hearing

15. Pursuant to 42 USC Section 11603(c), Jasjit shall be given notice pursuant to Michiana Civil Code Sections 5153 and 5154.

Attorney Fees and Costs (Convention Article 26 and/or 42 U.S.C. Section 11607)

16. Fiona has attached, as Exhibit B, a copy of all expenditures to date incurred by Fiona as a result of the wrongful removal and/or retention of the children by Jasjit.
17. Fiona will amend Exhibit B from time to time, according to proof and further expenditures required because of this wrongful removal and/or retention.
18. Fiona requests that this Court award all costs and fees incurred to date as required by 42 USC Section 11607, reserving jurisdiction over further expenses.

Verification

I am attorney for the Petitioner, Fiona Bindra. I make this verification on behalf of the Petitioner because Petitioner is absent from Hoynes County, Michiana. The above document is true of my own knowledge, except as to the matters that are stated in it on my information and belief and as to those matters I believe it to be true. I declare under penalty of perjury under the laws of the State of Michiana that the foregoing is true and correct.

EXECUTED on the _____ day of September, YR-0, at Southby, Michiana.

_____
Attorney for Petitioner,
Fiona Bindra

STATE OF MICHIANA) IN THE HOYNES CIRCUIT COURT
)
HOYNES COUNTY) CAUSE NO. DR-1992-112144

IN RE THE APPLICATION OF FIONA BINDRA

PETITIONER: FIONA BINDRA
AND
RESPONDENT: JASJIT BINDRA

RESPONSE TO PETITION FOR RETURN OF CHILDREN

Status of Petitioner and Child

1. Petitioner, Fiona Bindra (Fiona), has no right to custody of the children within the meaning of Articles Three and Five of the Hague Convention on the Civil Aspects of International Child Abduction (Convention) in that
    a. Fiona consented to the children's removal to the United States.
2. Fiona was not actually exercising custody of the children at the time of the alleged removal or retention.
3. Harinder Bindra, minor child of the parties, was born on 10-21-16, and will be over the age of sixteen before this Court considers the issues raised in the application by Fiona.

Removal of Children By Respondent

4. On May 30, YR-0, Respondent, Jasjit Bindra (Jasjit), with the consent and knowledge of Fiona, removed the children from the United Kingdom and thereafter retained the children outside the U.K. Since that date, Fiona has had and continues to have knowledge of the present whereabouts of the children and has acquiesced in the present custodial arrangement.
5. The removal and/or retention of the children is not in breach of custody rights under the laws of the United Kingdom for the following reasons:
    a. Fiona consented to the children's removal to the United States and retention of the children in the United States.

Provisional Remedies (42 U.S.C. Section 11604)

6. The children are presently in the custody of Jasjit in Southby, Michiana.
7. Jasjit requests that this Court order that the children remain in the care, custody and control of Jasjit pending further order of this Court.
8. Jasjit agrees that pending further action by this Court the children and Jasjit will remain within the jurisdiction of this Court.
9. Jasjit agrees to post a bond in the amount of $1,000.00.
10. Jasjit requests that each party bear their own attorney fees and costs.

Relief Requested

11. Jasjit respectfully requests that the Petition for Return of Children be denied.

Verification

I am the Respondent. The above document is true of my own knowledge, except as to the matters that are stated in it on my information and belief and as to those matters I believe it to be true. I declare under penalty of perjury under the laws of the State of Michiana that the foregoing is true and correct.

EXECUTED on October 24, YR-0, at Southby, Michiana.

_____
Respondent, Jasjit Bindra

Problem 79

In re Marriage of Singh

Philomena Singh is the only child of Ruta and Rafat Singh. Ruta, the mother, was born of Indian parents in Chicago and grew up in the United States. Rafat was born and reared in Bombay, India. Ruta and Rafat were married by arrangement in Bombay on June 30, YR-6. Philomena was born in Southby, Michiana, on November 1, YR-4. Ruta and Rafat agreed in writing that Philomena should live with her paternal grandparents in India. On July 5, YR-2, Philomena arrived in Bombay and has lived with her grandparents in India ever since.

Ruta and Rafat separated in December of YR-2. In June of YR-1, Ruta withdrew her written consent that Philomena live with her paternal grandparents and initiated divorce proceedings, seeking to invoke jurisdiction of the Michiana court. The Judge of the Hoynes Circuit Court in Southby, Michiana, ruled that, since there was not a continued agreement of both parents (that Philomena remain in India), Philomena was habitually a resident in the United States.

Rafat has appealed the decision of the Hoynes Circuit Court to the Michiana Court of Appeals.

Question

1. Was the Hoynes Circuit Court decision a correct interpretation of the Hague Convention and the International Child Abduction Remedies Act (ICARA)? (*See* Appendix.)

P. CHILD SUPPORT

1. Federal Intervention

Problem 80

In re Marriage of Morgan

Review the facts of Problem 63 and the Domestic Relations Counseling Bureau (DRCB) report on custody. Assume, for this problem, that custody of the parties' minor children was awarded to Barbara. The DRCB filed its temporary support study, which follows this Problem. Peter and Barbara are unable to reach agreement on allocation of their debts and Peter's weekly support obligation. Assume that on issues pertaining to child support Michiana law is identical to the Uniform Marriage and Divorce Act. The Hoynes Circuit Court support guidelines follow this problem.

Chapter Nine. Dissolution of Marriage

Questions

1. *See* the child support guideline that follow this Problem. According to the guideline, assuming Peter grosses $75,000 per year, what should his child support obligation be?
2. Should allocation of marital debt affect child support? Why or why not?
3. What type of legal action should be taken to enforce the support order? Who should bring the action? In what court should the action be brought?

DATE: September 14, YR-0

TO: Honorable Albert B. Simpson, Judge
Hoynes Circuit Court

FROM: Susan Sheehan, Chief Counselor
Domestic Relations Counseling Bureau

IN RE: The Marriage of Peter R. Morgan—Husband
and
Barbara S. Morgan—Wife

CAUSE NO: R-7138

TEMPORARY SUPPORT STUDY

On 8/27/YR-4, Mr. Peter R. Morgan and Mrs. Barbara S. Morgan were referred to DRCB by the Honorable Albert B. Simpson, Judge, Hoynes Circuit Court, for a domestic investigation. The special instructions from the Court indicated that it desired the temporary support study be expedited.

On 9/11/YR-4, Mrs. Morgan was seen in this office for 1¼ hours.

On 9/11/YR-4, Mr. Morgan was seen in this office for 1½ hours.

A copy of this original report is on file in DRCB. Two additional copies are attached for distribution to the respective attorneys.

Interviews with Husband and Wife

Both of the parties presented monthly living expense summaries to DRCB. Mr. Morgan has vacated the family and is living in an apartment. Mrs. Morgan continues to live in the family hoe with her mother and the four Morgan children. DRCB has summarized the living expenses for each of the households for purposes of comparison and establishing temporary support. That summary is attached to this report.

Mr. Morgan brought in a completed form giving his gross and net monthly incomes and the amounts deducted from his monthly checks. A copy of that form is attached.

When Mr. Morgan first took employment with Ripley College in YR-5, his yearly salary was $40,000 gross. In YR-0, he will be earning about $75,000 gross. He has indicated to DRCB that he and his wife have:

1. No savings

2. No educational funds set aside

3. No funds for emergency use

Mr. Morgan stated that he has let his wife run the household and that there have been serious financial problems that he has had to solve on several occasions in the past years.

Mrs. Morgan provided the information to DRCB that she had been unable to make the 8/1/YR-0 house payment. She indicated that this was due to the fact that she had been shorted $300 on her husband's payroll check for 7/1/YR-0 and $400 on the check that came to her on 8/1/YR-0. (Mr. Morgan was in Dublin, Ireland, at Trinity College during this period.)

Mr. Morgan indicated that the August YR-0 house payment of $754 was due but contended that his wife had received his checks in July and August, both being in the amount of at least $2,400. Since the Morgans had discussed his study abroad for about two years, he did not feel that Mrs. Morgan had been taken by surprise. He is concerned now that the house payments may not be made with him out of the home and as the house goes on the market for sale. He would like to take over the housing payments at this time to avert any problems that might arise to negate the orderly sale of the house.

Mr. Morgan stated that in January of YR-1, the family's credit accounts at Sears and Ayres were closed by agreement of the parties. Following his return from Ireland in late August, Mr. Morgan said that he discovered that Mrs. Morgan had reopened the accounts and had run up about $1,000 in bills at Sears and Ayres during his absence.

Mrs. Morgan reported that she had asked for the accounts to be reopened, particularly for the purchase of the children's clothing for school in September.

On 8/3/YR-0, Mrs. Morgan said she owed a $380 phone bill. Upset over Mr. Morgan's announcement before he left for Ireland that he was unhappy with the marriage, she said she made calls to Peoria to her family members and to Ireland to Mr. Morgan.

Mr. Morgan does not want Mrs. Morgan to have her phone removed, but he chooses not to volunteer to pay the bill at this time. (This is the telephone bill that the respective attorneys were to discuss following the haring on 9/27/YR-0, according to the comments of both parties.)

Mr. Morgan reported that a new sound system had been installed at the family home while he was gone during July and August. He can only estimate the cost as being in the neighborhood of $400.

Mr. Morgan questions Mrs. Morgan's $300 monthly item on the budget for utilities, maintaining that in the winter months the largest gas and electric bills they ever had were $250. He believes that the bill would be considerably less in the summer. Mrs. Morgan indicated she has not run the central air conditioning unit much this summer.

In presenting her budget to this office, Mrs. Morgan did cut down her monthly payment to Sears and to Ayres. DRCB made adjustments around those items. DRCB has also made an adjustment in lunch money allowed to the two high school students. The cut was made on the basis of school lunches being 90 cents per day per student. Thus DRCB cut the $80 lunch money item to $40 per month. Mr. Morgan indicated that the $754 per month house payment is now up to $804 per month. It is not clear to him why $50 was added on to the monthly mortgage bill. DRCB has used the figure of $754 for the mortgage payment on Mrs. Morgan's monthly expense report, but the figure $804 may be the true figure.

<u>Assessment</u>

Mr. Morgan reports gross earnings per month of $6,250.00. Following deductions for taxes, two loans, hospitalization, life insurance and United Fund, his net earnings for the month are $3,090. Mr. Morgan is straightforward in presenting his wages to the court, pointing out that during the period 8/15/YR-0 until 12/1/YR-0, his Social Security is paid up. That gives him additional income for the months of September, October, and November the sum of $385 per month. Thus, for those three months, his net wages will be $3,475.

Mrs. Morgan presents her monthly expenses as $2,659.50; Mr. Morgan presents his monthly expenses as $1,052. The combined expenses for the two households come to the amount of $3,711.50. Thus the joint budget taken from the single salary leaves a deficit of $621.50, except for the three-month period cited above, when there would be a deficit of only $236.50 per month.

Mr. Morgan is making a request that the mortgage payment be his responsibility. If that is done, Mrs. Morgan would have monthly expenses of $1,905.50, and Mr. Morgan would then have monthly expenses of $1,806.

There are certain items in Mrs. Morgan's budget that could conceivably be cut: perhaps $50 from the food item; $100 from the utilities item; $40 from the telephone item; $20 from the amusement item; and $80 from the duplicate clothing items that are listed under "Clothing" and "Ayres" on the budget sheet. HBO may also be cut, saving $20 per month.

Mr. Morgan has had to rent furniture for his recently rented apartment. His clothing item is somewhat high by virtue of the fact that he has purchased almost no clothing for himself in the last several years. In his position he must present an adequate appearance. Mrs. Morgan has maintained that Mr. Morgan took all of his meals at Ripley College. If that is true, his monthly food item may be cut to lessen his monthly expenses.

In an attempt to look at the situations of both of these parents in an equitable fashion, the most logical solution that can be reached is the following:

> The Court may wish to consider transfer of the mortgage payment to Mr. Morgan. As that is done, support for Mrs. Morgan and the children would have to be lowered to $340 per week or $1,460 for 4.3 weeks.
>
> The $131 removed from support payments for Mrs. Morgan and the children on a weekly basis would come to $563.30 for a period of 4.3 weeks. The sum would be applied to the mortgage payment of $754 or ($804).
>
> In any event, the slim budgets of each of the parents would be approximately $200 in deficit.

The Court may consider these two options or those of the respective counsel in arriving at a solution to the financial problem.

_____
Susan Sheehan, Chief Counselor
Domestic Relations Counseling Bureau

_____
John R. Connell, Director
Domestic Relations Counseling Bureau

Copies to: Counsel for Peter R. Morgan and Barbara S. Morgan

MONTHLY EXPENSES	WIFE + M/GRMO. + 4 CHIL.		HUSBAND	
FOOD	$500.00		$260.00	
GASOLINE	$ 50.00			
CHURCH	- 0 -		$ 45.00	
LUNCH (WORK)	- 0 -		$ 15.00	
LAUNDRY	- 0 -		$ 65.00	
SCHOOL LUNCH	$ 40.00 (2)		- 0 -	
PET CARE	$ 10.00		- 0 -	
SITTER	- 0 -		- 0 -	
MORTGAGE/RENT	$754.00		$225.00	
UTILITIES (GAS, ELECTRIC, OIL)	$300.00		$ 50.00	
WATER	- 0 -		- 0 -	
TELEPHONE	$ 75.00		$ 15.00	
TRASH P/UP	$ 6.00		- 0 -	
INSURANCE—CAR	- 0 -		- 0 -	
INSURANCE—HOME	- 0 -		- 0 -	
INSURANCE—LIFE	$ 20.00		$ 38.00	
MEDICAL	$100.00		$ 11.00	
CAR—PLATES, TAXES	- 0 -		- 0 -	
ALLOWANCES, AMUSEMENTS	$120.00		$ 80.00	
GROOMING	$ 60.00		$ 20.00	
HOME REPAIR	$ 40.00		- 0 -	
CABLE TV/HBO	$ 43.00		- 0 -	
NEWSPAPER	$ 6.50		$ 8.00	
CLOTHING	$150.00		$ 80.00	
COUNSELING	$130.00			
OTHER	$ 25.00	Florist		
OTHER	$ 30.00	Sears	$ 90.00	Furniture
OTHER (CLOTHING, HOME)	$100.00	Ayres	$ 50.00	Misc.
OTHER	$ 60.00	United Airlines		
SUB TOTAL	$2659.00		$1052.00	

TO WHOM IT MAY CONCERN:

Re: _____

Social Security Number: _____

FOR PERIOD 1-1-YR-0 to 9-1-YR-0

There is a child support investigation pending in the Hoynes County Circuit Court involving the above captioned person. It is our task to recommend to the Court the amount of support payments for the minor children. In fairness to your employee, may we have the following information:

Gross Earnings Per Month_____ Net_____

Overtime Earnings Per Week _____ Hours_____

Gross Earnings Per Year _____ Net_____

Hourly Rate _____ Dependents Claimed_____

Amount of Deductions as Follows (where applicable): per month

    Federal Withholding_____   Hospitalization_____
    F.I.C.A._____   Life Insurance_____
    State Tax_____   Retirement_____
    Unemployment Tax_____   United Fund_____
    Optional Tax_____   Bond Deductions_____
    Credit Union_____   Garnishment_____
    Union Dues_____   Other: Specify_____

Please state the number of weeks worked in any given yearly figure_____

We would appreciate an expeditious reply to this request. Thank you for your cooperation in this matter.

Sincerely,

John R. Connell, Director
Domestic Relations Counseling Bureau
1st Floor, County-City Building
Southby, Michiana
Telephone: (210) 239-5865

_____ _____ _____
Signature of person completing form   Title   Date

SUPPORT GUIDELINE
(preliminary draft)

WEEKLY INCOME	SPOUSE	1 CHILD B-5	1 CHILD 6-12	1 CHILD 13+	2 CHILDREN B-5	2 CHILDREN 6-12	2 CHILDREN 13+	3 CHILDREN B-5	3 CHILDREN 6-12	3 CHILDREN 13+	4 CHILDREN B-5	4 CHILDREN 6-12	4 CHILDREN 13+	5 CHILDREN 6-12	5 CHILDREN 13+	MAXIMUM SUPPORT
66- 75	16	25	28	30	45	50	54	63	70	75	78	87	93	101	108	45
76- 85	19	25	28	30	45	50	54	63	70	75	78	87	93	101	108	51
86- 95	21	25	28	30	45	50	54	63	70	75	78	87	93	101	108	57
96-105	23	25	28	30	45	50	54	63	70	75	78	87	93	101	108	63
106-115	25	25	28	30	45	50	54	63	70	75	78	87	93	101	108	69
116-125	27	25	28	30	45	50	54	63	70	75	78	87	93	101	108	75
126-135	30	25	28	30	45	50	54	63	70	75	78	87	93	101	108	81
136-145	32	25	28	30	45	50	54	63	70	75	78	87	93	101	108	87
146-155	34	25	28	30	45	50	54	63	70	75	78	87	93	101	108	93
156-165	36	25	29	32	46	52	58	64	72	77	78	87	93	101	108	99
166-175	38	26	30	34	47	54	62	65	74	80	79	90	97	104	113	105
176-185	41	26	31	36	47	56	66	66	77	83	80	93	101	108	118	111
186-195	43	27	32	39	48	58	70	67	80	86	81	96	105	112	123	117
196-205	45	27	33	41	49	60	74	68	83	89	82	99	109	116	129	123
206-215	54	28	34	43	51	62	77	70	86	94	84	103	114	120	135	129
216-225	56	29	35	45	53	64	80	73	89	99	87	107	120	125	142	135
226-235	59	30	36	47	55	66	83	76	93	104	90	111	126	130	149	141
236-245	61	31	37	49	57	69	86	79	97	109	93	115	132	135	156	147
246-255	64	32	38	51	59	72	89	82	101	115	96	120	138	140	163	153
256-265	66	33	40	53	61	75	92	85	105	121	100	125	144	145	170	159
266-275	69	34	42	55	63	78	95	88	109	126	104	130	151	150	177	165
276-285	71	35	44	57	65	81	98	91	113	132	108	135	158	156	184	171
286-295	74	36	46	59	67	84	101	94	117	138	112	140	165	162	192	177
296-305	76	38	48	61	69	87	104	97	121	144	116	145	172	168	200	183
306-315	79	40	50	63	71	90	108	100	125	150	120	150	179	174	208	189
316-325	81	41	51	65	73	93	112	103	129	155	124	155	185	180	216	195
326-335	84	42	52	67	75	96	116	106	133	160	128	160	192	186	223	201
336-345	86	43	53	69	77	99	120	109	137	165	132	165	198	192	231	207
346-355	89	44	54	71	79	102	124	113	141	170	136	170	204	198	239	213
356-365	91	45	55	73	81	105	128	117	145	175	140	175	211	204	247	219
366-375	94	46	57	75	83	108	132	121	149	180	144	180	218	210	255	225
376-385	96	47	59	77	85	111	136	125	153	185	148	185	225	216	263	231
386-395	99	48	61	79	87	114	140	129	157	190	152	190	232	222	271	237
396-405	101	50	63	81	90	117	144	132	161	196	156	195	239	228	279	243
406-415	104	51	65	83	93	120	148	135	165	202	160	200	246	234	287	249
416-425	106	52	67	85	96	123	152	138	169	208	164	205	253	240	295	255
426-435	109	54	69	87	99	125	156	141	173	214	168	210	260	246	303	261
436-445	111	56	71	89	102	128	160	144	177	220	172	215	267	252	311	267
446-455	114	58	73	91	105	131	164	147	182	226	176	220	274	258	319	273
456-465	116	60	75	93	108	135	168	150	187	232	181	226	281	264	327	279
456-465	116	60	75	93	108	135	168	150	187	232	186	232	288	270	335	279

244

Chapter Nine. Dissolution of Marriage

HOYNES CIRCUIT AND SUPERIOR COURTS
SUPPORT GUIDELINE INSTRUCTIONS

Guideline Usage

WEEKLY INCOME — Weekly income refers to the noncustodial spouse's net income which is defined as gross income from all sources, taxable and non-taxable, less all applicable federal and state income tax withholdings and/or reasonable reserves for quarterly estimated tax payments and FICA credits, less Social Security and mandatory union fees

CHILD SUPPORT — Look to the number of children, one through five, and within that column the age of the oldest child to determine the appropriate sub-column and support obligation for all children.

SPOUSAL SUPPORT — Locate the spousal obligation of each party based on his and/or her income. Subtract the lesser from the greater. The balance is the spousal support for the recipient who has the lesser obligation.

MAXIMUM SUPPORT — Look to the last column to determine the non-custodial spouse's maximum child and/or spousal support. He or she is not obligated to pay more than 60% of weekly income in support.

EXAMPLES:

1. A husband has net earnings of $200.00 per week, and the wife has net earnings of $100.00 per week. She has custody of the two minor children; the oldest is fourteen (14) years. To determine spousal support, go to husband's figure (196-205) in column one, which equals $45, and wife's figure (96-105), which equals $23. Subtract. Husband pays spousal support of $22 weekly. To determine his child support obligation, go to his income (196-205) in column one and sub-column 13+ for two children. The sum is $74.00 per week for child support. Add the two support obligations ($22 + $74 = $96). Compare with the maximum support ($123). Since $96 is less than $123, the support obligation is $22 spousal and $74 child support.

2. Given the same information in Example 1, but there are four children, the eldest being 13+. The result is $114 child support and $22 spousal support, or $136. Since this amount exceeds the maximum of $123, the order for child support and spousal support will be $123 ($101 child support and $22 spousal support).

3. Same example as Example 1, but the wife earns $200, and the husband earns $100. The wife is obligated to pay spousal support of $22. The husband is obligated to pay child support of $54.

4. Same example as Example 1, but neither party has custody, and there is no request for spousal support. The wife pays $54 and the husband pays $74 per week child support.

5. Same example as Example 2, but the husband has custody. He pays $22 spousal support and the wife pays $63 child support. Since the child sup-

port of $93 is in excess of 60% of her income, the amount is determined by the maximum support column.

FURTHER EXPLANATION:

If a spouse has no income, temporary spousal support is the full amount in that column. If the net weekly income exceeds $465 per week, the parties may negotiate or the court may order an amount without the mathematical progressions of the Guideline, but not to exceed 60%. Spousal and child support will be segregated. If the maximum support figure is used, the spousal and child support will be prorated on a percentage basis.

The Guideline amounts include allowances for food, housing, transportation, clothing, and personal care, as well as ordinary medical and dental care and other items the family consumes directly. it does not include unusual or extraordinary mandatory expense items. These matters should be individually brought to the attention of the court. Examples of such expenses are special medical or educations costs.

The dates in this guideline were generated on the basis of reports that appeared in the YR-1 and YR-0 *Monthly Labor Review*, published by the U.S. Bureau of Labor Statistics.

STATE OF MICHIANA : CIRCUIT COURT : SUPERIOR COURT : HOYNES COUNTY

_____ Petitioner

VS.

_____ Respondent

Case No._____

FINANCIAL DECLARATION OF HUSBAND

Dated:_____

Wife _____
Address _____

Soc. Sec. No.: _____
Occupation _____
Employer _____
Birth Date _____

Husband _____
Address _____

Soc. Sec. No. _____
Occupation _____
Employer _____
Birth Date _____

Name, Address and Telephone Number of Attorney(s)

Space Below for Use of Court Clerk only

NOTE: THIS DECLARATION MUST BE FILED WITH THE COURT 7 DAYS BEFORE ALL CONTESTED HEARINGS RE: SUPPORT OR ASSETS.
FAILURE BY EITHER PARTY TO COMPLETE, PRESENT, AND FILE THIS FORM AS REQUIRED WILL AUTHORIZE THE COURT TO ACCEPT THE STATEMENT OF THE OTHER PARTY AS THE BASIS FOR ITS DECISION.
ANY FALSE STATEMENT MADE HEREON SHALL SUBJECT YOU TO PENALTY FOR **PERJURY** AND MAY BE CONSIDERED A FRAUD UPON THE COURT.

STATEMENT OF INCOME, EXPENSES, ASSETS AND LIABILITIES
Attach copies of State and Federal Income Tax Returns for last two taxable years and wage statements from your employer for last 8 weeks.

PART I INCOME AND EXPENSE STATEMENT

	HUSBAND	WIFE
	$	$

A. Gross weekly income from:
  Salary and wages, including commissions, bonuses, allowances and overtime, payable _____ (pay period) _____
  Note: If paid monthly, determine weekly income by dividing monthly income by 4.3
  Pensions and Retirement _____
  Social Security _____
  Disability and unemployment insurance _____
  Public Assistance (welfare, AFDC payments, etc.) _____
  Child support received from any prior marriage (not the marriage at issue) _____
  Dividends and interest _____
  Rents _____
  All other sources (Specify) _____

  * A. TOTAL WEEKLY INCOME _____ $ _____ $ _____

	HUSBAND	WIFE
	$	$

B. Itemize weekly deductions from gross income:
  State and federal income taxes _____
  Number of exemptions taken _____
  Social security _____
  Medical insurance (list all persons covered) _____

  Coverage: Medical ( ) Dental ( ) Eye Care ( ) Psychiatric ( ) _____
  Union or other dues _____
  Retirement or pension fund: Mandatory ( ) Optional ( ) _____
  Child care: Baby Sitter ( ) Pre-school ( ) Both ( ) _____
  Child support paid relating to a previous marriage _____
    *B. TOTAL WEEKLY DEDUCTIONS _____ $ _____ $ _____

C. Weekly disposable income (*A minus *B) _____ $ _____ $ _____

COURT COPY

specify which party is the custodial parent and list name and relationship of all members of the household whose

	HUSBAND	WIFE
(residence)		
(residence)		
supplies		
ng water, electricity, gas and heat		
and cleaning		
ng		
dical		
Dental		
Insurance (life, health, accident, liability, disability: exclude payroll deducted and automobile)		
School		
Entertainment (includes clubs, social obligations, travel, recreation)		
Incidentals (grooming, tobacco, alcohol, gifts, and donations)		
Transportation (other than automobile)		
Auto expense (gas, oil, repair, insurance)		
Auto payments		
Installment payment(s). Insert total and attach itemized schedule if not fully set forth below		
Other expenses (Insert total and specify on attached schedule)		
MONTHLY TOTAL EXPENSES		
AVERAGE WEEKLY EXPENSES (Divide total monthly expenses by 4.3)		

E. Debts and obligations:

CREDITOR'S NAME	FOR	DATE PAYABLE	BALANCE	MONTHLY PAYMENT
TOTAL			$	$

PART 2 NET WORTH All property of the parties known to me individually or jointly (indicate who holds or how title held: (H) Husband, (W) Wife, or (J) Jointly). **WHERE SPACE IS INSUFFICIENT FOR COMPLETE INFORMATION OR LISTING PLEASE ATTACH SEPARATE SCHEDULE.**

	CHECK OWNERSHIP H / W / J	VALUE	OWED THERE ON
A. Household furnishings, furniture, appliances, and equipment		$	
B. Automobiles (Year and Make) _____ Check regular driver			

C. Securities — stocks, bonds

	HUSBAND	WIFE

D. Cash and Deposit Accounts (banks, savings and loans, credit unions— savings and checking)

	HUSBAND	WIFE

COURT COPY

STATE OF MICHIANA : CIRCUIT COURT : SUPERIOR COURT : HOYNES COUNTY

_____ Petitioner

VS.

_____ Respondent

Case No. _____

FINANCIAL DECLARATION OF WIFE

Dated: _____

Husband _____
Address _____

Soc. Sec. No.: _____
Occupation _____
Employer _____
Birth Date _____

Name, Address and Telephone Number of Attorney(s)

Wife _____
Address _____

Soc. Sec. No. _____
Occupation _____
Employer _____
Birth Date _____

Space Below for Use of Court Clerk only

NOTE: THIS DECLARATION MUST BE FILED WITH THE COURT 7 DAYS BEFORE ALL CONTESTED HEARINGS RE: SUPPORT OR ASSETS.
FAILURE BY EITHER PARTY TO COMPLETE, PRESENT, AND FILE THIS FORM AS REQUIRED WILL AUTHORIZE THE COURT TO ACCEPT THE STATEMENT OF THE OTHER PARTY AS THE BASIS FOR ITS DECISION.
ANY FALSE STATEMENT MADE HEREON SHALL SUBJECT YOU TO PENALTY FOR PERJURY AND MAY BE CONSIDERED A FRAUD UPON THE COURT.

STATEMENT OF INCOME, EXPENSES, ASSETS AND LIABILITIES
Attach copies of State and Federal Income Tax Returns for last two taxable years and wage statements from your employer for last 8 weeks.

PART I INCOME AND EXPENSE STATEMENT

	HUSBAND	WIFE
	$	$

A. Gross weekly income from:
  Salary and wages, including commissions, bonuses, allowances and overtime, payable _____ (pay period) _____
  Note: If paid monthly, determine weekly income by dividing monthly income by 4.3
  Pensions and Retirement _____
  Social Security _____
  Disability and unemployment insurance _____
  Public Assistance (welfare, AFDC payments, etc.) _____
  Child support received from any prior marriage (not the marriage at issue) _____
  Dividends and interest _____
  Rents _____
  All other sources (Specify) _____

  *A. TOTAL WEEKLY INCOME _____ $ $

	HUSBAND	WIFE
	$	$

B. Itemize weekly deductions from gross income:
  State and federal income taxes _____
  Number of exemptions taken _____
  Social security _____
  Medical insurance (list all persons covered) _____

  Coverage: Medical ( ) Dental ( ) Eye Care ( ) Psychiatric ( ) _____
  Union or other dues _____
  Retirement or pension fund: Mandatory ( ) Optional ( ) _____
  Child care: Baby Sitter ( ) Pre-school ( ) Both ( ) _____
  Child support paid relating to a previous marriage _____
  *B. TOTAL WEEKLY DEDUCTIONS _____ $ $

C. Weekly disposable income (*A minus *B) _____ $ $

Page 1

COURT COPY

D. Total monthly expenses: *(Specify which party is the custodial parent and list name and relationship of all members of the household whose expenses are included.)*

	HUSBAND	WIFE
Rent or mortgage payments *(residence)*		
Real property taxes *(residence)*		
Real property insurance *(residence)*		
Maintenance *(residence)*		
Food and household supplies		
Utilities including water, electricity, gas and heat		
Telephone		
Laundry and cleaning		
Clothing		
Medical		
Dental		
Insurance *(life, health, accident, liability, disability; exclude payroll deducted and automobile)*		
School		
Entertainment *(includes clubs, social obligations, travel, recreation)*		
Incidentals *(grooming, tobacco, alcohol, gifts, and donations)*		
Transportation *(other than automobile)*		
Auto expense *(gas, oil, repair, insurance)*		
Auto payments		
Installment payment(s). Insert total and attach itemized schedule if not fully set forth below		
Other expenses *(Insert total and specify on attached schedule)*		
MONTHLY TOTAL EXPENSES		
AVERAGE WEEKLY EXPENSES *(Divide total monthly expenses by 4.3)*		

E. Debts and obligations:

CREDITOR'S NAME	FOR	DATE PAYABLE	BALANCE	MONTHLY PAYMENT
TOTAL			$	$

PART 2 NET WORTH All property of the parties known to me individually or jointly *(indicate who holds or how title held: (H) Husband, (W) Wife, or (J) Jointly)*. **WHERE SPACE IS INSUFFICIENT FOR COMPLETE INFORMATION OR LISTING PLEASE ATTACH SEPARATE SCHEDULE.**

	CHECK OWNERSHIP H / W / J	VALUE	OWED THERE ON
A. Household furnishings, furniture, appliances, and equipment		$	
B. Automobiles *(Year and Make)* _____ Check regular driver			

C. Securities — stocks, bonds	HUSBAND	WIFE
D. Cash and Deposit Accounts *(banks, savings and loans, credit unions— savings and checking)*		

COURT COPY

2. Enforcement and Modification of Child Support Order

Problem 81

In re Marriage of Rose

The marriage of Raymond Rose (Husband) and Brenda Rose (Wife) was dissolved by the Hoynes Circuit Court on September 26, YR-4. The court's decree awarded custody of the parties' five minor children to Brenda and provided for Raymond's visitation at reasonable times and places to be arranged by the parties. The court further ordered that the net proceeds of $40,000 from sale of the parties' real estate be divided equally between Raymond and Brenda.

The sale of the parties' real estate was closed on August 7, YR-4. Following the closing, Brenda forged Raymond's endorsement on the check made out to both Raymond and Brenda Rose in the sum of $40,000, and cashed it at the bank. The same day, Brenda packed up the five children and the forty grand and drove to West Virginia to live with a friend and start a new life.

Thereafter, Raymond made only sporadic weekly support payments of $200 to the clerk's office as provided in the dissolution decree. During the periods of his visitation with the children (Christmas YR-3, Summer YR-2, Christmas YR-2, Summer YR-1, and Christmas YR-1), however, Raymond bought the children several items of clothing and toys, and gave them cash for school supplies and entertainment. Raymond's records and receipts show a total of these expenses (not including Christmas and birthday gifts) to be $6,000.

On January 2, YR-0, Brenda filed a verified information for a rule to show cause in Hoynes Circuit Court, alleging that Raymond was delinquent in payment of child support in the sum of $23,000. The court issued an order for Raymond to appear in Hoynes Circuit Court on January 25, YR-0, to show cause why he should not be held in contempt for violating the court's support order of September 26, YR-4. Raymond then filed a petition to determine arrearage and request credit, alleging that on August 7, YR-4, Brenda fraudulently misappropriated Raymond's one-half of the proceeds from the same of the parties' real estate, in the sum of $20,000, to which Raymond is entitled pursuant to the Court's dissolution decree of September 26, YR-4. Raymond requests a credit of $26,000 ($20,000 plus $6,000 for the above-mentioned expenses) against his child support arrearage and future obligation. Both parties have requested an order for payment of attorney fees.

Questions

1. What is a petition for a rule to show cause? Why did Brenda file this document with the court?
2. Why should actions regarding enforcement of child support be heard in Michiana rather than in the children's home state of West Virginia? (*See* the Uniform Interstate Family Support Act in the Appendix.)
3. How do Brenda's actions regarding the house proceeds affect child support enforcement?
4. Should the clothing, toys, and cash for school supplies and entertainment, which Raymond provided the children, be credited as setoff against his child support arrearage? Since the child support payments were supposed to go to Brenda, wouldn't allowing the "gifts" as an off-

set be tantamount to modifying Raymond's support obligations? If the court refuses Raymond's request for a setoff, will this discourage Raymond from paying child support?

5. What is a non-conforming child support payment? As a matter of public policy, should support payors receive credit for these payments? Should the court have discretion to order an equitable setoff?

6. Would granting credit to Raymond on his support obligation for providing the children with cash for school supplies violate the general rule that bars retroactive modification of child support orders?

7. Suppose Brenda obtains a court order garnishing Raymond's wages for payment of past-due support. Then Raymond moves to Arizona in YR-2 and takes a new job. Can Brenda still obtain wage garnishment for past-due support? How? (*See* the Uniform Interstate Family Support Act (UIFSA) in the Appendix.)

STATE OF MICHIANA, HOYNES COUNTY
IN THE HOYNES CIRCUIT COURT

IN RE THE MARRIAGE OF)
) CAUSE NO. D-4301
RAYMOND J. ROSE   )
)
AND   )
)
BRENDA J. ROSE   ) DECREE OF DISSOLUTION

  This cause being regularly set for trial this day, the Petitioner-Husband appears in his own proper person and by his attorney of record and makes proof of the service of summons on the Respondent-Wife by certified mail, return receipt requested and received, receipt number 120892 bearing the signature of Wife being attached to the copy of the summons appearing in the file. Wife fails to appear or otherwise comply with the rules of procedure and is defaulted. Husband files affidavit of Wife's non-military status.

  Hearing is had on the petition for dissolution of marriage; the Court now finds the material allegations of the petition are true and that there is an irretrievable breakdown in the marriage of the parties; their marriage should be dissolved and terminated and they should be restored to the state of unmarried persons; the parties are the parents of five (5) minor children hereinafter named and Wife should be granted the care, charge and custody of the children.

  The Court further finds that during their marriage the parties acquired certain personal and real property and that they entered into an oral agreement by which they established and settled their respective rights in and to their property, which agreement has been fully implemented by the parties except that Wife has in violation of the agreement of the parties appropriated to herself the entire proceeds of the sale of certain real property sold by the parties pursuant to their agreement, which appropriation was accomplished by Wife's deceit, fraud and unlawful forging of Husband's endorsement signature of the check issued and payable jointly to the parties representing the amount due them as the net proceeds of the sale, in consequence of which Husband has been deprived of $20,000, being one-half of the net proceeds of the sale and of the check aforesaid to which he is entitled pursuant to the agreement of the parties.

  IT IS ORDERED:

  1. The marriage of Raymond J. Rose and Brenda J. Rose be and it hereby is dissolved and terminated and they are restored to the state of unmarried persons.

  2. Wife is granted the care, charge and custody of the five (5) minor children of the parties: Deborah, age 14, Kimberly, age 11, Tamara, age 9, Timothy, age 8, and Kevin, age 6.

  3. Husband shall pay to the Clerk of this Court the sum of $200 per week for the support of the parties' five minor children.

  4. Husband shall have the right to see and visit the minor children of the parties in the State of Michiana at all reasonable times and places, to be arranged by the parties.

  5. Title to all of the articles of personal property now in the possession of the wife in the State of West Virginia shall be and is hereby transferred and set over to Wife and that property shall be her sole and separate property free and clear of any right, title or interest of Husband therein or thereto; provided, however, that Wife shall have as her sole and separate property only one-half of the net proceeds of the sale of the real estate aforesaid even although Wife has sequestered and ap-

propriated to herself all of the proceeds in the manner hereinbefore described and nothing herein shall be construed to establish any ownership interest of Wife in more than one-half of the proceeds, being $20,000.

6. The title to all of the articles of the personal property now in the possession of Husband in the State of Michiana shall be and is hereby transferred and set over to Husband and that property shall be his sole and separate property free and clear of any right, title or interest of Wife therein or thereto.

7. The title to one-half of the net proceeds of the sale of the real property used by the parties as the family residence and located at what is commonly known and described as 725 Ditmer Street, Mowaki, Hoynes County, Michiana (and not otherwise described in the record) shall be and is hereby transferred and set over to Husband, being $20,000, and Husband shall have and recover of and from Wife the sum of $20,000.

8. The title to the real estate in Hoynes County, Michiana, and located at what is commonly known and described as 260 LaSalle Street, Southby, Hoynes County, Michiana (and not otherwise described in the record) shall be and it hereby is transferred to and vested in Husband free and clear of any right, title or interest of Wife therein or thereto and Husband shall pay therefor and hold Wife harmless from any liability in respect of this real estate.

9. The parties are jointly indebted to the Teachers Credit Union of Southby, Michiana, in the approximate amount of $2,000.00 and shall pay said indebtedness in accordance with the terms of the instrument by which it was created.

10. The parties are ordered to do all things necessary or required to carry into execution the orders of this Court.

ORDERED September 26, YR-4.

_____
Judge, Hoynes Circuit Court

Chapter Nine. Dissolution of Marriage

3. *Emancipation*

Problem 82

In re Marriage of Rose

At the hearing in Hoynes Circuit Court on Raymond Rose's petition for determination of arrearage and credit, on January 25, YR-0, Raymond informs you that he spoke over the telephone a few days ago with his oldest daughter, Deborah. Raymond reports that Deborah, now eighteen years of age, took most of her clothing and personal effects and left Brenda's home on September 26, YR-1, and moved into the home of friends, the Browns, in Wheeling, West Virginia. Deborah, who will graduate from high school in June, YR-0, also obtained a part-time job at Pizza Hut on September 28, YR-1.

Raymond doesn't think he should have to pay support for Deborah if she's "on her own." He wants to know if the court will consider this evidence about Deborah at the January 25 hearing.

Questions

1. Should the court consider this undisclosed evidence at the January 25 hearing? Why or why not?
2. What is the definition of emancipation? When is/was Deborah emancipated? What factors indicate emancipation?
3. Assume for this question that Deborah moved in with the Browns and took the Pizza Hut job because she has a serious drug addiction, which will prevent her graduation from high school. Brenda still pays for Deborah's clothes but for nothing else. Is Deborah emancipated?
4. What are the implications for emancipation on the duty of a parent to pay child support?
5. Emancipation rules vary from state to state. Should there be a uniform emancipation statute? What policies would be served by uniformity?

4. *Educational Expenses—Private School*

Problem 83

In re Marriage of Tidmarsh

In YR-4, Lee and Lena Tidmarsh were divorced in a decree issued by the Hoynes Circuit Court. The Court ordered that Lee and Lena have joint legal custody of their three children (with shared decision-making on issues such as the children's health care, education, and religious training), with Joan being the primary residential custodian. The parties executed a written agreement providing for Lee's payment of child support and his payment of the children's tuition to Hoynes Country Day Christian School through the eighth grade.

Lee made the tuition payments through YR-1, but now objects to further payment. Lee states that he is a firm believer in the quality and value of public schools, and, as an agnostic, he objects to the mixing of religion with education. Lee further argues that any order requiring him to pay tuition to the Christian School is an unconstitutional violation of his First Amendment right of the freedom to practice religion as he sees fit.

Questions

1. Is a court order requiring Lee to pay tuition to a Christian school unconstitutional under the First Amendment?
2. What factors should the Hoynes Circuit Court consider when deciding if Lee will have to continue making the payments? Does it matter that Lee originally made the payments voluntarily? Is it significant that the children have been attending the school for three years?
3. Is it important that pursuant to the court's order Lee and Lena have joint legal custody of the children?

5. *College Expenses*

Problem 84

Meyer v. Meyer

John Meyer and Linda Meyer have filed for divorce. John and Linda agree for the most part on how their marital assets will be divided, and they agree that Linda will have primary physical custody of their two children. What they do not agree on is the amount of child support John will pay. Taking advantage of a new Michiana statute, the Michiana College Expenses Act, Linda has asked the court to order John to finance the children's undergraduate studies at Michiana University. The statute provides that "A court can order a parent, whether divorced, separated or unmarried, to help pay for his or her child's college education expenses, unless the parent can show that it would cause the parent undue financial hardship."

Despite having substantial income and assets, John vehemently objects to being forced to support his children past the age of eighteen and intends to challenge the constitutionality of the Michiana College Expenses Act.

Questions

1. Does the Michiana College Expense Act violate the Equal Protection Clause because it requires unmarried parents to pay for a child's college education while a married parent has no such obligation?
2. What are the policy arguments for forcing divorced parents to support their child(ren) past the age of eighteen?

Chapter Nine. Dissolution of Marriage

6. *Child Support Recovery Act*

Problem 85

United States v. Balboa

Juan and Karen Balboa were divorced in Southby, Michiana, in YR-6. Karen was granted sole physical custody of the parties' three children, and Juan was ordered to pay the lump sum of $500.00 per month in child support. Immediately after the divorce, Juan moved to Illinois and never made a single child support payment. Karen and the children continued to live in Southby, Michiana.

In YR-1, Juan was indicted under the 1992 Child Support Recovery Act, 18 U.S.C. Section 228, for failure to pay child support. The Child Support Recovery Act provides for criminal prosecution of parents who willfully refuse to pay child support obligations that are either one year overdue or more than $5,000.00 when the parent and child are residents of different states. Congress enacted the law pursuant to power granted by the Commerce Clause of the U.S. Constitution. The Commerce Clause gives Congress the power "[t]o regulate Commerce with foreign Nations and among the several States, and with the Indian Tribes." Juan argues that the Child Support Recovery Act violates the Commerce Clause because it attempts to regulate an activity that does not substantially affect interstate commerce.

Questions

1. Does a parent's failure to pay support to a child in another state substantially affect interstate commerce?
2. What if the child is forced to receive public assistance due to the lack of child support?

Q. DIVISION OF PROPERTY

1. *Defining Equitable Distribution*

Problem 86

Gibbons v. Gibbons

Elizabeth (Lizzie) and Lansford (Lans) Gibbons were married in YR-15. In YR-3, after several years of marital difficulty, Lizzie moved out of the home. In YR-2, Lans won $2.9 million dollars in the Michiana State Lottery, entitling him to annual payments of $70,000 a year for twenty years. In YR-1, Lizzie decided there was no hope of salvaging the marriage, after two years of living separate and apart, so she filed for divorce. The main point of contention in the divorce negotiations was whether the lottery winnings are marital property to which Lizzie is equitably entitled to a share. The Michiana trial court found that the lottery winnings were marital property, but because Lizzie had not contributed to attaining the income in any way, the court awarded the total winnings to Lans.

Lizzie contends that the court's decision is a miscarriage of justice and has decided to appeal on the ground that the trial court abused its discretion in finding that Lans was entitled to all of the lottery winnings.

Questions

1. Is the property in this problem marital property or separate property under the equitable distribution system? What about under the Uniform Marriage and Divorce Act (UMDA)? (*See* Appendix.)
2. When does the marriage end for the purpose of determining what is marital property?
3. What are the guidelines or standards for equitable distribution? How much discretion does the trial court have in distributing the marital estate?
4. What is the proper scope of appellate review of the trial court's decision on distribution of property?
5. How would this case be different if Lizzie and Lans were divorced in a community property state?

2. *What Constitutes Marital Property?*

Problem 87

In re Marriage of Mumfort

Willis and Trudi Mumfort were married in Dolton, Michiana, on August 3, YR-5. After a ten-day honeymoon in Montreal, Willis and Trudi moved into an apartment in nearby Southby, Michiana, where Willis began his first semester of study at Michiana University School of Law in late August, YR-5. Trudi got a job as a waitress at Gib and Dencil's Restaurant. With the funds from Willis's scholarship, his income from clerking in a Southby law firm during the summers, and Trudi's salary from the restaurant, they were able to "make ends meet" until Willis graduated Order of the Coif in June of YR-2. Willis and Trudi moved back to Dolton in June of YR-2, and Willis took the Michiana bar examination in late July. On September 1, YR-2, Willis began work as an associate with DeSisto and Hogan, a firm of 150 lawyers, specializing in defense of medical malpractice and personal injury claims and other insurance litigation. It didn't take long for Willis to impress the partners at DeSisto and Hogan, and in May of YR-1 he was given an increase from his starting salary of $75,000 to $95,500, and told by the senior partner, Mr. DeSisto, "Willis, my boy, the sky is the limit for you here at DeSisto and Hogan. You keep up the good work, young man, and someday you'll be sitting in my chair."

Chapter Nine. Dissolution of Marriage

In June of YR-1, Trudi announced to Willis that she was pregnant. Willis, thinking that Trudi was taking birth control pills regularly, was shocked and angry. He told Trudi that the time was not right for a child and urged Trudi to have an abortion. When Trudi refused, Willis accused her of trying to ruin his career. Willis and Trudi agreed that they had "grown apart" and were no longer happy with their marriage. In early July of YR-1, Trudi moved into her parents' home in suburban Dolton.

In January of YR-0, Trudi retained an attorney, who filed her petition for dissolution of marriage. Following a hearing on Trudi's petition for provisional relief, the only disputed matter between the parties is Trudi's contention that Willis's law degree, which was obtained during the marriage, is marital property and is therefore part of the "marital pot." Trudi claims she is entitled to an equitable portion of the value of the law degree upon final division of the parties' property by the court. The applicable Michiana Code provision states that "marital property is property, however titled, acquired by one or both spouses during marriage."

The only contested issue is whether Willis's law degree should be considered marital property for the purpose of equitable distribution, and what effect the court's ruling on this issue should have on other incidents of divorce, such as alimony or maintenance.

Questions

1. Is the law degree marital property?
2. If the law degree is marital property, how is it "titled"? Which spouse earned the degree, or did both? How tangible is a professional degree?
3. Is it necessary that there be a concerted family effort by both spouses for the law degree to be considered a divisible marital asset with an ascertainable value?
4. Assume the court finds that the law degree is marital property subject to equitable distribution. How is the value of the degree to be determined? Should the court consider Willis's salary to be proceeds of the degree? If so, then how is alimony to be calculated? If not, what value does the degree have other than merely nominal worth?
5. Divided marital property is nontaxable but is dischargeable in bankruptcy. Alimony is nondischargeable in bankruptcy but is taxable income to the recipient. What characterization of the law degree would be best for Trudi?
6. What if both spouses are lawyers and attended different law schools? Is a degree from School A worth more than a School B degree?
7. Would it matter if Willis, pursuant to his law school's loan forgiveness program, is employed as a legal services lawyer at the time of the divorce, but he intends to practice corporate law in a few years?
8. Would it matter if Willis ranked last in his class at Michiana University School of Law rather than graduated Order of the Coif?
9. Assume that Michiana has enacted a statute identical to Section 307 (Alternative A) of the Uniform Marriage and Divorce Act. How should the court rule in this case? If the court found the law degree to be marital property and awarded Trudi an equitable portion of its value, would Section 307 permit this order to be modified in the future?

3. Person or Property?

Problem 88

Scribner v. Scribner

Elaine and Jean-Paul Scribner were married in YR-7. For several years, Elaine and Jean-Paul were unsuccessful in their attempts to have a child. In YR-2, Elaine and Jean-Paul enrolled in a fertility program at Hoynes Charity Hospital, in hopes that one of Elaine's eggs fertilized with Jean-Paul's sperm could be successfully implanted in the uterus of Elaine's sister. In YR-1, Elaine filed a petition for divorce. The only issue that remains to be resolved is who will get possession of the six zygotes that still remain frozen at the hospital ready for attempts at implantation. Elaine seeks to recover the zygotes for the purpose of implanting them in herself. Jean-Paul, who no longer wants to have children with Elaine, believes that the zygotes should be turned over to the hospital for research.

Questions

1. Are these zygotes persons or property? Is this dispute better characterized as a custody dispute or a property settlement issue?
2. In cases of in vivo (in the body) fertilization, the father has virtually no legal right to impact the fate of the unborn child once the egg has been fertilized. Should there be a different standard when the eggs are fertilized in vitro and have not yet been implanted into the mother?

4. Lien Avoidance

Problem 89

In re Hanes

Mary and Robert Hanes owned a home as tenants by the entirety when Robert filed for divorce in YR-2. The Hoynes divorce court, pursuant to agreement of the parties, awarded Robert the home and gave Mary a $75,000 "property settlement" money judgment equal to her interest in the home to be paid over the next ten years. The money judgment was secured by a judicial lien on the property in order to insure payment.

In YR-0, after failing to make any payments on the settlement, Robert filed for Chapter 7 bankruptcy and claimed the house as an exemption, meaning that is was not subject to liquidation in order to pay his creditors, under the Hoynes Homestead Law. Robert then filed a motion under 11 U.S.C. Section 522(f) to avoid the judicial lien on the house, which was essentially a motion to grant him the house free and clear of Mary's interest.

The relevant portion of 11 U.S.C. Section 522(f)(1) reads as follows:

(f)(1) Notwithstanding any waiver of exemptions . . . , the debtor may avoid the fixing of a lien on an interest of the debtor in property to the extent that such a lien impairs an exemption to which the debtor would have been entitled . . . , if such lien is—

(A) a judicial lien, other than a judicial lien that secures a debt—

(i) to a spouse, former spouse, or child of the debtor, for alimony, maintenance for, or support of such spouse or child, in connection with a separation agreement, divorce decree or other order of a court of record . . . , or property settlement agreement; and

(ii) to the extent such debt—

(I) is not assigned to any other entity, voluntarily, by operation of law or otherwise; and

(II) includes a liability designated as alimony, maintenance, or support. . . .

Questions

1. When did the judicial lien "fix" onto Robert's interest in the house? Did Robert have an existing interest at the time the lien "fixed"?
2. What could Mary's lawyer have done in order to prevent Robert from attempting to avoid this lien? Would it make any difference if the divorce decree had labeled the money due Mary as alimony or child support instead of a property settlement?

5. Valuation of Assets

Problem 90

Fester v. Fester

Andrea and Bill Fester met in college in YR-23. They fell in love and were married after only six months. Andrea dropped out of college to support Bill and has never returned to school. Their children, Billy, Johnny, Teddy, and Fred, were born in YR-21, YR-20, YR-19, and YR-18, respectively.

When Bill's roof repair business failed in YR-14, he decided to enter law school. Andrea, a homemaker since YR-19, returned to her old secretarial position to put Bill through Michiana School of Law. In YR-11, Bill took a position with the Carnation Law Firm in New City. Bill made partner on October 3, YR-3.

Bill and Andrea began to have marital troubles after Teddy was hit and killed by a drunk driver in YR-4. Communication between spouses dwindled as Bill concentrated more heavily on his law practice. Citing irreconcilable differences, Andrea filed a divorce petition on June 6, YR-2.

The parties have been separated for the statutory period under Michiana's no-fault divorce statute. The only issue in this case is a division of the parties' assets.

Bill owns a 2.25 percent interest in the Carnation Law Firm. The firm owns its building, the old Stock Exchange, as well as a firm condominium in Puerto Rico. The firm's physical assets, less its outstanding business loans, are valued at $1.4 million.

In addition to the firm's physical assets, there are receivables and work in progress. Receivables, of which the firm typically collects 70 percent, are valued at $200,000. Work in progress is of two types. First, the firm has its regular litigation and transactional practice, at which the firm typically bills $120,000 per month. Bill earns none of the income, although he shares in the profits as a partner.

The other work in progress comes from the firm's substantial personal injury practice, in which Bill specializes. Bill's practice for all of YR-0 has been consumed by a class-action asbestos lawsuit against a major manufacturer. The case may settle, but trial is not likely for at least four years. Andrea has hired an expert accountant, who values the lawsuit at $14.4 million, of which the firm would collect 40 percent after trial, 30 percent if the case settles. The Carnation Law Firm recently filed a financial statement for a commercial loan in which they valued the asbestos suit at $2 million. Bill's only measurable interest in the suit is his proportionate share in the partnership's income, although a successful trial could launch Bill's reputation and substantially increase the value of the firm's goodwill. The firm has dropped all other personal injury cases to concentrate its resources on the asbestos suit.

This problem deals solely with the valuation of Bill's assets related to property settlement. Assume Michiana is a separate property state and that the Carnation Law Firm was organized under the Revised Uniform Partnership Act.

Questions

1. What is Bill's share of the physical assets? Is this share subject to property division?
2. What is Bill's share of the firm's accounts receivable? Is this number sufficiently fixed for valuation as a personal asset? How much of this amount should be subject to property divison?
3. What is Bill's share of the regular work in progress (not including the personal injury cases)? Should this share be included in property division?
4. What is Bill's share of the asbestos suit? Which number should be used to value the suit, if either? Since the suit may settle for an unknown amount, can the asset be valued at all? What amount should be subject to property division?
5. Should the property division include a calculation for the general goodwill of Bill's practice? How can this number be calculated?
6. Under what theories can Andrea claim an interest in Bill's business assets?
7. Can the court validly enter a "wait and see" property division order under the Uniform Marriage and Divorce Act (UMDA) or the Uniform Marital Property Act (UMPA)?
8. How would the property division be affected if Michiana was a community property state?
9. How would Bill's calculable share in firm assets be affected if all his work was spent on pro bono activities involving drunk driving awareness?

6. *Qualified Domestic Relations Orders*

Problem 91

Harris v. Harris

Clarence (C.J.) and Regina Harris were divorced in YR-1 after eleven years of marriage. Included as part of the divorce decree was the Qualified Domestic

Chapter Nine. Dissolution of Marriage

Relations Order (QDRO) that follows this problem. The QDRO provides that Regina is entitled to 50 percent of all interest C.J. was entitled to under his profit-sharing plans as of the date of divorce.

C.J. has now decided to appeal the QDRO, claiming that it is in fact not a Qualified Domestic Relations Order under I.R.C. Section 414(p) for four reasons:

1. It attempts to enjoin C.J. from receiving benefits to which he is entitled under his profit-sharing plans.
2. It fails to specify the amount of the participant's benefits to be paid to the alternate payee.
3. It fails to specify the number of payments to which the order applies.
4. In that the order requires the plan provider to make payments directly to Regina, it requires the plan to provide the alternative payee a form of benefits not provided for in the original plan.

Questions

1. Please read I.R.C. Section 414(p). Does this plan qualify as a QDRO? Can the court force C.J. to alienate or assign benefits to which he is entitled? Read I.R.C. Section 401 (a)(13)(A) and (B).
2. Does the order have to specify the amount of payments and the number of payments?
3. May the order require the plan provider to make payments directly to Regina?

IN RE THE MARRIAGE OF   )   HOYNES CIRCUIT COURT
REGINA R. HARRIS   )
    Petitioner,   )   CAUSE NO. 71CO1-8910
)
and   )
)
CLARENCE J. HARRIS   )
    Respondent   )

QUALIFIED DOMESTIC RELATIONS ORDER

Petitioner and Respondent, by their respective counsel, having filed their Property Settlement Agreement, and the Court having entered its Findings of Fact and Decree of Dissolution which read in the following words and figures, to wit: (H.I.)

And the Court, being duly advised in the premises, and having entered said Decree and approved said Property Settlement Agreement, now issues this Qualified Domestic Relations Order (QDRO) and reserves continuing jurisdiction over the implementation of this Order.

    1. <u>Identification of "Participant"</u>. The Participant is Clarence J. Harris, Social Security No. 321-45-7896, Employee No. 306526888, whose last know address is 1124 Oak Road, Southby, Michiana 42314, and who is a Participant under The First Interstate Bank Profit Sharing Plan and The First Interstate Bank Profit Sharing Trust/401K.

    2. <u>Identification of "Alternate Payee"</u>. The Alternate Payee is Regina R. Harris, Social Security No. 141-56-1928, whose last known address is 462 Fishback Road, Southby Michiana 42314.

The Alternate Payee is the former spouse of the Participant, having been married on August 11, YR-12, with the Alternate Payee's marriage having been dissolved on February 12, YR-1.

    3. <u>Identification of "Plans"</u>. The Alternate Payee will receive payments from the following retirement plans, hereafter collectively referred to as "Plans", as provided in this QDRO:

<u>Plans</u>:

    a. First Interstate Bank Profit Sharing Plan;
    b. First Interstate Bank Profit Sharing Trust—401K.

<u>Administrator of Plans</u>: First Interstate Bank of Northern Michiana, N.A.

    4.   <u>State Order</u>. This Order is issued pursuant to the laws of the State of Michiana relating to the provisions of child support, alimony payments or marital property rights between spouses and former spouses and actions for dissolution of marriage pursuant to M.C. 31-1-11.5-1, et seq.

    5.   <u>Assignment of Benefits</u>. The Participant assigns to the Alternate Payee a portion of benefits from the Participant's benefits from the Plans; and the Plans and any successor or transferee plan will pay benefits to the Alternate Payee as follows:

    a. <u>Account Balance</u>. For purposes of this order, the account balances of the Participant's interest in said account shall be determined as of December 31, YR-1.
    b. <u>Interest in the Plans</u>. The Participant and the Alternate Payee shall each be awarded an interest in the Plans. The Alternate Payee's interest shall consist of 50% of Participant's interest in and to the Plans.
    c. <u>Segregation of Account</u>. The Alternate Payee's interest in the Participant's account shall be segregated for accounting purposes. The amount so seg-

regated shall be credited with interest and accumulations earned thereon in accordance with the Plans until such time as the Alternate Payee matures her interest.

d. <u>Survivor Benefits</u>. The Alternate Payee shall waive her interest in any survivor benefits under the Plans, and shall execute whatever documents are necessary in order to effectuate such waiver; provided, however, that such waiver shall not apply to that portion of said Plans which are being assigned and set over to the Alternate Payee pursuant to this Order.

e. <u>Payment of Benefits</u>. The Plans will pay directly to the Alternate Payee her share of the benefits in the full amount to which she is entitled.

f. <u>Timing of Benefits</u>. The Alternate Payee shall have the right to elect to receive benefit payments under the Plans at the earlier of (1) any time beginning when the Participant attains (or would have attained) earliest retirement age under the Plans, as defined by IRC §414(p)(4), or (2) at any time otherwise permitted by law or by said Plans.

g. <u>Rights of Alternate Payee</u>. The Alternate Payee shall have all options available to her under the Plans, and the same options, opportunities, and elections available to the Participant under the Plans.

6. <u>Intended Tax Treatment</u>. The Alternate Payee shall include benefits received pursuant to the Participant's assignment of benefits herein in gross income for the tax year such payment is received.

For purposes of IRC §402, the Alternate Payee shall be treated as the distributee of any distribution or payment made to the Alternate Payee pursuant to this Order.

The benefits paid to the Alternate Payee hereunder shall not be taxable income or a deduction on the Participant's income tax returns. To the extent of any rollover of a lump sum distribution to the Alternate Payee, the portion of any such distribution so rolled over shall be treated as a nontaxable transfer pursuant to IRC §402(a)(6)(F) and IRC §408(d), provided that:

a. (1) The balance to be received by the Alternate Payee pursuant to this order is distributed or paid to the Alternate Payee during one taxable year of the Alternate Payee; and (2) the Alternate Payee transfers any portion of the property received from such distribution to an individual retirement account (as described in IRC § 408(b)) within 60 days of receipt of the distribution; and

b. In the case of distribution of property other than money, the amount so transferred consists of the property transferred.

7. <u>Covenants Regarding Non-Alienation of Benefits</u>. Nothing contained herein shall be construed to require the Plans or Plan Administrator:

a. To provide any type or form of benefit, or any option not otherwise provided under the Plans.
b. To provide increased benefits determined on the basis of actuarial value.
c. To provide benefits to the Alternate Payee which are required to be paid to another Alternate Payee under another order previously determined to be a qualified domestic relations order.

8. <u>Intent</u>. The Participant, the Alternate Payee, and the Court intend this Order to be a Qualified Domestic Relations Order.

9. <u>Jurisdiction of the Court</u>. If this Order is determined by the Administrator of the Plans <u>not</u> to be a Qualified Domestic Relations Order, the parties hereby agree to submit to and to request of the Court, which continues to have jurisdiction over

this issue, to modify this Order, to make it a Qualified Domestic Relations Order in such manner that will reflect the parties' intent and, thereafter, enter an Order modifying the Domestic Relations Order entered at the time the parties' marriage is dissolved, said modification order to be entered nunc pro tunc, if appropriate.

10. <u>Effective Date</u>. This order shall take effect not later than thirty (30) days after the Plan Administrator has received a copy of this order and shall remain in effect until further order of this Court.

Approved and so ordered this 12th day of February, YR-0.

_____
Regina R. Harris

_____
Clarence J. Harris

_____
Judge, Hoynes Circuit Court

Chapter Nine. Dissolution of Marriage

7. *Future Interests—Pensions*

Problem 92

In re Marriage of McDougal

Bruce McDougal, a public high school teacher, and Celeste McDougal, a homemaker, were married in YR-20. On March 1, YR-10, Bruce began his teaching career at Central High School in Southby, Michiana. Bruce has a pension that vests after ten years of teaching and pays 40 percent of his salary at the time of retirement. Bruce contributes 5 percent of his gross pay per year to the pension. If Bruce quits his teaching position or transfers before the ten years, he is entitled to receive his contribution, without interest, ten years later. Bruce filed his petition for dissolution of marriage on February 26, YR-0. A Michiana statute, MC 13-1-11.5-2(d)(3), which was enacted on February 3, YR-0, and became effective on April 3, YR-0, defines property to include the following:

(1) a present right to withdraw pension or retirement benefits;
(2) the right to receive pension or retirement benefits that are not forfeited upon termination of employment, or that are vested, as that term is defined in Section 411 of the Internal Revenue Code, but that are payable after the dissolution of marriage; and
(3) the right to receive disposable retired or retainer pay, as defined in 10 U.S.C. Section 1408(a), acquired in the marriage, that is or may be payable after dissolution of marriage.

Prior to enactment of the statute, Michiana courts could not allocate future pension plan benefits to a spouse in a dissolution proceeding.

The final hearing is set for September 3, YR-0, in Hoynes Circuit Court. The only contested matter at this hearing concerns Celeste's claim that she is entitled to one-half of Bruce's pension benefits.

Questions

1. What is the effective date of the statute? When are Bruce and Celeste no longer married? On what date are the parties' rights to be calculated for property distribution?
2. Does the fact that the divorce petition was filed before the statute giving Celeste a right in Bruce's pension went into effect necessarily mean that Celeste can claim no pension rights? Can the court apply the statute retroactively? Should it?
3. All pension payments came from Bruce's salary; Celeste contributed no cash to the pension plan. Should Celeste be granted a right in the pension per se? Would your answer be different if Celeste had been working and contributing to a pension of her own? Why or why not?
4. Traditionally, pensions that are currently paying their owners (i.e., mature pensions) are considered marital property. What makes this pension different is that it has not yet matured. As such, the precise amount of income the pension may pay in the future is difficult to calculate. Is the pension too speculative an asset to be considered properly as a marital asset?

5. Assume the pension is a marital asset to be divided up on September 3. How is it to be calculated? What methods of calculation can and/or should be applied to the pension?
6. Assume Bruce is in the military and that his pension comes from the federal government. What result in this case? See Uniformed Service Former Spouses' Protection Act.
7. Suppose Michiana enacted a statute regarding state employees' pensions in YR-57. That statute provides, inter alia: (a) pension rights vest at the later of the employee's 50th birthday and the employee's 20th anniversary as a state employee; (b) the employee's pension is not subject to attachment, garnishment, or any creditor's rights; (c) upon the employee's death, the employee's spouse has the right to one half of the employee's living benefits through a survivor's annuity; (d) if the employee's spouse divorces or dies before the employee dies, the survivor's annuity is extinguished. Furthermore, the Michiana Constitution of YR-17, Article XIII, Section 4, states, "All pension rights for Michiana residents shall be considered contractual in nature, and all pensions cited in Michiana shall be subject to the Michiana law of contracts." Finally, suppose Bruce has met the vesting requirements, that he is dying of a terminal illness, and that the sole purpose of his divorce petition is "to punish her for the rotten way she's treated me all these years." If the divorce goes through before Bruce dies, will Celeste lose her survivor's annuity? Under the Michiana statute, the Michiana Constitution, the U.S. Constitution, and the Uniform Marital Property Act, what legal arguments can Celeste make that the divorce will not divest her survivor's annuity? Against whom should she bring this claim? If she succeeds in maintaining her rights to the survivor's annuity, is that annuity marital property? If so, how can one get property rights in an annuity whose value depends entirely on one's death?

8. *Community Property*

Problem 93

Rollins v. Rollins

Reginald and Jacinda Rollins, having married in YR-4, decided to divorce in YR-1. The only issue that remains to be resolved is which party is entitled to stock options given to Reginald by his company, which options did not vest until after Reginald and Jacinda separated. Because Reginald and Jacinda were married in a community property state and still live in a community property state, it must be determined if the stock options are community property or Reginald's separate property.

Questions

1. What is community property? What is separate property? How much of the community property and separate property is each spouse entitled to upon divorce?

Chapter Nine. Dissolution of Marriage

2. What does it mean to say that a property right is not vested?
3. At what point does the marriage end for the purposes of determining what is community property and what is separate property?

9. Social Security Income

Problem 94

In re Marriage of Robinson

Robert and Julia Robinson have decided to divorce after thirty years of marriage, and Julia has asked you to represent her in the divorce. You have looked over the financial information provided to you by Julia and discovered that the major source of the Robinsons' income is Robert's monthly Social Security Disability check. The only major asset in the martial estate is a house owned free and clear of mortgage.

Julia is very concerned because she has heard that she can't get any of Robert's Social Security check because there is a law that prohibits the division of Social Security income upon divorce. The law that Julia is talking about is the Social Security Act found at 42 U.S.C. Section 407(a), which states as follows:

> The right of any person to any future payment under this subchapter shall not be transferable or assignable, at law or in equity, and none of the moneys paid or payable or rights existing under this subchapter shall be subject to execution, levy, attachment, garnishment, or other legal process, or to the operation of any bankruptcy or insolvency.

Questions

1. Assume that Julia and Robert live in an equitable distribution jurisdiction and that there are no additional circumstances that would warrant anything but a fifty-fifty division of their martial estate. Despite the fact that Robert will continue to be the sole beneficiary of the couple's only source of income, will the court still split the house fifty-fifty?
2. The court is prevented from dividing the Social Security income, but is the court also prevented from considering the income when making an equitable distribution of property?

10. Worker's Compensation

Problem 95

In re Marriage of Branch

In YR-9, Brent and Georgia Branch met and were married. In YR-8, Brent was injured at work when he fell from a ladder that had been negligently maintained by his employer. As a result, Brent was awarded $10,000.00 per year until the age of sixty-five to compensate him for loss of income and earning capacity. During their marriage, Brent and Georgia used the $10,000.00 to pay the mortgage on their home.

Georgia and Brent have now filed a joint petition for divorce. The only disputes in the settlement negotiation are whether or not the $80,000 of worker's compensation award money contributed to the house is marital property and whether the payments that Brent will receive from the time of the divorce until the time he turns sixty-five are marital property.

Questions

1. What is the worker's compensation award intended to compensate?
2. Did Loretta in any way contribute to the "earning" of the money? Was she harmed by the accident?
3. Is the worker's compensation received during the marriage separate property or marital property?
4. Is the worker's compensation received after the divorce marital property?

11. Application of RICO

Problem 96

Marriage of Sarducci

Joseph and Elisha Sarducci were married on a rainy day in June, YR-21. Rain was not good luck for their marriage, however. Within six months of their wedding, Joseph had his first love affair outside his marriage. That affair and the three that followed lasted less than three months each.

Joseph's fifth love affair, however, began on New Year's Eve, YR-10, and continues today. Joseph's paramour is Sharon Sharalike, a New City beautician. Joseph has fathered two children by Sharon but only one by Elisha.

Elisha discovered Joseph's affair with Sharon on June 3, YR-1, when she decided to try a new hairdresser. Elisha happened upon Sharon's salon, which, Sharon later confessed, Joseph had established for her. As Sharon prepared Elisha's hair, she struck up a conversation. Almost immediately, Elisha realized that Sharon knew entirely too much about her husband. Before the end of their conversation, Sharon had admitted that she and Joseph were lovers. Appalled, Elisha left the salon and headed straight for her lawyer.

Elisha filed for divorce on the grounds of mental cruelty and infidelity on June 30, YR-1. The divorce court has entered an interim order of separation and has docketed the divorce trial for November 10, YR+1. An interlocutory order of the divorce court has frozen all marital assets other than two individual bank accounts in each party's name.

On February 28, YR-0, Elisha filed a claim under the Federal Racketeering and Involvement in Corrupt Organizations Act (RICO), 18 U.S.C. Sections 161 et seq., in the U.S. District Court for the Southern District of Michiana. Sharon is the named defendant in Elisha's RICO action. Elisha's complaint alleges that Sharon aided Joseph while he systematically converted marital assets for Sharon's use.

On March 10, YR-0, Sharon filed a limited appearance and filed a motion to dismiss the RICO case for lack of jurisdiction under the decision in *Younger v. Harris*, 410 U.S. 37 (1971).

Questions

1. Why would RICO be used in a divorce proceeding? What kinds of divorce claims may be brought under RICO?
2. May a RICO claim be brought during the pendency of a divorce action?
3. What is the *Younger* abstention doctrine? How might it apply in this case? What is the *Burford* abstention doctrine? Does it foreclose the use of *Younger* abstention in this case?
4. Should the federal court dismiss Elisha's action? What is the federal court's proper response to Sharon's motion?
5. Should Elisha have named Joseph in her RICO claim? Why or why not?
6. How would this case be different if Elisha brought her case under the Michiana Racketeering Act, a state law identical to the RICO statute?

12. Negotiation of Settlement Agreement

Problem 97

In re Marriage of Miller

Helen Miller, age forty-two, and Joe Miller, age forty-four, were married in YR-22. Joe is an associate professor in the College of Business at Southby State University. Helen is a graduate student in cultural anthropology, working on a Ph.D degree, and an associate instructor in the department of anthropology at Southby State University. They have three children—Andrew, age seventeen, Susan, age twenty, and Matthew, age twenty-two. Helen admits to having an affair with Roscoe, an anthropology faculty member who is directing her doctoral thesis. Helen and Roscoe, who is also married, have attended faculty parties together and are often seen at restaurants and shopping centers in Southby. Joe retains you to initiate proceedings to dissolve his marriage and states that he has accepted a chaired professorship at the University of Maine and must relocate in early August of YR-0. Helen and Joe would like to work out an amicable separation agreement, if possible. They own the following real and personal property:

1. Family home located at 5280 Oakton Drive, Southby, Michiana, owned by Helen and Joe as tenants by the entirety, appraised in March of YR-0 for $200,000. The mortgage balance is $78,000, monthly payment of $1,000. The down payment of $65,000 for 5280 Oakton Drive was made with proceeds from the sale of 16871 Morning Glory. The parties' antenuptial agreement, dated October 25, YR-23, provided as follows:

It is understood that the real estate at 16871 Morning Glory in Southby, Michiana, was purchased in YR-23 by Joe from funds inherited from his mother's estate in YR-24 and is titled in the name of Joseph T. Miller. In the event of a dissolution of the parties' marriage, Helen agrees that 16871 Morning Glory, Southby, Michiana, is to be the sole and separate property of Joe, not subject to equitable distribution.

2. Joe's Teachers Insurance and Annuity Association College Retirement Equities Fund (TIAA-CREF) account valued at $79,949, as of March 1, YR-0, payable to Joe in monthly installments upon retirement and unavailable to him before retirement.

3. Cottage at Loon Lake, two miles west of Columbia, Michiana, inherited by Helen from her mother's estate in YR-2, appraised in YR-0 at $60,000, used as family summer home. Helen and Joe have paid for gas and electric bills and minor improvements to the cottage from their joint checking-savings account.

4. Joint checking-savings account at National Bank of Southby, balance $4,000.

5. YR-2 Volvo automobile, titled in joint name, monthly payment of $250 to National Bank of Southby, loan balance $7,500.

6. YR-3 Chevrolet station wagon, titled in joint name.

7. 425 shares of Sears Roebuck common stock, inherited by Joe from his mother's estate in YR-3, held in Joe's name, selling at $44 per share, paying dividends of $1.27 per share per year.

8. Prudential-Bache Moneymart account owned by Helen and Joe in joint name, balance $21,000.00. This account was opened by Joe in YR-1 with inheritance proceeds of $20,000 from Joe's aunt's estate.

9. Joe's life insurance policy in amount of $50,000, with Helen and three children as named beneficiaries, present cash value of $2,700.

10. Household furnishings:
    a. antique furniture, a wedding gift from Joe's family—appraised at $5,000
    b. 24-inch Sony color television, purchased in YR-2 for $600
    c. Goebel Hummel plate collection—appraised in YR-1 at $6,500
    d. walnut table, eight chairs—appraised at $5,500
    e. Mitsubishi VCR, purchased in YR-1 for $500.
    f. Zenith-IBM compatible personal computer, purchased in YR-0 for $5,000
    g. Flemish tapestry appraised in YR-0 at $12,500
    h. four French Impressionist oil paintings appraised in YR-1 as follows.
        1) Toulouse-Lautrec—$35,000
        2) Toulouse-Lautrec—$25,000
        3) Monet—$27,500
        4) Renoir—$45,000
    i. 25 pieces of Waterford crystal—appraised as collection at $7,000

11. Accounts—joint name
    a. Ayres—$2,500 (clothing, jewelry for Helen)
    b. Visa—$3,250 (Christmas gifts for Helen's parents and other clothing, jewelry for Helen)

Chapter Nine. Dissolution of Marriage

      c. J.C. Penney—$1,500 (birthday, Christmas gifts for children)
      d. Sears—$2,000 (household appliances)
      e. Nieman Marcus—$2,500 (clothing, jewelry for Helen)

12. five lacquer boxes imported from U.S.S.R., appraised in YR-9 at $1,000 each.

Joe's nine-month contract at the University of Maine for next year is $85,000. Joe also receives approximately $200 each quarter for book royalties. Joe will agree that Helen have custody of Matthew and Susan if Helen agrees that Joe receive custody of Andrew. Helen's projected income for teaching next year is $5000 per semester, plus a full tuition remission. She wants custody of the three children but agrees that Andrew probably feels closer to his father. Helen and the three children of the parties are presently covered on Joe's medical and hospitalization policy through his employer. The court has recently adopted child support guidelines, which follow this Problem.

For this Problem, assume that the applicable Michiana law is identical to the Uniform Marriage and Divorce Act and the Uniform Marital Property Act. (*See* Appendix.)

Questions

1. When negotiating with Helen's attorney, what points do you anticipate will be the most contentious between Helen and Joe?
2. On what points should Joe be flexible in order to negotiate an amicable settlement?
3. If Joe and Helen wish to negotiate their divorce amicably, should either of them be seeing an attorney?
4. What is a lawyer's duty in settlement negotiations? As Joe's attorney, do you have any duty toward Helen or the children?
5. What role should Helen's affair with Roscoe play in the negotiations?
6. Should property settlement be negotiated prior to the filing of a divorce petition or subsequently?
7. Should Joe negotiate all elements of the divorce with Helen or only some (for example, agree on child custody and support but not on spousal maintenance)?
8. What positive role could a professional mediator play in this case? What are the potential drawbacks of using mediation in this case?

Chapter Ten

Mediation in Dissolution Cases

Problem 98

In re Marriage of Gardner

Please review the facts of Problem 61. The student should be prepared to meet with his or her client (Glenn Gardner or Loretta Gardner) to discuss the mediation process. Students assigned to play the roles of Glenn and Loretta will be provided confidential instructions by the professor.

Questions

1. Should the court recommend that the parties mediate their disputes over custody?
2. Would you as counsel for Glenn or Loretta encourage either client to agree to mediation?
3. What should the client expect from the mediation process in terms of the following:
   a. how long the mediation process takes
   b. financial cost
   c. how the mediation process works
   d. the lawyer's role in mediation
   e. anticipated result

Chapter Eleven

Family Law Practice and Professional Responsibility

A. FAMILY LAW PRACTICE

1. Role of Guardian ad litem

Problem 99

In re Woods

Bill and Margaret Woods were married in YR-10 and had three children during the course of their marriage. In YR-2, they decided to divorce. The major area of contention was who would get custody of the children. At the first of many hearings prior to the trial, the judge appointed a guardian ad litem (GAL) to represent the best interests of the children and ordered that the children live with Bill until the case went to trial as it seemed that Bill was better able to provide for the children.

While Bill was preparing for trial, the children would often accompany him on his trips to his attorney's office. During the course of these visits, Bill's attorney often spoke to the children about the nature of their relationship with their mother. When Margaret and her attorney got wind of the fact that these meetings were taking place, they immediately filed a motion for sanctions to be imposed on Bill's attorney for interviewing a "party" without the presence or consent of their attorney or, in this case, GAL. Bill's attorney argues that the children are not parties and that there was no professional misconduct on his part because he had the consent of the children's parent to interview the children.

Questions

1. Are children "parties" to a divorce action?
2. What is the policy behind the rule preventing an attorney from communicating with a party without the presence or consent of the attorney for the party?
3. Is the GAL, who represents the best interests of a child, required (like an attorney) to obtain counsel's consent before communicating with the client-party?
4. What are the differences between the duties of the GAL and the child's attorney?

2. Attorney-Client Relations

Problem 100

In re Marriage of Constant

You represent Clay Constant in the divorce action filed by his wife, Shelley Constant. Clay and Shelley have one child, Damien, age eight.

The Hoynes Circuit Court recently entered a preliminary order granting custody of the parties' son to Shelley. Thereafter, your client sent you the letter that follows.

814 Whisper Way
Southby, Michiana 46615
February 15, YR-0

Mr. Arthur Attorney
Attorney at Law
309 E. Carter
Southby, Michiana 46601

Dear Mr. Attorney:

As I've suggested to you and I'm sure you understand, the future of my relationship with my son is something I take very seriously. I would not be exaggerating to say that it is the most important thing in my life, especially considering the circumstances of the breakup of my marriage.

The fact that I am deeply concerned about the outcome of my legal proceedings entails certain expectations about the services I should be able to expect from an attorney. Your efforts now will, to a great extent, determine the outcome I will have to live with for the next sixteen years. For the client, this is what justifies the hassle and the expense of retaining a lawyer.

Generally, I feel it is reasonable to expect a good working relationship where communication is not a problem. An attorney's relationship with his client should be a kind of partnership where both feel mutual concern and support toward achieving the goal. This, in turn, entails actively seeking and gathering any and all information relevant to the case, and exploring all its facets to see how it could be used in the preparation of the best possible argument. That argument should be thorough and convincing so that the client has the best possible chance of getting a fair and just outcome. Preparation and thorough knowledge of the client and his concerns also aids an attorney in better responding to the information and arguments presented by the other party's attorney in court. Finally, the condition that makes all these other things possible is time. It is self-defeating to not allow for the amount of time necessary to do each client's case well, because losing damages the attorney's reputation as well as the client's future chances for finding justice through the court system.

Needless to say, I feel you have not lived up to what I feel can be reasonably expected of you. I understand we may have a difference of opinion about exactly what is reasonable, and if that is the case, perhaps we should look into alternatives. It appears to me that a father (and his attorney) attempting to get custody can expect an uphill fight, and should expect to have to work a bit harder. I will repeat that I cannot afford to not have the best possible case prepared and presented for me, because my relationship with my son is at stake. Rather than be offended by my criticisms, I would hope that you'd be motivated to make the necessary adjustments. I've already expressed some of these concerns to you verbally and have been discouraged by your lack of responsiveness. I will mention here a few of the specific things that have concerned me, and I would appreciate an immediate written reply so that I can move forward with the case as soon as possible.

I invested a lot of time to prepare the five or so pages of notes that I submitted to you for review on your own time. I had to prepare them in the first place because you didn't have the time to discuss these matters with me in person. Frankly, I was shocked to find that you hadn't read them before the hearing. You also asked me to type a copy of the "contract" that was originally in Shelly's handwriting, and then you failed to review it, when it seemed to me that our case would have to rely heavily on it.

Shelley's case relied heavily on allegations about my violence that were utterly false. Some effort should have been made to at least present my version of the events, so as to not appear to be in agreement with those allegations. Rather, you did not mention them at all. Ms. Teahouse also made statements about me or about my relationship to Shelley that were false or that did not bear on the case and only served to slander or embarrass me (such as the statement that I've never had a real job in my life; and there were three or four other similar comments). Objections should have been raised or the record should have been set straight, at least by presenting my version.

It also seems important to me that some mention be made that the separation occurred under the false pretense that it was temporary, and that had Shelley told me the truth, that she was going to seek a divorce, I never would have left the home and Damien. It is only through an act of deliberate deception that she came to have custody of Damien. When I moved back home, it was through a desire to be with my family and not an act of intimidation as she claimed. It therefore should have been pointed out that no such harassment occurred (except perhaps that she harassed me when I had a right to be in my own home) and that Shelley committed perjury by claiming she was molested in order to acquire the restraining order denying me access to my son. Again, to not point these things out is to permit her an implied validity about her claims.

I felt that we should have had a briefing session to familiarize me with your presentation before the hearing, and to prepare me for what would happen and coach me somewhat about what I should do or say. Instead, you took me completely by surprise when you gave me an opportunity to comment to the judge, and I wish that I'd known ahead of time so that I could have better prepared my comments.

Perhaps it is normal procedure to wait until the last minute for prehearing negotiations. I thought it was a little absurd, and the information we gained about Shelley's position in those discussions could have greatly aided us in making our case. For instance, we assumed Shelley's ability to compromise and work things out up to that point, and had we known she would be so intransigent we would have realized that we would have to make a stronger case before the judge about her lack of suitability as custodial parent. I understand that in the absence of compelling reasons to do otherwise, the judge will just maintain the status quo. With what we learned about Shelley in the preliminary negotiations, we might have made a case that custody should be shifted to me. It will be much more difficult at this point to make that case. Also, in those negotiations, it was clear to me that you came into it completely cold when you asked me to brief you on what our position was with respect to custody, and this seems inappropriate to me.

In the hearing itself, you made a couple of statements that assumed Shelley would be getting custody, and I felt these statements made it appear as if we were expecting that outcome and were prepared to accept it. How do you think I felt hearing you make these statements?

Some of the problems I see in our style of relating and communicating have also perturbed me, because it seems they interfere with your ability to properly evaluate our situation. I feel it is inappropriate to end a conversation before reaching a conclusion about the matter being discussed. You have on many occasions frustrated me by insisting that you had to do something else and couldn't continue speaking to me, even though the conversation may have only been a couple of minutes long.

We should also have a sense that we are cooperating with each other. Instead, you have left me in the dark about what you're doing, how the case is developing, what I should expect from the court, what laws and precedents are established, and what angle we would use to best establish my own custodial rights. Consequently, I have had to seek a lot of outside advice on these matters. Then when you became aware of my efforts, you interpreted it that I was going around you or working behind your back. I would have gladly worked with you, but it was your own time constraints that made it impossible. It is solely because of my deep concern about these matters that I felt an urgent necessity to do and to learn everything I possibly could about divorce laws and precedents and my rights as a father.

You seem to feel that I should leave the whole matter up to you and trust that you will do the job well, and are offended that I would take some initiative. In my only other experience with a lawyer, I did leave it up to him to do the work on his own. We were suing for back wages owed to me, and it should have been a cut and dried case. But he did absolutely no research or preparation, and we lost. I had worked over 500 hours that I never got paid for.

That was just money. This time it is my son, and I have a wife who feels he is merely property to be fought over, as you would fight over a desk or a car. I am determined to do everything I can to see that the outcome is just and fair and protects my right to have a continuing relationship with my son. And if that means keeping track of what you're doing or not doing and holding you accountable for it, I have to ask you to understand and please accommodate.

To summarize how I feel about the preliminary hearing and your performance, I will say simply that I feel like we lost when we shouldn't have. Maybe we would have lost even had you been thoroughly prepared. I will never know. But because you were not prepared and didn't know me, Shelley, or the case very well, I am left with the feeling that it's the reason we lost. It will be extremely difficult to recover an advantage going into a divorce hearing, and will therefore require that much more work. At this point, I am not willing to remain as passive and removed from things as I've been until now. I urge you to think carefully about this and decide whether you can truly fulfill the expectations I have of you. Thank you for your time.

Sincerely,

Clay Constant

Questions

1. Prepare a written list of the problems and concerns of Mr. Constant.
2. What should Attorney do in response to Mr. Constant's letter?
3. What does Mr. Constant's letter tell you about the expectations divorce clients have of their lawyers?

B. PROFESSIONAL RESPONSIBILITY

1. Attorney-Client Relationship

Problem 101

In re Bellows

Myra and Fred Robins were married in YR-20 and subsequently had two sons and two daughters who are now teenagers. In YR-1, after the girls made accusations to a school counselor that Fred was sexually abusing them, the Hoynes County Department of Public Welfare (DPW) investigated the report and removed all four of the children from the home.

Myra immediately moved out of the home she shared with Fred, and both Myra and Fred were appointed an attorney ad litem for the pendency of the children in need of services (CHINS) proceedings. Because there were no allegations made against Myra, her attorney, John Bellows, explained to her that she had a good chance of having the children returned to her. Myra explained to Mr. Bellows that as she had just moved out and had gotten her first job in twenty years, making minimum wage, she didn't believe that she would be able to support all four of the children. Therefore, Myra decided that since the girls were the only ones who made allegations of abuse that she would ask for custody of them and request that the boys be returned to the care and custody of their father.

Myra instructed Mr. Bellows to appear at the next CHINS hearing and recommend to the Court that she get custody of the girls, that the boys return to their father's home, and that the investigation by Child Protection Services of the DPW be terminated. However, after hearing all four of the children testify in court, and based on his belief that Fred was also sexually abusing the boys, Mr. Bellows wrote a letter to the DPW asking them to continue their investigations and enclosed with the letter an unfiled motion requesting the court to grant custody of all four children to Myra.

When Myra learned what her attorney had done she was furious and petitioned the Michiana State Bar Association to file a complaint against Mr. Bellows, claiming which he violated Michiana Rule of Professional Conduct 10-1, that states in relevant part:

> A lawyer shall abide by a client's decisions concerning the objectives of representation and shall consult with the client as to the means by which they are to be pursued.

After the bar association filed the complaint, Bellows filed an answer stating as his defense that if he had carried out Myra's wishes he would have assisted her in criminal conduct by knowingly placing the children in a situation where they could be sexually abused. Mr. Bellows cited Michiana Rule of Professional Conduct 11-2, which states in relevant part:

> A lawyer shall not counsel a client to engage, or assist a client, in conduct that the lawyer knows or reasonably should know is criminal or fraudulent.

Questions

1. Does it matter that Mr. Bellows took this action based on his "belief" the boys were being sexually abused as opposed to being based on evidence that the boys were being abused?
2. What other options did Mr. Bellows have that would have prevented him from taking this drastic step in order to do what he thought was right?
3. Did Myra have other options that would have enabled her to keep and support all four of her children? Was it Mr. Bellows's responsibility to explain these options to her?

2. Conflicts of Interest

Problem 102

In re Matthews

Martha and Walter Matthews were married in YR-15, and during their marriage they had five children. Upon their divorce in YR-4, Walter was ordered to pay substantial child support, but no payments were ever made. As Martha had no employment history or significant job skills, she was unable to obtain a job, and before long she and the children were living on Aid to Families with Dependent Children (AFDC).

In YR-2, the State of Michiana created the Child Support Enforcement Task Force, a division of the Department of Public Welfare (DPW) designed to prosecute parents who were not paying child support and whose children were on AFDC. Cheryl Benedict was assigned to prosecute Walter. Through the course of the investigation and subsequent case she came to know Martha and the children quite well.

In YR-1, after reports by several of the children's teachers of suspicious cuts and bruises, the DPW removed the children from Martha's home, and an attorney was required to serve as the children's guardian ad litem (GAL). Because Cheryl was familiar with the children, she volunteered to take the case.

At the first hearing in the child abuse case, Martha, through her attorney, moved to have Cheryl removed from the case, citing a conflict of interest, as Cheryl had represented the state against Walter.

The conflict rule in the Michiana Code of Professional Responsibility reads as follows: "A lawyer may not represent a client if that representation may be materially limited by the lawyer's duties to another client or to a third party."

Questions

1. Is there a conflict of interest in this case?
2. Does it matter that all of the child support that the state collected from Walter went to the state because Martha and the children were receiving public assistance (AFDC)? Does it matter if the case against Walter is still open?

3. Ethical Dilemmas

Problem 103

In re Marriage of Hosinski

You've agreed to represent Casimer Hosinski (Casimer), owner of a jewelry store, in a divorce action against his wife, Roxanne (Roxie). Casimer pays you a $4000.00 retainer fee and states that Roxie is having an affair and that she uses cocaine. Casimer wants sole custody of the parties' three children, Terry, age fourteen, Dinah, age eight, and Joy, age six. On November 11, YR-1, Casimer requested that you meet with the children.

On January 5, YR-0, the Hoynes Circuit Court ordered that Casimer and the three children be evaluated by a psychologist. Casimer requests that you meet with him and the children to brief them on what to expect from the psychological evaluations. Casimer also would like to meet with another psychologist of his own choosing before he and the children are evaluated by the court-appointed psychologist.

Assume that before the final divorce hearing Casimer and Roxie have hired their own psychologists and have notified each other of these arrangements. Dr. Kubley, the psychologist who evaluated Casimer, calls you on the telephone and says, "Your client is crazy. Are you really going to pursue custody of the three children in his behalf?"

The sole issue in dispute is custody of the children. One week before trial, Casimer's sister, Barbara, informs you that "Casimer is a cocaine addict, and Roxie doesn't know this because he does his drugs in an apartment off the jewelry store." Barbara will not be available to testify at trial. You confront Casimer with this information, and he admits to regular use of cocaine. He claims, however, that he has enough money to support his habit and his drug use does not affect his relationship with the children. The children are willing to live with Casimer, and there has been no other mention of Casimer's drug use during discovery.

Questions

1. What factors should be considered before you meet with the children, as requested by Casimer, on November 11, YR-1?

2. If you meet with the children, do you have an obligation to notify anyone else?
3. Would you meet (as requested) with Casimer and the children before their evaluations by the court-appointed psychologist to brief them on what to expect?
4. What would you say to Dr. Kubley?
5. Would the telephone conversation with Dr. Kubley affect your representation of Casimer?
6. Would Casimer's admission of cocaine addiction affect your representation of Casimer? Is withdrawal an option?
7. Assess your obligation of zealous advocacy in behalf of Casimer on the custody issue.
8. As an officer of the court, do you have any other ethical/professional responsibility obligations in this situation?

4. Contingency Fee

Problem 104

Ketch v. Alstott

Heidi Ketch retained Edwin Alstott to represent Heidi in her divorce. The written retainer agreement stated that Heidi would pay Edwin a fee based on the number of hours worked multiplied by an hourly rate. Settlement negotiations continued for a year, until Heidi and her husband finally reached an agreement. On May 19, YR-1, Heidi executed the settlement agreement, which provided that she would get property worth fifteen times what her husband had originally offered her. Two days later, on May 21, Heidi's husband also signed the agreement.

On May 20, YR-1, Heidi and Edwin executed a performance fee agreement in which Heidi "in light of the results achieved by Edwin . . . agreed to pay a performance fee of $500,000." This fee was to be paid in addition to the $230,000 fee based on Edwin's hourly billing.

Heidi paid half of the $500,000 performance fee to Edwin and then retained other counsel. Heidi refuses to pay the remainder of Edwin's bill and demands repayment of the money already paid to Edwin. Heidi claims that she is entitled to repayment because the performance fee is a contingency fee, which is disallowed in domestic relations cases in the Michiana Rules of Professional Responsibility. Edwin claims that the performance fee was a bonus agreement and not a contingency fee, since the fee was not contingent on any future event (since Heidi executed the agreement and became liable for the debt regardless of whether her husband signed the agreement).

Questions

1. What public policy is served by the prohibition of contingency fees in domestic relations cases? Is the policy being served if the performance agreement in this case is found to be a contingency fee?
2. Is the performance fee in this case contingent on any event? What impact do the words "results achieved" have on the analysis?

3. Would Heidi have been liable for this fee if her husband had not signed the settlement agreement? If so, could this fee be considered excessive and in violation of another rule of professional responsibility?
4. Why are contingency fees allowed in some cases and not others?
5. In light of the ability of a non-monied spouse to ask the court for attorney fees, are contingency fees necessary in domestic relations cases?

Appendix

Statutes and Uniform Acts

Defense of Marriage Act (1996)
Public Law 104-199 [H.R. 3396]

[Below is the full text of the H.R. 3396, signed into law by President Clinton on September 21, 1996.]

An Act to define and protect the institution of marriage.

Be it enacted by the Senate and the House of Representatives of the United States of America in Congress assembled,

Section 1. Short Title.

This Act may be cited as the "Defense of Marriage Act."

Section 2. Powers Reserved to the States.

(a) In General—Chapter 115 of title 28, United States Code, is amended by adding after section 1738B the following:

"Section 1738C. Certain acts, records, and proceedings and the effect thereof."

"No State, territory, or possession of the United States, or Indian tribe, shall be required to give effect to any public act, record, or judicial proceeding of any other State, territory, possession, or tribe, or a right or claim arising form such relationship."

(b) Clerical Amendment—The table of sections at the beginning of chapter 115 of title 28, United States Code, is amended by inserting after the item relating to section 1738B the following new item:

"1738C. Certain acts, records, and proceedings and the effect thereof."

Section 3. Definition of Marriage.

(a) In General—Chapter 1 of title 1, United States code, is amended by adding at the end the following:

"Section 7. Definition of 'marriage' and 'spouse.'"

"In determining the meaning of any Act of Congress, or of any ruling, regulation, or interpretation of the various administrative bureaus and agencies of the United States, the word 'marriage' means only a legal union between one man and one woman as husband and wife, and the word 'spouse' refers only to a person of the opposite sex who is a husband or a wife."

(b) Clerical Amendment—The table of sections at the beginning of chapter 1 of title 1, United States Code, is amended by inserting after the item relating to section 6 the following new item:

"7. Definition of 'marriage' and 'spouse'."

Uniform Premarital Agreement Act (1983)
9B U.L.A. 369 (1987)

[Reprinted with permission from the National Conference of Commissioners on Uniform State Laws]

Section 1. Definitions.

As used in this Act:

(1) "Premarital agreement" means an agreement between prospective spouses made in contemplation of marriage and to be effective upon marriage.

(2) "Property" means an interest, present or future, legal or equitable, vested or contingent, in real or personal property, including income and earnings.

Section 2. Formalities.

A premarital agreement must be in writing and signed by both parties. It is enforceable without consideration.

Section 3. Content.

(a) Parties to a premarital agreement may contract with respect to:

(1) the rights and obligations of each of the parties in any of the property of either or both of them whenever and wherever acquired or located;

(2) the right to buy, sell, use, transfer, exchange, abandon, lease, consume, expend, assign, create a security interest in, mortgage, encumber, dispose of, or otherwise manage and control property;

(3) the disposition of property upon separation, marital dissolution, death, or the occurrence or nonoccurrence of any other event;

(4) the modification or elimination of spousal support;

(5) the making of a will, trust, or other arrangement to carry out the provisions of the agreement;

(6) the ownership rights in and disposition of the death benefit from a life insurance policy;

(7) the choice of law governing the construction of the agreement; and

(8) any other matter, including their personal rights and obligations, not in violation of public policy or a statute imposing a criminal penalty.

(b) The right of a child to support may not be adversely affected by a premarital agreement.

Section 4. Effect of Marriage.

A premarital agreement becomes effective upon marriage.

Section 5. Amendment, Revocation.

After marriage, a premarital agreement may be amended or revoked only by a written agreement signed by the parties. The amendment agreement or the revocation is enforceable without consideration.

Section 6. Enforcement.

(a) A premarital agreement is not enforceable if the party against whom enforcement is sought proves that:

(1) that party did not execute the agreement voluntarily; or

(2) the agreement was unconscionable when it was executed and, before execution of the agreement, that party:

(i) was not provided a fair and reasonable disclosure of the property or financial obligations of the other party;

(ii) did not voluntarily and expressly waive, in writing, any right to disclosure of the property or financial obligations of the other party beyond the disclosure provided; and

(iii) did not have, or reasonably could not have had, an adequate knowledge of the property or financial obligations of the other party.

(b) If a provision of a premarital agreement modifies or eliminates spousal support and that modification or elimination causes one party to the agreement to be eligible for support under a program of public assistance at the time of separation or marital dissolution, a court, notwithstanding the terms of the agreement, may require the other party to provide support to the extent necessary to avoid that eligibility.

(c) An issue of unconscionability of a premarital agreement shall be decided by the court as a matter of law.

Section 7. Enforcement; Void Marriage.

If a marriage is determined to be void, an agreement that would otherwise have been a premarital agreement is enforceable only to the extent necessary to avoid an inequitable result.

Section 8. Limitation of Actions.

Any statute of limitations applicable to an action asserting a claim for relief under a premarital agreement is tolled during the marriage of the parties to the agreement. However, equitable defenses limiting the time for enforcement, including laches and estoppel, are available to either party.

Section 9. Application and Construction.

This [Act] shall be applied and construed to effectuate its general purpose to make uniform the law with respect to the subject of this [Act] among states enacting it.

[Sections 10 through 13, dealing with the short title of the Act, severability, time of effect, and repeals, have been omitted.]

Uniform Parentage Act (1973)
9B U.L.A. 287 (1987)

[Reprinted with permission from the National Conference of Commissioners on Uniform State Laws]

Section 1. [Parent and Child Relationship Defined.]

As used in this Act, "parent and child relationship" means the legal relationship existing between a child and his natural or adoptive parents incident to which the law confers or imposes rights, privileges, duties, and obligations. It includes the mother and child relationship and the father and child relationship.

Section 2. [Relationship Not Dependent on Marriage.]

The parent and child relationship extends equally to every child and to every parent, regardless of the marital status of the parents.

Section 3. [How Parent and Child Relationship Established.]

The parent and child relationship between a child and

(1) the natural mother may be established by proof of her having given birth to the child, or under this Act;

(2) the natural father may be established under this Act;

(3) an adoptive parent may be established by proof of adoption or under the [Revised Uniform Adoption Act].

Section 4. [Presumption of Paternity.]

(a) A man is presumed to be the natural father of a child if:

(1) he and the child's natural mother are or have been married to each other and the child is born during the marriage, or within 300 days after the marriage is terminated by death, annulment, declaration of invalidity, or divorce, or after a decree of separation is entered by a court;

(2) before the child's birth, he and the child's natural mother have attempted to marry each other by a marriage solemnized in apparent compliance with law, although the attempted marriage is or could be declared invalid, and,

(i) if the attempted marriage could be declared invalid only be a court, the child is born during the attempted marriage, or within 300 days after its termination by death, annulment, declaration of invalidity, or divorce; or

(ii) if the attempted marriage is invalid without a court order, the child is born within 300 days after the termination of cohabitation;

(3) after the child's birth, he and the child's natural mother have married, or attempted to marry, each other by a marriage solemnized in apparent compliance with law, though the attempted marriage is or could be declared invalid, and

(i) he has acknowledged his paternity of the child in writing filed with the [appropriate court or Vital Statistics Bureau],

(ii) with his consent, he is named as the child's father on the child's birth certificate, or

(iii) he is obligated to support the child under a written voluntary promise or by court order;

(4) while the child is under the age of majority, he receives the child into his home and openly holds out the child as his natural child; or

(5) he acknowledges his paternity of the child in a writing filed with the [appropriate court or Vital Statistics Bureau], which shall promptly inform the mother of the filing of the acknowledgment, and she does not dispute the acknowledgment within a reasonable time after being informed thereof, in a writing filed with the [appropriate court of Vital Statistics Bureau]. If another man is presumed under this section to be the child's father, acknowledgment may be effected only with the written consent of the presumed father or after the presumption has been rebutted.

(b) A presumption under this section may be rebutted in an appropriate action only by clear and convincing evidence. If two or more presumptions arise which conflict with each other, the presumption which on the facts is founded on the weightier considerations of policy and logic controls. The presumption is rebutted by a court decree establishing paternity of the child by another man.

Section 5. [Artificial insemination.]

(a) If, under the supervision of a licensed physician and with the consent of her husband, a wife is inseminated artificially with semen donated by a man not her husband, the husband is treated in law as if he were th natural father of a child thereby conceived. The husband's consent must be in writing and signed by him and his wife. The physician shall certify their signatures and the date of the insemination, and file the husband's consent with the [State Department of Health], where it shall be kept confidential and in a sealed file. However, the physician's failure to do so does not affect the father and child relationship. All papers and records pertaining to the insemination, whether part of the permanent record of a court or of a file held by the supervising physician or elsewhere, are subject to inspection only upon an order of the court for good cause shown.

(b) The donor of semen provided to a licensed physician for use in artificial insemination of a married woman other than the donor's wife is treated in law as if he were not the natural father of a child thereby conceived.

Section 6. [Determination of Father and Child Relationship; Who May Bring Action; When Action May Be Brought.]

(a) A child, his natural mother, or a man presumed to be his father under Paragraph (1), (2), or (3) of Section 4(a), may bring an action

(1) at any time for the purpose of declaring the existence of the father and child relationship presumed under Paragraph (1), (2), or (3) of Section 4(a); or

(2) for the purpose of declaring the non-existence of the father and child relationship presumed under Paragraph (1), (2), or (3) of section 4(a) only if the action is brought within a reasonable time after obtaining knowledge of relevant facts, but in no event later than [5] years after the child's birth. After the presumption has been rebutted, paternity of the child by another man may be determined in the same action, if he has been made a party.

(b) Any interested party may bring an action at any time for the purpose of determining the existence or non-existence of the father and child relationship presumed under Paragraph (4) or (5) of Section 4(a).

(c) An action to determine the existence of the father and child relationship with respect to a child who has no presumed father under Section 4 may be brought by the child, the mother or personal representative of the child, the [appropriate state agency], the personal representative or a parent of the mother if the mother has died, a man alleged or alleging himself to be the father, or the personal representative or a parent of the alleged father if the alleged father has died or is a minor.

(d) Regardless of its terms, an agreement, other than an agreement approved by the court in accordance with Section 13(b), between an alleged or presumed father and the mother or child, does not bar an action under this section.

(e) If an action under this section is brought before the birth of the child, all proceedings shall be stayed until after the birth, except service of process and the taking of depositions to perpetuate testimony.

Section 7. [Statute of Limitations.]

An action to determine the existence of the father and child relationship as to a child who has no presumed father under Section 4 may not be brought later than [3] years after the birth of the child, or later than [3] years after the effective date of this Act, whichever is later. However, an action brought by or on behalf of a child whose paternity has not been determined is not barred until [3] years after the child reaches the age of majority. Sections 6 and 7 do not extend the times within which a right of inheritance or a right to a succession may be asserted beyond the time provided by law relating to distribution and closing of decedents' estates or to the determination of heirship, or otherwise.

Section 8. [Jurisdiction; Venue.]

(a) [Without limiting the jurisdiction of any other court,] [The] [appropriate] court has jurisdiction of an action brought under this Act. [The action may be joined with an action for divorce, annulment, separate maintenance, or support.]

(b) A person who has sexual intercourse in this State thereby submits to the jurisdiction of the courts of this State as to an action brought under this Act with respect to a child who may have been conceived by that act of intercourse. In addition to any other method provided by [rule or] statute, including [cross reference to "long arm statute"], personal jurisdiction may be acquired by [personal service of summons outside this State or by registered mail with proof of actual receipt] [service in accordance with (citation to long-arm statute)].

(c) The action may be brought in the county in which the child or the alleged father resides or is found or, if the father is deceased, in which proceedings for probate of his estate have been or could be commenced.

Section 9. [Parties.]

The child shall be made a party to the action. If he is a minor he shall be represented by his general guardian or a guardian ad litem appointed by the court. The child's mother or father may not represent the child as guardian or otherwise. The court may appoint the [appropriate state agency] as guardian ad litem for the child. The natural mother, each man presumed to be the father under Section 4, and each man alleged to be the natural father, shall be made parties or, if not subject to the jurisdiction of the court, shall be given notice of the action in a manner prescribed by the court and an opportunity to be heard. The court may align the parties.

Uniform Putative and Unknown Fathers Act (1988)
9B U.L.A. 76 (Supp 1996)

[Reprinted with permission from the National Conference of Commissioners on Uniform State Laws]

Section 1. Definitions
In this [Act]:

(1) "Man" means a male individual of any age;

(2) "Putative father" means a man who claims to be, or is named as, the biological father or a possible biological father of a particular child, and whose paternity of that child has not been judicially determined, excluding:

(i) a man whose parental rights with respect to that child have been previously judicially terminated or declared not to exist;

(ii) a donor of semen used in artificial insemination, whose identity is not known by the mother of the resulting child or whose semen was donated under circumstances indicating that the donor did not anticipate having an interest in the resulting child;

(iii) a man who is or was married to the mother of a particular child, and the child is born during the marriage [or within 300 days after the marriage was terminated by death, annulment, declaration of invalidity, divorce, or marital dissolution, or after a decree of separation was entered by a court];

(iv) a man who, before the birth of a particular child, attempted to marry the mother of the child in apparent compliance with law, although the attempted marriage is, or could be declared, invalid, and:

(A) if the attempted marriage could be declared invalid only by a court, the child is born during the attempted marriage [or within 300 days after its termination by death, annulment, declaration of invalidity, divorce, or marital dissolution]; or

(B) if the attempted marriage is invalid without a court order, the child is born during, or within 300 days after the termination of, cohabitation; and

(v) a man who, after the birth of a particular child, married or attempted to marry the mother of the child in apparent compliance with law, although the attempted marriage is, or could be declared, invalid, and:

(A) has acknowledged his paternity of the child in a writing filed with the [appropriate court or Vital Statistics Bureau],

(B) with his consent, he is named as the child's biological father on the child's birth certificate, or

(C) is obligated to support the child under a written promise or by court order;

(3) "Unknown father" means a particular child's biological father, whose identity is unascertained. However, the term does not include a donor of semen used in artificial insemination or in vitro fertilization whose identity is not known to the mother of the resulting child or whose semen was donated under circumstances indicating that the donor did not anticipate having an interest in the resulting child.

Section 2. Right to Determination of Paternity

(a) A putative father may bring an action to determine whether he is the biological father of a particular child [,in accordance with [applicable state law],] at any time, unless his paternity or his possible parental rights have already been determined or are in issue in a pending action.

(b) An agreement between a putative father and the mother or between him and the child does not bar an action under this section [, unless the agreement has been judicially approved [under applicable state law].]

Section 3. Notice of Judicial Proceedings for Adoption or Termination of Parental Rights

(a) In an adoption or other judicial proceeding that might result in termination of any man's parental rights with respect to a child, the person seeking termination shall give notice to every putative father of that child known to that person.

(b) The notice must be given at a time and place and in a manner (i) appropriate under the [rules of civil procedure for the service of process in a civil action in this State] or (ii) at a time and place and in a manner as the court directs to provide actual notice.

(c) A putative father may participate as a party in a proceeding described in subsection (a).

(d) If, at any time in the proceeding, it appears to the court that there is a putative father of the child who has not been given notice, the court shall require notice to be given to him in accordance with subsection (b).

(e) If, at any time in the proceeding, it appears to the court that an unknown father might not have been given notice, the court shall determine whether he can be identified. The determination must be based on evidence that includes inquiry of appropriate persons in an effort to identify the unknown father for the purpose of providing notice. The inquiry must include:

(1) whether the mother was married at the time of conception of the child or at a later time;

(2) whether the mother was cohabiting with a man at the probable time of conception of the child;

(3) whether the mother has received support payments or promises of support, other than from a governmental agency, with respect to the child or because of her pregnancy;

(4) whether the mother has named any man as the biological father in connection with applying for or receiving public assistance; and

(5) whether any man has formally or informally acknowledged or claimed paternity of the child in any jurisdiction in which the mother resided at the

time of or since conception of the child or in which the child has resided or resides at the time of the inquiry.

(f) If the inquiry required by subsection (e) identifies any man as the unknown father, notice of the proceeding must be given to each in accordance with subsection (b). If the inquiry so identifies a man, but his whereabouts are unknown, the court shall proceed in accordance with subsections (b) and (g).

(g) If, after the inquiry required by subsection (e), it appears that there might be an unknown father of the child, the court shall consider whether publication or public posting of notice of the proceeding is likely to lead to actual notice to him. The court may order publication or public posting of notice only if, on the basis of all information available, the court determines that the publication or posting is likely to lead to actual notice to him.

Section 4. Notice of Judicial Proceedings Regarding Custody or Visitation

(a) The petitioner in a judicial proceeding to change or establish legal or physical custody of or visitation rights with respect to a child shall give notice to every putative father of that child known to the petitioner, except a proceeding for annulment, declaration of invalidity, divorce, marital dissolution, legal separation, modification of child custody, or determination of paternity.

(b) The notice must be given (i) at a time and place and in a manner appropriate under the [rules of civil procedure for the service of process in a civil action in this State] or (ii) as the court directs and determines will likely provide actual notice.

(c) If, at any time in the proceeding, it appears to the court that there is a putative father of the child who has not been given notice of the proceeding, the court shall require notice of the proceeding to be given to him in accordance with subsection (b).

(d) If, at any time in the proceeding, it appears to the court that an unknown father might not have been given notice of the proceeding, the court may attempt to identify him pursuant to Section 3(e) and require notice of the proceeding to be given to him pursuant to Section 3(f) and (g).

(e) A putative father may participate as a party in a proceeding described in subsection (a).

Section 5. Factors in Determining Parental Rights of Father

In determining whether to preserve or terminate the parental rights of a putative father in a proceeding governed by Section 3 or 4, the court shall consider all of the following factors that are pertinent:

(1) the age of the child;

(2) the nature and quality of any relationship between the man and the child;

(3) the reasons for any lack of a relationship between the man and the child;

(4) whether a parent and child relationship has been established between the child and another man;

(5) whether the child has been abused or neglected;

(6) whether the man has a history of substance abuse or of abuse of the mother or the child;

(7) any proposed plan for the child;

(8) whether the man seeks custody and is able to provide the child with emotional or financial support and a home, whether or not he has had opportunity to establish a parental relationship with the child;

(9) whether the man visits the child, has shown any interest in visitation, or, desiring visitation, has been effectively denied opportunity to visit the child;

(10) whether the man is providing financial support for the child according to his means;

(11) whether the man provided emotional or financial support for the mother during her prenatal, natal, and postnatal care;

(12) the circumstances of the child's conception, including whether the child was conceived as a result of incest or forcible rape;

(13) whether the man has formally or informally acknowledged or declared his possible paternity of the child; and

(14) other factors the court considers relevant to the standards stated in Section 6(d) and (g).

Section 6. Court Determination and Orders

(a) If a man appears in a proceeding described in Section 3, other than as a petitioner or prospective adoptive parent, the court may:

(1) [in accordance with [applicable state law],] determine whether the man is the biological father of the child and, if the court determines that he is, enter an order in accordance with subsection (d); or

(2) without determining paternity, and consistent with the standards in subsection (d), enter an order, after considering the factors in Section 5, terminating any parental rights he may have, or declaring that he has no parental rights, with respect to the child.

(b) If the court makes an order under subsection (a), the court may also make an order (i) terminating the parental rights of any other man given notice who does not appear, or (ii) declaring that no man has any parental rights with respect to the child.

(c) If a man who appears in a proceeding described in Section 3 is determined by the court to be the father, the court, after considering evidence of the factors in Section 5, shall determine (i) whether a familial bond between the father and the child has been established; or (ii) whether the failure to establish a familial bond is justified, and the father has the desire and potential to establish the bond.

(d) If the court makes an affirmative determination under subsection (c), the court may terminate the parental rights of the father [, in accordance with [applicable state law],] only if failure to do so would be detrimental to the child. If the court does not make an affirmative determination, it may terminate the parental rights of the father if doing so is in the best interest of the child.

(e) If no man appears in a proceeding described in Section 3, the court may enter an order:

(1) terminating with respect to the child the parental rights of any man given notice; or

(2) declaring that no putative father or unknown father has any parental rights with respect to the child.

(f) If the court does not require notice under Section 3, it shall enter an order declaring that no putative father or unknown father has any parental rights with respect to the child.

(g) If a man appears in a proceeding described in Section 4 and requests custody or visitation based on a claim of paternity, the court shall either determine [, in accordance with [applicable state law],] whether he is the biological father of the child or, after considering the factors in Section 5, deny him the custody of or visitation with the child. If the court determines that he is the biological father, the court shall determine, after considering evidence of the factors listed in Section 5, whether or not to grant him custody or visitation and shall make such other orders as are appropriate. All orders issued under this subsection must be in the child's best interest.

(h) A court order under subsection (a)(2), (b), (d), or (e) terminating the parental rights of a man, or declaring that no man has parental rights, with respect to the child, is not a determination that the man is or is not the biological father of the child.

(i) [Six months] after the date of issuance of an order under this section terminating parental rights or declaring that no man has parental rights, no person may directly or collaterally challenge the order upon any ground, including fraud, misrepresentation, failure to give a required notice, or lack of jurisdiction over the parties or of the subject matter. The running of this period of limitation may not be extended for any reason.

[Sections 7 through 10, dealing with short title, severability, effective date, and repeals, have been omitted.]

Uniform Status of Children of Assisted Conception Act (1988)
9B U.L.A. 152 (Supp. 1994)

[Reprinted with permission from the National Conference of Commissioners on Uniform State Laws.]

Section 1. Definitions.
In this [Act]:

(1) "Assisted conception" means a pregnancy resulting from (i) fertilizing an egg of a woman with sperm of a man by means other than sexual intercourse or (ii) implanting an embryo, but the term does not include the pregnancy of a wife resulting from fertilizing her egg with sperm of her husband.

(2) "Donor" means an individual [other than a surrogate] who produces egg or sperm used for assisted conception, whether or not a payment is made for the egg or sperm used, but does not include a woman who gives birth to a resulting child.

[(3) "Intended parents" means a man and woman, married to each other, who enter into an agreement under this [Act] providing that they will be the parents of a child born to a surrogate through assisted conception using egg or sperm of one or both of the intended parents.]

(4) "Surrogate" means an adult woman who enters into an agreement to bear a child conceived through assisted conception for intended parents.

Section 2. Maternity.
[Except as provided in Sections 5 through 9,] a woman who gives birth to a child is the child's mother.

Section 3. Assisted Conception by Married Woman.
[Except as provided in Sections 5 through 9,] the husband of a woman who bears a child through assisted conception is the father of the child, notwithstanding a declaration of invalidity or annulment of the marriage obtained after the assisted conception, unless within two years after learning of the child's birth he commences an action in which the mother and child are parties and in which it is determined that he did not consent to the assisted conception.

Section 4. Parental Status of Donors and Deceased Persons.
[Except as otherwise provided in Sections 5 through 9:]

(a) A donor is not the parent of a child conceived through assisted conception.

(b) An individual who dies before implantation of an embryo, or before a child is conceived other than through sexual intercourse, using the individual's egg or sperm, is not a parent of the resulting child.

ALTERNATIVE A

Comment

A state which chooses Alternative A should also consider section 1(3) and the bracketed language in sections 1(3), 2, 3, and 4.

Section 5. Surrogacy Agreement.
(a) A surrogate, her husband, if she is married, and intended parents may enter into a written agreement whereby the surrogate relinquishes all her rights and duties as a parent of a child conceived through assisted conception, and the intended parents may become the parents of the child pursuant to Section 8.

(b) If the agreement is not approved by the court under Section 6 before conception, the agreement is void and the surrogate is the mother of a resulting child and the surrogate's husband, if a party to the agreement, is the father of the child. If the surrogate's husband is not a party to the agreement or the surrogate is unmarried, paternity of the child is governed by [the Uniform Parentage Act].

Section 6. Petition and Hearing for Approval of Surrogacy.
(a) The intended parents and the surrogate may file a petition in the [appropriate court] to approve a surrogacy agreement if one of them is a resident of this State. The surrogate's husband, if she is married, must join in the petition. A copy of the agreement must be attached to the petition. The court shall name a [guardian ad litem] to represent the interests of any child to be conceived by the surrogate through assisted conception and [shall] [may] appoint counsel to represent the surrogate.

(b) The court shall hold a hearing on the petition and shall enter an order approving the surrogacy agreement, authorizing assisted conception for a period of 12 months after the date of the order, declaring the intended parents to be the parents of a child to be conceived through assisted conception pursuant to the agreement and discharging the guardian ad litem and attorney for the surrogate, upon finding that:

(1) the court has jurisdiction and all parties have submitted to its jurisdiction under subsection (e) and have agreed that the law of this State shall govern all matters arising under this [Act] and the agreement;

(2) the intended mother is unable to bear a child or is unable to do so without unreasonable risk to an unborn child or to the physical or mental health of the intended mother or child, and the finding is supported by medical evidence;

(3) the [relevant child welfare agency] has made a home study of the intended parents and the surrogate and a copy of the report of the home study has been filed with the court;

(4) the intended parents, the surrogate, and the surrogate's husband, if any, meet the standards of fitness applicable to adoptive parents in this State;

(5) all parties have voluntarily entered into the agreement and understand its terms and the nature, and meaning, and the effect of the proceeding;

(6) the surrogate has had at least one pregnancy and delivery and bearing another child will not pose an unreasonable risk to the unborn child or to the physical or mental health of the surrogate or the child, and this finding is supported by medical evidence;

(7) all parties have received counseling concerning the effect of the surrogacy by [a qualified health-care professional or social worker] and a report containing conclusions about the capacity of the parties to enter into and fulfill the agreement has been filed with the court;

(8) a report of the results of any medical or psychological examination or genetic screening agreed to by the parties or required by law has been filed with the court and made available to the parties;

(9) adequate provision has been made for all reasonable health care costs associated with the surrogacy until the child's birth including responsibility for such costs if the agreement is terminated under Section 7; and

(10) the agreement will not be substantially detrimental to the interest of any of the affected individuals.

(c) Unless otherwise provided in the surrogacy agreement, all court costs, attorney's fees, and other costs and expenses associated with the hearing shall be assessed against the intended parents.

(d) Notwithstanding any other law concerning judicial proceedings or vital statistics, the court shall conduct all hearings and proceedings under this section in camera. The court shall keep all records confidential and subject to inspection under the same standards applicable to adoptions. At the request of any party, the court shall take steps necessary to insure that the identities of the parties are not disclosed.

(e) The court conducting the hearing has exclusive and continuing jurisdiction of all matters arising out of the surrogacy until a child born after entry of an order under this section is 180 days old.

Section 7. Termination of Surrogacy Agreement.

(a) After entry of an order under Section 6, but before the surrogate becomes pregnant through assisted conception, the court for cause, or the surrogate, her husband, or the intended parents may terminate the agreement by giving written notice of termination to all other parties and filing notice of the termination with the court. Thereupon, the court shall vacate the order entered under Section 6.

(b) A surrogate who has provided an egg for the assisted conception pursuant to an agreement approved under Section 6 may terminate the agreement by filing written notice with the court within 180 days after the last insemination pursuant to the agreement. Upon finding, after notice to the parties to the agreement and hearing that the surrogate has voluntarily terminated the surrogacy agreement and understands the nature, meaning, and effect of the termination the court shall vacate the order entered under Section 6.

(c) The surrogate is not liable to the intended parents for terminating the agreement pursuant to this section.

Section 8. Parentage Under Approved Surrogacy.

(a) The following rules of parentage apply to surrogacy agreements approved under Section 6:

(1) Upon birth of a child to the surrogate, the intended parents are the parents of the child and the surrogate and her husband, if she is married, are not parents of the child unless the court vacates the order pursuant to Section 7(b).

(2) If, after notice of termination by the surrogate, the court vacates the order under Section 7(b) the surrogate is the mother of the resulting child, and her husband, if a party to the agreement, is the father. If the surrogate's husband is not a party to the agreement or the surrogate is unmarried, paternity of the child is governed by [the Uniform Parentage Act].

(b) Upon birth of the child, the intended parents shall file a written notice with the court that a child has been born to the surrogate within 300 days after assisted conception. Thereupon, the court shall enter an order directing the [Department of Vital Statistics] to issue a new birth certificate naming the intended parents as parents and to seal the original birth certificate in the records of the [Department of Vital Statistics].

Section 9. Surrogacy: Miscellaneous Provisions.

(a) A surrogacy agreement that is the basis of an order under Section 6 may provide for the payment of consideration.

(b) A surrogacy agreement may not limit the right of the surrogate to make decisions regarding her health care or that of the embryo or fetus.

(c) After the entry of an order under Section 6, the marriage of the surrogate does not affect the validity of the order, and her husband's consent to the surrogacy agreement is not required, nor is he the father of an resulting child.

(d) A child born to a surrogate within 300 days after assisted conception pursuant to an order under Section 6 is presumed to result from the assisted conception. The presumption is conclusive as to all persons who have notice of the birth and who do not commence within 180 days after notice an action to assert the contrary in which the child and the parties to the agreement are named as parties. The action must be filed in the court that issued the order under Section 6.

(e) A health care provider is not liable for recognizing the surrogate as the mother before receipt of a copy of the order entered under Section 6 or for recognizing the intended parents as parents after receipt of an order entered under Section 6.

[End of Alternative A]

ALTERNATIVE B

Comment

A state which chooses Alternative B shall also consider sections 10, 11, 12, 13, 14, 15 and 16, renumbered 6, 7, 8, 9, 10, 11 and 12, respectively.

[Section 5. Surrogate Agreements.

An agreement in which a woman agrees to become a surrogate or to relinquish her rights and duties as parent of a child conceived through assisted conception is void. However, she is the mother of a resulting child and the surrogate's husband, if a party to the agreement, is the father of the child. If her husband is not a party to the agreement or the surrogate is unmarried, paternity of the child is governed by [the Uniform Parentage Act].]

[End of Alternative B]

Section 10. Parent and Child Relationship; Status of Child.

(a) A child whose status as a child is declared or negated by this [Act] is the child only of his or her parents as determined under this [Act].

(b) Unless superseded by later events forming or terminating a parent and child relationship, the status of parent and child declared or negated by this [Act] as to a given individual and a child born alive controls for purposes of:

(1) intestate succession;

(2) probate law exemptions, allowances, or other protections for children in a parent's estate; and

(3) determining eligibility of the child or its descendants to share in a donative transfer from any person as a member of a class determined by reference to the relationship.

[Sections 11 through 15, dealing with uniformity of application and construction, severability, short title, effective date, and repeals, have been omitted. Section 14, which covers effective date, provides that the provisions of the Act are to be applied prospectively.]

Section 16. Application to Existing Relationships.

This [Act] applies to surrogacy agreements entered into after its effective date.

Uniform Adoption Act (1994)
9 (Part 1) U.L.A. 1 (Supp. 1996)

[Reprinted with permission from the National Council of Commissioners on Uniform State Laws.]

[ARTICLE] 1. GENERAL PROVISIONS

Section 1-101. Definitions.
In this [Act]:

(1) "Adoptee" means an individual who is adopted or is to be adopted.

(2) "Adult" means an individual who has attained 18 years of age.

(3) "Agency" means a public or private entity, including the Department, that is authorized by the law of this State to place individuals for adoption.

(4) "Child" means a minor or adult son or daughter, by birth or adoption.

(5) "Court," with reference to a court of this State, means the [designate] court.

(6) "Department" means the [Department of Social Services, or Health Services, or Children's Services.]

(7) "Guardian" means an individual, other than a parent, appointed by a court under [applicable law] as general guardian or guardian of the person of a minor.

(8) "Legal custody" means the right and duty to exercise continuing general supervision of a minor as authorized by law.

(9) "Minor" means an individual who has not attained 18 years of age.

(10) "Parent" means an individual who is legally recognized as a mother or father or whose consent to the adoption of a minor is required under section 2-401(a)(1). The term does not include an individual whose parental relationship to a child has been terminated judicially or by operation of law.

(11) "Person" means an individual, corporation, limited liability company, business trust, estate, trust, partnership, association, agency, joint venture, government, governmental subdivision or instrumentality, public corporation, or any other legal or commercial entity.

(12) "Physical custody" means the physical care and supervision of a minor.

(13) "Place for adoption" means to select a prospective adoptive parent for a minor and transfer physical custody of the minor to the prospective adoptive parent.

(14) "Relative" means a grandparent, great grandparent, sibling, first cousin, aunt, uncle, great-aunt, great-uncle, niece, or nephew of an individual by the whole or the half blood, affinity, or adoption. The term does not include an individual's stepparent.

(15) "Relinquishment" means the voluntary surrender to an agency by a minor's parent or guardian, for purposes of the minor's adoption, of the rights of the parent or guardian with respect to the minor, including legal and physical custody of the minor.

(16) "State" means a State of the United States, the District of Columbia, the Commonwealth of Puerto Rico, or any territory or insular possession subject to the jurisdiction of the United States.

(17) "Stepparent" means an individual who is the spouse or surviving spouse of a parent of a child but who is not a parent of the child.

Section 1-102. Who May Adopt or Be Adopted.

Subject to this [Act], any individual may adopt or be adopted by another individual for the purpose of creating the relationship of parent and child between them.

Section 1-103. Name of Adoptee After Adoption.

The name of an adoptee designated in a decree of adoption takes effect as specified in the decree.

Section 1-104. Legal Relationship Between Adoptee and Adoptive Parent After Adoption.

After a decree of adoption becomes final, each adoptive parent and the adoptee have the legal relationship of parent and child and have all the rights and duties of that relationship.

Section 1-105. Legal Relationship Between Adoptee and Former Parent After Adoption.

Except as otherwise provided in section 4-102, after a decree of adoption becomes final:

(1) the legal relationship of parent and child between each of the adoptee's former parents and the adoptee terminates, except for a former parent's duty to pay arrearages for child support; and

(2) a prior court order for visitation or communication with an adoptee terminates.

Section 1-106. Other Rights of Adoptee.

A decree of adoption does not affect any right or benefit vested in the adoptee before the decree becomes final.

Section 1-107. Proceedings Subject to Indian Child Welfare Act.

A proceeding under this [Act] which pertains to an Indian child, as defined in the Indian Child Welfare Act, 25 U.S.C. §§1901 et seq., is subject to that Act.

Section 1-108. Recognition of Adoption in Another Jurisdiciton.

A decree or order of adoption issued by a court of any other State which is entitled to full faith and credit in this State, or a decree or order of adoption entered by a court or administrative entity of another country acting pursuant to that country's law or to any convention or treaty on intercountry adoption law which the United States has ratified, has the same effect as a decree or order of this State. The rights and obligations of the parties as to matters within the jurisdiction of this State must be determined as though the decree or order were issued by a court of this State.

[ARTICLE] 2. ADOPTION OF MINORS
[PART] 1. PLACEMENT OF MINOR FOR ADOPTION

Section 2-101. Who May Place Minor for Adoption.

(a) The only persons who may place a minor for adoption are:

(1) a parent having legal and physical custody of the minor, as provided in subsections (b) and (c);

(2) a guardian expressly authorized by the court to place the minor for adoption;

(3) an agency to which the minor has been relinquished for purposes of adoption; or

(4) an agency expressly authorized to place the minor for adoption by a court order terminating the relationship between the minor and the minor's parent or guardian.

(b) Except as provided in subsection (c), a parent having legal and physical custody of a minor may place the minor for adoption, even if the other parent has not executed a consent or relinquishment or the other parent's relationship to the minor has not been terminated.

(c) A parent having legal and physical custody of a minor may not place the minor for adoption if the other parent has legal custody or a right of visitation with the minor and the parent's whereabouts are known, unless the other parent agrees in writing to the placement or, before the placement, the parent sends notice by certified mail to the other parent's last known address that the parent intends to place the child for adoption.

(d) An agency authorized under this [Act] to place a minor for adoption may place the minor for adoption, even if only one parent has executed a relinquishment or has had his or her parental relationship to the minor terminated.

Section 2-102. Direct Placement for Adoption by Parent or Guardian.

(a) A parent or guardian authorized to place a minor directly for adoption may place the minor only with a prospective adoptive parent for whom a favorable preplacement evaluation has been prepared pursuant to sections 2-201 through 2-206 or for whom a preplacement evaluation is not required under section 2-201(b) or (c).

(b) A parent or guardian shall personally select a prospective adoptive parent for the direct placement of a minor. Subject to the direct limitations of [Article] 7, the parent or guardian may be assisted by another person, including a lawyer, health-care provider, or agency, in locating a prospective adoptive parent or transferring legal or physical custody of the minor to that individual.

(c) A prospective adoptive parent shall furnish a copy of the preplacement evaluation to the parent or guardian and may provide additional information requested by the parent or guardian. The evaluation and any additional information must be edited to exclude identifying information, except that information identifying a prospective adoptive parent need not be edited if that individual agrees to its disclosure. Subject to the limitations of [Article] 7, a prospective adoptive parent may be assisted by another person in locating a minor who is available for adoption.

(d) If a consent to a minor's adoption is not executed at the time the minor is placed for adoption, the parent or guardian who places the minor shall furnish to the prospective adoptive parent a signed writing stating that the transfer of physical custody is for the purposes of adoption and that the parent or guardian has been informed of the provisions of this [Act] relevant to placement for adoption, consent, relinquishment, and termination of parental rights. The writing must authorize the prospective adoptive parent to provide medical and other care and support for the minor pending the execution of the consent within a time specified in the writing, and the prospective adoptive parent shall acknowledge in a signed writing responsibility for the minor's medical and other care and support and for returning the minor to the custody of the parent or guardian if the consent is not executed within the time specified.

(e) A person who provides services with respect to direct placements for adoption shall furnish to an individual who inquires about the person's services a written statement of the person's services and a schedule of fees.

Section 2-104. Preferences for Placement When Agency Places Minor.

(a) An agency may place a minor for adoption only with an individual for whom a favorable preplacement evaluation has been prepared pursuant to Sections 2-201 through 2-206. Placement must be made in the following order:

(1) if the agency has agreed to place the minor with a prospective adoptive parent selected by the parent or guardian, the individual selected by the parent or guardian;

(2) an individual selected by the agency in accordance with the best interest of the minor.

(b) In determining best interest under subsection (a)(2), the agency shall consider the following individuals in order of preference:

(1) an individual who has previously adopted a sibling of the minor and who makes a written request to adopt the minor;

(2) an individual with characteristics requested by a parent or guardian, if the agency agrees to comply with the request and locates the individual within a time agreed to by the parent or guardian and the agency;

(3) an individual who has had physical custody of the minor for six months or more within the preceding 24 months or for half of the minor's life, whichever is less, and makes a written request to adopt the minor;

(4) a relative with whom the minor has established a positive emotional relationship and who makes a written request to adopt the minor; and

(5) any other individual selected by the agency.

(c) Unless necessary to comply with a request under subsection (b)(2), an agency may not delay or deny a minor's placement for adoption solely on the basis of the minor's race, national origin, or ethnic background. A guardian ad litem of a minor or an individual with a favorable preplacement evaluation who makes a written request to an agency to adopt the minor may maintain an action or proceeding for equitable relief against an agency that violates this subsection.

(d) If practicable and in the best interest of minors who are siblings, an agency shall place siblings with the same prospective adoptive parent selected in accordance with subsections (a) through (c).

(e) If an agency places a minor pursuant to subsection (a)(2), an individual described in paragraph (b)(3) may commence an action or proceeding within 30 days after the placement to challenge the agency's placement. If the individual proves by a preponderance of the evidence that the minor has substantial emotional ties to the individual and that an adoptive placement of the minor with the individual would be in the best interest of the minor, the court shall place the minor with the individual.

Section 2-107. Interstate Placement.

An adoption in this State of a minor brought into this State from another State by a prospective adoptive parent, or by a person who places the minor for adoption in this State, is governed by the laws of this State including this [Act] and the Interstate Compact on the Placement of Children.

Section 2-108. Intercountry Placement.

An adoption in this State of a minor brought into this State from another country by a prospective adoptive parent, or by a person who places the minor for adoption in this State, is governed by this [Act], subject to any convention or treaty on intercountry adoption which the United States has ratified and any relevant federal law.

[PART] 4. CONSENT TO AND RELINQUISHMENT FOR ADOPTION

Section 2-401. Persons Whose Consent Required.

(a) Unless consent is not required or is dispensed with by Section 2-402, in a direct placement of a minor for adoption by a parent or guardian authorized under this [Act] to place the minor, a petition to adopt the minor may be granted only if consent to the adoption has been executed by:

(1) the woman who gave birth to the minor and the man, if any, who:

(i) is or has been married to the woman if the minor was born during the marriage or within 300 days after the marriage was terminated or a court issued a decree of separation;

(ii) attempted to marry the woman before the minor's birth by a marriage solemnized in apparent compliance with law, although the attempted marriage is or could be declared invalid, if the minor was born during the attempted marriage or within 300 days after the attempted marriage was terminated;

(iii) under applicable law, has been judicially determined to be the father of the minor, or has signed a document which has the effect of establishing his parentage of the minor, and;

(A) has provided, in accordance with his financial means, reasonable and consistent payments for the support of the minor and has visited or communicated with the minor; or

(B) after the minor's birth, but before the minor's placement for adoption, has married or attempted to marry the woman who gave birth to the minor by a marriage solemnized in apparent compliance with law, although the attempted marriage is or could be declared invalid; or

(iv) has received the minor into his home and openly held out the minor as his child;

(2) the minor's guardian if expressly authorized by a court to consent to the minor's adoption; or

(c) Unless the court dispenses with the minor's consent, a petition to adopt a minor who has attained 12 years of age may be granted only if, in addition to any consent required by subsections (a) and (b), the minor has executed an informed consent to the adoption.

Section 2-402. Persons Whose Consent Not Required.

(a) Consent to an adoption of a minor is not required of:

(1) an individual who has relinquished the minor to an agency for purposes of adoption;

(2) an individual whose parental relationship to a minor has been terminated or determined not to exist;

(3) a parent who has been judicially declared incompetent;

(4) a man who has not been married to the woman who gave birth to the minor and who, after the conception of the minor, executes a verified statement, denying paternity or disclaiming any interest in the minor and acknowledging that his statement shall be irrevocable when executed;

(5) the personal representative of a deceased parent's estate; or

(6) a parent or other person who has not executed a consent or a relinquishment and who fails to file an answer or an appearance in a proceeding for adoption or for termination of a parental relationship within the requisite time after service of notice of the proceeding.

(b) The court may dispense with the consent of:

(1) a guardian or an agency whose consent is otherwise required upon a finding that the consent is being withheld contrary to the best interest of a minor adoptee; or

(2) a minor adoptee who has attained 12 years of age upon a finding that it is not in the best interest of the minor to require the consent.

Section 2-403. Individuals Who May Relinquish Minor.

A parent or guardian whose consent to the adoption of a minor is required by Section 2-401 may relinquish to an agency all of that individual's rights with respect to the minor, including legal and physical custody and the right to consent to the minor's adoption.

Section 2-404. Time for Execution of Consent or Relinquishment.

(a) A parent whose consent to the adoption of a minor is required by Section 2-401 may execute a consent or a relinquishment only after the minor is born. A parent who executes a consent or relinquishment may revoke the consent or relinquishment within 192 hours after the birth of the minor.

(b) A guardian may execute a consent to the adoption of a minor or a relinquishment at any time after being authorized by a court to so do;

(c) An agency that places a minor for adoption may execute its consent at any time at or before the hearing on the petition for adoption.

(d) A minor adoptee whose consent is required may execute a consent at any time at or before the hearing on the petition for adoption.

(e) Before executing a consent or relinquishment, a parent must have been informed of the meaning and consequences of adoption, the availability of personal and legal counseling, the procedure for releasing information about the health and other characteristics of the parent which may affect the physical or psychological well-being of the adoptee, and the procedure for the consensual release of the parent's identity to an adoptee, an adoptee's direct descendant, or an adoptive parent pursuant to Article 6. The parent must have had an opportunity to indicate in a signed document whether and under what circumstances the parent is or is not willing to release identifying information, and must have been informed of the procedure for changing the document at a later time.

Section 2-405. Procedure for Execution of Consent or Relinquishment.

(a) A consent or relinquishment executed by a parent or guardian must be signed or confirmed in the presence of

(1) a judge of a court of record;

(2) an individual designated by a judge to take consents or relinquishments;

(3) an employee designated by an agency to take consents or relinquishments, but not an employee of an agency to which a minor is relinquished;

(4) a lawyer other than a lawyer who is representing an adoptive parent or the agency to which a minor is relinquished;

(5) a commissioned officer on active duty in the military service of the United States; if the individual executing the consent or relinquishment is in military service; or

(6) an officer of the foreign service or a consular officer of the United States in another country, if the individual executing the consent or relinquishment is in that country.

(b) A consent executed by a minor adoptee must be signed or confirmed in the presence of the court in the proceeding for adoption or in a manner the court directs.

(c) Minority of a parent does not affect competency to execute a consent or relinquishment, but a parent who is a minor must have had access to counseling and must have had the advice of a lawyer who is not representing an adoptive parent or the agency to which the parent's child is relinquished.

(d) An individual before whom a consent or relinquishment is signed or confirmed under subsection (a) shall certify in writing that he or she orally explained the contents and consequences of the consent or relinquishment, and to the best of his or her knowledge or belief, the individual executing the consent or relinquishment:

(1) read or was read the consent or relinquishment and understood it;

(2) signed the consent or relinquishment voluntarily;

(3) received or was offered a copy of the consent or relinquishment and the information described by Section 2404(e) and was afforded an opportunity to sign the document described in that section;

(4) was offered counseling services and information about adoption; and

(5) if the individual executing the consent or relinquishment is a parent who is a minor, was advised by a lawyer who is not representing an adoptive parent or the agency to which the parent's child is being relinquished, and, if an adult, was informed of the right to have a lawyer who is not representing an adoptive parent or an agency to which the parent's child is being relinquished.

(e) A prospective adoptive parent named or described in a consent to the adoption of a minor shall sign a statement indicating an intention to adopt the minor, acknowledging an obligation to return legal and physical custody of the minor to the minor's parent if the parent revokes the consent within the time specified in Section 2-404(a), and acknowledging responsibility for the minor's medical and other care and support if the consent is not revoked.

(f) An employee of an agency to which a minor child is being relinquished shall sign a statement indicating the agency's willingness to accept the relinquishment, acknowledging its obligation to return legal and physical custody of the child to the minor's parent if the parent revokes the relinquishment within the time indicated in Section 2-404(a), and acknowledging responsibility for the minor's medical and other care and support if the relinquishment is not revoked.

(g) An individual before whom a consent or a relinquishment is signed or confirmed shall certify that the statements required by subsections (e) and (f) were given to him or her.

(h) A consent by an agency to the adoption of a minor in the agency's legal custody must be executed by the executive head or another authorized employee and must be signed or confirmed under oath in the presence of an individual authorized to take acknowledgments.

(i) A consent or relinquishment executed and signed or confirmed in another State or in another country is valid if in accord with this [Act] or with the law and procedure of the State or country in which executed.

Section 2-407. Consequences of Consent or Relinquishment.

(a) Except under a circumstance stated in Section 2408, a consent to the adoption of a minor which is executed by a parent or guardian in substantial compliance with Sections 2-405 and 2-406 is final and irrevocable, and:

(1) unless a court orders otherwise to protect the welfare of the minor, entitles the prospective adoptive parent named or described in the consent to the legal and physical custody of the minor and imposes on that individual responsibility for the medical and other care and support of the minor;

(2) terminates any duty of a parent who executed the consent with respect to the minor, except for arrearages of child support; and

(3) terminates any right of a parent or guardian who executed the consent to object to the minor's adoption by the prospective adoptive parent and any right to notice of the proceeding for adoption unless the adoption is contested, appealed, or denied.

(b) Except under a circumstance stated in Section 2409, a relinquishment of a minor to an agency which is executed by a parent or guardian in substantial compliance with Sections 2-405 and 2-406 is final and irrevocable, and:

(1) unless a court orders otherwise to protect the welfare of the minor, entitles the agency to the legal custody of the minor until a decree of adoption becomes final;

(2) empowers the agency to place the minor for adoption, consent to the minor's adoption, and delegate to a prospective adoptive parent responsibility for the medical and other care and support of the minor;

(3) terminates any duty of the individual who executed the relinquishment with respect to the minor except for arrearages of child support; and

(4) terminates any right of the individual who executed the relinquishment to object to the minor's adoption and, unless otherwise provided in the relinquishment, any right to notice of the proceeding for adoption.

Section 2-408. Revocation of Consent.

(a) In a direct placement of a minor for adoption by a parent or guardian, a consent is revoked if:

(1) within 192 hours after the birth of the minor, a parent who executed the consent notifies in writing the prospective adoptive parent, or the adoptive parent's lawyer, that the parent revokes the consent, or the parent complies with any other instructions for revocation specified in the consent;

(2) the individual who executed the consent and the prospective adoptive parent named or described in the consent agree to its revocation.

(b) In a direct placement of a minor for adoption by a parent or guardian, the court shall set aside the consent if the individual who executed the consent establishes:

(1) by clear and convincing evidence, before a decree of adoption is issued, that the consent was obtained by fraud or duress;

(2) by a preponderance of the evidence that, without good cause shown, a petition to adopt was not filed within 60 days after the minor was placed for adoption; or

(3) by a preponderance of the evidence, that a condition permitting revocation has occurred, as expressly provided for in the consent pursuant to Section 2-406(f)(1) through (3).

(c) If the consent of an individual who had legal and physical custody of a minor when the minor was placed for adoption or the consent was executed is revoked under subsection (a)(1) or (2), the prospective adoptive parent shall immediately return the minor to that individual's custody and move to dismiss any proceeding for adoption or termination of the individual's parental relationship to the minor. If the minor is not returned immediately, the individual may petition the court named in the consent for appropriate relief. The court shall hear the petition expeditiously.

(d) If the consent of an individual who had legal and physical custody of a minor when the minor was placed for adoption or the consent was executed is set aside under subsection (b)(1), the court shall order the return of the minor to the custody of the individual and dismiss a pending proceeding for adoption.

(e) If the consent of an individual who had legal and physical custody of a minor when the minor was placed for adoption or the consent was executed is set aside under subsection (b)(2) or (3) and no ground exists under Article 3, Part 5, for terminating the parental relationship between the individual and the minor, the court shall dismiss a pending proceeding for adoption and order the return of the minor to the custody of the individual, unless the court finds that return will be detrimental to the minor.

(f) If the consent of an individual who did not have physical custody of a minor when the minor was placed for adoption or the consent was executed is revoked under subsection (a) or set aside under subsection (b) and no ground exists under Article 3, Part 5, for terminating the parental relationship between the individual and the minor, the court shall dismiss a

Appendix. Statutes and Uniform Acts

pending proceeding for adoption and issue an order providing for the care and custody of the minor according to the best interest of the minor.

[PART] 4. NOTICE OF PENDENCY OF PROCEEDING

Section 3-401. Service of Notice.

(a) Unless notice has been waived, notice of a proceeding for adoption of a minor must be served, within 20 days after a petition for adoption is filed, upon:

(1) an individual whose consent to the adoption is required under Section 2-401, but notice need not be served upon an individual whose parental relationship to the minor or whose status as a guardian has been terminated;

(2) an agency whose consent to the adoption is required under Section 2-401;

(3) an individual who the petitioner knows is claiming to be or who is named as the father or possible father of the minor adoptee and whose paternity of the minor has not been judicially determined, but notice need not be served upon a man who has executed a verified statement, as described in Section 2-402(a)(4), denying paternity or disclaiming any interest in the minor;

(4) an individual other than the petitioner who has legal or physical custody of the minor adoptee or who has a right of visitation with the minor under an existing court order issued by a court in this or another State;

(5) the spouse of the petitioner if the spouse has not joined in the petition; and

(6) a grandparent of a minor adoptee if the grandparent's child is a deceased parent of the minor and before death, the deceased parent had not executed a consent or relinquishment or the deceased parent's parental relationship to the minor had not been terminated.

(b) The court shall require notice of a proceeding for adoption of a minor to be served upon any person the court finds, at any time during the proceeding, is:

(1) a person described in subsection (a) who has not been given notice;

(2) an individual who has revoked a consent or relinquishment pursuant to Section 2-408(a) or 2-409(a) or is attempting to have a consent or relinquishment set aside pursuant to Section 2-408(b) or 2-409(b); or

(3) a person who, on the basis of a previous relationship with the minor adoptee, a parent, an alleged parent, or the petitioner, can provide information that is relevant to the proposed adoption and that the court in its discretion wants to hear.

Section 3-404. Investigation and Notice to Unknown Father.

(a) If, at any time in a proceeding for adoption or for termination of a relationship of parent and child under Part 5, the court finds that an unknown father of a minor adoptee may not have received notice, the court shall determine whether he can be identified. The determination must be based on evidence that includes inquiry of appropriate persons in an effort to identify an unknown father for the purpose of providing notice.

(b) The inquiry required by subsection (a) must include whether:

(1) the woman who gave birth to the minor adoptee was married at the probable time of conception of the minor, or at a later time;

(2) the woman was cohabiting with a man at the probable time of conception of the minor;

(3) the woman has received payments or promises of support, other than from a governmental agency, with respect to the minor or because of her pregnancy;

(4) the woman has named any individual as the father on the birth certificate of the minor or in connection with applying for or receiving public assistance; and

(5) any individual has formally or informally acknowledged or claimed paternity of the minor in a jurisdiction in which the woman resided during or since her pregnancy, or in which the minor has resided or resides, at the time of the inquiry.

(c) If inquiry pursuant to subsection (b) identifies as the father of the minor an individual who has not received notice of the proceeding, the court shall require notice to be served upon him pursuant to Section 3-403, unless service is not possible because his whereabouts are unknown.

(d) If, after inquiry pursuant to subsection (b), the court finds that personal service cannot be made upon the father of the minor because his identity or whereabouts is unknown, the court shall order publication or public posting of the notice only if, on the basis of all information available, the court determines that publication or posting is likely to lead to receipt of notice by the father. If the court determines that publication or posting is not likely to lead to receipt of notice, the court may dispense with the publication or posting of a notice.

(e) If, in an inquiry pursuant to this section, the woman who gave birth to the minor adoptee fails to disclose the identity of a possible father or reveal his whereabouts, she must be advised that the proceeding for adoption may be delayed or subject to challenge if a possible father is not given notice of the proceeding and that the lack of information about the father's medical and genetic history may be detrimental to the adoptee.

[PART] 5. PETITION TO TERMINATE RELATIONSHIP BETWEEN PARENT AND CHILD

A petition to terminate the relationship between a parent or an alleged parent and a minor child may be filed in a proceeding for adoption under this [Act] by:

(1) a parent or a guardian who has selected a prospective adoptive parent for a minor and who intends to place, or has placed, the minor with that individual;

(2) a parent whose spouse has filed a petition under Article 4 to adopt the parent's minor child;

(3) a prospective adoptive parent of the minor who has filed a petition to adopt under this Article or Article 4; or

(4) an agency that has selected a prospective adoptive parent for the minor and intends to place, or has placed, the minor with that individual.

Section 3-503. Service of Petition and Notice.

(a) A petition to terminate under this Part and a notice of hearing on the petition must be served upon the respondent, with notice of the proceeding for adoption, in the manner prescribed in Sections 3-403 and 3-404.

(b) The notice of the hearing must inform the respondent of the method for responding and that:

(1) the respondent has a right to be represented by a lawyer, and may be entitled to have a lawyer appointed by the court; and

(2) failure to respond within 20 days after service, and, in the case of an alleged father, failure to file a claim of paternity within 20 days after service, unless a claim of paternity is pending, will result in termination of the relationship of parent and child between the respondent and the minor, unless the proceeding for adoption is dismissed.

Section 3-504. Grounds for Terminating Relationship.

(a) If the respondent is served with a petition to terminate under this Part and the accompanying notice and does not respond, and, in the case of an alleged father, file a claim of paternity within 20 days after the service, unless a claim of paternity is pending, the court shall order the termination of any relationship of parent and child between the respondent and the minor unless the proceeding for adoption is dismissed.

(b) If under Section 3-404, the court dispenses with service of the petition upon the respondent, the court shall order the termination of any relationship of parent and child between the respondent and the minor unless the proceeding for adoption is dismissed.

(c) If the respondent asserts parental rights, the court shall proceed with the hearing expeditiously and may order the termination of any relationship of parent and child between the respondent and the minor upon finding, upon clear and convincing evidence, that one of the following grounds exists and, by a preponderance of the evidence, that termination is in the best interest of the minor.

(1) in the case of a minor who has not attained six months of age at the time the petition for adoption is filed, unless the respondent proves by a preponderance of the evidence a compelling reason for not complying with this paragraph, the respondent has failed to:

(i) pay reasonable prenatal, natal, and postnatal expenses in accordance with the respondent's financial means;

(ii) make reasonable and consistent payments, in accordance with the respondent's financial means, for the support of the minor;

(iii) visit regularly with the minor; and

(iv) manifest an ability and willingness to assume legal and physical custody of the minor, if, during this time, the minor was not in the physical custody of the other parent;

(2) in the case of a minor who has attained six months of age at the time a petition for adoption is filed, unless the respondent proves by a preponderance of the evidence a compelling reason for not complying with this paragraph, the respondent, for a period of at least six consecutive months immediately preceding the filing of the petition has failed to:

(i) make reasonable and consistent payments, in accordance with the respondent's means, for the support of the minor;

(ii) communicate or visit regularly with the minor; and

(iii) manifest an ability and willingness to assume legal and physical custody of the minor, if, during this time, the minor was not in the physical custody of the other parent;

(3) the respondent has been convicted of a crime of violence or of violating a restraining or protective order, and the facts of the crime or violation and the respondent's behavior indicate that the respondent is unfit to maintain a relationship of parent and child with the minor;

(4) the respondent is a man who was not married to the minor's mother when the minor was conceived or born and is not the biological or adoptive father of the minor; or

(5) termination is justified on a ground specified in [the State's statute for involuntary termination of parental rights].

(d) If the respondent proves by a preponderance of the evidence that he or she had a compelling reason for not complying with the requirements of subsection (c)(1) or (2) and termination is not justified on a ground stated in subsection (c)(3) through (5), the court may terminate the respondent's parental relationship to a minor only upon a finding, upon clear and convincing evidence, that one of the following grounds exists and, by a preponderance of the evidence that termination is in the best interest of the minor:

(1) if the minor is not in the legal and physical custody of the other parent, the respondent is not able or willing promptly to assume legal and physical custody of the minor, and to pay for the minor's support, in accordance with the respondent's financial means;

(2) if the minor is in the legal and physical custody of the other parent and a stepparent, and the stepparent is the prospective adoptive parent, the respondent is not able or willing promptly to establish and maintain contact with the minor and to pay for the minor's support, in accordance with the respondent's financial means;

(3) placing the minor in the respondent's legal and physical custody would pose a risk of substantial harm to the physical or psychological well-being of the minor because the circumstances of the minor's conception, the respondent's behavior during the mother's pregnancy or since the minor's birth, or the respondent's behavior with respect to other minors, indicates that the respondent is unfit to maintain a relationship of parent and child with the minor; or

(4) failure to terminate would be detrimental to the minor.

(e) In determining whether to terminate under subsection (d)(4), the court shall consider any relevant factor, including the respondent's efforts to obtain or maintain legal and physical custody of the minor, the role of other persons in thwarting the respondent's efforts to assert parental rights, the respondent's ability to care for the minor, the age of the minor, the quality of any previous relationship between the respondent and the minor and between the respondent and any other minor children, the duration and suitability of the minor's present custodial environment, and the effect of a change of physical custody on the minor.

Section 3-505. Effect of Order Granting Petition.
An order issued under this Part granting the petition:

(1) terminates the relationship of parent and child between the respondent and the minor, except for arrearages of child support;

(2) extinguishes any right the respondent had to withhold consent to a proposed adoption of the minor or to further notice of a proceeding for adoption; and

(3) is a final order for purposes of appeal.

Section 3-506. Effect of Order Denying Petition.

(a) If the court denies the petition to terminate a relationship of parent and child, the court shall dismiss the proceeding for adoption and shall determine the legal and physical custody of the minor according to the criteria stated in Section 3-704.

(b) An order issued under this Part denying a petition to terminate a relationship of parent and child is a final order for purposes of appeal.

[PART] 7. DISPOSITIONAL HEARING; DECREE OF ADOPTION

Section 3-703. Granting Petition for Adoption.

(a) A court shall grant a petition for adoption if it determines that the adoption will be in the best interest of the minor, and that:

(1) at least 90 days have elapsed since the filing of the petition for adoption unless the court for good cause shown waives this requirement;

(2) the adoptee has been in the physical custody of the petitioner for at least 90 days unless the court for good cause shown waives this requirement;

(3) notice of the proceeding for adoption has been served or dispensed with as to any person entitled to receive notice under Part 4;

(4) every necessary consent, relinquishment, waiver, disclaimer of paternal interest, or judicial order terminating parental rights, including an order issued under Part 5, has been obtained and filed with the court;

(5) any evaluation required by this [Act] has been filed with and considered by the court;

(6) the petitioner is a suitable adoptive parent for the minor;

(7) if applicable, any requirement of this [Act] governing an interstate or intercountry placement for adoption has been met;

(8) the Indian Child Welfare Act, 25 U.S.C. §§1901 et seq., is not applicable to the proceeding or, if applicable, its requirements have been met;

(9) an accounting and affidavit required by Section 3-702 has been reviewed by the court, and the court has denied, modified, or ordered reimbursement of any payment or disbursement that is not authorized by Article 7 or is unreasonable or unnecessary when compared with the expenses customarily incurred in connection with an adoption;

(10) the petitioner has received each report required by Section 2-106; and

(11) any document signed pursuant to Section 2404(e) concerning the release of a former parent's identity to the adoptee after the adoptee attains 18 years has been filed with the court.

(b) Notwithstanding a finding by the court that an activity prohibited by Article 7 or another section of this [Act] has occurred, if the court makes the determinations required by subsection (a), the court shall grant the petition for adoption and report the violation to the appropriate authorities.

(c) Except as otherwise provided in Article 4, the court shall inform the petitioner and any other individual affected by an existing order for visitation or communication with the minor adoptee that the decree of adoption terminates any existing order for visitation or communication. . . .

Section 3-705. Decree of Adoption.

(a) A decree of adoption must state or contain:

(1) the original name of the minor adoptee, if the adoption is by a stepparent or relative and, in all other adoptions, the original name or a pseudonym;

(2) the name of the petitioner for adoption;

(3) whether the petitioner is married or unmarried;

(4) whether the petitioner is a stepparent of the adoptee;

(5) the name by which the adoptee is to be known and when the name takes effect;

(6) information to be incorporated into a new birth certificate to be issued by the State [Registrar of Vital Records], unless the petitioner or an adoptee who has attained 12 years of age requests that a new certificate not be issued;

(7) the adoptee's date and place of birth, if known, or in the case of an adoptee born outside the United States, as determined pursuant to subsection (b);

(8) the effect of the decree of adoption as stated in Sections 1-104 through 1-106; and

(9) that the adoption is in the best interest of the adoptee.

(b) In determining the date and place of birth of an adoptee born outside the United States, the court shall:

(1) enter the date and place of birth as stated in the birth certificate from the country of origin, the United States Department of State's report of birth abroad, or the documents of the United States Immigration and Naturalization Service;

(2) if the exact place of birth is unknown, enter the information that is known and designate a place of birth according to the best information known with respect to the country of origin;

(3) if the exact date of birth in unknown, determine a date of birth based upon medical evidence as to the probable age of the adoptee and other evidence the court considers appropriate; and

(4) if documents described in paragraph (1) are not available, determine the date and place of birth based upon evidence the court finds appropriate to consider.

(c) Unless a petitioner requests otherwise, the decree of adoption may not name a former parent of the adoptee.

(d) Except for a decree of adoption of a minor by a stepparent which is issued pursuant to Article 4, a decree of adoption of a minor must contain a statement that the adoption terminates any order for visitation or communication with the minor that was in effect before the decree is issued.

(e) A decree that substantially complies with the requirements of this section is not subject to challenge solely because one or more items required by this section are not contained in the decree.

Section 3-706. Finality of Decree.

A decree of adoption is a final order for purposes of appeal when it is issued and becomes final for other purposes upon the expiration of the time for filing an appeal, if no appeal is filed, or upon the denial or dismissal of any appeal filed within the requisite time.

Section 3-707. Challenges to Decree.

(a) An appeal from a decree of adoption or other appealable order issued under this [Act] must be heard expeditiously.

(b) A decree or order issued under this [Act] may not be vacated or annulled upon application of a person who waived notice, or who was properly served with notice pursuant to this [Act] and failed to respond or appear, file an answer, or file a claim of paternity within the time allowed.

(c) The validity of an adoption may not be challenged for failure to comply with an agreement for visitation or communication with an adoptee.

(d) A decree of adoption or other order issued under this [Act] is not subject to a challenge begun more than six months after the decree or order is issued. If a challenge is brought by an individual whose parental relationship to an adoptee is terminated by a decree or order under this [Act], the court shall deny the challenge, unless the court finds by clear and convincing evidence that the decree or order is not in the best interest of the adoptee. . . .

ARTICLE 4. ADOPTION OF MINOR STEPCHILD BY STEPPARENT

Section 4-101. Other Provisions Applicable to Adoption of Stepchild.

Except as otherwise provided by this [article], [Article] 3 applies to an adoption of a minor stepchild by a stepparent.

Section 4-102. Standing to Adopt Minor Stepchild.

(a) A stepparent has standing under this Article to petition to adopt a minor stepchild who is the child of the stepparent's spouse if:

(1) the spouse has sole legal and physical custody of the child and the child has been in the physical custody of the spouse and the stepparent during the 60 days next preceding the filing of a petition for adoption;

(2) the spouse has joint legal custody of the child with the child's other parent and the child has resided primarily with the spouse and the stepparent during the 12 months next preceding the filing of the petition;

(3) the spouse is deceased or mentally incompetent, but before dying or being judicially declared mentally incompetent, had legal and physical custody of the child, and the child has resided primarily with the stepparent during the 12 months next preceding the filing of the petition; or

(4) an agency placed the minor stepchild with the stepparent pursuant to Section 2-104.

(b) For good cause shown, a court may allow an individual who does not meet the requirements of paragraphs (a)(1) through (4), but has the consent of the custodial parent of a minor to file a petition for adoption under this Article. A petition allowed under this subsection shall be treated as a petition for adoption by a stepparent.

(c) A petition for adoption by a stepparent may be joined with a petition under Article 3, Part 5, to terminate the parental relationship between the minor adoptee and the adoptee's parent who is not the stepparent's spouse.

Section 4-103. Legal Consequences of Adoption of Stepchild.

(a) Except as otherwise provided in subsections (b) and (c), the legal consequences of an adoption of a stepchild by a stepparent are the same as under Sections 1-103 through 1-106.

(b) An adoption by a stepparent does not affect:

(1) the relationship between the adoptee and the adoptee's parent who is the adoptive stepparent's spouse or deceased spouse;

(2) an existing court order for visitation or communication with a minor adoptee by an individual related to the adoptee through the parent who is the adoptive stepparent's spouse or deceased spouse;

(3) the right of the adoptee or a descendant of the adoptee to inheritance or intestate succession through or from the adoptee's former parent; or

(4) a court order or agreement for visitation or communication with a minor adoptee approved by the court pursuant to Section 4-113.

(c) Failure to comply with an agreement or order is not a ground for challenging the validity of the adoption.

Section 4-104. Consent to Adoption.

Unless consent is not required under Section 2-402, a petition to adopt a minor stepchild may be granted only if consent to the adoption has been executed by a stepchild who has attained 12 years of age; and

(1) the minor's parents as described in Section 2401(a);

(2) the minor's guardian if expressly authorized by a court to consent to the minor's adoption; or

(3) an agency that placed the minor for adoption by the stepparent. . . .

Section 4-110. Notice of Pendency of Proceeding.

(a) Within 30 days after a petition to adopt a minor stepchild is filed, the petitioner shall serve notice of the proceeding upon

(1) the petitioner's spouse;

(2) any other person whose consent to the adoption is required under this Article;

(3) any person described in Section 3-401(a)(3), (4), and (6) and (b); and

(4) the parents of the minor's parent whose parental relationship will be terminated by the adop-

tion unless the identity or the whereabouts of those parents are unknown. . . .

Section 4-112. Dispositional Hearing: Decree of Adoption.

Sections 3-701 through 3-707 apply to a proceeding for adoption of a minor stepchild by a stepparent, but the court may waive the requirements of Section 3-702.

[ARTICLE] 5. ADOPTION OF ADULTS AND EMANCIPATED MINORS

Section 5-101. Who May Adopt Adult or Emancipated Minor.

(a) An adult may adopt another adult or an emancipated minor pursuant to this Article, but:

(1) an adult may not adopt his or her spouse; and

(2) an incompetent individual of any age may be adopted only pursuant to Articles 2, 3 and 4.

(b) An individual who has adopted an adult or emancipated minor may not adopt another adult or emancipated minor within one year after the adoption unless the prospective adoptee is a sibling of the existing adoptee.

Section 5-102. Legal Consequences of Adoption

The legal consequences of an adoption of an adult or emancipated minor are the same as under Sections 1-103 through 1-106, but the legal consequences of adoption of an adult stepchild by an adult stepparent are the same as under Section 4-103.

Section 5-103. Consent to Adoption.

(a) Consent to the adoption of an adult or emancipated minor is required only of:

(1) the adoptee;

(2) the prospective adoptive parent; and

(3) the spouse of the prospective adoptive parent, unless they are legally separated, or the court finds that the spouse is not capable of giving consent or is withholding consent contrary to the best interest of the adoptee and the prospective adoptive parent.

(b) The consent of the adoptee and the prospective adoptive parent must:

(1) be in writing and be signed or confirmed by each of them in the presence of the court or an individual authorized to take acknowledgments;

(2) state that they agree to assume toward each other the legal relationship of parent and child and to have all of the rights and be subject to all of the duties of that relationship; and

(3) state that they understand the consequences the adoption may have for any right of inheritance, property, or support each has.

(c) The consent of the spouse of the prospective adoptive parent:

(1) must be in writing and be signed or confirmed in the presence of the court or an individual authorized to take acknowledgments;

(2) must state that the spouse:

(i) consents to the proposed adoption; and

(ii) understands the consequences the adoption may have for any right of inheritance, property, or support the spouse has; and

(3) may waive notice of the adoption proceeding.

[ARTICLE] 7. PROHIBITED AND PERMISSIBLE ACTIVITIES IN CONNECTION WITH ADOPTION

Section 7-101. Prohibited Activities in Placement.

(a) Except as provided in Article 2, Part 1:

(1) a person, other than a parent, guardian, or agency, as specified in Sections 2-101 through 2-103, may not place a minor for adoption or advertise in any public medium that the person knows of a minor who is available for adoption;

(2) a person, other than an agency or an individual with a favorable preplacement evaluation, as required by Section 2-201 through 2-207, may not advertise in any public medium that the person is willing to accept a minor for adoption;

(3) an individual, other than a relative or stepparent of a minor, who does not have a favorable preplacement evaluation or a court-ordered waiver of the evaluation, or who has an unfavorable evaluation, may not obtain legal or physical custody of a minor for purposes of adoption; and

(4) a person may not place or assist in placing a minor for adoption with an individual, other than a relative or stepparent, unless the person knows that the individual has a favorable preplacement evaluation or a waiver pursuant to Section 2-201.

(b) A person who violates subsection (a) is liable for a [civil penalty] not to exceed [$5,000] for the first violation, and not to exceed [$10,000] for each succeeding violation in an action brought by the [appropriate official]. The court may enjoin from further violations any person who violates subsection (a) and shall refer the person to an appropriate licensing authority for disciplinary proceedings.

Interstate Compact on the Placement of Children (1961)
Council of State Governments, Suggested State Legislation 49 (1961)

ARTICLE I—PURPOSE AND POLICY

It is the purpose and policy of the party states to cooperate with each other in the interstate placement of children to the end that:

(a) Each child requiring placement shall receive the maximum opportunity to be placed in a suitable environment and with persons or institutions having appropriate qualifications and facilities to provide a necessary and desirable degree and type of care.

(b) The appropriate authorities in a state where a child is to be placed may have full opportunity to ascertain the circumstances of the proposed placement, thereby promoting full compliance with applicable requirements for the protection of the child.

(c) The proper authorities of the state from which the placement is made may obtain the most complete information on the basis of which to evaluate a projected placement before it is made.

(d) Appropriate jurisdictional arrangements for the care of children will be promoted.

Article II—Definitions

As used in this compact:

(a) "Child" means a person who, by reason of minority, is legally subject to parental, guardianship, or similar control.

(b) "Sending agency" means a party state, or officer or employee thereof; a subdivision of a party state, or officer or employee thereof; a court of a party state; a person, corporation, association, charitable agency, or other entity which sends, brings, or causes to be sent or brought any child to another party state.

(c) "receiving state" means the state to which a child is sent, brought, or caused to be sent or brought, whether by public authorities or private persons or agencies, and whether for placement with state or local public authorities or for placement with private agencies or persons.

(d) "Placement" means the arrangement for the care of a child in a family free or boarding home or in a child-caring agency or institution but does not include any institution caring for the mentally ill, mentally defective, or epileptic or any institution primarily educational in character, and any hospital or other medical facility.

Article III—Conditions for Placement

(1) No sending agency shall send, bring, or cause to be sent or brought into any other party state any child for placement in foster care or as a preliminary to a possible adoption unless the sending agency shall comply with each and every requirement set forth in this article and with the applicable laws of the receiving state governing the placement of children therein.

(2) Prior to sending, bringing, or causing any child to be sent or brought into a receiving state for placement in foster care or as a preliminary to a possible adoption, the sending agency shall furnish the appropriate public authorities in the receiving state written notice of the intention to send, bring, or place the child in the receiving state. The notice shall contain:

(a) The name, date, and place of birth of the child.

(b) The identity and address or addresses of the parents or legal guardian.

(c) The name and address of the person, agency, or institution to or with which the sending agency proposes to send, bring, or place the child.

(d) A full statement of the reasons for such proposed action and evidence of the authority pursuant to which the placement is proposed to be made.

(3) Any public officer or agency in a receiving state which is in receipt of a notice pursuant to subsection (2) of this article may request of the sending agency, or any other appropriate officer or agency of or in the sending agency's state, and shall be entitled to receive therefrom, such supporting or additional information as it may deem necessary under the circumstances to carry out the purpose and policy of this compact.

(4) The child shall not be sent, brought, or caused to be sent or brought into the receiving state until the appropriate public authorities in the receiving state shall notify the sending agency, in writing, to the effect that the proposed placement does not appear to be contrary to the interests of the child.

Article IV—Penalty for Illegal Placement

The sending, bringing, or causing to be sent or brought into any receiving state of a child in violation of the terms of this compact shall constitute a violation of the laws respecting the placement of children of both the state in which the sending agency is located or from which it sends or brings the child and of the receiving state. Such violation may be punished or subjected to penalty in either jurisdiction in accordance with its laws. In addition to liability for any such punishment or penalty, any such violation shall constitute full and sufficient grounds for the suspension or revocation of any license, permit, or other legal authorization held by the sending agency which empowers or allows it to place, or care for children.

Article V—Retention of Jurisdiction

(1) the sending agency shall retain jurisdiction over the child sufficient to determine all matters in relation to the custody, supervision, care, treatment, and disposition of the child which it would have had if the child had remained in the sending agency's state, until the child is adopted, reaches majority, becomes self-supporting, or is discharged with the concurrence of the appropriate authority in the receiving state. Such jurisdiction shall also include the power to effect or cause the return of the child or its transfer to another location and custody pursuant to law. The sending agency shall continue to have financial responsibility for support and maintenance of the child during the period of the placement. Nothing contained herein shall defeat a claim of jurisdiction by a receiving state sufficient to deal with an act of delinquency or crime committed therein.

(2) When the sending agency is a public agency, it may enter into an agreement with an authorized public or private agency in the receiving state providing for the performance of 1 or more services in respect of such case by the latter as agent for the sending agency.

(3) Nothing in this compact shall be construed to prevent a private charitable agency authorized to place children in the receiving state from performing services or acting as agent in that state for a private charitable agency of the sending state; nor to prevent the agency in the receiving state from discharging financial responsibility for the support and maintenance of a child who has been placed on behalf of the sending agency without relieving the responsibility set forth in subsection (1) of this article.

Article VI—Institutional Care of Delinquent Children

A child adjudicated delinquent may be placed in an institution in another party jurisdiction pursuant to this compact but no such placement shall be made unless the child is given a court hearing on notice to the parent or guardian with opportunity to be heard, prior to his or her being sent to such other party jurisdiction for institutional care and the court finds that:

(a) Equivalent facilities for the child are not available in the sending agency's jurisdiction; and

(b) Institutional care in the other jurisdiction is in the best interest of the child and will not produce undue hardship.

Article VII—Compact Administrator

The executive head of each jurisdiction party to this compact shall designate an officer who shall be general coordinator of activities under this compact in the officer's jurisdiction and who, acting jointly with like officers of other party jurisdictions, shall have power to promulgate rules and regulations to carry out more effectively the terms and provisions of this compact.

ARTICLE VIII—LIMITATIONS

This compact shall not apply to:

(a) The sending or bringing of a child into a receiving state by the child's parent, stepparent, grandparent, adult brother or sister, adult uncle or aunt, or the child's guardian and leaving the child with any such relative or nonagency guardian in the receiving state.

(b) Any placement, sending, or bringing of a child into a receiving state pursuant to any other interstate compact to which both the state from which the child is sent or brought and the receiving state are party, or to any other agreement between said states which has the force of law.

The Indian Child Welfare Act
Subchapter I—Child Custody Proceedings
25 U.S.C.A. Sections 1911 et seq.

Section 1911. Indian Tribe Jurisdiction over Indian Child Custody Proceedings.

(a) Exclusive jurisdiction. An Indian tribe shall have jurisdiction exclusive as to any State over any child custody proceeding involving an Indian child who resides or is domiciled within the reservation of such tribe, except where such jurisdiction is otherwise vested in the State by existing Federal law. Where an Indian child is a ward of a tribal court, the Indian tribe shall retain exclusive jurisdiction, notwithstanding the residence or domicile of the child.

(b) Transfer of proceedings; declination by tribal court. In any State court proceeding for the foster care placement of, or termination of parental rights to, an Indian child not domiciled or residing within the reservation of the Indian child's tribe, the court, in the absence of good cause to the contrary, shall transfer such proceeding to the jurisdiction of the tribe, absent objection by either parent, upon the petition of either parent or the Indian custodian or the Indian child's tribe: Provided, That such transfer shall be subject to declination by the tribal court of such tribe.

(c) State court proceedings; intervention. In any state court proceeding for the foster care placement of, or termination of parental rights to, an Indian child, the Indian custodian of the child and the Indian child's tribe shall have a right to intervene at any point in the proceeding.

(d) Full faith and credit to public acts, records, and judicial proceedings of Indian tribes. The United States, every State, every territory or possession of the United States, and every Indian tribe shall give full faith and credit to the public acts, records, and judicial proceedings of any Indian tribe applicable to Indian child custody proceedings to the same extent that such entities give full faith and credit to the public acts, records, and judicial proceedings of any other entity.

Section 1912. Pending Court Proceedings.

(a) Notice; time for commencement of proceedings; additional time for preparation. In any involuntary proceeding in a State court, where the court knows or has reason to know that an Indian child is involved, the party seeking the foster care placement of, or termination of parental rights to, an Indian child shall notify the parent or Indian custodian and the Indian child's tribe, by registered mail with return receipt requested, of the pending proceedings and of their right of intervention. If the identity or location of the parent or Indian custodian and the tribe cannot be determined, such notice shall be given to the Secretary in like manner, who shall have fifteen days after receipt to provide the requisite notice to the parent or Indian custodian and the tribe. No foster care placement or termination of parental rights proceeding shall be held until at least ten days after receipt of notice by the parent or Indian custodian and the tribe or the Secretary: Provided, That the parent or Indian custodian or the tribe shall, upon request, be granted up to twenty additional days to prepare for such proceeding.

(b) Appointment of counsel. In any case in which the court determines indigence, the parent or Indian custodian shall have the right to court-appointed counsel in any removal, placement, or termination proceeding. The court may, in its discretion, appoint counsel for the child upon a finding that such appointment is in the best interests of the child. Where State law makes no provision for appointment of counsel in such proceedings, the court shall promptly notify the Secretary upon appointment of counsel, and the Secretary, upon certification of the presiding judge, shall pay reasonable fees and expenses out of funds which may be appropriated pursuant to section 13 of this title.

(c) Examination of reports or other documents. Each party to a foster care placement or termination of parental rights proceeding under State law involving an Indian child shall have the right to examine all reports or other documents filed with the court upon which any decision with respect to such action may be based.

(d) Remedial services and rehabilitative programs; preventive measures. Any party seeking to effect a foster care placement of, or termination of parental rights to, an Indian child under State law shall satisfy the court that active efforts have been made to provide remedial services and rehabilitative programs designed to prevent the breakup of the Indian family and that these efforts have proved unsuccessful.

(e) Foster care placement orders; evidence; determination of damage to child. No foster care placement may be ordered in such proceeding in the absence of a determination, supported by clear and convincing evidence, including testimony of qualified expert witnesses, that the continued custody of the child by the parent or Indian custodian is likely to result in serious emotional or physical damage to the child.

(f) Parental rights termination orders; evidence; determination of damage to child. No termination of parental rights may be ordered in such proceeding in the absence of a determination, supported by evidence beyond a reasonable doubt, including testimony of qualified expert witnesses, that the continued custody of the child by the parent or Indian custodiam is likely to result in serious emotional or physical damage to the child.

Section 1913. Parental Rights, Voluntary Termination.

(a) Consent; record; certification matters; invalid consents. Where any parent or Indian custodian voluntarily consents to a foster care placement or to termination of parental rights, such consent shall not be valid unless executed in writing and recorded before a judge of a court of competent jurisdiction and accompanied by the presiding judge's certificate that the terms and consequences of the consent were fully explained in detail and were fully understood by the parent or Indian custodian. The court shall also certify that either the parent or Indian custodian fully understood the explanation in English or that it was interpreted into a language that the parent or Indian custodian understood. Any consent given prior to, or within ten days after birth of the Indian child shall not be valid.

(b) Foster care placement, withdrawal of consent. Any parent or Indian custodian may withdraw consent to a foster care placement under State law at any time and, upon such withdrawal, the child shall be returned to the parent or Indian custodian.

(c) Voluntary termination of parental rights or adoptive placement; withdrawal of consent; return of custody. In any voluntary proceeding for termination of parental rights to, or adoptive placement of, an Indian child, the consent of the parent may be withdrawn for any reason at any time prior to the entry of a final decree of termination or adoption, as the case may be, and the child shall be returned to the parent.

(d) Collateral attack; vacation of decree and return of custody; limitations. After the entry of a final decree of adoption of an Indian child in any State court, the parent may withdraw consent thereto upon the grounds that consent was obtained through fraud or duress and may petition the court to vacate such decree. Upon a finding that such consent was obtained through fraud or duress, the court shall vacate such decree and return the child to the parent. No adoption which has been effective for at least two years may be invalidated under the provisions of this subsection unless otherwise permitted under State law.

Section 1914. Petition to Court of Competent Jurisdiction to Invalidate Action Upon Showing of Certain Violations.

Any Indian child who is the subject of any action for foster care placement or termination of parental rights under State law, any parent or Indian custodian from whose custody such child was removed, and the Indian child's tribe may petition any court of competent jurisdiction to invalidate such action upon a showing that such action violated any provision of sections 1911, 1912, and 1913 of this title.

Section 1915. Placement of Indian Children.

(a) Adoptive placements; preferences. In any adoptive placement of an Indian child under State law, a preference shall be given, in absence of good cause to the contrary, to a placement with (1) a member of the child's extended family; 2) other members of the Indian child's tribe; or (3) other Indian families.

(b) Foster care of preadoptive placements, criteria; preferences. Any child accepted for foster care or preadoptive placement shall be placed in the least restrictive setting which most approximates a family and in which his special needs, if any, may be met. The child shall also be placed within reasonable proximity to his or her home, taking into account any special needs of the child. In any foster care or preadoptive placement, a preference shall be given, in the absence of good cause to the contrary, to a placement with—

(i) a member of the Indian child's extended family;

(ii) a foster home licensed, approved, or specified by the Indian child's tribe;

(iii) an Indian foster home licensed or approved by an authorized non-Indian licensing authority; or

(iv) an institution for children approved by an Indian tribe or operated by an Indian organization which has a program suitable to meet the Indian child's needs.

(c) Tribal resolution for different order of preference; personal preference considered; anonymity in application of preferences. In the case of a placement under subsection (a) or (b) of this section, if the Indian child's tribe shall establish a different order of preference by resolution, the agency or court effecting the placement shall follow such order so long as the placement is the least restrictive setting appropriate to the particular needs of the child, as provided in subsection (b) of this section. Where appropriate, the preference of the Indian child or parent shall be considered: Provided, That where a consenting parent evidences a desire for anonymity, the court or agency shall give weight to such desire in applying the preferences.

(d) Social and cultural standards applicable. The standards to be applied in meeting the preference requirements of this section shall be the prevailing social and cultural standards of the Indian community in which the parent or extended family resides or with which the parent or extended family members maintain social and cultural ties.

(e) Record of placement; availability. A record of each such placement, under State law, of an Indian child shall be maintained by the State in which the placement was made, evidencing the efforts to comply with the order of preference specified in this section. Such record shall be made available at any time upon the request of the Secretary or the Indian child's tribe.

Section 1916. Return of Custody

(a) Petition; best interests of child. Notwithstanding State law to the contrary, whenever a final decree of adoption of an Indian child has been vacated or set aside or the adoptive parents voluntarily consent to the termination of their parental rights to the child, a biological parent or prior Indian custodian may petition for return of custody and the court shall grant such petition unless there is a showing, in a proceeding subject to the provisions of section 1912 of this title, that such return of custody is not in the best interests of the child.

(b) Removal from foster care home; placement procedure. Whenever an Indian child is removed from a foster care home or institution for the purpose of further foster care, preadoptive, or adoptive placement, such placement shall be in accordance with the provisions of this chapter, except in the case where an Indian child is being returned to the parent or Indian custodian from whose custody the child was originally removed.

Section 1920. Improper Removal of Child from Custody; Declination of Jurisdiction; Forthwith Return of Child: Danger Exception.

Where any petitioner in an Indian child custody proceeding before a State court has improperly removed the child from custody of the parent or Indian custodian or has improperly retained custody after a visit or other temporary relinquishment of custody, the court shall decline jurisdiction over such petition and shall forthwith return the child to his parent or Indian custodian unless returning the child to his parent or custodian would subject the child to a substantial and immediate danger or threat of such danger.

Section 1922. Emergency Removal or Placement of Child; Termination Appropriate Action.

Nothing in this subchapter shall be construed to prevent the emergency removal of an Indian child who is resident of or is domiciled on a reservation, but temporarily located off the reservation, from his parent or Indian custodian or the emergency placement of such child in a foster home or institution, under applicable State law, in order to prevent imminent physical damage or harm to the child. The State authority, official, or agency involved shall insure that the emergency removal or placement terminates immediately when such removal or placement is no longer necessary to prevent imminent physical damage or harm to the child and shall expeditiously initiate a child custody proceeding subject to the provisions of this subchapter, transfer the child to the jurisdiction of the appropriate Indian tribe, or restore the child to the parent or Indian custodian, as may be appropriate. . . .

Uniform Marriage and Divorce Act (1970)
9A U.L.A. 156 (1987)

[The Uniform Marriage and Divorce Act is reprinted with permission from the National Conference of Commissioners on State Laws.]

Section 101. [Short Title].
This Act may be cited as the "Uniform Marriage and Divorce Act."

Section 102. [Purposes: Rules of Construction].
This Act shall be liberally construed and applied to promote its underlying purposes, which are to:

(1) provide adequate procedures for the solemnization and registration of marriage;

(2) strengthen and preserve the integrity of marriage and safeguard family relationships;

(3) promote the amicable settlement of disputes that have arisen between parties to a marriage;

(4) mitigate the potential harm to the spouses and their children caused by the process of legal dissolution of marriage;

(5) make reasonable provision for spouse and minor children during and after litigation; and

(6) make the law of legal dissolution of marriage effective for dealing with the realities of matrimonial experience by making irretrievable breakdown of the marriage relationship the sole basis for its dissolution.

Section 201. [Formalities].
Marriage is a personal relationship between a man and a woman arising out of a civil contract to which the consent of the parties is essential. A marriage licensed, solemnized, and registered as provided in this Act is valid in this State. A marriage may be contracted, maintained, invalidated, or dissolved only as provided by law.

Section 202. [Marriage License and Marriage Certificate].

(a) The [Secretary of State, Commissioner of Public Health] shall prescribe the form for an application for a marriage license, which shall include the following information:

(1) name, sex, occupation, address, social security number, date and place of birth of each party to the proposed marriage;

(2) if either party was previously married, his name, and the date, place, and court in which the marriage was dissolved or declared invalid or the date and place of death of the former spouse;

(3) name and address of the parents or guardian of each party; and

(4) whether the parties are related to each other and, if so, their relationship;

(5) the name and date of birth of any child of which both parties are parents, born before the making of the application, unless their parental rights and the parent and child relationship with respect to the child have been terminated.

(b) The [Secretary of State, Commissioner of Public Health] shall prescribe the forms for the marriage license, the marriage certificate, and the consent to marriage.

Section 203. [License to Marry].
When a marriage application has been completed and signed by both parties to a prospective marriage and at least one party has appeared before the [marriage license] clerk and paid the marriage license fee of [$_____], the [marriage license] clerk shall issue a license to marry and a marriage certificate form upon being furnished:

(1) satisfactory proof that each party to the marriage will have attained the age of 18 years at the time the marriage license is effective, or will have attained the age of 16 years and has either the consent to the marriage of both parents or his guardian, or judicial approval; [or, if under the age of 16 years, has both the consent of both parents or his guardian and judicial approval;] and

(2) satisfactory proof that the marriage is not prohibited; [and]

[(3) a certificate of the results of any medical examination required by the laws of this State].

Section 204. [License, Effective Date].
A license to marry becomes effective throughout this state 3 days after the date of issuance, unless the [_____] court orders that the license is effective

when issued, and expires 180 days after it becomes effective.

Section 205. [Judicial Approval].

(a) The [_____] court, after a reasonable effort has been made to notify the parents or guardian of each underage party, may order the [marriage license] clerk to issue a marriage license and a marriage certificate form:

[(1)] to a party aged 16 or 17 years who has no parent capable of consenting to his marriage, or whose parent or guardian has not consented to this marriage; [or

(2) to a party under the age of 16 years who has the consent of both parents to his marriage, if capable of giving consent, or his guardian].

(b) A marriage license and a marriage certificate form may be issued under this section only if the court finds that the underage party is capable of assuming the responsibilities of marriage and the marriage will serve his best interest. Pregnancy alone does not establish that the best interest of the party will be served.

(c) The [_____] court shall authorize performance of a marriage by proxy upon the showing required by the provisions on solemnization.

Section 206. [Solemnization and Registration].

(a) A marriage may be solemnized by a judge of a court of record, by a public official whose powers include solemnization of marriages, or in accordance with any mode of solemnization recognized by any religious denomination, Indian Nation or Tribe, or Native Group. Either the person solemnizing the marriage, or, if no individual acting alone solemnized the marriage, a party to the marriage, shall complete the marriage certificate form and forward it to the [marriage license] clerk.

(b) If a party to a marriage is unable to be present at the solemnization, he may authorize in writing a third person to act as his proxy. If the person solemnizing the marriage is satisfied that the absent party is unable to be present and has consented to the marriage, he may solemnize the marriage by proxy. If he is not satisfied, the parties may petition the [_____] court for an order permitting the marriage to be solemnized by proxy.

(c) Upon receipt of the marriage certificate, the [marriage license] clerk shall register the marriage.

(d) The solemnization of the marriage is not invalidated by the fact that the person solemnizing the marriage was not legally qualified to solemnize it, if neither party to the marriage believed him to be so qualified.

Section 207. [Prohibited Marriages].

(a) The following marriages are prohibited:

(1) a marriage entered into prior to the dissolution of an earlier marriage of one of the parties;

(2) a marriage between an ancestor and a descendant, or between a brother and a sister, whether the relationship is by the half or the whole blood, or by adoption;

(3) a marriage between an uncle and a niece or between an aunt and a nephew, whether the relationship is by the half or the whole blood, except as to marriages permitted by the established customs of aboriginal cultures.

(b) Parties to a marriage prohibited under this section who cohabit after removal of the impediment are lawfully married as of the date of the removal of the impediment.

(c) Children born of a prohibited marriage are legitimate.

Section 208. [Declaration of Invalidity].

(a) The [_____] court shall enter its decree declaring the invalidity of a marriage entered into under the following circumstances:

(1) a party lacked capacity to consent to the marriage at the time the marriage was solemnized, either because of mental incapacity or infirmity or because of the influence of alcohol, drugs, or other incapacitating substances, or a party was induced to enter into a marriage by force or duress, or by fraud involving the essentials of marriage;

(2) a party lacks the physical capacity to consummate the marriage by sexual intercourse, and at the time the marriage was solemnized the other party did not know of the incapacity;

(3) a party [was under the age of 16 years and did not have the consent of his parents or guardian and judicial approval or] was aged 16 or 17 years and did not have the consent of his parents or guardian or judicial approval; or

(4) the marriage is prohibited.

(b) A declaration of invalidity under subsection (a)(1) through (3) may be sought by any of the following persons and must be commenced within the times specified, but in no event may a declaration of invalidity be sought after the death of either party to the marriage:

(1) for a reason set forth in subsection (a)(1), by either party or by the legal representative of the party who lacked capacity to consent, no later than 90 days after the petitioner obtained knowledge of the described condition;

(2) for the reason set forth in subsection (a)(2), by either party, no later than one year after the petitioner obtained knowledge of the described condition;

(3) for the reason set forth in subsection (a)(3), by the underage party, his parent or guardian, prior to the time the underage party reaches the age at which he could have married without satisfying the omitted requirement.

ALTERNATIVE A

[(c) A declaration of invalidity for the reason set forth in subsection (a)(4) may be sought by either party, the legal spouse in case of a bigamous marriage, the [appropriate state official], or a child of either party, at any time prior to the death of one of the parties.]

ALTERNATIVE B

[(c) A declaration of invalidity for the reason set forth in subsection (a)(4) may be sought by either party, the legal spouse in case of a bigamous marriage, the [appropriate state official] or a child of either party, at any time, not to exceed 5 years following the death of either party.]

(d) Children born of a marriage declared invalid are legitimate.

(e) Unless the court finds, after a consideration of all relevant circumstances, including the effect of a retroactive decree on third parties, that the interests of justice would be served by making the decree not retroactive, it shall declare the marriage invalid as of the date of the marriage. The provisions of this Act relating to property rights of the spouses, maintenance, support, and custody of children on dissolution of marriage are applicable to non-retroactive decrees of invalidity.

Section 209. [Putative Spouse].

Any person who has cohabited with another to whom he is not legally married in the good faith belief that he was married to that person is a putative spouse until knowledge of the fact that he is not legally married terminates his status and prevents acquisition of further rights. A putative spouse acquires the rights conferred upon a legal spouse, including the right to maintenance following termination of his status, whether or not the marriage is prohibited (Section 207) or declared invalid (Section 208). If there is a legal spouse or other putative spouses, rights acquired by a putative spouse do not supersede the rights of the legal spouse or those acquired by other putative spouses, but the court shall apportion property, maintenance, and support rights among the claimants as appropriate in the circumstances and in the interests of justice:

Section 210. [Application].

All marriages contracted within this State prior to the effective date of this Act, or outside this State, that were valid at the time of the contract or subsequently validated by the laws of the place in which they were contracted or by the domicile of the parties, are valid in this State.

ALTERNATIVE A

[Section 211. [Validity of Common Law Marriage].

Common law marriages are not invalidated by this Act.]

ALTERNATIVE B

[Section 211. [Invalidity of Common Law Marriage].

Common law marriages contracted in this State after the effective date of this Act are invalid.]

Section 302. [Dissolution of Marriage; Legal Separation].

(a) The [_____] court shall enter a decree of dissolution of marriage if:

(1) the court finds that one of the parties, at the time the action was commenced, was domiciled in this State, or was stationed in this State while a member of the armed services, and that the domicile or military presence has been maintained for 90 days next preceding the making of the findings;

(2) the court finds that the marriage is irretrievably broken, if the finding is supported by evidence that (i) the parties have lived separate and apart for a period of more than 180 days next preceding the commencement of the proceeding, or (ii) there is serious marital discord adversely affecting the attitude of one or both of the parties toward the marriage;

(3) the court finds that the conciliation provisions of Section 305 either do not apply or have been met;

(4) to the extent it has jurisdiction to do so, the court has considered, approved, or provided for child custody, the support of any child entitled to support, the maintenance of either spouse, and the disposition of property; or has provided for a separate, later hearing to complete these matters.

(b) If a party requests a decree of legal separation rather than a decree of dissolution of marriage, the court shall grant the decree in that form unless the other party objects.

Section 303. [Procedure; Commencement; Pleadings; Abolition of Existing Defenses].

(a) All proceedings under this Act are commenced in the manner provided by the [Rules of Civil Practice].

(b) The verified petition in a proceeding for dissolution of marriage or legal separation shall allege that the marriage is irretrievably broken and shall set forth:

(1) the age, occupation, and residence of each party and his length of residence in this State;

(2) the date of the marriage and the place at which it was registered;

(3) that the jurisdictional requirements of Section 302 exist and the marriage is irretrievably broken in that either (i) the parties have lived separate and apart for a period of more than 180 days next preceding the commencement of the proceeding or (ii) there is serious marital discord adversely affecting the attitude of one or both of the parties toward the marriage, and there is no reasonable prospect of reconciliation;

(4) the names, ages, and addresses of all living children of the marriage, and whether the wife is pregnant;

(5) any arrangements as to support, custody, and visitation of the children and maintenance of a spouse, and

(6) the relief sought.

(c) Either or both parties to the marriage may initiate the proceeding.

(d) If a proceeding is commenced by one of the parties, the other party must be served in the manner provided by the [Rules of Civil Practice] and may within [30] days after the date of service file a verified response.

(e) Previously existing defenses to divorce and legal separation, including but not limited to condonation, connivance, collusion, recrimination, insanity, and lapse of time, are abolished.

(f) The court may join additional parties proper for the exercise of its authority to implement this Act.

Section 304. [Temporary Order or Temporary Injunction].

(a) In a proceeding for dissolution of marriage or for legal separation or in a proceeding for disposition of property or for maintenance or support following dissolution of the marriage by a court which lacked personal jurisdiction over the absent spouse, either party may move for temporary maintenance or temporary support of a child of the marriage entitled to support. The motion shall be accompanied by an affidavit setting forth the factual basis for the motion and the amounts requested.

(b) As a part of a motion for temporary maintenance or support or by independent motion accompanied by affidavit, either party may request the court to issue a temporary injunction for any of the following relief:

(1) restraining any person from transferring, encumbering, concealing, or otherwise disposing of any property except in the usual course of business or for the necessities of life, and, if so restrained, requiring him to notify the moving party of any proposed extraordinary expenditures made after the order is issued;

(2) enjoining a party from molesting or disturbing the peace of the other party or of any child;

(3) excluding a party from the family home or from the home of the other party upon a showing that physical or emotional harm would otherwise result;

(4) enjoining a party from removing a child from the jurisdiction of the court; and

(5) providing other injunctive relief proper in the circumstances.

(c) The court may issue a temporary restraining order without requiring notice to the other party only if it finds on the basis of the moving affidavit or other evidence that irreparable injury will result to the moving party if no order is issued until the time for responding has elapsed.

(d) A response may be filed within [20] days after service of notice of motion or at the time specified in the temporary restraining order.

(e) On the basis of the showing made and in conformity with Sections 308 and 309, the court may issue a temporary injunction and an order for temporary maintenance or support in amounts and on terms just and proper in the circumstance.

(f) A temporary order or temporary injunction:

(1) does not prejudice the rights of the parties or the child which are to be adjudicated at subsequent hearings in the proceeding;

(2) may be revoked or modified before final decree on a showing by affidavit of the facts necessary to revocation or modification of a final decree under Section 316; and

(3) terminates when the final decree is entered or when the petition for dissolution or legal separation is voluntarily dismissed.

Section 305. [Irretrievable Breakdown].

(a) If both of the parties by petition or otherwise have stated under oath or affirmation that the marriage is irretrievably broken, or one of the parties has so stated and the other has not denied it, the court, after hearing, shall make a finding whether the marriage is irretrievably broken.

(b) If one of the parties has denied under oath or affirmation that the marriage is irretrievably broken, the court shall consider all relevant factors, including the circumstances that gave rise to filing the petition and the prospect of reconciliation, and shall:

(1) make a finding whether the marriage is irretrievably broken; or

(2) continue the matter for further hearing not fewer than 30 nor more than 60 days later, or as soon thereafter as the matter may be reached on the court's calendar, and may suggest to the parties that they seek counseling. The court, at the request of either party shall, or on its own motion may, order a conciliation conference. At the adjourned hearing the court shall make a finding whether the marriage is irretrievably broken.

(c) A finding of irretrievable breakdown is a determination that there is no reasonable prospect of reconciliation.

Section 306. [Separation Agreement].

(a) To promote amicable settlement of disputes between parties to a marriage attendant upon their separation or the dissolution of their marriage, the parties may enter into a written separation agreement containing provisions for disposition of any property owned by either of them, maintenance of either of them, and support, custody, and visitation of their children.

(b) In a proceeding for dissolution of marriage or for legal separation, the terms of the separation agreement, except those providing for the support, custody, and visitation of children, are binding upon the court unless it finds, after considering the economic circumstances of the parties and any other relevant evidence produced by the parties, on their own motion or on request of the court, that the separation agreement is unconscionable.

(c) If the court finds the separation agreement unconscionable, it may request the parties to submit a revised separation agreement or may make orders for the disposition of property, maintenance, and support.

(d) If the court finds that the separation agreement is not unconscionable as to disposition of property or maintenance, and not unsatisfactory as to support:

(1) unless the separation agreement provides to the contrary, its terms shall be set forth in the decree of dissolution or legal separation and the parties shall be ordered to perform them, or

(2) if the separation agreement provides that its terms shall not be set forth in the decree, the decree shall identify the separation agreement and state that the court has found the terms not unconscionable.

(e) Terms of the agreement set forth in the decree are enforceable by all remedies available for enforcement of a judgment, including contempt, and are enforceable as contract terms.

(f) Except for terms concerning the support, custody, or visitation of children, the decree may expressly preclude or limit modification of terms set forth in the decree if the separation agreement so provides. Otherwise, terms of a separation agreement set forth in the decree are automatically modified by modification of the decree.

ALTERNATIVE A

Section 307. [Disposition of Property].

(a) In a proceeding for dissolution of a marriage, legal separation, or disposition of property following a decree of dissolution of marriage or legal separation by a court which lacked personal jurisdiction over the absent spouse or lacked jurisdiction to dispose of the property, the court, without regard to marital misconduct, shall, and in a proceeding for legal separation may, finally equitably apportion between the parties the property and assets belonging to either or both however and whenever acquired, and whether the title thereto is in the name of the husband or wife or both. In making apportionment the court shall consider the duration of the marriage, and prior marriage of either party, antenuptial agreement of the parties, the age, health, station, occupation, amount and sources of income, vocational skills, employability, estate, liabilities, and needs of each of the parties, custodial provisions, whether the apportionment is in lieu of or in addition to maintenance, and the opportunity of each for future acquisition of capital assets and income. The court shall also consider the contribution or dissipation of each party in the acquisition, preservation, depreciation, or appreciation in value of the respective estates, and the contribution of a spouse as a homemaker or to the family unit.

(b) In a proceeding, the court may protect and promote the best interests of the children by setting aside a portion of the jointly and separately held estates of the parties in a separate fund or trust for the support, maintenance, education, and general welfare of any minor, dependent, or incompetent children of the parties.]

ALTERNATIVE B

[Section 307. [Disposition of Property.]

In a proceeding for dissolution of the marriage, legal separation, or disposition of property following a decree of dissolution of the marriage or legal separation by a court which lacked personal jurisdiction over the absent spouse or lacked jurisdiction to dispose of the property, the court shall assign each spouse's separate property to that spouse. It also shall divide community property, without regard to martial misconduct, in just proportions after considering all relevant factors including:

(1) contribution of each spouse to acquisition of the marital property, including contribution of a spouse as homemaker;

(2) value of the property set apart to each spouse;

(3) duration of the marriage; and

(4) economic circumstances of each spouse when the division of property is to become effective, including the desirability of awarding the family home or the right to live therein for a reasonable period to the spouse having custody of any children.]

Section 308. [Maintenance].

(a) In a proceeding for dissolution of marriage, legal separation, or maintenance following a decree of dissolution of the marriage by a court which lacked personal jurisdiction over the absent spouse, the court may grant a maintenance order for either spouse only if it finds that the spouse seeking maintenance:

(1) lacks sufficient property to provide for his reasonable needs; and

(2) is unable to support himself through appropriate employment or is the custodian of a child whose condition or circumstances make it appropriate that the custodian not be required to seek employment outside the home.

(b) The maintenance order shall be in amounts and for periods of time the court deems just, without regard to marital misconduct and after considering all relevant factors including:

(1) the financial resources of the party seeking maintenance, including marital property apportioned to him, his ability to meet his needs independently, and the extent to which a provision for support of a child living with the party includes a sum for that party as custodian;

(2) the time necessary to acquire sufficient education or training to enable the party seeking maintenance to find appropriate employment;

(3) the standard of living established during the marriage;

(4) the duration of the marriage;

(5) the age and the physical and emotional condition of the spouse seeking maintenance; and

(6) the ability of the spouse from whom maintenance is sought to meet his needs while meeting those of the spouse seeking maintenance.

Section 309. [Child Support].

In a proceeding for dissolution of marriage, legal separation, maintenance or child support, the court may order either or both parents owing a duty of support to a child to pay an amount reasonable or necessary for his support, without regard to marital misconduct, after considering all relevant factors including:

(1) the financial resources of the child;

(2) the financial resources of the custodial parent;

(3) the standard of living the child would have enjoyed had the marriage not been dissolved;

(4) the physical and emotional condition of the child and his educational needs; and

(5) the financial resources and needs of the noncustodial parent.

Section 310. [Representation of Child].

The court may appoint an attorney to represent the interests of a minor or dependent child with respect to his support, custody, and visitation. The court shall enter an order for costs, fees, and disbursements in favor of the child's attorney. The order shall be made against either or both parents, except that, if the responsible party is indigent, the costs, fees, and disbursements shall be born by the [appropriate agency].

Section 311. [Payment of Maintenance or Support to Court].

(a) Upon its own motion or upon motion of either party, the court may order at any time that maintenance or support payments be made to the [clerk of court, court trustee, probation officer] as trustee for remittance to the person entitled to receive the payments.

(b) The [clerk of court, court trustee, probation officer] shall maintain records listing the amount of payments, the date payments are required to be made, and the names and addresses of the parties affected by the order.

(c) The parties affected by the order shall inform the [clerk of court, court trustee, probation officer] of any change of address or of other condition that may affect the administration of the order.

(d) If a party fails to make a required payment, the [clerk of court, court trustee, probation officer] shall send by registered or certified mail notice of the arrearage to the obligor. If payment of the sum due is not made to the [clerk of court, court trustee, probation officer] within 10 days after sending notice, the [clerk of court, court trustee, probation officer] shall certify the amount due to the [prosecuting attorney]. The [prosecuting attorney] shall promptly initiate contempt proceedings against the obligator.

(e) The [prosecuting attorney] shall assist the court on behalf of a person entitled to receive maintenance or support in all proceedings initiated under this section to enforce compliance with the order. The person to whom maintenance or support is awarded may also initiate action to collect arrearages.

(f) If the person obligated to pay support has left or is beyond the jurisdiction of the court, the [prosecuting attorney] may institute any other proceeding available under the laws of this State for enforcement of the duties of support and maintenance.

Section 313. [Attorney's Fees].

The court from time to time after considering the financial resources of both parties may order a party to pay a reasonable amount for the cost to the other party of maintaining or defending any proceeding under this Act and for attorney's fees, including sums for legal services rendered and costs incurred prior to the commencement of the proceeding or after entry of judgment. The court may order that the amount be paid directly to the attorney, who may enforce the order in his name.

Section 314. [Decree].

(a) A decree of dissolution of marriage or of legal separation is final when entered, subject to the right of appeal. An appeal from the decree of dissolution that does not challenge the finding that the marriage is irretrievably broken does not delay the finality of that provision of the decree which dissolves the marriage beyond the time for appealing from that provision, and either of the parties may remarry pending appeal.

(b) No earlier than 6 months after entry of a decree of legal separation, the court on motion of either party shall convert the decree to a decree of dissolution of marriage.

(c) The Clerk of Court shall give notice of the entry of a decree of dissolution or legal separation:

(1) if the marriage is registered in this State, to the [marriage license] clerk of the [county, judicial district] where the marriage is registered who shall enter the fact of dissolution or separation in the [Registry of Marriage]; or

(2) if the marriage is registered in another jurisdiction, to the appropriate official of that jurisdiction, with the request that he enter the fact of dissolution in the appropriate record.

(d) Upon request by a wife whose marriage is dissolved or declared invalid, the court may, and if there are no children of the parties shall, order her maiden name or former name restored.

Section 316. [Modification and Termination of Provisions for Maintenance, Support and Property Disposition].

(a) Except as otherwise provided in subsection (f) of Section 306, the provisions of any decree respecting maintenance or support may be modified only as to installments accruing subsequent to the motion for modification and only upon a showing of changed circumstances so substantial and continuing as to make the terms unconscionable. The provisions as to property disposition may not be revoked or modified, unless the court finds the existence of conditions that justify the reopening of a judgment under the laws of this state.

(b) Unless otherwise agreed in writing or expressly provided in the decree, the obligation to pay future maintenance is terminated upon the death of either party or remarriage of the party receiving maintenance.

(c) Unless otherwise agreed in writing or expressly provided in the decree, provisions for the support of a child are terminated by emancipation of the child but not by the death of a parent obligated to support the child. When a parent obligated to pay support dies, the amount of support may be modified, revoked, or commuted to a lump sum payment, to the extent just and appropriate in the circumstances.

Section 401. [Jurisdiction; Commencement of Proceeding].

(a) A court of this State competent to decide child custody matters has jurisdiction to make a child custody determination by initial or modification decree if:

(1) this State (i) is the home state of the child at the time of commencement of the proceeding, or (ii) had been the child's home state within 6 months before commencement of the proceeding and the child is absent from this State because of his removal or retention by a person claiming his custody or for other reasons, and a parent or person acting as parent continues to live in this State; or

(2) it is in the best interest of the child that a court of this State assume jurisdiction because (i) the child and his parents, or the child and at least one contestant, have a significant connection with this State, and (ii) there is available in this State substantial evidence concerning the child's present or future care, protection, training, and personal relationships; or

(3) the child is physically present in this State and (i) has been abandoned or (ii) it is necessary in an emergency to protect him because he has been subjected to or threatened with mistreatment or abuse or is neglected or dependent; or

(4)(i) no other state has jurisdiction under prerequisites substantially in accordance with paragraphs (1), (2) or (3), or another state has declined to exercise jurisdiction on the ground that this State is the more appropriate forum to determine custody of the child, and (ii) it is in his best interest that the court assume jurisdiction.

(b) Except under paragraphs (3) and (4) of subsection (a), physical presence in this State of the child, or of the child and one of the contestants, is not alone sufficient to confer jurisdiction on a court of this State to make a child custody determination.

(c) Physical presence of the child, while desirable, is not a prerequisite for jurisdiction to determine his custody.

(d) A child custody proceeding is commenced in the [_____] court:

(1) by a parent, by filing a petition (i) for dissolution or legal separation; or (ii) for custody of the child in the [county, judicial district] in which he is permanently resident or found; or

(2) by a person other than a parent, by filing a petition for custody of the child in the [county, judicial district] in which he is permanently resident or found, but only if he is not in the physical custody of one of his parents.

(e) Notice of a child custody proceeding shall be given to the child's parent, guardian, and custodian, who may appear, be heard, and file a responsive pleading. The court, upon a showing of good cause, may permit intervention of other interested parties.

Section 402. [Best Interest of Child].

The court shall determine custody in accordance with the best interest of the child. The court shall consider all relevant factors including:

(1) the wishes of the child's parent or parents as to his custody;

(2) the wishes of the child as to his custodian;

(3) the interaction and interrelationship of the child with his parent or parents, his siblings, and any other person who may significantly affect the child's best interest;

(4) the child's adjustment to his home, school, and community; and

(5) the mental and physical health of all individuals involved.

The court shall not consider conduct of a proposed custodian that does not affect his relationship to the child.

Section 403. [Temporary Orders].

(a) A party to a custody proceeding may move for a temporary custody order. The motion must be supported by an affidavit as provided in Section 410. The court may award temporary custody under the standards of Section 402 after a hearing, or, if there is no objection, solely on the basis of the affidavits.

(b) If a proceeding for dissolution of marriage or legal separation is dismissed, any temporary custody order is vacated unless a parent or the child's custodian moves that the proceeding continue as a custody proceeding and the court finds, after a hearing, that the circumstances of the parents and the best interest of the child require that a custody decree be issued.

(c) If a custody proceeding commenced in the absence of a petition for dissolution of marriage or legal separation under subsection (1)(ii) or (2) or Section 401 is dismissed, any temporary custody order is vacated.

Section 404. [Interview].

(a) The court may interview the child in chambers to ascertain the child's wishes as to his custodian and as to visitation. The court may permit counsel to be present at the interview. The court shall cause a record of the interview to be made and to be part of the record in the case.

(b) The court may seek the advice of professional personnel, whether or not employed by the court on a regular basis. The advice given shall be in writing and made available by the court to counsel upon request. Counsel may examine as a witness any professional personnel consulted by the court.

Section 405. [Investigations and Reports].

(a) In contested custody proceedings, and in other custody proceedings if a parent or the child's custodian so requests, the court may order an investigation and report concerning custodial arrangements for the child. The investigation and report may be made by [the court social service agency, the staff of the juvenile court, the local probation or welfare department, or a private agency employed by the court for the purpose].

(b) In preparing his report concerning a child, the investigator may consult any person who may have information about the child and his potential custodial arrangements. Upon order of the court, the investigator may refer the child to professional personnel for diagnosis. The investigator may consult with and obtain information from medical, psychiatric, or other expert persons who have served the child in the past without obtaining the consent of the parent or the child's custodian; but the child's consent must be obtained if he has reached the age of 16, unless the court finds that he lacks mental capacity to consent. If the requirements of subsection (c) are fulfilled, the investigator's report may be received in evidence at the hearing.

(c) The court shall mail the investigator's report to counsel and to any party not represented by counsel at least 10 days prior to the hearing. The investigator shall make available to counsel and to any party not represented by counsel the investigator's file of underlying data, and reports, complete texts of diagnostic reports made to the investigator pursuant to the provisions of subsection (b), and the names and addresses of all persons whom the investigator has consulted. Any party to the proceeding may call the investigator and any person whom he has consulted for cross-examination. A party may not waive his right of cross-examination prior to the hearing.

Section 406. [Hearings].

(a) Custody proceedings shall receive priority in being set for hearing.

(b) The court may tax as costs the payment of necessary travel and other expenses incurred by any person whose presence at the hearing the court deems necessary to determine the best interest of the child.

(c) The court without a jury shall determine questions of law and fact. If it finds that a public hearing may be detrimental to the child's best interest, the court may exclude the public from a custody hearing, but may admit any person who has a direct and legitimate interest in the particular case or a legitimate educational or research interest in the work of the court.

(d) If the court finds it necessary to protect the child's welfare that the record of any interview report, investigation, or testimony in a custody proceeding be kept secret, the court may make an appropriate order sealing the record.

Section 407. [Visitation].

(a) A parent not granted custody of the child is entitled to reasonable visitation rights unless the court finds, after a hearing, that visitation would endanger seriously the child's physical, mental, moral, or emotional health.

(b) The court may modify an order granting or denying visitation rights whenever modification would serve the best interest of the child; but the court shall not restrict a parent's visitation rights unless it finds that the visitation would endanger seriously the child's physical, mental, moral, or emotional health.

Section 408. [Judicial Supervision].

(a) Except as otherwise agreed by the parties in writing at the time of the custody decree, the custodian may determine the child's upbringing, including his education, health care, and religious training, unless the court after hearing, finds, upon motion by the non-custodial parent, that in the absence of a specific limitation of the custodian's authority, the child's physical health would be endangered or his emotional development significantly impaired.

(b) If both parents or all contestants agree to the order, or if the court finds that in the absence of the order the child's physical health would be endangered or his emotional development significantly impaired, the court may order the [local probation or welfare department, court social service agency] to exercise continuing supervision over the case to assure that the custodial or visitation terms of the decree are carried out.

Section 409. [Modification].

(a) No motion to modify a custody decree may be made earlier than 2 years after its date, unless the court permits it to be made on the basis of affidavits that there is reason to believe the child's present environment may endanger seriously his physical, mental, moral, or emotional health.

(b) If a court of this State has jurisdiction pursuant to the Uniform Child Custody Jurisdiction Act, the court shall not modify a prior custody decree unless it finds, upon the basis of facts that have arisen since the prior decree or that were unknown to the court at the time of entry of the prior decree, that a change has occurred in the circumstances of the child or his custodian, and that the modification is necessary to serve the best interest of the child. In applying these standards the court shall retain the custodian appointed pursuant to the prior decree unless:

(1) the custodian agrees to the modification;

(2) the child has been integrated into the family of the petitioner with consent of the custodian; or

(3) the child's present environment endangers seriously his physical, mental, moral, or emotional health, and the harm likely to be caused by a change of environment is outweighed by its advantages to him.

(c) Attorney fees and costs shall be assessed against a party seeking modification if the court finds that the modification action is vexatious and constitutes harassment.

[Sections 501-503, dealing with time of taking effect, application to pending actions, and severability, and Section 105, dealing with general repealer, have been omitted.]

Uniform Child Custody Jurisdiction Act (1968)
9 U.L.A. (1988)

[The Uniform Child Custody Jurisdiction Act was drafted by the National Conference of Commissioners on Uniform State Laws and it is reproduced with their permission. Selected portions of the official Comments are included, and some citations in the Comments have been omitted.]

Section 1. [Purposes of Act; Construction of Provisions.]

(a) The general purposes of this Act are to:

(1) avoid jurisdictional competition and conflict with courts of other states in matters of child custody which have in the past resulted in the shifting of children from state to state with harmful effects on their well-being;

(2) promote cooperation with the courts of other states to the end that a custody decree is rendered in that state which can best decide the case in the interest of the child;

(3) assure that litigation concerning the custody of a child take place ordinarily in the state with which the child and his family have the closest connection and where significant evidence concerning his care, protection, training, and personal relationships is most readily available, and that courts of this state decline the exercise of jurisdiction when the child and his family have a closer connection with another state;

(4) discourage continuing controversies over child custody in the interest of greater stability of home environment and of secure family relationships for the child;

(5) deter abductions and other unilateral removals of children undertaken to obtain custody awards;

(6) avoid re-litigation of custody decisions of other states in this state insofar as feasible;

(7) facilitate the enforcement of custody decrees of other states;

(8) promote and expand the exchange of information and other forms of mutual assistance between the courts of this state and those of other states concerned with the same child; and

(9) make uniform the law of those states which enact it.

(b) This Act shall be construed to promote the general purposes stated in this section.

Section 2. [Definitions] As used in this Act:

(1) "contestant" means a person, including a parent, who claims a right to custody or visitation rights with respect to a child;

(2) "custody determination" means a court decision and court orders and instructions providing for the custody of a child, including visitation rights; it does not include a decision relating to child support or any other monetary obligation of any person;

(3) "custody proceeding" includes proceedings in which a custody determination is one of several issues, such as an action for divorce or separation, and includes child neglect and dependency proceedings;

(4) "decree" or "custody decree" means a custody determination contained in a judicial decree or

order made in a custody proceeding, and includes an initial decree and a modification decree;

(5) "home state" means the state in which the child immediately preceding the time involved lived with his parents, a parent, or a person acting as a parent, for at least 6 consecutive months, and in the case of a child less than 6 months old the state in which the child lived from birth with any of the persons mentioned. Periods of temporary absence of any of the named persons are counted as part of the 6-month or other period;

(6) "initial decree" means the first custody decree concerning a particular child;

(7) "modification decree" means a custody decree which modifies or replaces a prior decree, whether made by the court which rendered the prior decree or by another court;

(8) "physical custody" means actual possession and control of a child;

(9) "person acting as parent" means a person, other than a parent, who has physical custody of a child and who has either been awarded custody by a court or claims a right to custody; and

(10) "state" means any state, territory, or possession of the United States, the Commonwealth of Puerto Rico, and the District of Columbia.

Section 3. [Jurisdiction].

(a) A court of this State which is competent to decide child custody matters has jurisdiction to make a child custody determination by initial or modification decree if:

(1) this State (i) is the home state of the child at the time of commencement of the proceeding, or (ii) had been the child's home state within 6 months before commencement of the proceeding and the child is absent from this State because of his removal or retention by a person claiming his custody or for other reasons, and a parent or person acting as parent continues to live in this State; or

(2) it is in the best interest of the child that a court of this State assume jurisdiction because (i) the child and his parents, or the child and at least one contestant, have a significant connection with this State, and (ii) there is available in this State substantial evidence concerning the child's present or future care, protection, training, and personal relationships; or

(3) the child is physically present in this State and (i) the child has been abandoned or (ii) it is necessary in an emergency to protect the child because he has been subjected to or threatened with mistreatment or abuse or is otherwise neglected [or dependent]; or

(4) (i) it appears that no other state would have jurisdiction under prerequisites substantially in accordance with paragraphs (1), (2), or (3), or another state has declined to exercise jurisdiction on the ground that this State is the more appropriate forum to determine the custody of the child, and (ii) it is in the best interest of the child that this court assume jurisdiction.

(b) Except under paragraphs (3) and (4) of subsection (a), physical presence in this State of the child, or of the child and one of the contestants, is not alone sufficient to confer jurisdiction on a court of this State to make a child custody determination.

(c) Physical presence of the child, while desirable, is not a prerequisite for jurisdiction to determine his custody.

Comment

Paragraphs (1) and (2) of subsection (a) establish the two major bases for jurisdiction. In the first place, a court in the child's home state has jurisdiction, and secondly, if there is no home state or the child and his family have equal or stronger ties with another state, a court in that state has jurisdiction. If this alternative test produces concurrent jurisdiction in more than one state, the mechanisms provided in sections 6 and 7 are used to assure that only one state makes the custody decision.

"Home state" is defined in section 2(5). A 6-month period has been selected in order to have a definite and certain test which is at the same time based on a reasonable assumption of fact. See Ratner, Child Custody in a Federal System, 62 Mich. L. Re. 795, 818 (1964) who explains:

> Most American children are integrated into an American community after living there six months; consequently this period of residence would seem to provide a reasonable criterion for identifying the established home.

Subparagraph (ii) of paragraph (1) extends the home state rule for an additional six-month period in order to permit suit in the home state after the child's departure. The main objective is to protect a parent who has been left by his spouse taking the child along. The provision makes clear that the stay-at-home parent, if he acts promptly, may start proceedings in his own state if he desires, without the necessity of attempting to base jurisdiction on paragraph (2). This changes the law in those states which required presence of the child as a condition for jurisdiction and consequently forced the person left behind to follow the departed person to another state, perhaps to several states in succession. See also subsection (c).

Paragraph (2) comes into play either when the home state test cannot be met or as an alternative to that test. The first situation arises, for example, when a family has moved frequently and there is no state where the child has lived for 6 months prior to suit, or if the child has recently been removed from his home state and the person who was left behind has also moved away. See paragraph (1), last clause. A typical example of alternative jurisdiction is the case in which the stay-at-home parent chooses to follow the departed spouse to state 2 (where the child has lived for several months with the other parent) and starts proceedings there. Whether the departed parent also has access to a court in state 2 depends on the strength of the family ties in that state and on the applicability of the clean hands provision of section 8. If state 2, for example, was the state of the matrimonial home where the entire family lived for two years before moving to the "home state" for 6 months, and the wife returned to state 2 with the child with the consent of the husband, state 2 might well have jurisdiction upon petition of the wife. The same may be true if the wife returned to her parents in her former home state where the child had spent several months every year before. Compare Willmore v. Willmore, 273 Minn. 537, 143 N.W. 2d 630 (1966), *cert. denied*, 385 U.S. 898 (1966). While jurisdiction may exist in two states in these instances it will not be *exercised* in both states. See sections 6 and 7.

Paragraph (2) of subsection (a) is supplemented by subsection (b) which is designed to discourage unilateral removal of children to other states and to guard generally against too liberal an interpretation of paragraph (2). Short-term presence in the state is not enough even though there may be an intent to stay longer, perhaps an intent to establish a technical "domicile" for divorce or other purposes.

Paragraph (2) perhaps more than any other provision of the Act requires that it be interpreted in the spirit of the legislative purposes expressed in section 1. The paragraph was phrased in general terms in order to be flexible enough to cover many fact situations too diverse to lend themselves to exact description. But its purpose is to limit jurisdiction rather than to proliferate it. The first clause of the paragraph is important: jurisdiction exists only if it is in the *child's* interest, not merely the interest or convenience of the feuding parties, to determine custody in a particular state. The interest of the child is served when the forum has optimum access to relevant evidence about the child and family. There must be maximum rather than minimum contact with the state. The submission of the parties to a forum, perhaps for purposes of divorce, is not sufficient without additional factors establishing closer ties with the state. Divorce jurisdiction does not necessarily include custody jurisdiction. See Clark, Domestic Relations 578 (1968).

Paragraph (3) of subsection (a) retains and reaffirms *parens patriae* jurisdiction, usually exercised by a juvenile court, which a state must assume when a child is in a situation requiring immediate protection. This jurisdiction exists when a child has been abandoned and in emergency cases of child neglect. Presence of the child in the state is the only prerequisite. This extraordinary jurisdiction is reserved for extraordinary circumstances. See Application of Lang, 9 App. Div. 2d 401, 193 N.Y.S.2d 763 (1959). When there is child neglect without emergency or abandonment, jurisdiction cannot be based on this paragraph.

Section 4. [Notice and Opportunity to Be Heard].

Before making a decree under this Act, reasonable notice and opportunity to be heard shall be given to the contestants, any parent whose parental rights have not been previously terminated, and any person who has physical custody of the child. If any of these persons is outside this State, notice and opportunity to be heard shall be given pursuant to section 5.

Section 5. [Notice to Persons Outside This State; Submission to Jurisdiction].

(a) Notice required for the exercise of jurisdiction over a person outside this State shall be given in a manner reasonably calculated to give actual notice, and may be:

(1) by personal delivery outside this State in the manner prescribed for service of process within this State;

(2) in the manner prescribed by the law of the place in which the service is made for service of process in that place in an action in any of its courts of general jurisdiction;

(3) by any form of mail addressed to the person to be served and requesting a receipt; or

(4) as directed by the court [including publication, if other means of notification are ineffective].

(b) Notice under this section shall be served, mailed, or delivered, [or last published] at least [10, 20] days before any hearing in this State.

(c) Proof of service outside this State may be made by affidavit of the individual who made the service, or in the manner prescribed by the law of this State, the order pursuant to which the service is made, or the law of the place in which the service is made. If service is made by mail, proof may be a receipt signed by the addressee or other evidence of delivery to the addressee.

(d) Notice is not required if a person submits to the jurisdiction of the court.

Section 6 [Simultaneous Proceedings in Other States].

(a) A court of this State shall not exercise its jurisdiction under this Act if at the time of filing the petition a proceeding concerning the custody of the child was pending in a court of another state exercising jurisdiction substantially in conformity with this Act, unless the proceeding is stayed by the court of the other state because this State is a more appropriate forum or for other reasons.

(b) Before hearing the petition in a custody proceeding the court shall examine the pleadings and other information supplied by the parties under section 9 and shall consult the child custody registry established under section 16 concerning the pendency of proceedings with respect to the child in other states. If the court has reason to believe that proceedings may be pending in another state it shall direct an inquiry to the state court administrator or other appropriate official of the other state.

(c) If the court is informed during the course of the proceeding that a proceeding concerning the custody of the child was pending in another state before the court assumed jurisdiction it shall stay the proceeding and communicate with the court in which the other proceeding is pending to the end that the issue may be litigated in the more appropriate forum and that information be exchanged in accordance with sections 19 through 22. If a court of this state has made a custody decree before being informed of a pending proceeding in a court of another state it shall immediately inform that court of the fact. If the court is informed that a proceeding was commenced in another state after it assumed jurisdiction it shall likewise inform the other court to the end that the issues may be litigated in the more appropriate forum.

Section 7. [Inconvenient Forum].

(a) A court which has jurisdiction under this Act to make an initial or modification decree may decline to exercise its jurisdiction any time before making a decree if it finds that it is an inconvenient forum to make a custody determination under the circumstances of the case and that a court of another state is a more appropriate forum.

(b) A finding of inconvenient forum may be made upon the court's own motion or upon motion of a party or a guardian ad litem or other representative of the child.

(c) In determining if it is an inconvenient forum, the court shall consider if it is in the interest of the child that another state assume jurisdiction. For this purpose it may take into account the following factors, among others:

(1) if another state is or recently was the child's home state;

(2) if another state has a closer connection with the child and his family or with the child and one or more of the contestants;

(3) if substantial evidence concerning the child's present or future care, protection, training, and personal relationships is more readily available in another state;

(4) if the parties have agreed on another forum which is no less appropriate; and

(5) if the exercise of jurisdiction by a court of this state would contravene any of the purposes stated in section 1.

(d) Before determining whether to decline or retain jurisdiction the court may communicate with a court of another state and exchange information pertinent to the assumption of jurisdiction by either court with a view to assuring that jurisdiction will be exercised by the more appropriate court and that a forum will be available to the parties.

(e) If the court finds that it is an inconvenient forum and that a court of another state is a more appropriate forum, it may dismiss the proceedings, or it may stay the proceedings upon condition that a custody proceeding be promptly commenced in another named state or upon any other conditions which may be just and proper, including the condition that a moving party stipulate his consent and submission to the jurisdiction of the other forum.

(f) The court may decline to exercise its jurisdiction under this Act if a custody determination is incidental to an action for divorce or another proceeding while retaining jurisdiction over the divorce or other proceeding.

(g) If it appears to the court that it is clearly an inappropriate forum it may require the party who commenced the proceedings to pay, in addition to the costs of the proceedings in this State, necessary travel and other expenses, including attorneys' fees, incurred by other parties or their witnesses. Payment is to be made to the clerk of the court for remittance to the proper party.

(h) Upon dismissal or stay of proceedings under this section the court shall inform the court found to be the more appropriate forum of this fact, or if the court which would have jurisdiction in the other state is not certainly known, shall transmit the information to the court administrator or other appropriate official for forwarding to the appropriate court.

(i) Any communication received from another state informing this State of a finding of inconvenient forum because a court of this State is the more appropriate forum shall be filed in the custody registry of the appropriate court. Upon assuming jurisdiction the court of this State shall inform the original court of this fact.

Section 8. [Jurisdiction Declined by Reason of Conduct].

(a) If the petitioner for an initial decree has wrongfully taken the child from another state or has engaged in similar reprehensible conduct the court may decline to exercise jurisdiction if this is just and proper under the circumstances.

(b) Unless required in the interest of the child, the court shall not exercise its jurisdiction to modify a custody decree of another state if the petitioner, without consent of the person entitled to custody, has improperly removed the child from the physical custody of the person entitled to custody or has improperly retained the child after a visit or other temporary relinquishment of physical custody. If the petitioner has violated any other provision of a custody decree of another state the court may decline to exercise its jurisdiction if this is just and proper under the circumstances.

(c) In appropriate cases a court dismissing a petition under this section may charge the petitioner with necessary travel and other expenses, including attorneys' fees, incurred by other parties or their witnesses.

Comment

This section incorporates the "clean hands doctrine," so named by Ehrenzweig, Interstate Recognition of Custody Decrees, 51 Mich. L. Rev. 345 (1953). Under this doctrine courts refuse to assume jurisdiction to re-examine an out-of-state custody decree when the petitioner has abducted the child or has engaged in some other objectionable scheme to gain or retain physical custody of the child in violation of the decree. But when adherence to this rule would lead to punishment of the parent at the expense of the well being of the child, it is often not applied.

Subsection (a) extends the clean hands principle to cases in which a custody decree has not yet been rendered in any state. For example, if upon a de facto separation the wife returned to her own home with the children without objection by her husband and lived there for two years without hearing from him, and the husband without warning forcibly removes the children one night and brings them to another state, a court in that state although it has jurisdiction after 6 months may decline to hear the husband's custody petition. "Wrongfully" taking under this subsection does not mean that a "right" has been violated—both husband and wife as a rule have a right to custody until a court determination is made—but that one party's conduct is so objectionable that a court in the exercise of its inherent equity power cannot in good conscience permit that party access to its jurisdiction.

Subsection (b) does not come into operation unless the court has power under section 14 to modify the custody decree of another state. It is a codification of the clean hands rule, except that it differentiates between (1) a taking or retention of the child and (2) other violations of custody decrees. In the case of illegal removal or retention refusal of jurisdiction is mandatory unless the harm done to the child by a denial of jurisdiction outweighs the parental misconduct. Compare Smith v. Smith and In Re Guardianship of Rodgers, supra; and see In re Walter, 228 Cal. App. 2d 217, 39 Cal. Rptr. 243 (1964) where the court assumed jurisdiction after both parents had been guilty of misconduct. The qualifying word "improperly" is added to exclude cases in which a child is withheld because of illness or other emergency or in which there are other special justifying circumstances.

The most common violation of the second category is the removal of the child from the state by the parent who has the right to custody, thereby frustrating the exercise of visitation rights of the other parent. The second sentence of subsection (b) makes refusal of jurisdiction entirely discretionary in this situation because it depends on the circumstances whether noncompliance with the court order is serious enough to warrant the drastic action of denial of jurisdiction.

Subsection (c) adds a financial deterrent to child stealing and similar reprehensible conduct.

Section 9. [Information Under Oath to Be Submitted to the Court].

(a) Every party in a custody proceeding in his first pleading or in an affidavit attached to that pleading shall give information under oath as to the child's present address, the places where the child has lived within the last 5 years, and the names and present addresses of the persons with whom the child has lived during that period. In this pleading or affidavit every party shall further declare under oath whether:

(1) he has participated (as a party, witness, or in any other capacity) in any other litigation concerning the custody of the same child in this or any other state;

(2) he has information of any custody proceeding concerning the child pending in a court of this or any other state; and

(3) he knows of any person not a party to the proceedings who has physical custody of the child or claims to have custody or visitation rights with respect to the child.

(b) If the declaration as to any of the above items is in the affirmative the declarant shall give additional information under oath as required by the court. The court may examine the parties under oath as to details of the information furnished and as to other matters pertinent to the court's jurisdiction and the disposition of the case.

(c) Each party has a continuing duty to inform the court of any custody proceeding concerning the child in this or in any other state of which he obtained information during this proceeding.

Section 10. [Additional Parties].

If the court learns from information furnished by the parties pursuant to section 9 or from other sources that a person not a party to the custody proceeding has physical custody of the child or claims to have custody or visitation rights with respect to the child, it shall order that person to be joined as a party and to be duly notified of the pendency of the proceeding and of his joinder as a party. If the person joined as a party is outside this State he shall be served with process or otherwise notified in accordance with section 5.

Section 11. [Appearance of Parties and the Child].

[(a) The court may order any party to the proceeding who is in this State to appear personally before the court. If that party has physical custody of the child the court may order that he appear personally with the child.]

(b) If a party to the proceeding whose presence is desired by the court is outside this State with or without the child the court may order that the notice given under section 5 include a statement directing that party to appear personally with or without the child and declaring that failure to appear may result in a decision adverse to that party.

(c) If a party to the proceeding who is outside this State is directed to appear under subsection (b) or desires to appear personally before the court with or without the child, the court may require another party to pay to the clerk of the court travel and other necessary expenses of the party so appearing and of the child if this is just and proper under the circumstances.

Section 12. [Binding Force and Res Judicata Effect of Custody Decree].

A custody decree rendered by a court of this State which had jurisdiction under section 3 binds all parties who have been served in this State or notified in accordance with section 5 or who have submitted to the jurisdiction of the court and who have been given an opportunity to be heard. As to these parties the custody decree is conclusive as to all issues of law and fact decided and as to the custody determination made unless and until that determination is modified pursuant to law, including the provisions of this Act.

Section 13. [Recognition of Out-of-State Custody Decrees].

The courts of this State shall recognize and enforce an initial or modification decree of a court of another state which had assumed jurisdiction under statutory provisions substantially in accordance with this Act or which was made under factual circumstances meeting the jurisdictional standards of the Act, so long as this decree has not been modified in accordance with jurisdictional standards substantially similar to those of this Act.

Comment

This section and sections 14 and 15 are the key provisions which guarantee a great measure of security and stability of environment to the "interstate child" by discouraging relitigations in other states. See Section 1, and see Ratner, Child Custody in a Federal System, 62 Mich. L. Rev. 795, 828 (1964).

Although the full faith and credit clause may perhaps not require the recognition of out-of-state custody decrees, the states are free to recognize and enforce them. See Restatement of the Law Second, Conflict of Law, Proposed Official Draft, section 109 (1967), and see the Prefatory Note, supra. This section declares as a matter of state law that custody decrees of sister states will be recognized and enforced. Recognition and enforcement is mandatory if the state in which the prior decree was rendered 1) has adopted this Act, 2) has statutory jurisdictional requirements substantially like this Act, or 3) would have had jurisdiction under the facts of the case if this Act had been the law in the state. Compare Comment, Ford v. Ford: Full Faith and Credit to Child Custody Decrees? 73 Yale L.J. 134, 148 (1963).

"Jurisdiction" or "jurisdictional standards" under this section refers to the requirements of section 3 in the case of initial decrees and to the requirements of sections 3 and 14 in the case of modification decrees. The section leaves open the possibility of discretionary recognition of custody decrees of other states beyond the enumerated situations of mandatory acceptance. For the recognition of custody decrees of other nations, see section 23.

Recognition is accredited to a decree which is valid and binding under section 12. This means, for example, that a court in the state where the father resides will recognize and enforce a custody decree rendered in the home state where the child lives with the mother if the father was duly notified and given enough time to appear in the proceedings. Personal jurisdiction over the father is not required. See Comment to section 12. This is in accord with a common interpretation of the inconclusive decision in May v. Anderson, 345 U.S. 528, 72 S. Ct. 840, 97 L. Ed. 1221 (1953). See Restatement of the Law Second, Conflict of Law, Proposed Official Draft, section 79 and comment thereto, p. 298 (1967). Under this interpretation a state is permitted to recognize a custody decree of another state regardless of lack of personal jurisdiction, as long as due process requirements of notice and opportunity to be heard have been met. . . . The Act emphasizes the need for the personal appearance of the contestants rather than any technical requirement for personal jurisdiction.

The mandate of this section could cause problems if the prior decree is a punitive or disciplinary measure. See Ehrenzweig, Inter-state Recognition of Custody Decrees, 51 Mich. L. Rev. 345, 370 (1953). If, for example, a court grants custody to the mother and after 5 years' of continuous life with the mother the child is awarded to the father by the same court for the sole reason that the mother who had moved to another state upon remarriage had not lived up to the visitation requirements of the decree, courts in other states may be reluctant to recognize the changed decree. Disciplinary decrees of this type can be avoided under this Act by enforcing the visitation provisions of the decree directly in another state. See Section 15. If the original plan for visitation does not fit the new conditions, a petition for modification of the visiting arrangements would be filed in a court which has jurisdiction, that is, in many cases the original court. See section 14.

Section 14. [Modification of Custody Decree of Another State].

(a) If a court of another state has made a custody decree, a court of this State shall not modify that decree unless (1) it appears to the court of this State that the court which rendered the decree does not now have jurisdiction under jurisdictional prerequisites substantially in accordance with this Act or has declined to assume jurisdiction to modify the decree and (2) the court of this State has jurisdiction.

(b) If a court of this State if authorized under subsection (a) and section 8 to modify a custody decree of another state it shall give due consideration to the transcript of the record and other documents of all previous proceedings submitted to it in accordance with section 22.

Comment

Courts which render a custody decree normally retain continuing jurisdiction to modify the decree under local law. Courts in other states have in the past often assumed jurisdiction to modify the out-of-state decree themselves without regard to the preexisting jurisdiction of the other state. See People ex rel. Halvey v. Halvey, 330 U.S. 610, 67 S. Ct. 903, 91 L. Ed. 1133 (1947). In order to achieve greater stability of custody arrangements and avoid forum shopping, subsection (a) declares that other states will defer to the continuing jurisdiction of the court of another state as long as that state has jurisdiction under the standards of this Act. In other words, all petitions for modification are to be addressed to the prior state if that state has sufficient contact with the case to satisfy section 3. The fact that the court had previously considered the case may be one factor favoring its continued jurisdiction. If, however, all the parsons involved have moved away or the contact with the state has otherwise become slight, modification jurisdiction would shift elsewhere. Compare Ratner, Child Custody in a Federal System, 62 Mich. L. Rev. 795, 821-2 (1964).

For example, if custody was awarded to the father in state 1 where he continued to live with the children for two years and thereafter his wife kept the children in state 2 for 6 1/2 months (3 1/2 months beyond her visitation privileges) with or without permission of the husband, state 1 has preferred jurisdiction to modify the degree despite the fact that state 2 has in the meantime become the "home state" of the child. If, however, the father also moved away from state 1, that state loses modification jurisdiction interstate, whether or not its jurisdiction continues under the local law. See Clark, Domestic Relations 322-23 (1968). Also, if the father in the same case continued to live in state 1, but let his wife keep the children for several years without asserting his custody rights and without visits of the children in state 1, modification jurisdiction of state 1 would ceases. Compare Brengle v. Hurst, 408 S.W.2d 418 (Ky. 1966). The situation would be different if the children had been abducted and their whereabouts could not be discovered by the legal custodian for several years. The abductor would be denied access to the court of another state under section 8(b) and state 1 would have modification jurisdiction in any event under section 3(a)(4). Compare Crocker v. Crocker, 122 Colo. 49, 219 P.2d 311 (1950).

The prior court has jurisdiction to modify under this section even though its original assumption of jurisdiction did not meet the standards of this Act, as long as it would have jurisdiction *now*, that is, at the time of the petition for modification.

If the state of the prior decree declines to assume jurisdiction to modify the decree, another state with jurisdiction under section 3 can proceed with the case. That is not so if the prior court dismissed the petition on its merits.

Respect for the continuing jurisdiction of another state under this section will serve the purposes of this Act only if the prior court will assume a corresponding obligation to make no changes in the existing custody arrangement which are not required for the good of the child. If the court overturns its own decree in order to discipline a mother or father, with whom the child had lived for years, for failure to comply with an order of the court, the objective of greater stability of custody decrees is not achieved. See Comment to section 13 last paragraph, and cases there cited. See also Sharpe v. Sharpe, 77 Ill. App. 2925, 222 N.E.2d 340 (1966). Under section 15 of this Act an order of a court contained in a custody decree can be directly enforced in another state.

Under subsection (b) transcripts of prior proceedings if received under section 22 are to be considered by the modifying court. The purpose is to give the judge the opportunity to be as fully informed as possible before making a custody decision. "One court will seldom have so much of the story that another's inquiry is unimportant" says Paulsen, Appointment of a Guardian in the Conflict of Laws, 45 Iowa L. Rev. 212, 226 (1960). How much consideration is "due" this transcript, whether or under what conditions it is received in evidence, are matters of local, internal law which are not affected by this interstate act.

Section 15. [Filing and Enforcement of Custody Decree of Another State].

(a) A certified copy of a custody decree of another state may be filed in the office of the clerk of any [District Court, Family Court] of this State. The clerk shall treat the decree in the same manner as a custody decree of the [District Court, Family Court] of this State. A custody decree so filed has the same effect and shall be enforced in like manner as a custody decree rendered by a court of this State.

(b) A person violating a custody decree of another state which makes it necessary to enforce the decree in this State may be required to pay necessary travel and other expenses, including attorneys' fees, incurred by the party entitled to the custody or his witnesses.

Section 16. [Registry of Out-of-State Custody Decrees and Proceedings].

The clerk of each [District Court, Family Court] shall maintain a registry in which he shall enter the following:

(1) certified copies of custody decrees of other states received for filing;

(2) communications as to the pendency of custody proceedings in other states;

(3) communications concerning a finding of inconvenient forum by a court of another state; and

(4) other communications or documents concerning custody proceedings in another state which may affect the jurisdiction of a court of this State or the disposition to be made by it in a custody proceeding.

Section 17. [Certified Copies of Custody Decree].

The Clerk of the [District Court, Family Court] of this State, at the request of the court of another sate or at the request of any person who is affected by or has a legitimate interest in a custody decree, shall certify and forward a copy of the decree to that court or person.

Section 18. [Taking Testimony in Another State].

In addition to other procedural devices available to a party, any party to the proceeding or a guardian ad litem or other representative of the child may adduce testimony of witnesses, including parties and the child, by deposition or otherwise, in another state. The court on its own motion may direct that the testimony of a person be taken in another state and may prescribe the manner in which and the terms upon which the testimony shall be taken.

Section 19. [Hearings and Studies in Another State; Orders to Appear].

(a) A court of this State may request the appropriate court of another state to hold a hearing to adduce evidence, to order a party to produce or give evidence under other procedures of that state, or to have social studies made with respect to the custody of a child involved in proceedings pending in the court of this State; and to forward to the court of this State certified copies of the transcript of the record of the hearing, the evidence otherwise adduced, or any social studies prepared in compliance with the request. The cost of the services may be assessed against the parties or, if necessary ordered paid by the [County, State].

(b) A court of this State may request the appropriate court of another state to order a party to custody proceedings pending in the court of this State to appear in the proceedings, and if that party has physical custody of the child, to appear with the child. The request may state that travel and other necessary expenses of the party and of the child whose appearance is desired will be assessed against another party or will otherwise be paid.

Section 20. [Assistance to Courts of Other States].

(a) Upon request of the court of another state the courts of this State which are competent to hear custody matters may order a person in this State to appear at a hearing to adduce evidence or to produce or give evidence under other procedures available in this State [or may order social studies to be made for use in a custody proceeding in another state]. A certified copy of the transcript of the record of the hearing or the evidence otherwise adduced [and any social studies prepared] shall be forwarded by the clerk of the court to the requesting court.

(b) A person within this State may voluntarily give his testimony or statement in this State for use in a custody proceeding outside this state.

(c) Upon request of the court of another state a competent court of this State may order a person in this State to appear alone or with the child in a custody proceeding in another state. The court may condition compliance with the request upon assurance by the other state that state travel and other necessary expenses will be advanced or reimbursed.

Section 21. [Preservation of Documents for Use in Other States].

In any custody proceeding in this State the court shall preserve the pleadings, orders and decrees, any record that has been made of its hearings, social studies, and other pertinent documents until the child reaches [18, 21] years of age. Upon appropriate request of the court of another state the court shall forward to the other court certified copies of any or all of such documents.

Section 22. [Request for Court Records of Another State].

If a custody decree has been rendered in another state concerning a child involved in a custody proceeding pending in a court of this State, the court of this State upon taking jurisdiction of the case shall request of the court of the other state a certified copy of the transcript of any court record and other documents mentioned in section 21.

Section 23. [International Application].

The general policies of this Act extend to the international area. The provisions of this Act relating to the recognition and enforcement of custody decrees of other states apply to custody decrees and decrees involving legal institutions similar in nature to custody institutions rendered by appropriate authorities of other nations if reasonable notice and opportunity to be heard were given to all affected persons.

Section 24. [Priority].

Upon the request of a party to a custody proceeding which raises a question of existence or exercise of jurisdiction under this Act the case shall be given calendar priority and handled expeditiously.

[Sections 25-28, dealing with the Act's short title, severability, repeal of other legislation, and time of taking effect, have been omitted.]

Parental Kidnapping Prevention Act (1980)
Public Law 96-611, 96th Congress, 2d Session

Section 7.

(a) The Congress finds that—

(1) there is a large and growing number of cases annually involving disputes between persons claiming rights of custody and visitation of children under the laws, and in the courts, of different States, the District of Columbia, the Commonwealth of Puerto Rico, and the territories and possessions of the United States;

(2) the laws and practices by which the courts of those jurisdictions determine their jurisdiction to decide such disputes, and the effect to be given the decisions of such disputes by the courts of other jurisdictions, are often inconsistent and conflicting;

(3) those characteristics of the law and practice in such cases, along with the limits imposed by a Federal system on the authority of each such jurisdiction to conduct investigations and take other actions outside its own boundaries, contribute to a tendency of parties involved in such disputes to frequently resort to the seizure, restraint, concealment, and interstate transportation of children, the disregard of court orders, excessive relitigation of cases, obtaining of conflicting orders by the courts of various jurisdictions, and interstate travel and communication that is so expensive and time consuming as to disrupt their occupations and commercial activities; and

(4) among the results of those conditions and activities are the failure of the courts of such jurisdictions to give full faith and credit to the judicial proceedings of the other jurisdictions, the deprivation of rights of liberty and property without due process of law, burdens on commerce among such jurisdictions and with foreign nations, and harm to the welfare of children and their parents and other custodians.

(b) For those reasons it is necessary to establish a national system for locating parents and children who travel from one such jurisdiction to another and are concealed in connection with such disputes, and to establish national standards under which the courts of such jurisdictions will determine ther jurisdiction to decide such disputes and the effect to be given by each such jurisdiction to such decisions by the courts of other such jurisdictions.

(c) The general purposes of sections 6 to 10 of this Act are to—

(1) promote cooperation between State courts to the end that a determination of custody and visitation is rendered in the State which can best decide the case in the interest of the child;

(2) promote and expand the exchange of information and other forms of mutual assistance between States which are concerned with the same child;

(3) facilitate the enforcement of custody and visitation decrees of sister States;

(4) discourage continuing interstate controversies over child custody in the interest of greater stability of home environment and of secure family relationships for the child;

(5) avoid jurisdictional competition and conflict between State courts in matters of child custody and visitation which have in the past resulted in the shifting of children from State to State with harmful effects on their well-being; and

(6) deter interstate abductions and other unilateral removals of children undertaken to obtain custody and visitation awards.

Section 8.

(a) Chapter 115 of title 28, United States Code, is amended by adding immediately after section 1738 the following new section:

"Section 1738A. Full faith and credit given to child custody determinations

"(a) The appropriate authorities of every State shall enforce according to its terms, and shall not modify except as provided in subsection (f) of this section, any child custody determination made consistently with the provisions of this section by a court of another State.

"(b) As used in this section, the term—

"(1) "child" means a person under the age of eighteen;

"(2) "contestant" means a person, including a parent, who claims a right to custody or visitation of a child;

"(3) "custody determination" means a judgment, decree, or other order of a court providing for the custody or visitation of a child, and includes permanent and temporary orders, and initial orders and modifications;

"(4) "home State" means the State in which, immediately preceding the time involved, the child lived with his parents, a parent, or a person acting as parent, for at least six consecutive months, and in the case of a child less than six months old, the State in which the child lived from birth with any of such persons. Periods of temporary absence of any of such persons are counted as part of the six-month or other periods;

"(5) "modifications" and "modify" refer to a custody determination which modifies, replaces, supersedes, or otherwise is made subsequent to, a prior custody determination concerning the same child, whether made by the same court or not;

"(6) "person acting as a parent" means a person, other than a parent, who has physical custody of a child and who has either been awarded custody by a court or claims a right to custody;

"(7) "physical custody" means actual possession and control of a child; and

"(8) "State" means a State of the United States, the District of Columbia, the Commonwealth of

Puerto Rico, or a territory or possession of the United States.

"(c) A child custody determination made by a court of a State is consistent with the provisions of this section only if—

"(1) "such court has jurisdiction under the law of such State; and

"(2) "one of the following conditions is met:

"(A) "such State (i) is the home State of the child on the date of the commencement of the proceeding, or (ii) had been the child's home State within six months before the date of the commencement of the proceeding and the child is absent from such State because of his removal or retention by a contestant or for other reasons, and a contestant continues to live in such State;

"(B) (i) it appears that no other State would have jurisdiction under subparagraph (A), and (ii) it is in the best interest of the child that a court of such State assume jurisdiction because (I) the child and his parents, or the child and at least one contestant, have a significant connection with such State other than mere physical presence in such State, and (II) there is available in such State substantial evidence concerning the child's present or future care, protection, training, and personal relationships;

"(C) the child is physically present in such State and (i) the child has been abandoned, or (ii) it is necessary in an emergency to protect the child because he has been subjected to or threatened with mistreatment or abuse;

"(D) (i) it appears that no other State would have jurisdiction under subparagraph (A), (B), (C) or (E), or another State has declined to exercise jurisdiction on the ground that the State whose jurisdiction is in issue is the more appropriate forum to determine the custody of the child, and (ii) it is in the best interest of the child that such court assume jurisdiction; or

"(E) the court has continuing jurisdiction pursuant to subsection (d) of this section.

"(d) "The jurisdiction of a court of a State which has made a child custody determination consistently with the provisions of this section continues as long as the requirement of subsection (c)(1) of this section continues to be met and such State remains the residence of the child or of any contestant.

"(e) Before a child custody determination is made, reasonable notice and opportunity to be heard shall be given to the contestants, any person whose parental rights have not been previously terminated and any person who has physical custody of a child.

"(f) A court of a State may modify a determination of the custody of the same child made by a court of another State, if—

"(1) "it has jurisdiction to make such a child custody determination; and

"(2) the court of the other State no longer has jurisdiction, or it has declined to exercise such jurisdiction to modify such determination.

"(g) "A court of a State shall not exercise jurisdiction in any proceeding for a custody determination commenced during the pendency of a proceeding in a court of another State where such court of that other State is exercising jurisdiction consistently with the provisions of this section to make a custody determination."

(b) The table of sections at the beginning of chapter 115 of title 28, United States Code, is amended by inserting after the item relating to section 1738 the following new item:

"1738A. Full faith and credit given to child custody determinations."

(c) In furtherance of the purposes of section 1738A of title 28, United States code, as added by subsection (a) of this section, State courts are encouraged to—

(1) afford priority to proceedings for custody determinations; and

(2) award to the person entitled to custody or visitation pursuant to a custody determination which is consistent with the provisions of such section 1738A, necessary travel expenses, attorneys' fees, costs of private investigations, witness fees or expenses, and other expenses incurred in connection with such custody determination in any case in which—

(A) a contestant has, without the consent of the person entitled to custody or visitation pursuant to a custody determination which is consistent with the provisions of such section 1738A, (i) wrongfully removed the child from the physical custody of such person, or (ii) wrongfully retained the child after a visit or other temporary relinquishment of physical custody; or

(B) the court determines it is appropriate.

Section 9. . . .

(b) Part D of title IV of the Social Security Act is amended by adding at the end thereof the following new section:

Use of Federal Parent Locator Service in Connection with the Enforcement or Determination of Child Custody and in Cases of Parental Kidnapping of a Child

"Section 463.

(a) The secretary shall enter into an agreement with any State which is able and willing to do so, under which the services of the Parent Locator Service established under section 453 shall be made available to such State for the purpose of determining the whereabouts of any absent parent or child when such information is to be used to locate such parent or child for the purpose of—

"(1) enforcing any State or Federal Law with respect to the unlawful taking or restraint of a child; or

"(2) making or enforcing a child custody determination.

"(b) An agreement entered into under this section shall provide that the State agency described in section 454 will, under procedures prescribed by the Secretary in regulations, receive and transmit to the Secretary requests from authorized persons for information as to (or useful in determining) the whereabouts of any absent parent or child when such information is to be used to locate such parent or child for the purpose of—

"(1) enforcing any State or Federal law with respect to the unlawful taking or restraint of a child; or

"(2) making or enforcing a child custody determination.

"(c) Information authorized to be provided by the Secretary under this section shall be subject to the same conditions with respect to disclosure as information authorized to be provided under section 453, and a request for information by the Secretary under this section shall be considered to be a request for information under section 453 which is authorized to be provided under such section. Only information as to the most recent address and place of employment of any absent parent or child shall be provided under this section.

"(d) For purposes of this section—

"(1) the term "custody determination" means a judgment, decree, or other order of a court providing for the custody or visitation of a child, and includes permanent and temporary orders, and initial orders and modification;

"(2) the term "authorized person" means—

"(A) any agent or attorney of any State having an agreement under this section, who has the duty or authority under the law of such State to enforce a child custody determination;

"(B) any court having jurisdiction to make or enforce such a child custody determination, or any agent of such court; and

"(C) any agent or attorney of the United States, or of a State having an agreement under this section, who has the duty or authority to investigate, enforce, or bring a prosecution with respect to the unlawful taking or restraint of a child.".

(c) Section 455(a) of such Act is amended by adding after paragraph (3) the following: "except that no amount shall be paid to any State on account of amounts expended to carry out an agreement which it has entered into pursuant to section 463."

(d) No agreement entered into under section 463 of the Social Security Act shall become effective before the date on which section 1738A of title 28, United States Code (as added by this title) becomes effective.

Section 10.

(a) In view of the findings of the Congress and the purposes of sections 6 to 10 of this Act set forth in section 302, the Congress hereby expressly declares its intent that section 1073 of title 18, United States code, apply to cases involving parental kidnaping and interstate or international flight to avoid prosecution under applicable State felony statutes.**

(b) The Attorney General of the United States, not later than 120 days after the date of the enactment of this section (and once every 6 months during the 3 years period following such 120 day period) shall submit a report to the Congress with respect to steps taken to comply with the intent of the Congress set forth in subsection (a). Each such report shall include—

(1) date relating to the number of applications for complaints under section 1073 of title 18, United States Code, in cases involving parental kidnapping:

(2) data relating to the number of complaints issued in such cases; and

(3) such other information as may assist in describing the activities of the Department of Justice in conformance with such intent.

Hague Conference on Private International Law: Convention on the Civil Aspects of International Child Abduction
(October 25, 1980)

The States signatory to the present Convention, Firmly convinced that the interests of children are of paramount importance in matters relating to their custody,

Desiring to protect children internationally from the harmful effects of their wrongful removal or retention and to establish procedures to ensure their prompt return to the State of their habitual residence, as well as to secure protection for rights of access,

Have resolved to conclude a Convention to this effect, and have agreed upon the following provisions—

CHAPTER I—SCOPE OF THE CONVENTION

Article 1
The objects of the present Convention are—a) to secure the prompt return of children wrongfully removed to or retained in any Contracting State; and b) to ensure that rights of custody and of access under the law of one Contracting State are effectively respected in the other Contracting States.

Article 2
Contracting States shall take all appropriate measures to secure within their territories the implementation of

---

**U.S.C. title 18, Section 1073 provides that:

Whoever moves or travels in interstate or foreign commerce with intent either (1) to avoid prosecution, or custody or confinement after conviction, under the laws of the place from which he flees, for a crime, or an attempt to commit a crime, punishable by death or which is a felony under the laws of the place from which the fugitive flees, or which, in the case of New Jersey, is a high misdemeanor under the laws of said State, or (2) to avoid giving testimony in any criminal proceedings in such place in which the commission of an offense punishable by death or which is a felony under the laws of such place, or which in the case of New Jersey, is a high misdemeanor under the laws of said State, is charged, or (3) to avoid service of, or contempt proceedings for alleged disobedience of, lawful process requiring attendance and the giving of testimony or the production of documentary evidence before an agency of a State empowered by the law of such State to conduct investigations of all alleged criminal activities, shall be fined not more than $5,000 or imprisoned not more than five years, or both.

Violations of this section may be prosecuted only in the Federal judicial district in which the original crime was alleged to have been committed, or in which the person was held in custody or confinement, or in which an avoidance of service of process or a contempt referred to in clause (3) of the first paragraph of this section is alleged to have been committed, and only upon formal approval in writing by the Attorney General or an Assistant Attorney General of the United States, which function of approving prosecutions may not be delegated.

the objects of the Convention. For this purpose they shall use the most expeditious procedures available.

Article 3

The removal or the retention of a child is to be considered wrongful where—a) it is in breach of rights of custody attributed to a person, an institution or any other body, either jointly or alone, under the law of the State in which the child was habitually resident immediately before the removal or retention; and b) at the time of removal or retention those rights were actually exercised, either jointly or alone, or would have been so exercised but for the removal or retention. The rights of custody mentioned in sub-paragraph a above, may arise in particular by operation of law or by reason of a judicial or administrative decision, or by reason of an agreement having legal effect under the law of that State.

Article 4

The Convention shall apply to any child who was habitually resident in a Contracting State immediately before any breach of custody or access rights. The Convention shall cease to apply when the child attains the age of 16 years.

Article 5

For the purposes of this Convention—a) 'rights of custody' shall include rights relating to the care of the person of the child and, in particular, the right to determine the child's place of residence; b) 'rights of access' shall include the right to take a child for a limited period of time to a place other than the child's habitual residence.

CHAPTER II—CENTRAL AUTHORITIES

Article 6

A Contracting State shall designate a Central Authority to discharge the duties which are imposed by the Convention upon such authorities.

Federal States, States with more than one system of law or States having autonomous territorial organizations shall be free to appoint more than one Central Authority and to specify the territorial extent of their powers. Where a State has appointed more than one Central Authority, it shall designate the Central Authority to which applications may be addressed for transmission to the appropriate Central Authority within that State.

Article 7

Central Authorities shall co-operate with each other and promote co-operation amongst the competent authorities in their respective States to secure the prompt return of children and to achieve the other objects of this Convention.

In particular, either directly or through any intermediary, they shall take all appropriate measures—a) to discover the whereabouts of a child who has been wrongfully removed or retained; b) to prevent further harm to the child or prejudice to interested parties by taking or causing to be taken provisional measures; c) to secure the voluntary return of the child or to bring about an amicable resolution of the issues; d) to exchange, where desirable, information relating to the social background of the child; e) to provide information of a general character as to the law of their State in connection with the application of the Convention; f) to initiate or facilitate the institution of judicial or administrative proceedings with a view to obtaining the return of the child and, in a proper case, to make arrangements for organizing or securing the effective exercise of rights of access; g) where the circumstances so require, to provide or facilitate the provision of legal aid and advice, including the participation of legal counsel and advisers; h) to provide such administrative arrangements as may be necessary and appropriate to secure the safe return of the child; i) to keep each other informed with respect to the operation of this Convention and, as far as possible, to eliminate any obstacles to its application.

CHAPTER III—RETURN OF CHILDREN

Article 8

Any person, institution or other body claiming that a child has been removed or retained in breach of custody rights may apply either to the Central Authority of the child's habitual residence or to the Central Authority of any other Contracting State for assistance in securing the return of the child.

The application shall contain—a) information concerning the identity of the applicant, of the child and of the person alleged to have removed or retained the child; b) where available, the date of birth of the child; c) the grounds on which the applicant's claim for return of the child is based; d) all available information relating to the whereabouts of the child and the identity of the person with whom the child is presumed to be.

The application may be accompanied or supplemented by—e) an authenticated copy of any relevant decision or agreement; f) a certificate or an affidavit emanating from a Central Authority, or other competent authority of the State of the child's habitual residence, or from a qualified person, concerning the relevant law of that State; g) any other relevant document.

Article 9

If the Central Authority which receives an application referred to in Article 8 has reason to believe that the child is in another Contracting State, it shall directly and without delay transmit the application to the Central Authority of that Contracting State and inform the requesting Central Authority, or the applicant, as the case may be.

Article 10

The Central Authority of the State where the child is shall take or cause to be taken all appropriate measures in order to obtain the voluntary return of the child.

Article 11

The judicial or administrative authorities of Contracting States shall act expeditiously in proceedings for the return of children.

If the judicial or administrative authority concerned has not reached a decision within six weeks from the date of commencement of the proceedings, the applicant or the Central Authority of the requested State, on its own initiative or if asked by the Central Authority of the requesting State, shall have the right to request a statement of the reasons for the delay. If a reply is received by the Central Authority of the requested State, that Authority shall transmit the reply to the Central Authority of the requesting State, or to the applicant, as the case may be.

Article 12

Where a child has been wrongfully removed or retained in terms of Article 3 and, at the date of the commencement of the proceedings before the judicial or administrative authority of the Contracting State where the child is, a period of less than one year has elapsed from the date of the wrongful removal or retention, the authority concerned shall order the return of the child forthwith. The judicial or administrative authority, even where the proceedings have been commenced after the expiration of the period of one year referred to in the preceding paragraph, shall also order the return of the child, unless it is demonstrated that the child is now settled in its new environment.

Where the judicial or administrative authority in the requested State has reason to believe that the child has been taken to another State, it may stay the proceedings or dismiss the application for the return of the child.

Article 13

Notwithstanding the provisions of the preceding Article, the judicial or administrative authority of the requested State is not bound to order the return of the child if the person, institution or other body which opposes its return establishes that—a) the person, institution or other body having the care of the person of the child was not actually exercising the custody rights at the time of removal or retention, or had consented to or subsequently acquiesced in the removal or retention; or b) there is a grave risk that his or her return would expose the child to physical or psychological harm or otherwise place the child in an intolerable situation. The judicial or administrative authority may also refuse to order the return of the child if it finds that the child objects to being returned and has attained an age and degree of maturity at which it is appropriate to take account of its views.

In considering the circumstances referred to in this Article, the judicial and administrative authorities shall take into account the information relating to the social background of the child provided by the Central Authority or other competent authority of the child's habitual residence.

Article 14

In ascertaining whether there has been a wrongful removal or retention within the meaning of Article 3, the judicial or administrative authorities of the requested State may take notice directly of the law of, and of judicial or administrative decisions, formally recognized or not in the State of the habitual residence of the child, without recourse to the specific procedures for the proof of that law or for the recognition of foreign decisions which would otherwise be applicable.

Article 15

The judicial or administrative authorities of a Contracting State may, prior to the making of an order for the return of the child, request that the applicant obtain from the authorities of the State of the habitual residence of the child a decision or other determination that the removal or retention was wrongful within the meaning of Article 3 of the Convention, where such a decision or determination may be obtained in that State. The Central Authorities of the Contracting States shall so far as practicable assist applicants to obtain such a decision or determination.

Article 16

After receiving notice of a wrongful removal or retention of a child in the sense of Article 3, the judicial or administrative authorities of the Contracting State to which the child has been removed or in which it has been retained shall not decide on the merits of rights of custody until it has been determined that the child is not to be returned under this Convention or unless an application under this Convention is not lodged within a reasonable time following receipt of the notice.

Article 17

The sole fact that a decision relating to custody has been given in or is entitled to recognition in the requested State shall not be a ground for refusing to return a child under this Convention, but the judicial or administrative authorities of the requested State may take account of the reasons for that decision in applying this Convention.

Article 18

The provisions of this Chapter do not limit the power of a judicial or administrative authority to order the return of the child at any time.

Article 19

A decision under this Convention concerning the return of the child shall not be taken to be a determination on the merits of any custody issue.

Article 20

The return of the child under the provisions of Article 12 may be refused if this would not be permitted by the fundamental principles of the requested State relating to the protection of human rights and fundamental freedoms.

CHAPTER IV—RIGHTS OF ACCESS

Article 21

An application to make arrangements for organizing or securing the effective exercise of rights of access may be presented to the Central Authorities of the Contracting States in the same way as an application for the return of a child.

The Central Authorities are bound by the obligations of co-operation which are set forth in Article 7 to promote the peaceful enjoyment of access rights and the fulfillment of any conditions to which the exercise of those rights may be subject. The Central Authorities shall take steps to remove, as far as possible, all obstacles to the exercise of such rights.

The Central Authorities either directly or through intermediaries, may initiate or assist in the institution of proceedings with a view to organizing or protecting these rights and securing respect for the conditions to which the exercise of these rights may be subject.

CHAPTER V—GENERAL PROVISIONS

Article 22

No security, bond or deposit, however described, shall be required to guarantee the payment of costs and expenses in the judicial or administrative proceedings falling within the scope of this Convention.

Article 23

No legalization or similar formality may be required in the context of this Convention.

Article 24

Any application, communication or other document sent to the Central Authority of the requested State shall be in the original language, and shall be accompanied by a translation into the official language or one of the official languages of the requested State or, where that is not feasible, a translation into French or English.

However, a Contracting State may, by making a reservation in accordance with Article 42, object to the use of either French or English, but not both, in any application, communication or other document sent to its Central Authority.

Article 25

Nationals of the Contracting States and persons who are habitually resident within those States shall be entitled in matters concerned with the application of this Convention to legal aid and advice in any other Contracting State on the same conditions as it they themselves were nationals of and habitually resident in that State.

Article 26

Each Central Authority shall bear its own costs in applying this Convention.

Central Authorities and other public services of Contracting States shall not impose any charges in relation to applications submitted under this Convention. In particular, they may not require any payment from the applicant towards the costs and expenses of the proceedings or, where applicable, those arising from the participation of legal counsel or advisers. However, they may require the payment of the expenses incurred or to be incurred in implementing the return of the child.

However, a Contracting State may, by making a reservation in accordance with Article 42, declare that it shall not be bound to assume any costs referred to in the preceding paragraph resulting from the participation of legal counsel or advisers or from court proceedings, except insofar as those costs may be covered by its system of legal aid and advice.

Upon ordering the return of a child or issuing an order concerning rights of access under this Convention, the judicial or administrative authorities may, where appropriate, direct the person who removed or retained the child, or who prevented the exercise of rights of access, to pay necessary expenses incurred by or on behalf of the applicant, including travel expenses, any costs incurred or payments made for locating the child, the costs of legal representation of the applicant, and those of returning the child.

Article 27

When it is manifest that the requirements of this Convention are not fulfilled or that the application is otherwise not well founded, a Central Authority is not bound to accept the application. In that case, the Central Authority shall forthwith inform the applicant or the Central Authority through which the application was submitted, as the case may be, of its reasons.

Article 28

A Central Authority may require that the application be accompanied by a written authorization empowering it to act on behalf of the applicant, or to designate a representative so to act.

Article 29

This Convention shall not preclude any person, institution or body who claims that there has been a breach of custody or access rights within the meaning of Article 3 or 21 from applying directly to the judicial or administrative authorities of a Contracting State, whether or not under the provisions of this Convention.

Article 30

Any application submitted to the Central Authorities or directly to the judicial or administrative authorities of a Contracting State in accordance with the terms of this Convention, together with documents and any other information appended thereto or provided by a Central Authority, shall be admissible in the courts or administrative authorities of the Contracting States.

Article 31

In relation to a State which in matters of custody of children has two or more systems of law applicable in different territorial units—a) any reference to habitual residence in that State shall be construed as referring to habitual resident in a territorial unit of that State; b) any reference to the law of the State of habitual residence shall be construed as referring to the law of the territorial unit in that State where the child habitually resides.

Article 32

In relation to a State which in matters of custody of children has two or more systems of law applicable to different categories of persons, any reference to the law of that State shall be construed as referring to the legal system specified by the law of that State.

Article 33

A State within which different territorial units have their own rules of law in respect of custody of children shall not be bound to apply this Convention where a State with a unified system of law would not be bound to do so.

Article 34

This Convention shall take priority in matters within its scope over the Convention of 5 October 1961 concerning the powers of authorities and the law applicable in respect of the protection of minors, as between Parties to both Conventions. Otherwise the present Convention shall not restrict the application of an international instrument in force between the State of origin and the State addressed or other law of the State addressed for the purposes of obtaining the return of a child who has been wrongfully removed or retained or of organizing access rights.

Article 35

This Convention shall apply as between Contracting States only to wrongful removals or retention occurring after its entry into force in those states.

Where a declaration has been made under Article 39 or 40, the reference in the preceding paragraph to a Contracting State shall be taken to refer to the territorial unit or units in relation to which this Convention applies.

Article 36

Nothing in this Convention shall prevent two or more Contracting States, in order to limit the restrictions to which the return of the child may be subject, from agreeing among themselves to derogate from any provisions of this Convention which may imply such a restriction.

International Child Abduction Remedies Act
Title 42, United States Code Annotated

Section 11601. Findings and declarations

(a) Findings

The Congress makes the following findings:

(1) The international abduction or wrongful retention of children is harmful to their well-being.

(2) Persons should not be permitted to obtain custody of children by virtue of their wrongful removal or retention.

(3) International abductions and retentions of children are increasing, and only concerted cooperation pursuant to an international agreement can effectively combat this problem.

(4) The Convention on the Civil Aspects of International Child Abduction, done at The Hague on October 25, 1980, established legal rights and procedures for the prompt return of children who have been wrongfully removed or retained, as well as for securing the exercise of visitation rights. Children who are wrongfully removed or retained within the meaning of the Convention are to be promptly returned unless one of the narrow exceptions set forth in the Convention applies. The Convention provides a sound treaty framework to help resolve the problem of international abduction and retention of children and will deter such wrongful removals and retentions.

(b) Declarations. The Congress makes the following declarations:

(1) It is the purpose of this chapter to establish procedures for the implementation of the Convention in the United States.

(2) The provisions of this chapter are in addition to and not in lieu of the provisions of the Convention.

(3) In enacting this chapter the Congress recognizes—

(A) the international character of the Conventions; and

(B) the need for uniform international interpretation of the Convention.

(4) The Convention and this chapter empower courts in the United States to determine only rights under the Convention and not the merits of any underlying child custody claims.

Section 11602. Definitions

For the purposes of this chapter—

(1) the term "applicant" means any person who, pursuant to the Convention, files an application with the United States Central Authority or Central Authority of any other party to the Convention for the return of a child alleged to have been wrongfully removed or retained or for arrangements for organizing or securing the effective exercise of rights of access pursuant to the Convention;

(2) the term "Convention" means the Convention on the Civil Aspects of International Child Abduction, done at The Hague on October 25, 1980;

(3) the term "Parent Locator Service" means the service established by the Secretary of Health and Human Services under section 653 of this title;

(4) the term "petitioner" means any person who, in accordance with this chapter, files a petition in court seeking relief under the Convention;

(5) the term "person" includes any individual, institution, or other legal entity or body;

(6) the term "respondent" means any person against whose interests a petition is filed in court, in accordance with this chapter, which seeks relief under the Convention;

(7) the term "rights of access" means visitation rights;

(8) the term "State" means any of the several States, the District of Columbia, and any commonwealth, territory, or possession of the United States; and

(9) the term "United States Central Authority" means the agency of the Federal Government designated by the President under section 11606(a) of this title.

Section 11603. Judicial remedies

(a) Jurisdiction of the courts. The courts of the States and the United States district courts shall have concurrent original jurisdiction of actions arising under the Convention.

(b) Petitions. Any person seeking to initiate judicial proceedings under the Convention for the return of a child or for arrangements for organizing or securing the effective exercise of rights of access to a child may do so by commencing a civil action by filing a petition for the relief sought in any court which has jurisdiction of such action and which is authorized to exercise its jurisdiction in the place where the child is located at the time the petition is filed.

(c) Notice. Notice of an action brought under subsection (b) of this section shall be given in accordance with the applicable law governing notice in interstate child custody proceedings.

(d) Determination of case. The court in which an action is brought under subsection (b) of this section shall decide the case in accordance with the Convention.

(e) Burdens of proof

(1) A petitioner in an action brought under subsection (b) of this section shall establish by a preponderance of the evidence—

(A) in the case of an action for the return of a child, that the child has been wrongfully removed or retained within the meaning of the Convention; and

(B) in the case of an action for arrangements for organizing or securing the effective exercise of rights of access, that the petitioner has such rights.

(2) In the case of an action for the return of a child, a respondent who opposes the return of the child has the burden of establishing—

    (A) by clear and convincing evidence that one of the exceptions set forth in article 13b or 20 of the Convention applies; and

    (B) by a preponderance of the evidence that any other exception set forth in article 12 or 13 of the Convention applies.

(f) Application of the Convention. For purposes of any action brought under this chapter—

    (1) the term" authorities", as used in article 15 of the Convention to refer to the authorities of the state of the habitual residence of a child, includes courts and appropriate government agencies;

    (2) the terms "wrongful removal or retention: and Wrongfully removed or retained", as used in the Convention, include a removal or retention of a child before the entry of a custody order regarding that child; and

    (3) the term "commencement of proceedings", as used in article 12 of the Convention, means, with respect to the return of a child located in the United States, the filing of a petition in accordance with subsection (b) of this section.

(g) Full faith and credit. Full faith and credit shall be accorded by the courts of the States and the courts of the United States to judgment of any other such court ordering or denying the return of a child, pursuant to the Convention, in an action brought under this chapter.

(h) Remedies under the Convention not exclusive. The remedies established by the Convention and this chapter shall be in addition to remedies available under other laws or international agreements.

Section 11604. Provisional remedies

(a) Authority of courts. In furtherance of the objectives of article 7(b) and other provisions of the Convention, and subject to the provisions of subsection (b) of this section, any court exercising jurisdiction of an action brought under section 11603(b) of this title may take or cause to be taken measures under Federal or State law, as appropriate, to protect the well-being of the child involved or to prevent the child's further removal or concealment before the final disposition of the petition.

(b) Limitation on authority. No court exercising jurisdiction of an action brought under section 11603(b) of this title, may under subsection (a) of this section, order a child removed from a person having physical control of the child unless the applicable requirements of State law are satisfied.

[The United States deposited its instrument of ratification of the Hague Convention on the Civil Aspects of International Child Abduction on April 29, 1988. The Convention entered into force for the United States on July 1, 1988. On August 8, 1988, President Reagan designated the Department of State as the Central Authority of the United States for purposes of the Convention, authorizing and empowering the Secretary of State, in accordance with such regulations as he or she may prescribe, to perform all lawful acts necessary and proper to execute the functions of the Central Authority in a timely and efficient manner.]

International Parental Kidnapping Act
Title 18, U.S. Code Annotated

Section 1204. International parental kidnapping

(a) Whoever removes a child from the United States or retains a child (who has been in the United States) outside the United States with intent to obstruct the lawful exercise of parental rights shall be fined under this title or imprisoned not more than 3 years, or both.

(b) As used in this section—

    (1) the term "child" means a person who has not attained the age of 16 years; and

    (2) the term "parental rights", with respect to a child, means the right to physical custody of the child—

        (A) whether joint or sole (and includes visiting rights); and

        (B) whether arising by operation of law, court order, or legally binding agreement of the parties.

(c) It shall be an affirmative defense under this section that—

    (1) the defendant acted within the provisions of a valid court order granting the defendant legal custody or visitation rights and that order was obtained pursuant to the Uniform Child Custody Jurisdiction Act and was in effect at the time of the offense;

    (2) the defendant was fleeing an incidence or pattern of domestic violence;

    (3) the defendant had physical custody of the child pursuant to a court order granting legal custody or visitation rights and failed to return the child as a result of circumstances beyond the defendant's control, and the defendant notified or made reasonable attempts to notify the other parent or lawful custodian of the child of such circumstances within 24 hours after the visitation period had expired and returned the child as soon as possible.

(d) This section does not detract from The Hague Convention on the Civil Aspects of International Parental Child Abduction, done at The Hague on October 25, 1980.

Uniform Interstate Family Support Act (1992)
9 U.L.A. 255 (Supp. 1996)

[Reproduced with the permission of the National Conference of Commissioners on Uniform State Laws. Only selected parts of the Commentary have been included.]

ARTICLE 1. GENERAL PROVISIONS

Section 101. Definitions.

In this [Act]:

(1) "Child" means an individual, whether over or under the age of majority, who is or is alleged to be owed a duty of support by the individual's parent or who is or is alleged to be the beneficiary of a support order directed to the parent.

(2) "Child support order" means a support order for a child, including a child who has attained the age of majority under the law of the issuing state.

(3) "Duty of support" means an obligation imposed or imposable by law to provide support for a child, spouse, or former spouse, including an unsatisfied obligation to provide support.

(4) "Home State" means the state in which a child lived with a parent or a person acting as parent for at least six consecutive months immediately preceding the time of filing of a [petition] or comparable pleading for support and, if a child is less than six months old, the state in which the child lived from birth with any of them. A period of temporary absence of any of them is counted as part of the six-month or other period.

(5) "Income" includes earnings or other periodic entitlements to money from any source and any other property subject to withholding for support under the law of this State.

(6) "Income-withholding order" means an order or other legal process directed to an obligor's employer [or other debtor], as defined by [the income-withholding law of this State], to withhold support from the income of the obligor.

(7) "Initiating state" means a state in which a proceeding under this [Act] or a law substantially similar to this [Act], the Uniform Reciprocal Enforcement of Support Act, or the Revised Uniform Reciprocal Enforcement of Support Act is filed for forwarding to a responding state.

(8) "Initiating tribunal" means the authorized tribunal in an initiating state.

(9) "Issuing state" means the state in which a tribunal issues a support order or renders a judgment determining parentage.

(10) "Issuing tribunal" means the tribunal that issues a support order or renders a judgment determining parentage.

(11) "Law" includes decisional and statutory law and rules and regulations having the force of law.

(12) "Obligee" means:

(i) an individual to whom a duty of support is or is alleged to be owed or in whose favor a support order has been issued or a judgment determining parentage has been rendered;

(ii) a state or political subdivision to which the rights under a duty of support or support order have been assigned or which has independent claims based on financial assistance provided to an individual obligee; or

(iii) an individual seeking a judgment determining parentage of the individual's child.

(13) "Obligor" means an individual, or the estate of a decedent:

(i) who owes or is alleged to owe a duty of support;

(ii) who is alleged but has not been adjudicated to be a parent of a child; or

(iii) who is liable under a support order.

(14) "Register" means to [record; file] a support order or judgment determining parentage in the [appropriate location for the recording or filing of foreign judgments generally or foreign support orders specifically].

(15) "Registering tribunal" means a tribunal in which a support order is registered.

(16) "Responding state" means a state to which a proceeding is forwarded under this [Act] or a law substantially similar to this [Act], the Uniform Reciprocal Enforcement of Support Act, or the Revised Uniform Reciprocal Enforcement of Support Act.

(17) "Responding tribunal" means the authorized tribunal in a responding state.

(18) "Spousal-support order" means a support order for a spouse or former spouse of the obligor.

(19) "State" means a state of the United States, the District of Columbia, the Commonwealth of Puerto Rice, or any territory or insular possession subject to the jurisdiction of the United States. The term "state" includes an Indian tribe and includes a foreign jurisdiction that has established procedures for issuance and enforcement of support orders which are substantially similar to the procedures under this [Act].

(20) "Support enforcement agency" means a public official or agency authorized to seek:

(i) enforcement of support orders or laws relating to the duty of support;

(ii) establishment or modification of child support;

(iii) determination of parentage; or

(iv) to locate obligors or their assets.

(21) "Support order" means a judgment, degree, or order, whether temporary, final, or subject to modification, for the benefit of a child, a spouse, or a former spouse, which provides for monetary support, health care, arrearage, or reimbursement, and may include related costs and fees, interest, income withholding, attorney's fees, and other relief.

(22) "Tribunal" means a court, administrative agency, or quasi-judicial entity authorized to establish, enforce, or modify support orders or to determine parentage.

Comment

Several additional terms are defined in this section as compared to the parallel RURESA §2, which has fourteen entries. Many crucial definitions continue to be left to local law. For example, the definitions of "child" and "child support order" provided by Subsections (1) and (2) refer to "the age of majority" without further elaboration. The exact age at which a child becomes an adult for different purposes is a matter for the law of each state, as is the age at which a parent's duty to furnish child support terminates. Similarly, a wide variety of other terms of art are implicitly left to state law. For example, Subsection (21) refers inter alia to "health care, arrearage, or reimbursement. . . ." All of these terms are subject to individualized definitions on a state-by-state basis.

Subsection (3) defines "duty of support" to mean the legal obligation to provide support before it has been reduced to judgment. It is broadly defined to include both prospective and retrospective obligations, to the extent they are imposed by the relevant state law.

In order to resolve certain conflicts in the exercise of jurisdiction, for limited purposes Subsection (4) borrows the concept of the "home state" of a child from the Uniform Child Custody Jurisdiction Act, versions of which have been adopted in all 50 states, and from the federal Parental Kidnapping Prevention Act, 42 U.S.C. §1738A.

Subsection (6) is written broadly so that states that direct income withholding by an obligor's employer based on "other legal process," as distinguished from an order of a tribunal, may have that "legal process" recognized as an "income-withholding order." Federal law requires that each state provide for income withholding "without the necessity of any application therefor . . . or for any further . . . by the court or other entity which issued such order." 42 U.S.C. 666(b)(2). States have complied with this directive in a variety of ways. For example, New York provides a method for obtaining income withholding of court-ordered support by authorizing an attorney, clerk of court, sheriff or agent of the child support enforcement agency to serve upon the defaulting obligor's employer an "income execution for support enforcement." New York McKinney's C.P.L.R. 5241. This "other legal process" reportedly is the standard method for obtaining income withholding in that state, while the statutory provision for an income withholding order, C.P.L.R. 5242, is rarely used by either the courts or the litigants.

Subsections (7) and (8) define "initiating state" and "initiating tribunal" similarly to RURESA §2(d). It is important to note, however, that this Act permits the direct filing of an interstate action in the responding state without an initial filing in an initiating tribunal. Thus, a petitioner in one state could seek to establish a support order in a second state by either filing in the second state's tribunal or seeking the assistance of the support enforcement agency in the second state.

The term "obligee" in Subsection (12) is defined in a broad manner similar to RURESA §2(f), which is consistent with common usage. In instances of spousal support, the person owed the duty of support and the person receiving the payments are almost always the same. Use of the term is more complicated in the context of a child support order. The child is the person to whom the duty of support is owed and therefore can be viewed as the ultimate obligee. However, "obligee" usually refers to the individual receiving the payments. While this is most commonly the custodial parent or other legal custodian, the "obligee" may be a support enforcement agency which has been assigned the right to receive support payments in order to recoup AFDC (Aid to Families with Dependent Children, 42 U.S.C. §601 et seq.). Even in the absence of such an assignment, a state may have an independent statutory claim for reimbursement for general assistance provided to a spouse, a former spouse, or a child of an obligor. The Act also uses "obligee" to identify an individual who is asserting a claim for support, not just or a person whose right to support is unquestioned, presumed, or has been established in a legal action. Subsection (13) provides the correlative definition of an "obligor," which includes an individual who is alleged to owe a duty of support as well as a person whose obligation has previously been determined.

Note that the definitions of "responding state" and "responding tribunal" in Subsections (16) and (17) accommodate the direct filing of a petition under this Act without the intervention of an initiating tribunal. Both definitions acknowledge the possibility that there might be a responding state or tribunal in a situation where there is no initiating state or tribunal.

Subsection (19) withdraws the requirement of reciprocity demanded by RURESA and URESA. A state need not enact UIFSA in order for support orders issued by its tribunal to be enforced by other states. Public policy favoring such enforcement is sufficiently strong to warrant waiving any quid pro quo among the states. This policy extends to foreign jurisdictions, as well, which is intended to facilitate establishment and enforcement of orders from those jurisdictions. Specifically, if a support order from a Canadian province or Mexican state conforms to the principles of UIFSA, that order should be honored when it crosses the border in a spirit of comity.

Subsection (20), "Support Enforcement Agency," includes the state IV-D agency (Part IV-D, Social Security Act, 42 U.S.C. §651 et seq.), and other state or local governmental entities charged with establishing or enforcing support.

Subsection (22) introduces a completely new term, "tribunal," which replaces the term "court" used in RURESA. With the advent of the federal IV-D program, a number of states have delegated various aspects of child support establishment and enforcement to quasi-judicial bodies and administrative agencies. UIFSA adopts the term "tribunal" to account for the breadth of state variations in dealing with support orders.

Throughout the Act the term refers to a tribunal of the enacting state unless expressly noted otherwise. To avoid confusion, however, when actions of tribunals of the enacting state and another state are contrasted in the same section or subsection, the phrases "tribunal of this State" and "tribunal of another state" are used for the sake of clarity.

ARTICLE 2. JURISDICTION

Section 201. Bases for Jurisdiction over Nonresident.

In a proceeding to establish, enforce, or modify a support order or to determine parentage, a tribunal of this State may exercise personal jurisdiction over a nonresident individual [or the individual's guardian or conservator] if:

(1) the individual is personally served with [citation, summons, notice] within this State;

(2) the individual submits to the jurisdiction of this State by consent, by entering a general appearance, or by filing a responsive document having the effect of waiving any contest to personal jurisdiction;

(3) the individual resided with the child in this State;

(4) the individual resided in this State and provided prenatal expenses or support for the child;

(5) the child resides in this State as a result of the acts or directives of the individual;

(6) the individual engaged in sexual intercourse in this State and the child may have been conceived by that act of intercourse;

[(7) the individual asserted parentage in the [putative father registry] maintained in this State by the [appropriate agency];] or

(8) there is any other basis consistent with the constitutions of this State and the United States for the exercise of personal jurisdiction.

Section 202. Procedure When Exercising Jurisdiction over Nonresident.

A tribunal of this State exercising personal jurisdiction over a nonresident under Section 201 may apply Section 316 (Special Rules of Evidence and Procedure) to receive evidence from another state, and Section 318 (Assistance with Discovery) to obtain discovery through a tribunal of another state. In all other respects, Articles 3 through 7 do not apply and the tribunal shall apply the procedural and substantive law of this State, including the rules on choice of law other than those established by this [Act].

Section 203. Initiating and Responding Tribunal of This State.

Under this [Act], a tribunal of this State may serve as an initiating tribunal to forward proceedings to another state and as a responding tribunal for proceedings initiated in another state.

Section 204. Simultaneous Proceedings in Another State.

(a) A tribunal of this State may exercise jurisdiction to establish a support order if the [petition] or comparable pleading is filed after a [petition] or comparable pleading is filed in another state only if:

(1) the [petition] or comparable pleading in this State is filed before the expiration of the time allowed in the other state for filing a responsive pleading challenging the exercise of jurisdiction by the other state;

(2) the contesting party timely challenges the exercise of jurisdiction in the other state; and

(3) if relevant, this State is the home state of the child.

(b) A tribunal of this State may not exercise jurisdiction to establish a support order if the [petition] or comparable pleading is filed before a [petition] or comparable pleading is filed in another state if:

(1) the [petition] or comparable pleading in the other state is filed before the expiration of the time allowed in this State for filing a responsive pleading challenging the exercise of jurisdiction by this State;

(2) the contesting party timely challenges the exercise of jurisdiction in this State; and

(3) if relevant, the other state is the home state of the child.

Section 205. Continuing, Exclusive Jurisdiction.

(a) A tribunal of this State issuing a support order consistent with the law of this State has continuing, exclusive jurisdiction over a child support order:

(1) as long as this State remains the residence of the obligor, the individual obligee, or the child for whose benefit the support order is issued; or

(2) until each individual party has filed written consent with the tribunal of this State for a tribunal of another state to modify the order and assume continuing, exclusive jurisdiction.

(b) A tribunal of this State issuing a child support order consistent with the law of this State may not exercise its continuing jurisdiction to modify the order if the order has been modified by a tribunal of another state pursuant to a law substantially similar to this [Act].

(c) If a child support order of this State is modified by a tribunal of another state pursuant to a law substantially similar to this [Act], a tribunal of this State loses its continuing, exclusive jurisdiction with regard to prospective enforcement of the order issued in this State, and may only:

(1) enforce the order that was modified as to amounts accruing before the modification;

(2) enforce nonmodifiable aspects of that order; and

(3) provide other appropriate relief for violations of that order which occurred before the effective date of the modification.

(d) A tribunal of this State shall recognize the continuing, exclusive jurisdiction of a tribunal of another state which has issued a child support order pursuant to a law substantially similar to this [Act].

(e) A temporary support order issued ex parte or pending resolution of a jurisdictional conflict does not create continuing, exclusive jurisdiction in the issuing tribunal.

(f) A tribunal of this State issuing a support order consistent with the law of this State has continuing, exclusive jurisdiction over a spousal support order throughout the existence of the support obligation. A tribunal of this State may not modify a spousal support order issued by a tribunal of another state having continuing, exclusive jurisdiction over that order under the law of that state.

Comment

This section is perhaps the most crucial provision in UIFSA. It established the principle that the issuing tribunal retains continuing, exclusive jurisdiction over the support order except in very narrowly defined circumstances. If all parties and the child reside elsewhere, the issuing state loses its continuing, exclusive jurisdiction—which in practical terms means the issuing tribunal loses its authority to modify its order. The issuing state no longer has a nexus with the parties or child and, furthermore, the issuing tribunal has no current information about the circumstances of anyone involved. Note, however, that the one-order of the issuing tribunal remains valid and enforceable. That order is in effect not only in the issuing state and those states in which the order has been registered, but also may be enforced in additional states in which the one-order is registered for enforcement after the issuing state loses its power to modify the original order, see Sections 601-604 (Registration and Enforcement of Support Order), *infra*. The one-order remains in effect until it is properly modified in accordance with the narrow terms of the Act, see Sections 609-612 (Registration and Modification of Child Support Order), *infra*.

Child support orders may be modified under certain, specific conditions: (1) on the agreement of both parties; or, (2) if all the relevant persons, that is, the obligor, the individual obligee, and the child, have permanently left the issuing state. Note that while Subsection (b)(2) identifies the method for the release of continuing, exclusive jurisdiction by the issuing tribunal, it does not confer jurisdiction to modify on another tribunal. Modification requires that a tribunal have personal jurisdiction over both parties, as provided in Article 6, Part C. It should also be noted that nothing in this section is intended to deprive a court which has lost continuing, exclusive jurisdiction of the power to enforce arrearage which have accrued during the existence of a valid order.

With regard to spousal support, the issuing tribunal retains continuing, exclusive jurisdiction over an order of spousal support throughout the entire existence of the support obligation. The prohibition against a modification of an existing spousal support order of another state imposed by Sections 205 and 206 marks a radical departure from RURESA, which treats spousal and child support orders identically. Under UIFSA, modification of spousal support is permitted in the interstate context only if an action is initiated outside of, and modified by the original issuing state. While UIFSA revises RURESA in this regard, in fact this will have a minimal effect on actual practice. Interstate modification of spousal support has been relatively rare under RURESA. Moreover, the prohibition of modification of spousal support is consistent with the basic principle that a tribunal should apply local law if at all possible to insure efficient handling of cases and to minimize choice-of-law problems. Avoiding conflict-of-law problems is almost impossible if spousal support orders are subject to modification in a second state. For example, there is wide variation among state laws on the effect on a spousal support order following the obligee's remarriage or nonmarital cohabitation with another person.

The distinction between spousal and child support is further justified because the standards for modification of child support and spousal support are so different. In most jurisdictions a drastic improvement in the obligor's economic circumstances will have little or no relevance in an action seeking an upward modification of spousal support, while a similar change in an obligor's situation typically is a primary basis for an increase in child support. This disparity is founded on a policy choice that post-divorce success should benefit the obligor's child, but not an ex-spouse.

Section 206. Enforcement and Modification of Support Order by Tribunal Having Continuing Jurisdiction.

(a) A tribunal of this State may serve as an initiating tribunal to request a tribunal of another state to enforce or modify a support order issued in that state.

(b) A tribunal of this State having continuing, exclusive jurisdiction over a support order may act as a responding tribunal to enforce or modify the order. If a party subject to the continuing, exclusive jurisdiction of the tribunal no longer resides in the issuing state, in subsequent proceedings the tribunal may apply Section 316 (Special Rules of Evidence and Procedure) to receive evidence from another state and Section 318 (Assistance with Discovery) to obtain discovery through a tribunal of another state.

(c) A tribunal of this State which lacks continuing, exclusive jurisdiction over a spousal support order may not serve as a responding tribunal to modify a spousal support order of another state.

Section 207. Recognition of Child Support Orders.

(a) If a proceeding is brought under this [Act], and one or more child support orders have been issued in this or another state with regard to an obligor and a child, a tribunal of this State shall apply the following rules in determining which order to recognize for purposes of continuing, exclusive jurisdiction.

(1) If only one tribunal has issued a child support order, the order of that tribunal must be recognized.

(2) If two or more tribunals have issued child support orders for the same obligor and child, and only one of the tribunals would have continuing, exclusive jurisdiction under this [Act], the order of that tribunal must be recognized.

(3) If two or more tribunals have issued child support orders for the same obligor and child, and more than one of the tribunals would have continuing, exclusive jurisdiction under this [Act], an order issued by a tribunal in the current home state of the child must be recognized, but if an order has not been issued in the current home state of the child, the order most recently issued must be recognized.

(4) If two or more tribunals have issued child support orders for the same obligor and child, and none of the tribunals would have continuing, exclusive jurisdiction under this [Act], the tribunal of this State may issue a child support order, which must be recognized.

(b) The tribunal that has issued an order recognized under subsection (a) is the tribunal having continuing, exclusive jurisdiction.

Comment

This section establishes a priority scheme for recognition and enforcement of existing multiple orders regarding the same obligor, obligee or obligees, and the same child. Even assuming universal enactment of UIFSA, many years will pass before its one-order system will be completely in place. Part C is designed to span the gulf between the one-order system and the multiple order system in place under RURESA. If only one order has been issued, it is to be treated as if it had been issued under UIFSA if it was issued under a statute which is consistent with the principles of UIFSA. But, multiple orders issued under RURESA number in the tens of thousands; it can be reasonably anticipated that those orders, covering the same parties and child, will continue in effect far into the future.

Assuming multiple orders exist, none of which can be distinguished as being in conflict with the principles of UIFSA, an order issued by a tribunal of the child's home state is given the higher priority. If more than one of these orders exists, priority is given to the order most recently issued. If none of the priorities apply, the forum tribunal is directed to issue a new order. Note, however, that multiple orders issued by different states may be entitled to full faith and credit. While this section cannot and does not attempt to interfere with that constitutional directive with regard to accrued arrearages, it may and does establish a system for prospective enforcement of competing orders.

Section 208. Multiple Child Support Orders for Two or More Obligees.

In responding to multiple registrations or [petitions] for enforcement of two or more child support orders in effect at the same time with regard to the same obligor and different individual obligees, at least one of which was issued by a tribunal of another state, a tribunal of this State shall enforce those orders in the same manner as if the multiple orders had been issued by a tribunal of this State.

Comment

Multiple orders may involve two or more families of the same obligor. Although all such orders are entitled to future enforcement, practical difficulties are often presented. For example, full enforcement of all orders may exceed the maximum allowed for income withholding, i.e., the federal statute, 42 U.S.C. 666(b)(1), requires that states cap the maximum to be withheld in accordance with the federal consumer credit code limitations on wage garnishment, 15 US.C. 1673(b). In order to allocate resources between competing families, the Act refers to state law. The basic principle is that one or more foreign orders for the support of the obligor's families are of equal dignity and should be treated as if all of the multiple orders had been issued by a tribunal of the forum state.

Section 209. Credit for Payments.

Amounts collected and credited for a particular period pursuant to a support order issued by a tribunal of another state must be credited against the amounts accruing or accrued for the same period under a support order issued by the tribunal of this State.

ARTICLE 3. CIVIL PROVISIONS OF GENERAL APPLICATION

Section 301. Proceedings Under This [Act].

(a) Except as otherwise provided in this [Act], this article applies to all proceedings under this [Act].

(b) This [Act] provides for the following proceedings:

(1) establishment of an order for spousal support or child support pursuant to Article 4;

(2) enforcement of a support order and income-withholding order of another state without registration pursuant to Article 5;

(3) registration of an order for spousal support or child support of another state for enforcement pursuant to Article 6;

(4) modification of an order for child support or spousal support issued by a tribunal of this State pursuant to Article 2, Part B;

(5) registration of an order for child support of another state or modification pursuant to Article 6;

(6) determination of parentage pursuant to Article 7 and

(7) assertion of jurisdiction over nonresidents pursuant to Article 2, Part A.

(c) An individual [petitioner] or a support enforcement agency may commence a proceeding authorized under this [Act] by filing a [petition] in an initiating tribunal for forwarding to a responding tribunal or by filing a [petition] or a comparable pleading directly in a tribunal of another state which has or can obtain personal jurisdiction over the [respondent].

Section 302. Action by Minor Parent.

A minor parent may maintain a proceeding on behalf of or for the benefit of the minor's child.

Section 303. Application of Law of This State.

Except as otherwise provided by this [Act], a responding tribunal of this State:

(1) shall apply the procedural and substantive law, including the rules on choice of law, generally applicable to similar proceedings originating in this State and may exercise all powers and provide all remedies available in those proceedings; and

(2) shall determine the duty of support and the amount payable in accordance with the law and support guidelines of this State.

Section 304. Duties of Initiating Tribunal.

Upon the filing of a [petition] authorized by this [Act,] an initiating tribunal of this State shall forward three copies of the [petition] and its accompanying documents:

(1) to the responding tribunal or appropriate support enforcement agency in the responding state; or

(2) if the identity of the responding tribunal is unknown, to the state information agency of the responding state with a request that they be forwarded to the appropriate tribunal and that receipt be acknowledged.

Section 305. Duties and Powers of Responding Tribunal.

(a) When a responding tribunal of this State receives a [petition] or comparable pleading from an initiating tribunal or directly pursuant to Section 301(c) (Proceedings Under this [Act]), it shall cause the pleading to be filed and notify the [petitioner] by first class mail where and when it was filed.

(b) A responding tribunal of this State, to the extent otherwise authorized by law, may do one or more of the following:

(1) issue or enforce a support order, modify a child support order, or render a judgment to determine parentage;

(2) order an obligor to comply with a support order and the manner of compliance;

(3) order income withholding;

(4) determine the amount of any arrearages;

(5) enforce orders by civil or criminal contempt;

(6) set aside property for satisfaction of the support order;

(7) place liens and order execution on the obligor's property;

(8) order an obligor to keep the tribunal informed of the obligor's current residential address, telephone number at the place of employment;

(9) issue a [bench warrant; capias] for an obligor who has filed after proper notice to appear at a hearing ordered by the tribunal and enter the [bench warrant; capias] in any local and state computer systems for criminal warrants;

(10) order the obligor to seek appropriate employment by specified methods;

(11) award reasonable attorney's fees and other fees and costs; and

(12) grant any other available remedy.

(c) A responding tribunal of this State shall include in a support order issued under this [Act], or in the documents accompanying the order, the calculations on which the support order is based.

(d) A responding tribunal of this State may not condition the payment of a support order issued under this [Act] upon compliance by a party with provisions for visitation.

(e) If a responding tribunal of this State issues an order under this [Act] the tribunal shall send a copy of the order by first class mail to the [petitioner] and the [respondent] and to the initiating tribunal, if any.

Section 306. Inappropriate Tribunal.

If a [petition] or comparable pleading is received by an inappropriate tribunal of this State, it shall forward the pleading and accompanying documents to an appropriate tribunal in this State or another state and notify the [petitioner] by first class mail where and when the pleading was sent.

Section 307. Duties of Support Enforcement Agency.

(a) A support enforcement agency of this State, upon request, shall provide services to a [petitioner] in a proceeding under this [Act].

(b) A support enforcement agency that is providing services to the [petitioner] as appropriate shall:

(1) take all steps necessary to enable an appropriate tribunal in this State or another state to obtain jurisdiction over the [respondent];

(2) request an appropriate tribunal to set a date, time, and place for a hearing;

(3) make a reasonable effort to obtain all relevant information as to income and property of the parties;

(4) within [two] days, exclusive of Saturdays, Sundays and legal holidays, after receipt of a written notice from an initiating, responding or registering tribunal, send a copy of the communication by first class mail to the [petitioner]; and

(5) within [two] days, exclusive of Saturdays, Sundays and legal holidays, after receipt of a written communication from the [respondent[or the [respondent's] attorney, send a copy of the communication to the [petitioner]; and

(6) notify the [petitioner] if jurisdiction over the [respondent] cannot be obtained.

(c) This [Act] does not create or negate a relationship of attorney and client or other fiduciary relationship between a support enforcement agency or the attorney for the agency and the individual being assisted by the agency.

Section 308. Duty of [Attorney General].

If the [Attorney General] determines that the support enforcement agency is neglecting or refusing to provide services to an individual, the [Attorney General] may order the agency to perform its duties under this [Act] or may provide those services directly to the individual.

Section 309. Private Counsel.

An individual may employ private counsel to represent the individual in proceedings authorized by this [Act].

Section 310. Duties of [State Information Agency].

(a) The [Attorney General's Office, State Attorney's Office, State Central Registry or other information agency] is the state information agency under this [Act].

(b) The state information agency shall:

(1) compile and maintain a current list, including addresses, of the tribunals in this State which have jurisdiction under this [Act] and any support enforcement agencies in this State and transmit a copy to the state information agency of every other state;

(2) maintain a register of tribunals and support enforcement agencies received from other states;

(3) forward to the appropriate tribunal in the place in this State in which the individual obligee or the obligor resides, or in which the obligor's property is believed to be located, all documents concerning a proceeding under this [Act] received from an initiating tribunal or the state information agency of the initiating state; and

(4) obtain information concerning the location of the obligor and the obligor's property within this State not exempt from execution, by such means as postal verification and federal or state locator services, examination of telephone directories, requests for the obligor's address from employers, and examination of governmental records, including, to the extent not prohibited by law, those relating to real property, vital statistics, law enforcement, taxation, motor vehicles, driver's licenses, and social security.

Section 311. Pleadings and Accompanying Documents.

(a) A [petitioner] seeking to establish or modify a support order or to determine parentage in a proceeding under this [Act] must verify the [petition]. Unless otherwise ordered under Section 312 (Nondisclosure of Information in Exceptional Circumstances), the [petition] or accompanying documents must provide, so far as known, the name, sex, residence address, social security number, and date of birth of each child for whom support is sought. The [petition] must be accompanied by a certified copy of any support order in effect. The [petition] may include any other information that may assist in locating or identifying the [respondent].

(b) the [petition] must specify the relief sought. The [petition] and accompanying documents must conform substantially with the requirements imposed by the forms mandated by federal law for use in cases filed by a support enforcement agency.

Section 312. Nondisclosure of Information in Exceptional Circumstances.

Upon a finding, which may be made ex parte, that the health, safety, or liberty of a party or child would be unreasonably put at risk by the disclosure of identifying information, or if an existing order so provides, a tribunal shall order that the address of the child or party or other identifying information not be disclosed in a pleading or other document filed in a proceeding under this [Act].

Section 313. Costs and Fees.

(a) The [petitioner] may not be required to pay a filing fee or other costs.

(b) If an obligee prevails, a responding tribunal may assess against an obligor filing fees, reasonable attorney's fees, other costs, and necessary travel and other reasonable expenses incurred by the obligee and the obligee's witnesses. The tribunal may not assess fees, costs, or expenses against the obligee or the support enforcement agency of either the initiating or the responding state, except as provided by other law. Attorney's fees may be taxed as costs, and may be ordered paid directly to the attorney, who may enforce the order in the attorney's own name. Payment of support owed to the obligee has priority over fees, costs and expenses.

(c) The tribunal shall order the payment of costs and reasonable attorney's fees if it determines that a hearing was requested primarily for delay. In a proceeding under Article 6 (Enforcement and Modification of Support Order After Registration), a hearing is presumed to have been requested primarily for delay if a registered support order is confirmed or enforced without change.

Section 314. Limited Immunity of [Petitioner].

(a) Participation by a [petitioner] in a proceeding before a responding tribunal, whether in person, by private attorney, or through services provided by the support enforcement agency, does not confer personal jurisdiction over the [petitioner] in another proceeding.

(b) A [petitioner] is not amenable to service of civil process while physically present in this State to participate in a proceeding under this [Act].

(c) The immunity granted by this section does not extend to civil litigation based on acts unrelated to a proceeding under this [Act] committed by a party while present in this State to participate in the proceeding.

Section 315. Nonparentage as Defense.

A party whose parentage of a child has been previously determined by or pursuant to law may not plead nonparentage as a defense to a proceeding under this [Act].

Section 316. Special Rules of Evidence and Procedure.

(a) The physical presence of the [petitioner] in a responding tribunal of this State is not required for the establishment, enforcement, or modification of a support order or the rendition of a judgment determining parentage.

(b) A verified [petition], affidavit, document substantially complying with federal mandated forms, and a document incorporated by reference in any of them, not excluded under the hearsay rule if given in person, is admissible in evidence if given under oath by a party or witness residing in another state.

(c) A copy of the record of child support payments certified as a true copy of the original by the custodian of the record may be forwarded to a responding tribunal. The copy is evidence of facts asserted in it and is admissible to show whether payments were made.

(d) Copies of bills for testing for parentage, and for prenatal and postnatal health care of the mother and child, furnished to the adverse party at least [ten] days before trial, are admissible in evidence to prove the amount of the charges billed and that the charges were reasonable, necessary, and customary.

(e) Documentary evidence transmitted from another state to a tribunal of this State by telephone, telecopier, or other means that do not provide an original writing may not be excluded from evidence on an objection based on the means of transmission.

(f) In a proceeding under this [Act], a tribunal of this State may permit a party or witness residing in another state to be deposed or to testify by telephone, audiovisual means, or other electronic means at a designated tribunal or other location in that state. A tribunal of this State shall cooperate with tribunals of other states in designating an appropriate location for the deposition or testimony.

(g) If a party called to testify at a civil hearing refuses to answer on the ground that the testimony may be self-incriminating, the trier of fact may draw an adverse inference from the refusal.

(h) A privilege against disclosure of communications between spouses does not apply in a proceeding under this [Act].

(i) The defense of immunity based on the relationship of husband and wife or parent and child does not apply in a proceeding under this [Act].

Section 317. Communications Between Tribunals.

A tribunal of this State may communicate with a tribunal of another state in writing, or by telephone or other means, to obtain information concerning the laws of that state, the legal effect of a judgment, decree, or order of that tribunal, and the status of a proceeding in the other state. A tribunal of this State may furnish similar information by similar means to a tribunal of another state.

Section 318. Assistance with Discovery.

A tribunal of this State may:

(1) request a tribunal of another state to assist in obtaining discovery; and

(2) upon request, compel a person over whom it has jurisdiction to respond to a discovery order issued by a tribunal of another state.

Section 319. Receipt and Disbursement of Payments.

A support enforcement agency or tribunal of this State shall disburse promptly any amounts received pursuant to a support order, as directed by the order. The agency or tribunal shall furnish to a requesting party or tribunal of another state a certified statement by the custodian of the record of the amounts and dates of all payments received.

ARTICLE 4. ESTABLISHMENT OF SUPPORT ORDER

Section 401. [Petition] to Establish Support Order.

(a) If a support order entitled to recognition under this [Act] has not been issued, a responding tribunal of this State may issue a support order if:

(1) the individual seeking the order resides in another state; or

(2) the support enforcement agency seeking the order is located in another state.

(b) The tribunal may issue a temporary child support order if:

(1) the [respondent] has signed a verified statement acknowledging parentage; or

(2) the [respondent] has been determined by or pursuant to law to be the parent; or

(3) there is other clear and convincing evidence that the [respondent] is the child's parent.

(c) Upon finding, after notice and opportunity to be heard, that an obligor owes a duty of support, the tribunal shall issue a support order directed to the obligor and may issue other orders pursuant to Section 305 (Duties and Powers of Responding Tribunal).

ARTICLE 5. DIRECT ENFORCEMENT OF ORDER OF ANOTHER STATE WITHOUT REGISTRATION

Section 501. Recognition of Income-Withholding Order of Another State.

(a) An income-withholding order issued in another state may be sent by first class mail to the person or entity defined as the obligor's employer under [the income-withholding law of this State] without first filing a [petition] or comparable pleading or registering the order with a tribunal of this State. Upon receipt of the order, the employer shall:

(1) treat an income-withholding order issued in another state which appears regular on its face as if it had been issued by a tribunal of this State;

(2) immediately provide a copy of the order to the obligor; and

(3) distribute the funds as directed in the withholding order.

(b) An obligor may contest the validity or enforcement of an income-withholding order issued in another state in the same manner as if the order had been issued by a tribunal of this State. Section 604 (Choice of Law) applies to the contest. The obligor shall give notice of the contest to any support enforcement agency providing services to the obligee and to:

(1) the person or agency designated to receive payments in the income-withholding order; or

(2) if no person or agency is designated, the obligee.

Section 502. Administrative Enforcement of Orders.

(a) A party seeking to enforce a support order or an income-withholding order, or both, issued by a tribunal of another state may send the documents required for registering the order to a support enforcement agency of this State.

(b) Upon receipt of the documents, the support enforcement agency, without initially seeking to register the order, shall consider and, if appropriate, use any administrative procedure authorized by the law of this State to enforce a support order or an income-withholding order, or both. If the obligor does not contest administrative enforcement, the order need not be registered. If the obligor contests the validity or administrative enforcement of the order, the support enforcement agency shall register the order pursuant to this [Act].

ARTICLE 6. ENFORCEMENT AND MODIFICATION OF SUPPORT ORDER AFTER REGISTRATION

Part A
Registration and Enforcement of Support Order

Section 601. Registration of Order for Enforcement.

A support order or an income-withholding order issued by a tribunal of another state may be registered in this State for enforcement.

Section 602. Procedure to Register Order for Enforcement.

(a) A support order or income-withholding order of another state may be registered in this State by sending the following documents and information to the [appropriate tribunal] in this State:

(1) a letter of transmittal to the tribunal requesting registration and enforcement;

(2) two copies, including one certified copy, of all orders to be registered, including any modification of an order;

(3) a sworn statement by the party seeking registration or a certified statement by the custodian of the records showing the amount of any arrearage;

(4) the name of the obligor and, if known:

(i) the obligor's address and social security number;

(ii) the name and address of the obligor's employer and any other source of income of the obligor; and

(iii) a description and the location of property of the obligor in this State not exempt from execution; and

(5) the name and address of the obligee and, if applicable, the agency or person to whom support payments are to be remitted.

(b) On receipt of a request for registration, the registering tribunal shall cause the order to be filed as a foreign judgment, together with one copy of the documents and information, regardless of their form.

(c) A [petition] or comparable pleading seeking a remedy that must be affirmatively sought under other law of this State may be filed at the same time as the request for registration or later. The pleading must specify the grounds for the remedy sought.

Section 603. Effect of Registration for Enforcement.

(a) A support order or income-withholding order issued in another state is registered when the order is filed in the registering tribunal of this State.

(b) A registered order issued in another state is enforceable in the same manner and is subject to the same procedures as an order issued by a tribunal of this State.

(c) Except as otherwise provided in this article, a tribunal of this State shall recognize and enforce, but may not modify, a registered order if the issuing tribunal had jurisdiction.

Section 604. Choice of Law.

(a) The law of the issuing state governs the nature, extent, amount, and duration of current payments and other obligations of support and the payment of arrearages under the order.

(b) In a proceeding for arrearages, the statute of limitation under the laws of this State or of the issuing state, whichever is longer, applies.

Section 605. Notice of Registration of Order.

(a) When a support order or income-withholding order issued in another state is registered, the registering tribunal shall notify the nonregistering party. Notice must be given by first class, certified, or registered mail or by any means of personal service authorized by the law of this State. The notice must be accompanied by a copy of the registered order and the documents and relevant information accompanying the order.

(b) The notice must inform the nonregistering party:

(1) that a registered order is enforceable as of the date of registration in the same manner as an order issued by a tribunal of this State;

(2) that a hearing to contest the validity or enforcement of the registered order must be requested within [20] days after the date of mailing or personal service of the notice;

(3) that failure to contest the validity or enforcement of the registered order in a timely manner will result in confirmation of the order and enforce-

ment of the order and the alleged arrearages and precludes further contest of that order with respect to any matter that could have been asserted; and

(4) of the amount of any alleged arrearages.

(c) Upon registration of an income-withholding order for enforcement, the registering tribunal shall notify the obligor's employer pursuant to [the income-withholding law of this State].

Section 606. Procedure to Contest Validity or Enforcement of Registered Order.

(a) A nonregistering party seeking to contest the validity or enforcement of a registered order in this State shall request a hearing within [20] days after the date of mailing or personal service of notice of the registration. The nonregistering party may seek to vacate the registration, to assert any defense to an allegation of noncompliance with the registered order, or to contest the remedies being sought or the amount of any alleged arrearages pursuant to Section 607 (Contest of Registration or Enforcement).

(b) If the nonregistering party fails to contest the validity or enforcement of the registered order in a timely manner, the order is confirmed by operation of law.

(c) If a nonregistering party requests a hearing to contest the validity or enforcement of the registered order, the registering tribunal shall schedule the matter for hearing and give notice to the parties by first class mail of the date, time, and place of the hearing.

Section 607. Contest of Registration or Enforcement.

(a) A party contesting the validity or enforcement of a registered order or seeking to vacate the registration has the burden of proving one of more of the following defenses:

(1) the issuing tribunal lacked personal jurisdiction over the contesting party;

(2) the order was obtained by fraud;

(3) the order has been vacated, suspended, or modified by a later order;

(4) the issuing tribunal has stayed the order pending appeal;

(5) there is a defense under the law of this State to the remedy sought;

(6) full or partial payment has been made; or

(7) the statute of limitation under Section 604 (Choice of Law) precludes enforcement of some or all of the arrearages.

(b) If a party presents evidence establishing a full or partial defense under subsection (a), a tribunal may stay enforcement of the registered order, continue the proceeding to permit production of additional relevant evidence, and issue other appropriate orders. An uncontested portion of the registered order may be enforced by all remedies available under the law of this State.

(c) If the contesting party does not establish a defense under subsection (a) to the validity or enforcement of the order, the registering tribunal shall issue an order confirming the order.

Section 608. Confirmed Order.

Confirmation of a registered order, whether by operation of law or after notice and hearing, precludes further contest of the order with respect to any matter that could have been asserted at the time of registration.

Section 609. Procedure to Register Child Support Order of Another State for Modification.

A party or support enforcement agency seeking to modify, or to modify and enforce, a child support order issued in another state shall register that order in this State in the same manner provided in Part A of this article if the order has not been registered. A [petition] for modification may be filed at the same time as a request for registration, or later. The pleading must specify the grounds for modification.

Section 610. Effect of Registration for Modification.

A tribunal of this State may enforce a child support order of another state registered for purposes of modification, in the same manner as if the order had been issued by a tribunal of this State, but the registered order may be modified only if the requirements of Section 611 (Modification of Child Support Order of Another State) have been met.

Section 611. Modification of Child Support Order of Another State.

(a) After a child support order issued in another state has been registered in this State, the responding tribunal of this State may modify that order only if, after notice and hearing, it finds that:

(1) the following requirements are met:

(i) the child, the individual obligee, and the obligor do not reside in the issuing state;

(ii) a [petitioner] who is a nonresident of this State seeks modifications; and

(iii) the [respondent] is subject to the personal jurisdiction of the tribunal of this State; or

(2) an individual party or the child is subject to the personal jurisdiction of the tribunal and all of the individual parties have filed a written consent in the issuing tribunal providing that a tribunal of this State may modify the support order and assume continuing, exclusive jurisdiction over the order.

(b) Modification of a registered child support order is subject to the same requirements, procedures, and defenses that apply to the modification of an order issued by a tribunal of this State and the order may be enforced and satisfied in the same manner.

(c) A tribunal of this State may not modify any aspect of a child support order that may not be modified under the law of the issuing state.

(d) On issuance of an order modifying a child support order issued in another state, a tribunal of this State becomes the tribunal of continuing, exclusive jurisdiction.

(e) Within [30] days after issuance of a modified child support order, the party obtaining the modification shall file a certified copy of the order with the issuing tribunal which had continuing, exclusive jurisdiction over the earlier order, and in each tribunal in which the party knows that earlier order has been registered.

Section 612. Recognition of Order Modified in Another State.

A tribunal of this State shall recognize a modification of its earlier child support order by a tribunal of another state which assumed jurisdiction pursuant to a law substantially similar to this [Act] and, upon request, except as otherwise provided in this [Act], shall:

(1) enforce the order that was modified only as to amounts accruing before the modification;

(2) enforce only nonmodifiable aspects of that order;

(3) provide other appropriate relief only for violations of that order which occurred before the effective date of the modification; and

(4) recognize the modifying order of the other state, upon registration, for the purpose of enforcement.

Article 7. Determination of Parentage

Section 701. Proceeding to Determine Parentage.

(a) A tribunal of this State may serve as an initiating or responding tribunal in a proceeding brought under this [Act] or a law substantially similar to this [Act], the Uniform Reciprocal Enforcement of Support Act, or the Revised Uniform Reciprocal Enforcement of Support Act to determine that the [petitioner] is a parent of a particular child or to determine that a [respondent] is a parent of that child.

(b) In a proceeding to determine parentage, a responding tribunal of this State shall apply the [Uniform Parentage Act; procedural and substantive law of this State] and the rules of this State on choice of law.

Article 8. Interstate Rendition

Section 801. Grounds for Rendition.

(a) For purposes of this article, "governor" includes an individual performing the functions of governor or the executive authority of a state covered by this [Act].

(b) The governor of this State may:

(1) demand that the governor of another state surrender an individual found in the other state who is charged criminally in this State with having failed to provide for the support of an obligee; or

(2) on the demand by the governor of another state, surrender an individual found in this State who is charged criminally in the other state with having failed to provide for the support of an obligee.

(c) A provision for extradition of individuals not inconsistent with this [Act] applies to the demand even if the individual whose surrender is demanded was not in the demanding state when the crime was allegedly committed and has not fled therefrom.

Section 802. Condition of Rendition.

(a) Before making demand that the governor of another state surrender an individual charged criminally in this State with having failed to provide for the support of an obligee, the governor of this State may require a prosecutor of this State to demonstrate that at least [60] days previously the obligee had initiated proceedings for support pursuant to this [Act] or that the proceeding would be of no avail.

(b) If, under this [Act] or a law substantially similar to this [Act], the Uniform Reciprocal Enforcement of Support Act, or the Revised Uniform Reciprocal Enforcement of Support Act, the governor of another state makes a demand that the governor of this State surrender an individual charged criminally in that state with having failed to provide for the support of a child or other individual to whom a duty of support is owed, the governor may require a prosecutor to investigate the demand and report whether a proceeding for support has been initiated or would be effective. If it appears that a proceeding would be effective but has not been initiated, the governor may delay honoring the demand for a reasonable time to permit the initiation of a proceeding.

(c) If a proceeding for support has been initiated and the individual whose rendition is demanded prevails, the governor may decline to honor the demand. If the [petitioner] prevails, and the individual whose rendition is demanded is subject to a support order, the governor may decline to honor the demand if the individual is complying with the support order.

[The provisions of Article 9, dealing with uniformity of application and construction, severability, repeals, effective date, and short title, have been omitted.]

Child Support Recovery Act of 1992
18 U.S.C. §228

Section 228. Failure to pay legal child support obligations

(a) Offense.—Whoever willfully fails to pay a past due support obligation with respect to a child who resides in another State shall be punished as provided in subsection (b).

(b) Punishment.—The punishment for an offense under this section is—

(1) in the case of a first offense under this section, a fine under this title, imprisonment for not more than 6 months, or both; and

(2) in any other case, a fine under this title, imprisonment for not more than 2 years, or both.

(c) Restitution.—Upon a conviction under this section, the court shall order restitution under section 3663 in an amount equal to the past due support obligation as it exists at the time of sentencing.

(d) Definitions.—As used in this section—

(1) the term "past due support obligation" means any amount—

(A) determined under a court order or an order of an administrative process pursuant to the law of a State to be due from a person for the support and maintenance of a child or of a child and the parent with whom the child is living; and

(B) that has remained unpaid for a period longer than one year, or is greater than $5,0000; and

(2) the term "State" includes the District of Columbia, and any other possession or territory of the United States.

Full Faith and Credit for Child Support Orders Act (1994)
28 U.S. Code Annotated

[The following section was added to 28 U.S.C.A. §1738 by P.O. 103-383 (the Act designated above) on October 20, 1994.]

Section 1738B. Full faith and credit for child support orders

(a) General rule.—The appropriate authorities of each State—

(1) shall enforce according to its terms a child support order made consistently with this section by a court of another State; and

(2) shall not seek or make a modification of such an order except in accordance with subsection (e).

(b) Definitions.—In this section:

"child" means:

(A) a person under 18 years of age; and

(B) a person 18 or more years of age with respect to whom a child support order has been issued pursuant to the laws of a state.

"child's State" means the State in which a child resides.

"child support" means a payment of money, continuing support, or arrearages or the provision of a benefit (including payment of health insurance, child care, and educational expenses) for the support of a child.

"child support order"—

(A) means a judgment, decree, or order of a court requiring the payment of child support in periodic amounts or in a lump sum; and

(B) includes—

(i) permanent or temporary order;

(ii) an initial order or a modification of an order.

"contestant" means—

(A) a person (including a parent) who—

(i) claims a right to receive child support;

(ii) is a party to a proceeding that may result in the issuance of a child support order; or

(iii) is under a child support order; and

(B) a State or political subdivision of a State to which the right to obtain child support has been assigned.

"court" means a court or administrative agency of a State that is authorized by State law to establish the amount of child support payable by a contestant or make a modification of a child support order.

"modification" means a change in a child support order that affects the amount, scope, or duration of the order and modifies, replaces, supersedes, or otherwise is made subsequent to the child support order.

"State" means a State of the United States, the District of Columbia, the Commonwealth of Puerto Rico, the territories and possessions of the United States, and Indian country (as defined in section 1151 of title 18).

(c) Requirements of child support orders.—A child support order is made consistent with this section if—

(1) a court that makes the order, pursuant to the laws of the State in which the court is located—

(A) has subject matter jurisdiction to hear the matter and enter such an order; and

(B) has personal jurisdiction over the contestants; and

(2) reasonable notice and opportunity to be heard is given to the contestants.

(d) Continuing jurisdiction.—A court of a State that has made a child support order consistently with this section has continuing, exclusive jurisdiction over the order if the State is the child's State or the residence of any contestant unless the court of another State, acting in accordance with subsection (e), has made a modification of the order.

(e) Authority to modify orders.—A court of a State may make a modification of a child support order with respect to a child that is made by a court of another State if—

(1) the court has jurisdiction to make such a child support order; and

(2) (A) the court of the other State no longer has continuing, exclusive jurisdiction of the child support order because that State no longer is the child's State or the residence of any contestant; or

(B) each contestant has filed written consent to that court's making the modification and assuming continuing, exclusive jurisdiction over the order.

(f) Enforcement of prior orders.—A court of a State that no longer has continuing, exclusive jurisdiction of a child support order may enforce the order with respect to nonmodifiable obligations and unsatisfied obligations that accrued before the date on which a modification of the order is made under subsection (e)

(g) Choice of law

(1) In general.—In a proceeding to establish, modify, or enforce a child support order, the forum State's law shall apply except as provided in paragraphs (2) and (3).

(2) Law of State of Issuance of order.—In interpreting a child support order, a court shall apply the law of the State of the court that issued the order.

(3) Period of limitation.—In an action to enforce a child support order, a court shall apply the statute of limitation of the forum State or the State of the court that issued the order, whichever statute provides the longer period of limitation.

[Ed.—Section 2 of Public Law 103-383 includes the following findings and explanation of the purpose of the preceding statutory provision.]

Section 2. Findings and Purposes

"(a) Findings.—The Congress finds that—

"(1) there is a large and growing number of child support cases annually involving disputes between parents who reside in different states;

"(2) the laws by which the courts of different jurisdictions determine their authority to establish child support orders are not uniform;

"(3) those laws, along with the limits imposed by the Federal system on the authority of each State to take certain actions outside its own boundaries—

"(A) encourage noncustodial parents to relocate outside the States where their children and the custodial parents reside to avoid the jurisdiction of the courts of such States, resulting in an increase in the amount of interstate travel and communication required to establish and collect on child support orders and a burden on custodial parents that is expensive, time consuming, and disruptive of occupations and commercial activity;

"(B) contribute to the pressing problem of relatively low levels of child support payments in interstate cases and to inequities in child support payments levels that are based solely on the noncustodial parent's choice of residence.

"(C) encourage a disregard of court orders resulting in massive arrearages nationwide;

"(D) allow noncustodial parents to avoid the payment of regularly scheduled child support payments for extensive periods of time, resulting in substantial hardship for the children for whom support is due and for their custodians; and

"(E) lead to the excessive relitigation of cases and to the establishment of conflicting orders by the courts of various jurisdictions, resulting in confusion, waste of judicial resources, disrespect for the courts, and a diminution of public confidence in the rule of law; and

"(4) among the results of the conditions described in this subsection are—

"(A) the failure of the courts of the States to give full faith and credit to the judicial proceedings of the other States;

"(B) the deprivation of rights of liberty and property without due process of law;

"(C) burdens on commerce among the States; and

"(D) harm to the welfare of children and their parents and other custodians.

"(b) Statement of police.—In view of the findings made in subsection (a) it is necessary to establish national standards under which the courts of the various States shall determine their jurisdiction to issue a child support order and the effect to be given by each State to child support orders issued by the courts of other States.

"(c) Purposes.—The purposes of this Act [enacting this section and a provision set out as a note under section 1 of this title] are—

"(1) to facilitate the enforcement of child support orders among the States;

"(2) to discourage continuing interstate controversies over child support in the interest of greater financial stability and secure family relationships for the child; and

"(3) to avoid jurisdictional competition and conflict among State courts in the establishment of child support orders."